Writing and Sexual Difference

Writing and Sexual Difference

Edited by Elizabeth Abel

The University of Chicago Press

The articles in this volume originally appeared in the Winter 1980, Winter 1981, and Spring and Summer 1982 issues of *Critical Inquiry*.

The University of Chicago Press, Chicago 60637
The University of Chicago Press, Ltd., London

Library of Congress Cataloging in Publication Data
Main entry under title:

Writing and sexual difference.

   "The articles in this volume originally appeared in
Critical inquiry"—Verso t.p.
   Includes index.
   1. Women and literature—Addresses, essays, lectures.
I. Abel, Elizabeth.
PN481.W75 1982   809'.89287   82-11131
ISBN 0-226-00076-1 (pbk.)

Contents

Introduction

> If human beings were not divided into two biological sexes, there
> would probably be no need for literature. And if literature could
> truly say what the relations between the sexes are, we would
> doubtless not need much of it then, either. . . . It is not the life of
> sexuality that literature cannot capture; it is literature that inhabits
> the very heart of what makes sexuality problematic for us speaking
> animals. Literature is not only a thwarted investigator but also an
> incorrigible perpetrator of the problem of sexuality.
> —BARBARA JOHNSON, *The Critical Difference*

Sexuality and textuality both depend on difference. Deconstructive criticism has made us attend to notions of textual difference, but the complexities of sexual difference, more pervasively engrained in our culture,
have largely been confined to the edges of critical debate. In the last
decade, however, feminist critics have demonstrated that gender informs and complicates both the writing and the reading of texts. This
volume indicates the scope of feminist inquiry in essays that examine
how writing relates to gender, how attitudes toward sexual difference
generate and structure literary texts, and how critical methods can effectively disclose the traces of gender in literature.

The notion of difference has only recently emerged as a focus of
feminist criticism. Initially, feminist theorists bolstered claims for equality with claims of similarity. This perspective found expression in literary
criticism which focused primarily on blind spots in male texts, cataloged
masculine stereotypes of women, and documented the transmission of
rigid and exaggerated notions of sexual difference. Feminist readings,
overtly polemical, typically progressed from text to author to society in
order to explain the limited array of female roles in literature. As
feminist theorists began to reconceptualize sexual difference to women's
advantage, however, feminist literary criticism shifted its focus to the
reading of texts by women. Female experience displaced male bias as the
center of analysis; female literary genealogies jostled male traditions.
Literary studies emphasized the distinctive features of female texts and
traced lines of influence connecting women in a fertile and partially autonomous tradition. Recently, analyses of sexual difference have stressed
interrelationship as well as opposition, difference *between* as well as difference *from*. Feminist critical attention has shifted from recovering a
lost tradition to discovering the terms of confrontation with the domi-

1

nant tradition. Aware that women writers inevitably engage a literary history and system of conventions shaped primarily by men, feminist critics now often strive to elucidate the acts of revision, appropriation, and subversion that constitute a female text. The analysis of female talent grappling with a male tradition translates sexual difference into literary differences of genre, structure, voice, and plot.

This concern with textual conventions dispels one litany of familiar accusations: reductiveness, dogmatism, insensitivity to literary values. Since the new focus integrates literary history, moreover, unwieldy global questions about female writing have yielded to specific historical studies of the ways women revise prevailing themes and styles. The more acutely literary perspective has also regenerated interest in male texts, examined less as documents of sexism than as artful renditions of sexual difference. Women emerge in these analyses no longer as the passive victims of male authorial desire but rather as powerful figures that elicit texts crafted to appropriate or mute their difference.

Such sophisticated reading may belatedly accord the feminist critic a position closer to the mainstream of critical debate. It may also generate a litany of new accusations: that the concern with textuality augurs a return to formalism; that feminist critics have betrayed political commitments in pursuit of academic credibility. These complaints may be inevitable, and also just; yet textual politics are neither trivial nor obvious: they reflect larger political contexts. The essays in this volume focus on texts, but by raising issues that extend beyond texts, they embody the allegiances that motivated them.

A single ideology is not, however, the source of unity in this volume. Nor is a single methodology. Deciphering the interplay of writing and sexual difference requires a variety of critical approaches. The celebrated pluralism of feminist criticism is apparent in these pages, which include psychoanalytic, deconstructive, historical, formalist, generic, and biographical studies. These essays, diverse in content and method, are united by a shared attempt to map the shifting boundaries of sexual difference. The readings of female texts accentuate the revision of male conventions; the readings of male texts emphasize the encounter with female difference; readings of both female and male texts focus on the literary dynamics of sexual difference rather than the characteristics of either sex. The unifying thread emerges not from method but from shared participation in a moment of inquiry.

The volume opens with a theoretical overview that situates feminist literary theory in the encounter between muted and dominant literary cultures. In "Feminist Criticism in the Wilderness," Elaine Showalter distinguishes two modes of feminist criticism: the "feminist critique," focused on the feminist reader, and "gynocritics," focused on the woman writer. If the feminist critique must invoke pluralism as the only adequately comprehensive critical stance, gynocritics offers the possibility of a distinctive feminist critical theory committed to elucidating the "difference" of female writing. After surveying the models of female difference offered by biology, linguistics, and psychoanalysis, Showalter adapts from cultural anthropology a model of women's writing and of feminist critical practice. The specificity of female writing will emerge, she claims, from the study of the woman writer's interaction with both her male and female literary heritages, for "in the reality to which we must address ourselves as critics, women's writing is a 'double-voiced discourse' that always embodies the social, literary, and cultural heritages of both the muted and the dominant."

The emphasis on the woman writer's vexed relation to male literary culture persists in the next three essays. Mary Jacobus and Margaret Homans both seek in George Eliot the means by which a female writer asserts her identity within philosophical, literary, and linguistic traditions shaped by men. By juxtaposing a chapter from *The Mill on the Floss* with a chapter from Luce Irigaray's *Ce sexe qui n'en est pas un,* Jacobus argues in "The Question of Language: Men of Maxims and *The Mill on the Floss*" that the woman writer (and the feminist critic) can express her difference only through a posture critical of prevailing discourse. Since she has no alternative to discourse, however, the woman writer must inscribe her disaffection either through a deliberate mimicry that, by its very imitation, gestures toward unthinkable alternatives, or through metaphors of female desire (such as those which conclude both these texts) which enact Eliot's own realization that "we can so seldom declare what a thing is, except by saying it is something else." Subversive imitation is also the focus of Margaret Homans' analysis of Eliot's response to a particular male authority. In "Eliot, Wordsworth, and the Scenes of the Sisters' Instruction," Homans argues that Eliot defends herself from engulfment in male influence by copying Wordsworth literally, thereby transforming his Romantic poetry into realist fiction. The seemingly docile imitation that Homans claims is our model of feminine reading shifts in Eliot's hands into a canny process of revision. Homans' brother-sister paradigm of influence not only links Eliot's creativity with a relationship central to her work (and life) but also expands our repertoire of family models of literary influence. A broad perspective on the burden of male influence governs Susan Gubar's study of sexual metaphors of literary creativity. In " 'The Blank Page' and the Issues of Female Creativity," Gubar documents the association of the female body with the empty page awaiting the male author's pen, then explores the impact of this equation on the female imagination. The continuity of life and art, biography and text, and the recurrent identification of writing with violation, with a process of "bleeding into print," reflect the woman writer's recognition that her body is the text. Yet, as Gubar's reading of Isak Dinesen's "The Blank Page" suggests, apparent imitation can become appropriation and the empty page evolve into an emblem of resistance.

The focus shifts to male texts in the next four essays, which pose the question of sexual difference not in terms of female defenses against a silencing male tradition but in terms of male appropriations of female creativity. The power struggle persists, though the terms have changed. Nancy J. Vickers opens the discussion with a reading of Petrarch's influential *Rime sparse* in terms of the recurrent myth in which Actaeon sees the naked Diana and is subsequently dismembered. In "Diana Described: Scattered Woman and Scattered Rhyme," Vickers argues that Petrarch's fragmentation of Laura's body is his defense against the threat of the female body: "His response to the threat of imminent dismemberment is the neutralization, through descriptive dismemberment, of the threat. He transforms the visible totality into scattered words, the body into signs." If Petrarchan description scatters woman as text, it also implies a story of origins that designates woman as the source of the text. Nina Auerbach pursues a similar argument about the covert sources of male creativity. In "Magi and Maidens: The Romance of the Victorian Freud," she allies Freud with Svengali and Dracula as turn-of-the-century magi who required the transformative power of their seemingly passive female prey. Freud's dismay at Dora's abrupt termination of analysis, Auerbach claims, reveals his dependence on her "boundlessly suggestive dreams" to trigger his interpretative faculties. Auerbach's reading of the magus and the maiden revises Gubar's model of male author/female text as an equal, dynamic interchange.

The active role of the feminine in male (theories of) art is also the subject of Froma I. Zeitlin's and Annette Kolodny's essays. Auerbach concludes her essay with reflections on H. D.'s *Helen in Egypt;* Zeitlin explores the dual accounts of Helen (Egypt/Troy) as a source of Helen's association in classical poetics with the problematic relation between truth and imitation. In "Travesties of Gender and Genre in Aristophanes' *Thesmophoriazousae*," Zeitlin examines the "intrinsic connection between the ambiguities of the feminine and those of art, linked together in various ways in Greek notions of poetics from their earliest formulations." Helen's skill at storytelling, at verbal as well as erotic seduction, provokes distrust as well as delight; yet as the principle of verbal ingenuity, she is as vital to the masculine poet as Dora's fluent dreaming is essential to the analyst. The role of female storytelling within the context of male writing also draws Kolodny's critical attention. In "Turning the Lens on 'The Panther Captivity': A Feminist Exercise in Practical Criticism," Kolodny subjects a captivity narrative, dated from the close of the American Revolution, to a feminist reading of the interplay between the interpolated female narrative and the masculine adventure story that encloses it. By examining both the role of women in the historical context of "The Panther Captivity" and the symbolic significance of gender in the text, Kolodny demonstrates that the "lady" 's narrative is essential to provide a positive image of woman's survival in the wilderness and to offer a choice between contending responses to the wilderness: accommodation, represented by the lady's agriculture; and mastery, enacted in the male pursuit of hunting and commerce. The conventions of male hunting tales could not incorporate the values represented in the lady's narrative.

The next group of essays returns to women's writing, now stressing its divergence from dominant conventions. These essays trace the imprint of female perceptions of gender and identity on twentieth-century fiction by women. Judith Kegan Gardiner introduces the section by revising the theories of Erik Erikson, Heinz Lichtenstein, and Norman Holland in the light of Nancy Chodorow's differentiation between male and female personality structures. Gardiner explains in "On Female Identity and Writing by Women" that an identity theory attuned to sexual difference provides a "multivariant theoretical apparatus" for distinguishing between male and female literary strategies. The fluid character of female identity, emerging from the symbiotic mother-daughter bond, finds literary form in the defiance of generic boundaries, the dissolution of integrated characters, and the distinctive identification among female authors, characters, and readers that Gardiner represents by the metaphor, "The hero is her author's daughter." In "Costumes of the Mind: Transvestism as Metaphor in Modern Literature," Sandra M. Gilbert begins where Gardiner concludes, analyzing male and female fictional portrayals of gender roles. The fluidity Gardiner ascribes to female identity, Gilbert detects in the female modernist's playful equation of costumes with the self, an imaginative audacity that contrasts with the male modernist's cautious representation of a gendered identity subsisting through all disguise. When James Joyce, D. H. Lawrence, and T. S. Eliot dramatize transvestism, Gilbert shows, they ultimately affirm the traditional gender hierarchy. Virginia Woolf and Djuna Barnes, by contrast, undermine that hierarchy by detaching identity from a notion of definitive, unalterable gender.

Female relationships provide a good arena for exploring interchangeable gender roles. Carolyn Burke and Catharine R. Stimpson examine the flexibility of gender and genre in twentieth-century narratives of female bonding. In "Gertrude Stein, the Cone Sisters, and the Puzzle of Female Friendship," Burke dissects the psychological and formal patterns differentiating "Ada" and "Two Women," two portraits of female relationships by a founder of female modernism. While these portraits depict significantly different modes of symbiosis, they both blur the boundary between the author's life and text. Stein's use of the genre demonstrates the self-reflexive nature of female accounts of female relationships and calls on feminists to reassess biography as a critical tool. Stimpson's analysis of lesbian fiction contracts the critical focus to one mode of female bonding and expands it to incorporate writers excluded from literary history. In "Zero Degree Deviancy: The Lesbian Novel in English," Stimpson charts the evolution of lesbian fiction from the narrative of damnation to the narrative of enabling escape and describes the assimilation of traditional forms to these patterns of lesbian narrative. By celebrating a "return to primal origins, to primal loves, when female/female, not male/female, relationships structured the world," lesbian fiction replaces the binary structure of gender with fluid and multiple relationships. Though most lesbian writers have preferred accessibility to formal innovation, the narrative experiments of Bertha Harris show how suitable modernist techniques are to the "polymorphic, amorphic, transmorphic, and orphic" spirit Harris sees in lesbian sexuality.

The final entry furthers the goal implicit in Stimpson's analysis: broadening the notion of sexual difference. Gayatri Chakravorty Spivak extends the cultural boundary of these essays by introducing and translating a story by Mahasveta Devi, an important Bengali woman novelist. With this story the volume shifts from West to East, from criticism to fiction, from implicit to explicit political perspective. Set in the Naxalite peasant rebellion against the central government of India, "Draupadi" culminates in the captured heroine's encounter with the Indian army officer responsible for her rape and torture. Sexual and political difference here explosively coalesce; the fragmented female body shifts from metaphor to fact. "Draupadi" lays bare the physical violence sublimated in metaphors of textual production. Yet, as Spivak reminds us, Draupadi's shattered body is itself a text that silences both her male interrogator and his allies in exegesis: us. As a well-educated pluralist aesthete, the literate army officer is our intellectual representative within the text; like his, our interpretative strategies should be shaken by Draupadi. As Western readers, female and male, we are blind to the radical difference of Third World sexual politics. Mahasveta's story, and Spivak's foreword, remind us that sexual difference is no invariant entity. Acknowledging its import in Western texts should be a step toward fracturing other assumptions about (racial, historical, economic) uniformity.

Draupadi's survival is unusually heroic, but as survival it exemplifies the faith in women's resiliency evident throughout these essays. Female characters and female authors alike emerge as ingenious strategists who succeed in devising some mode of assertion. Even Maggie Tulliver, an obvious exception, here dies in the service of her author's self-discovery, not as a victim of society. With the exploration of women's ingenuity comes an unlikely cast of female heroes: Helen of Troy, Petrarch's Laura, and Freud's Dora to name a few. The critical focus on sexual difference may increase our recognition of unorthodox female creative strategies. In addition to refining our mythologies of difference, this moment of feminist inquiry allows new figures to provide a different and enabling mythology.

This mythology, however, assumes diverse shapes, and "difference" is the term that best reveals this diversity. The responses that conclude this volume dispute the value of sexual difference as a focus of feminist criticism. Writing from a perspective informed by Lacanian psychoanalysis, Jane Gallop insists on the intrinsic difference *within* both sexuality and literature, each fractured by the inevitable presence of the other. The feminist critic is especially attuned to this interior division because of her dual and partially incompatible inheritance from feminism and criticism, which together confer "the at once enabling and disabling tension of a difference within." Writing within an American critical context, by contrast, Carolyn G. Heilbrun questions the emphasis on sexual difference and on differences of sexual preference. Now that feminist critics have documented the constraints deforming female experience and writing, Heilbrun argues, it may be time to rediscover shared capacities, the common ground of humanism. The debate between Carolyn J. Allen and Elaine Showalter provides an alternative focus for the controversy over difference. Allen insists that feminist theorists acknowledge differences of class and race as well as sex, yet she also attempts to reconcile feminist activism and criticism by replacing Showalter's distinction between feminist critique and gynocritics with a comprehensive focus on the politics of feminist reading. In reply Showalter claims that a clear distinction has never divided feminist criticism from political analysis, that interpretations of literary texts provided the germinal treatises of twentieth-century feminism, and that her model of gynocritics incorporates the variables of class, race, and nationality. The varying positions that conclude this collection contribute to a picture of an emerging theory marked by a new self-consciousness and a balance of tensions and tolerance.

Acknowledgments

Many people helped to create this volume. W. J. T. Mitchell, editor of *Critical Inquiry,* enthusiastically supported the special issue that was the basis for this collection (vol. 8, no. 2 [Winter 1981]). Toby Gordon, editorial consultant for *Critical Inquiry,* provided indispensable expertise in editing, and Carolyn Williams, editorial assistant, helped proofread and edit the issue. I am also grateful to a large community of feminist scholars, particularly to Marianne Hirsch, Janel Mueller, and Marta Peixoto, for their encouragement and advice. By far my greatest debt is to Janet Silver, managing editor of *Critical Inquiry,* who helped select, edit, and organize these essays, and who served in all respects as coeditor of this book. *Writing and Sexual Difference* would not exist without her outstanding generosity and skill, which exceed all the thanks that I can offer.

Elizabeth Abel

Feminist Criticism in the Wilderness

Elaine Showalter

1. Pluralism and the Feminist Critique

> Women have no wilderness in them,
> They are provident instead
> Content in the tight hot cell of
>   their hearts
> To eat dusty bread.
>
> —Louise Bogan, "Women"

In a splendidly witty dialogue of 1975, Carolyn Heilbrun and Catharine Stimpson identified two poles of feminist literary criticism. The first of these modes, righteous, angry, and admonitory, they compared to the Old Testament, "looking for the sins and errors of the past." The second mode, disinterested and seeking "the grace of imagination," they compared to the New Testament. Both are necessary, they concluded, for only the Jeremiahs of ideology can lead us out of the "Egypt of female servitude" to the promised land of humanism.[1] Matthew Arnold also thought that literary critics might perish in the wilderness before they reached the promised land of disinterestedness; Heilbrun and Stimpson were neo-Arnoldian as befitted members of the Columbia and Barnard faculties. But if, in 1981, feminist literary critics are still wandering in the

---

1. Carolyn G. Heilbrun and Catharine R. Stimpson, "Theories of Feminist Criticism: A Dialogue," in *Feminist Literary Criticism,* ed. Josephine Donovan (Lexington, Ky., 1975), p. 64. I also discuss this distinction in my "Towards a Feminist Poetics," in *Women Writing and Writing about Women,* ed. Mary Jacobus (New York, 1979), pp. 22–41; a number of the ideas in the first part of the present essay are raised more briefly in the earlier piece.

wilderness, we are in good company; for, as Geoffrey Hartman tells us, *all* criticism is in the wilderness.[2] Feminist critics may be startled to find ourselves in this band of theoretical pioneers, since in the American literary tradition the wilderness has been an exclusively masculine domain. Yet between feminist ideology and the liberal ideal of disinterestedness lies the wilderness of theory, which we too must make our home.

Until very recently, feminist criticism has not had a theoretical basis; it has been an empirical orphan in the theoretical storm. In 1975, I was persuaded that no theoretical manifesto could adequately account for the varied methodologies and ideologies which called themselves feminist reading or writing.[3] By the next year, Annette Kolodny had added her observation that feminist literary criticism appeared "more like a set of interchangeable strategies than any coherent school or shared goal orientation."[4] Since then, the expressed goals have not been notably unified. Black critics protest the "massive silence" of feminist criticism about black and Third-World women writers and call for a black feminist aesthetic that would deal with both racial and sexual politics. Marxist feminists wish to focus on class along with gender as a crucial determinant of literary production.[5] Literary historians want to uncover a lost tradition. Critics trained in deconstructionist methodologies wish to "synthesize a literary criticism that is both textual and feminist."[6] Freudian and Lacanian critics want to theorize about women's relationship to language and signification.

An early obstacle to constructing a theoretical framework for feminist criticism was the unwillingness of many women to limit or

2. No women critics are discussed in Hartman's *Criticism in the Wilderness* (New Haven, Conn., 1980), but he does describe a feminine spirit called "the Muse of Criticism": "more a governess than a Muse, the stern daughter of books no longer read under trees and in the fields" (p. 175).

3. See my "Literary Criticism," *Signs* 1 (Winter 1975): 435–60.

4. Annette Kolodny, "Literary Criticism," *Signs* 2 (Winter 1976): 420.

5. On black criticism, see Barbara Smith, "Towards a Black Feminist Criticism," *Conditions Two* 1 (1977): 25, and Mary Helen Washington, "New Lives and New Letters: Black Women Writers at the End of the Seventies," *College English* 43 (January 1981): 1–11. On Marxist criticism, see the Marxist-Feminist Literature Collective's "Women's Writing," *Ideology and Consciousness* 3 (Spring 1978): 27, a collectively written analysis of several nineteenth-century women's novels which gives equal weight to gender, class, and literary production as textual determinants.

6. Margaret Homans, *Women Writers and Poetic Identity* (Princeton, N.J., 1980), p. 10.

Elaine Showalter is professor of English at Rutgers University and author of *A Literature of Their Own: British Women Novelists from Brontë to Lessing*.

bound an expressive and dynamic enterprise. The openness of feminist criticism appealed particularly to Americans who perceived the structuralist, post-structuralist, and deconstructionist debates of the 1970s as arid and falsely objective, the epitome of a pernicious masculine discourse from which many feminists wished to escape. Recalling in *A Room of One's Own* how she had been prohibited from entering the university library, the symbolic sanctuary of the male *logos,* Virginia Woolf wisely observed that while it is "unpleasant to be locked out . . . it is worse, perhaps, to be locked in." Advocates of the antitheoretical position traced their descent from Woolf and from other feminist visionaries, such as Mary Daly, Adrienne Rich, and Marguerite Duras, who had satirized the sterile narcissism of male scholarship and celebrated women's fortunate exclusion from its patriarchal methodolatry. Thus for some, feminist criticism was an act of resistance to theory, a confrontation with existing canons and judgments, what Josephine Donovan calls "a mode of negation within a fundamental dialectic." As Judith Fetterley declared in her book, *The Resisting Reader,* feminist criticism has been characterized by "a resistance to codification and a refusal to have its parameters prematurely set." I have discussed elsewhere, with considerable sympathy, the suspicion of monolithic systems and the rejection of scientism in literary study that many feminist critics have voiced. While scientific criticism struggled to purge itself of the subjective, feminist criticism reasserted the authority of experience.[7]

Yet it now appears that what looked like a theoretical impasse was actually an evolutionary phase. The ethics of awakening have been succeeded, at least in the universities, by a second stage characterized by anxiety about the isolation of feminist criticism from a critical community increasingly theoretical in its interests and indifferent to women's writing. The question of how feminist criticism should define itself with relation to the new critical theories and theorists has occasioned sharp debate in Europe and the United States. Nina Auerbach has noted the absence of dialogue and asks whether feminist criticism itself must accept responsibility:

> Feminist critics seem particularly reluctant to define themselves to the uninitiated. There is a sense in which our sisterhood has become too powerful; as a school, our belief in ourself is so potent that we decline communication with the networks of power and respectability we say we want to change.[8]

7. Donovan, "Afterward: Critical Revision," *Feminist Literary Criticism,* p. 74. Judith Fetterley, *The Resisting Reader: A Feminist Approach to American Fiction* (Bloomington, Ind., 1978), p. viii. See my "Towards a Feminist Poetics," pp. 37–39. *The Authority of Experience* is the title of an anthology edited by Lee Edwards and Arlyn Diamond (Amherst, Mass., 1977).

8. Nina Auerbach, "Feminist Criticism Reviewed," in *Gender and Literary Voice,* ed. Janet Todd (New York, 1980), p. 258.

But rather than declining communication with these networks, feminist criticism has indeed spoken directly to them, in their own media: *PMLA, Diacritics, Glyph, Tel Quel, New Literary History,* and *Critical Inquiry.* For the feminist critic seeking clarification, the proliferation of communiqués may itself prove confusing.

There are two distinct modes of feminist criticism, and to conflate them (as most commentators do) is to remain permanently bemused by their theoretical potentialities. The first mode is ideological; it is concerned with the feminist as *reader,* and it offers feminist readings of texts which consider the images and stereotypes of women in literature, the omissions and misconceptions about women in criticism, and woman-as-sign in semiotic systems. This is not all feminist reading can do; it can be a liberating intellectual act, as Adrienne Rich proposes:

> A radical critique of literature, feminist in its impulse, would take the work first of all as a clue to how we live, how we have been living, how we have been led to imagine ourselves, how our language has trapped as well as liberated us, how the very act of naming has been till now a male prerogative, and how we can begin to see and name—and therefore live—afresh.[9]

This invigorating encounter with literature, which I will call *feminist reading* or the *feminist critique,* is in essence a mode of interpretation, one of many which any complex text will accommodate and permit. It is very difficult to propose theoretical coherence in an activity which by its nature is so eclectic and wide-ranging, although as a critical practice feminist reading has certainly been very influential. But in the free play of the interpretive field, the feminist critique can only compete with alternative readings, all of which have the built-in obsolescence of Buicks, cast away as newer readings take their place. As Kolodny, the most sophisticated theorist of feminist interpretation, has conceded:

> All the feminist is asserting, then, is her own equivalent right to liberate new (and perhaps different) significances from these same texts; and, at the same time, her right to choose which features of a text she takes as relevant because she is, after all, asking new and different questions of it. In the process, she claims neither definitiveness nor structural completeness for her different readings and reading systems, but only their usefulness in recognizing the particular achievements of woman-as-author and their applicability in conscientiously decoding woman-as-sign.

Rather than being discouraged by these limited objectives, Kolodny found them the happy cause of the "playful pluralism" of feminist criti-

9. Adrienne Rich, "When We Dead Awaken: Writing as Re-Vision," *On Lies, Secrets, and Silence* (New York, 1979), p. 35.

cal theory, a pluralism which she believes to be "the only critical stance consistent with the current status of the larger women's movement."[10] Her feminist critic dances adroitly through the theoretical minefield.

Keenly aware of the political issues involved and presenting brilliant arguments, Kolodny nonetheless fails to convince me that feminist criticism must altogether abandon its hope "of establishing some basic conceptual model." If we see our critical job as interpretation and reinterpretation, we must be content with pluralism as our critical stance. But if we wish to ask questions about the process and the contexts of writing, if we genuinely wish to define ourselves to the uninitiated, we cannot rule out the prospect of theoretical consensus at this early stage.

All feminist criticism is in some sense revisionist, questioning the adequacy of accepted conceptual structures, and indeed most contemporary American criticism claims to be revisionist too. The most exciting and comprehensive case for this "revisionary imperative" is made by Sandra Gilbert: at its most ambitious, she asserts, feminist criticism "wants to decode and demystify all the disguised questions and answers that have always shadowed the connections between textuality and sexuality, genre and gender, psychosexual identity and cultural authority."[11] But in practice, the revisionary feminist critique is redressing a grievance and is built upon existing models. No one would deny that feminist criticism has affinities to other contemporary critical practices and methodologies and that the best work is also the most fully informed. Nonetheless, the feminist obsession with correcting, modifying, supplementing, revising, humanizing, or even attacking male critical theory keeps us dependent upon it and retards our progress in solving our own theoretical problems. What I mean here by "male critical theory" is a concept of creativity, literary history, or literary interpretation based entirely on male experience and put forward as universal. So long as we look to androcentric models for our most basic principles—even if we revise them by adding the feminist frame of reference—we are learning nothing new. And when the process is so one-sided, when male critics boast of their ignorance of feminist criticism, it is disheartening to find feminist critics still anxious for approval from the "white fathers" who will not listen or reply. Some feminist critics have taken upon themselves a revisionism which becomes a kind of homage; they have made Lacan

10. Kolodny, "Dancing through the Minefield: Some Observations on the Theory, Practice, and Politics of a Feminist Literary Criticism," *Feminist Studies* 6 (Spring 1980): 19, 20. The complete theoretical case for a feminist hermeneutics is outlined in Kolodny's essays, including "Some Notes on Defining a 'Feminist Literary Criticism,'" *Critical Inquiry* 2 (Autumn 1975): 75–92; "A Map for Rereading; or, Gender and the Interpretation of Literary Texts," *New Literary History* (1980): 451–67; and "The Theory of Feminist Criticism" (paper delivered at the National Center for the Humanities Conference on Feminist Criticism, Research Triangle Park, N.C., March 1981).

11. Sandra M. Gilbert, "What Do Feminist Critics Want?; or, A Postcard from the Volcano," *ADE Bulletin* (Winter 1980): 19.

the ladies' man of *Diacritics* and have forced Pierre Macherey into those dark alleys of the psyche where Engels feared to tread. According to Christiane Makward, the problem is even more serious in France than in the United States: "If neofeminist thought in France seems to have ground to a halt," she writes, "it is because it has continued to feed on the discourse of the masters."[12]

It is time for feminist criticism to decide whether between religion and revision we can claim any firm theoretical ground of our own. In calling for a feminist criticism that is genuinely women centered, independent, and intellectually coherent, I do not mean to endorse the separatist fantasies of radical feminist visionaries or to exclude from our critical practice a variety of intellectual tools. But we need to ask much more searchingly what we want to know and how we can find answers to the questions that come from *our* experience. I do not think that feminist criticism can find a usable past in the androcentric critical tradition. It has more to learn from women's studies than from English studies, more to learn from international feminist theory than from another seminar on the masters. It must find its own subject, its own system, its own theory, and its own voice. As Rich writes of Emily Dickinson, in her poem "I Am in Danger—Sir—," we must choose to have the argument out at last on our own premises.

2. Defining the Feminine: Gynocritics and the Woman's Text

> A woman's writing is always feminine; it cannot help being feminine; at its best it is most feminine; the only difficulty lies in defining what we mean by feminine.
> —Virginia Woolf

> It is impossible to *define* a feminine practice of writing, and this is an impossibility that will remain, for this practice will never be theorized, enclosed, encoded—which doesn't mean that it doesn't exist.
> —Hélène Cixous, "The Laugh of the Medusa"

In the past decade, I believe, this process of defining the feminine has started to take place. Feminist criticism has gradually shifted its center from revisionary readings to a sustained investigation of literature by women. The second mode of feminist criticism engendered by this process is the study of women *as writers,* and its subjects are the history, styles, themes, genres, and structures of writing by women; the

12. Christiane Makward, "To Be or Not to Be. . . . A Feminist Speaker," in *The Future of Difference,* ed. Hester Eisenstein and Alice Jardine (Boston, 1980), p. 102. On Lacan, see Jane Gallop, "The Ladies' Man," *Diacritics* 6 (Winter 1976): 28–34; on Macherey, see the Marxist-Feminist Literature Collective's "Women's Writing."

psychodynamics of female creativity; the trajectory of the individual or collective female career; and the evolution and laws of a female literary tradition. No English term exists for such a specialized critical discourse, and so I have invented the term "gynocritics." Unlike the feminist critique, gynocritics offers many theoretical opportunities. To see women's writing as our primary subject forces us to make the leap to a new conceptual vantage point and to redefine the nature of the theoretical problem before us. It is no longer the ideological dilemma of reconciling revisionary pluralisms but the essential question of difference. How can we constitute women as a distinct literary group? What is *the difference* of women's writing?

Patricia Meyer Spacks, I think, was the first academic critic to notice this shift from an androcentric to a gynocentric feminist criticism. In *The Female Imagination* (1975), she pointed out that few feminist theorists had concerned themselves with women's writing. Simone de Beauvoir's treatment of women writers in *The Second Sex* "always suggests an a priori tendency to take them less seriously than their masculine counterparts"; Mary Ellmann, in *Thinking about Women,* characterized women's literary success as escape from the categories of womanhood; and, according to Spacks, Kate Millett, in *Sexual Politics,* "has little interest in woman imaginative writers."[13] Spacks' wide-ranging study inaugurated a new period of feminist literary history and criticism which asked, again and again, how women's writing had been different, how womanhood itself shaped women's creative expression. In such books as Ellen Moers' *Literary Women* (1976), my own *A Literature of Their Own* (1977), Nina Baym's *Woman's Fiction* (1978), Gilbert and Susan Gubar's *The Madwoman in the Attic* (1979), and Margaret Homans' *Women Writers and Poetic Identity* (1980), and in hundreds of essays and papers, women's writing asserted itself as the central project of feminist literary study.

This shift in emphasis has also taken place in European feminist criticism. To date, most commentary on French feminist critical discourse has stressed its fundamental dissimilarity from the empirical American orientation, its unfamiliar intellectual grounding in linguistics, Marxism, neo-Freudian and Lacanian psychoanalysis, and Derridean deconstruction. Despite these differences, however, the new French feminisms have much in common with radical American feminist theories in terms of intellectual affiliations and rhetorical energies. The concept of *écriture féminine,* the inscription of the female body and female difference in language and text, is a significant theoretical formulation in French feminist criticism, although it describes a Utopian possibility rather than a literary practice. Hélène Cixous, one of the leading advocates of *écriture féminine,* has admitted that, with only a few exceptions, "there has not yet been any writing that inscribes femininity," and Nancy

13. Patricia Meyer Spacks, *The Female Imagination* (New York, 1975), pp. 19, 32.

Miller explains that *écriture féminine* "privileges a textuality of the avant-garde, a literary production of the late twentieth century, and it is therefore fundamentally a hope, if not a blueprint, for the future."[14] Nonetheless, the concept of *écriture féminine* provides a way of talking about women's writing which reasserts the *value* of the feminine and identifies the theoretical project of feminist criticism as the analysis of difference. In recent years, the translations of important work by Julia Kristeva, Cixous, and Luce Irigaray and the excellent collection *New French Feminisms* have made French criticism much more accessible to American feminist scholars.[15]

English feminist criticism, which incorporates French feminist and Marxist theory but is more traditionally oriented to textual interpretation, is also moving toward a focus on women's writing.[16] The emphasis in each country falls somewhat differently: English feminist criticism, essentially Marxist, stresses oppression; French feminist criticism, essentially psychoanalytic, stresses repression; American feminist criticism, essentially textual, stresses expression. All, however, have become gynocentric. All are struggling to find a terminology that can rescue the feminine from its stereotypical associations with inferiority.

Defining the unique difference of women's writing, as Woolf and Cixous have warned, must present a slippery and demanding task. Is difference a matter of style? Genre? Experience? Or is it produced by the reading process, as some textual critics would maintain? Spacks calls the difference of women's writing a "delicate divergency," testifying to the subtle and elusive nature of the feminine practice of writing. Yet the delicate divergency of the woman's text challenges us to respond with equal delicacy and precision to the small but crucial deviations, the cumulative weightings of experience and exclusion, that have marked the history of women's writing. Before we can chart this history, we must uncover it, patiently and scrupulously; our theories must be firmly grounded in reading and research. But we have the opportunity, through gynocritics, to learn something solid, enduring, and real about the relation of women to literary culture.

Theories of women's writing presently make use of four models of difference: biological, linguistic, psychoanalytic, and cultural. Each is an

14. Hélène Cixous, "The Laugh of the Medusa," trans. Keith and Paula Cohen, *Signs* 1 (Summer 1976): 878. Nancy K. Miller, "Emphasis Added: Plots and Plausibilities in Women's Fiction," *PMLA* 96 (January 1981): 37.

15. For an overview, see Domna C. Stanton, "Language and Revolution: The Franco-American Dis-Connection," in *Future of Difference*, pp. 73–87, and Elaine Marks and Isabelle de Courtivron, eds., *New French Feminisms* (Amherst, Mass., 1979); all further references to *New French Feminisms*, abbreviated *NFF*, will hereafter be included with translator's name parenthetically in the text.

16. Two major works are the manifesto of the Marxist-Feminist Literature Collective, "Women's Writing," and the papers from the Oxford University lectures on women and literature, *Women Writing and Writing about Women*, ed. Jacobus.

effort to define and differentiate the qualities of the woman writer and the woman's text; each model also represents a school of gynocentric feminist criticism with its own favorite texts, styles, and methods. They overlap but are roughly sequential in that each incorporates the one before. I shall try now to sort out the various terminologies and assumptions of these four models of difference and evaluate their usefulness.

3. Women's Writing and Woman's Body

> More body, hence more writing.
> —Cixous, "The Laugh of the Medusa"

Organic or biological criticism is the most extreme statement of gender difference, of a text indelibly marked by the body: anatomy is textuality. Biological criticism is also one of the most sibylline and perplexing theoretical formulations of feminist criticism. Simply to invoke anatomy risks a return to the crude essentialism, the phallic and ovarian theories of art, that oppressed women in the past. Victorian physicians believed that women's physiological functions diverted about twenty percent of their creative energy from brain activity. Victorian anthropologists believed that the frontal lobes of the male brain were heavier and more developed than female lobes and thus that women were inferior in intelligence.

While feminist criticism rejects the attribution of literal biological inferiority, some theorists seem to have accepted the *metaphorical* implications of female biological difference in writing. In *The Madwoman in the Attic,* for example, Gilbert and Gubar structure their analysis of women's writing around metaphors of literary paternity. "In patriarchal western culture," they maintain, ". . . the text's author is a father, a progenitor, a procreator, an aesthetic patriarch whose pen is an instrument of generative power like his penis." Lacking phallic authority, they go on to suggest, women's writing is profoundly marked by the anxieties of this difference: "If the pen is a metaphorical penis, from what organ can females generate texts?"[17]

To this rhetorical question Gilbert and Gubar offer no reply; but it is a serious question of much feminist theoretical discourse. Those critics who, like myself, would protest the fundamental analogy might reply that women generate texts from the brain or that the word-processor of the near future, with its compactly coded microchips, its inputs and outputs, is a metaphorical womb. The metaphor of literary paternity, as Auerbach has pointed out in her review of *The Madwoman,* ignores "an

17. Gilbert and Gubar, *The Madwoman in the Attic: The Woman Writer and the Nineteenth-Century Literary Imagination* (New Haven, Conn., 1979), pp. 6, 7; all further references to this work will hereafter be included parenthetically in the text.

equally timeless and, for me, even more oppressive metaphorical equation between literary creativity and childbirth."[18] Certainly metaphors of literary *maternity* predominated in the eighteenth and nineteenth centuries; the process of literary creation is analogically much more similar to gestation, labor, and delivery than it is to insemination. Describing Thackeray's plan for *Henry Esmond,* for example, Douglas Jerrold jovially remarked, "You have heard, I suppose, that Thackeray is big with twenty parts, and unless he is wrong in his time, expects the first installment at Christmas."[19] (If to write is metaphorically to give birth, from what organ can males generate texts?)

Some radical feminist critics, primarily in France but also in the United States, insist that we must read these metaphors as more than playful; that we must seriously rethink and redefine biological differentiation and its relation to women's unity. They argue that "women's writing proceeds from the body, that our sexual differentiation is also our source."[20] In *Of Woman Born,* Rich explains her belief that

> female biology . . . has far more radical implications than we have yet come to appreciate. Patriarchal thought has limited female biology to its own narrow specifications. The feminist vision has recoiled from female biology for these reasons; it will, I believe, come to view our physicality as a resource rather than a destiny. In order to live a fully human life, we require not only *control* of our bodies . . . we must touch the unity and resonance of our physicality, the corporeal ground of our intelligence.[21]

Feminist criticism written in the biological perspective generally stresses the importance of the body as a source of imagery. Alicia Ostriker, for example, argues that contemporary American women poets use a franker, more pervasive anatomical imagery than their male counterparts and that this insistent body language refuses the spurious transcendence that comes at the price of denying the flesh. In a fascinating essay on Whitman and Dickinson, Terence Diggory shows that physical nakedness, so potent a poetic symbol of authenticity for Whit-

18. Auerbach, review of *Madwoman, Victorian Studies* 23 (Summer 1980): 506.

19. Douglas Jerrold, quoted in Kathleen Tillotson, *Novels of the Eighteen-Forties* (London, 1961), p. 39 n. James Joyce imagined the creator as female and literary creation as a process of gestation; see Richard Ellmann, *James Joyce: A Biography* (London, 1959), pp. 306–8.

20. Carolyn Burke, "Report from Paris: Women's Writing and the Women's Movement," *Signs* 3 (Summer 1978): 851.

21. Rich, *Of Woman Born: Motherhood as Experience and Institution* (New York, 1977), p. 62. Biofeminist criticism has been influential in other disciplines as well: e.g., art critics, such as Judy Chicago and Lucy Lippard, have suggested that women artists are compelled to use a uterine or vaginal iconography of centralized focus, curved lines, and tactile or sensuous forms. See Lippard, *From the Center: Feminist Essays on Women's Art* (New York, 1976).

man and other male poets, had very different connotations for Dickinson and her successors, who associated nakedness with the objectified or sexually exploited female nude and who chose instead protective images of the armored self.[22]

Feminist criticism which itself tries to be biological, to write from the critic's body, has been intimate, confessional, often innovative in style and form. Rachel Blau DuPlessis' "Washing Blood," the introduction to a special issue of *Feminist Studies* on the subject of motherhood, proceeds, in short lyrical paragraphs, to describe her own experience in adopting a child, to recount her dreams and nightmares, and to meditate upon the "healing unification of body and mind based not only on the lived experiences of motherhood as a social institution . . . but also on a biological power speaking through us."[23] Such criticism makes itself defiantly vulnerable, virtually bares its throat to the knife, since our professional taboos against self-revelation are so strong. When it succeeds, however, it achieves the power and the dignity of art. Its existence is an implicit rebuke to women critics who continue to write, according to Rich, "from somewhere outside their female bodies." In comparison to this flowing confessional criticism, the tight-lipped Olympian intelligence of such texts as Elizabeth Hardwick's *Seduction and Betrayal* or Susan Sontag's *Illness as Metaphor* can seem arid and strained.

Yet in its obsessions with the "corporeal ground of our intelligence," feminist biocriticism can also become cruelly prescriptive. There is a sense in which the exhibition of bloody wounds becomes an initiation ritual quite separate and disconnected from critical insight. And as the editors of the journal *Questions féministes* point out, "it is . . . dangerous to place the body at the center of a search for female identity. . . . The themes of otherness and of the Body merge together, because the most visible difference between men and women, and the only one we know for sure to be permanent . . . is indeed the difference in body. This difference has been used as a pretext to 'justify' full power of one sex over the other" (trans. Yvonne Rochette-Ozzello, *NFF*, p. 218). The study of biological imagery in women's writing is useful and important as long as we understand that factors other than anatomy are involved in it. Ideas about the body are fundamental to understanding how women conceptualize their situation in society; but there can be no expression of the body which is unmediated by linguistic, social, and literary structures. The difference of woman's literary practice, therefore, must be

22. See Alicia Ostriker, "Body Language: Imagery of the Body in Women's Poetry," in *The State of the Language*, ed. Leonard Michaels and Christopher Ricks (Berkeley, 1980), pp. 247–63, and Terence Diggory, "Armoured Women, Naked Men: Dickinson, Whitman, and Their Successors," in *Shakespeare's Sisters: Feminist Essays on Women Poets*, ed. Gilbert and Gubar (Bloomington, Ind., 1979), pp. 135–50.

23. Rachel Blau DuPlessis, "Washing Blood," *Feminist Studies* 4 (June 1978): 10. The entire issue is an important document of feminist criticism.

sought (in Miller's words) in "the body of her writing and not the writing of her body."[24]

4. Women's Writing and Women's Language

> The women say, the language you speak poisons your glottis tongue palate lips. They say, the language you speak is made up of words that are killing you. They say, the language you speak is made up of signs that rightly speaking designate what men have appropriated.
>
> —MONIQUE WITTIG, *Les Guérillères*

Linguistic and textual theories of women's writing ask whether men and women use language differently; whether sex differences in language use can be theorized in terms of biology, socialization, or culture; whether women can create new languages of their own; and whether speaking, reading, and writing are all gender marked. American, French, and British feminist critics have all drawn attention to the philosophical, linguistic, and practical problems of women's use of language, and the debate over language is one of the most exciting areas in gynocritics. Poets and writers have led the attack on what Rich calls "the oppressor's language," a language sometimes criticized as sexist, sometimes as abstract. But the problem goes well beyond reformist efforts to purge language of its sexist aspects. As Nelly Furman explains, "It is through the medium of language that we define and categorize areas of difference and similarity, which in turn allow us to comprehend the world around us. Male-centered categorizations predominate in American English and subtly shape our understanding and perception of reality; this is why attention is increasingly directed to the inherently oppressive aspects for women of a male-constructed language system."[25] According to Carolyn Burke, the language system is at the center of French feminist theory:

> The central issue in much recent women's writing in France is to find and use an appropriate female language. Language is the place to begin: a *prise de conscience* must be followed by a *prise de la parole*. . . . In this view, the very forms of the dominant mode of discourse show the mark of the dominant masculine ideology. Hence, when a woman writes or speaks herself into existence, she is

24. Miller, "Women's Autobiography in France: For a Dialectics of Identification," in *Women and Language in Literature and Society,* ed. Sally McConnell-Ginet, Ruth Borker, and Nelly Furman (New York, 1980), p. 271.

25. Furman, "The Study of Women and Language: Comment on Vol. 3, No. 3," *Signs* 4 (Autumn 1978): 182.

forced to speak in something like a foreign tongue, a language with which she may be personally uncomfortable.[26]

Many French feminists advocate a revolutionary linguism, an oral break from the dictatorship of patriarchal speech. Annie Leclerc, in *Parole de femme,* calls on women "to invent a language that is not oppressive, a language that does not leave speechless but that loosens the tongue" (trans. Courtivron, *NFF,* p. 179). Chantal Chawaf, in an essay on "La chair linguistique," connects biofeminism and linguism in the view that women's language and a genuinely feminine practice of writing will articulate the body:

> In order to reconnect the book with the body and with pleasure, we must disintellectualize writing. . . . And this language, as it develops, will not degenerate and dry up, will not go back to the fleshless academicism, the stereotypical and servile discourses that we reject.
> . . . Feminine language must, by its very nature, work on life passionately, scientifically, poetically, politically in order to make it invulnerable. [Trans. Rochette-Ozzello, *NFF,* pp. 177–78]

But scholars who want a women's language that *is* intellectual and theoretical, that works *inside* the academy, are faced with what seems like an impossible paradox, as Xavière Gauthier has lamented: "As long as women remain silent, they will be outside the historical process. But, if they begin to speak and write *as men do,* they will enter history subdued and alienated; it is a history that, logically speaking, their speech should disrupt" (trans. Marilyn A. August, *NFF,* pp. 162–63). What we need, Mary Jacobus has proposed, is a women's writing that works within "male" discourse but works "ceaselessly to deconstruct it: to write what cannot be written," and according to Shoshana Felman, "the challenge facing the woman today is nothing less than to 'reinvent' language, . . . to speak not only against, but outside of the specular phallogocentric structure, to establish a discourse the status of which would no longer be defined by the phallacy of masculine meaning."[27]

Beyond rhetoric, what can linguistic, historical, and anthropological research tell us about the prospects for a women's language? First of all, the concept of a women's language is not original with feminist criticism; it is very ancient and appears frequently in folklore and myth. In such myths, the essence of women's language is its secrecy; what is really being described is the male fantasy of the enigmatic nature of the feminine.

26. Burke, "Report from Paris," p. 844.
27. Jacobus, "The Difference of View," in *Women's Writing and Writing about Women,* pp. 12–13. Shoshana Felman, "Women and Madness: The Critical Phallacy," *Diacritics* 5 (Winter 1975): 10.

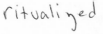

Herodotus, for example, reported that the Amazons were able linguists who easily mastered the languages of their male antagonists, although men could never learn the women's tongue. In *The White Goddess,* Robert Graves romantically argues that a women's language existed in a matriarchal stage of prehistory; after a great battle of the sexes, the matriarchy was overthrown and the women's language went underground, to survive in the mysterious cults of Eleusis and Corinth and the witch covens of Western Europe. Travelers and missionaries in the seventeenth and eighteenth centuries brought back accounts of "women's languages" among American Indians, Africans, and Asians (the differences in linguistic structure they reported were usually superficial). There is some ethnographic evidence that in certain cultures women have evolved a private form of communication out of their need to resist the silence imposed upon them in public life. In ecstatic religions, for example, women, more frequently than men, speak in tongues, a phenomenon attributed by anthropologists to their relative inarticulateness in formal religious discourse. But such ritualized and unintelligible female "languages" are scarcely cause for rejoicing; indeed, it was because witches were suspected of esoteric knowledge and possessed speech that they were burned.[28]

From a political perspective, there are interesting parallels between the feminist problem of a women's language and the recurring "language issue" in the general history of decolonization. After a revolution, a new state must decide which language to make official: the language that is "psychologically immediate," that allows "the kind of force that speaking one's mother tongue permits"; or the language that "is an avenue to the wider community of modern culture," a community to whose movements of thought only "foreign" languages can give access.[29] The language issue in feminist criticism has emerged, in a sense, after our revolution, and it reveals the tensions in the women's movement between those who would stay outside the academic establishments and the institutions of criticism and those who would enter and even conquer them.

The advocacy of a women's language is thus a political gesture that also carries tremendous emotional force. But despite its unifying appeal, the concept of a women's language is riddled with difficulties. Unlike Welsh, Breton, Swahili, or Amharic, that is, languages of minority or colonized groups, there is no mother tongue, no genderlect spoken by the female population in a society, which differs significantly from the dominant language. English and American linguists agree that "there is absolutely no evidence that would suggest the sexes are pre-

---

28. On women's language, see Sarah B. Pomeroy, *Goddesses, Whores, Wives, and Slaves: Women in Classical Antiquity* (New York, 1976), p. 24; McConnell-Ginet, "Linguistics and the Feminist Challenge," in *Women and Language,* p. 14; and Ioan M. Lewis, *Ecstatic Religion* (1971), cited in Shirley Ardener, ed., *Perceiving Women* (New York, 1977), p. 50.

29. Clifford Geertz, *The Interpretation of Cultures* (New York, 1973), pp. 241–42.

programmed to develop structurally different linguistic systems." Furthermore, the many specific differences in male and female speech, intonation, and language use that have been identified cannot be explained in terms of "two separate sex-specific languages" but need to be considered instead in terms of styles, strategies, and contexts of linguistic performance.[30] Efforts at quantitative analysis of language in texts by men or women, such as Mary Hiatt's computerized study of contemporary fiction, *The Way Women Write* (1977), can easily be attacked for treating words apart from their meanings and purposes. At a higher level, analyses which look for "feminine style" in the repetition of stylistic devices, image patterns, and syntax in women's writing tend to confuse innate forms with the overdetermined results of literary choice. Language and style are never raw and instinctual but are always the products of innumerable factors, of genre, tradition, memory, and context.

The appropriate task for feminist criticism, I believe, is to concentrate on women's access to language, on the available lexical range from which words can be selected, on the ideological and cultural determinants of expression. The problem is not that language is insufficient to express women's consciousness but that women have been denied the full resources of language and have been forced into silence, euphemism, or circumlocution. In a series of drafts for a lecture on women's writing (drafts which she discarded or suppressed), Woolf protested against the censorship which cut off female access to language. Comparing herself to Joyce, Woolf noted the differences between their verbal territories: "Now men are shocked if a woman says what she feels (as Joyce does). Yet literature which is always pulling down blinds is not literature. All that we have ought to be expressed—mind and body—a process of incredible difficulty and danger."[31]

"All that we have ought to be expressed—mind and body." Rather than wishing to limit women's linguistic range, we must fight to open and extend it. The holes in discourse, the blanks and gaps and silences, are not the spaces where female consciousness reveals itself but the blinds of a "prison-house of language." Women's literature is still haunted by the ghosts of repressed language, and until we have exorcised those ghosts, it ought not to be in language that we base our theory of difference.

5. *Women's Writing and Woman's Psyche*

Psychoanalytically oriented feminist criticism locates the difference of women's writing in the author's psyche and in the relation of gender to the creative process. It incorporates the biological and linguistic models of gender difference in a theory of the female psyche or self, shaped

30. McConnell-Ginet, "Linguistics and the Feminist Challenge," pp. 13, 16.

31. Woolf, "Speech, Manuscript Notes," *The Pargiters*, ed. Mitchell A. Leaska (London, 1978), p. 164.

by the body, by the development of language, and by sex-role socialization. Here too there are many difficulties to overcome; the Freudian model requires constant revision to make it gynocentric. In one grotesque early example of Freudian reductivism, Theodor Reik suggested that women have fewer writing blocks than men because their bodies are constructed to facilitate release: "Writing, as Freud told us at the end of his life, is connected with urinating, which physiologically is easier for a woman—they have a wider bladder."[32] Generally, however, psychoanalytic criticism has focused not on the capacious bladder (could this be the organ from which females generate texts?) but on the absent phallus. Penis envy, the castration complex, and the Oedipal phase have become the Freudian coordinates defining women's relationship to language, fantasy, and culture. Currently the French psychoanalytic school dominated by Lacan has extended castration into a total metaphor for female literary and linguistic disadvantage. Lacan theorizes that the acquisition of language and the entry into its symbolic order occurs at the Oedipal phase in which the child accepts his or her gender identity. This stage requires an acceptance of the phallus as a privileged signification and a consequent female displacement, as Cora Kaplan has explained:

> The phallus as a signifier has a central, crucial position in language, for if language embodies the patriarchal law of the culture, its basic meanings refer to the recurring process by which sexual difference and subjectivity are acquired. . . . Thus the little girl's access to the Symbolic, i.e., to language and its laws, is always negative and/or mediated by intro-subjective relation to a third term, for it is characterized by an identification with lack.[33]

In psychoanalytic terms, "lack" has traditionally been associated with the feminine, although Lac(k)anian critics can now make their statements linguistically. Many feminists believe that psychoanalysis could become a powerful tool for literary criticism, and recently there has been a renewed interest in Freudian theory. But feminist criticism based in Freudian or post-Freudian psychoanalysis must continually struggle with the problem of feminine disadvantage and lack. In *The Madwoman in the Attic,* Gilbert and Gubar carry out a feminist revision of Harold Bloom's Oedipal model of literary history as a conflict between fathers and sons and accept the essential psychoanalytic definition of the woman artist as displaced, disinherited, and excluded. In their view, the nature and "difference" of women's writing lies in its troubled and even tormented relationship to female identity; the woman writer experiences

32. Quoted in Erika Freeman, *Insights: Conversations with Theodor Reik* (Englewood Cliffs, N.J., 1971), p. 166. Reik goes on, "But what the hell, writing! The great task of a woman is to bring a child into the world."
33. Cora Kaplan, "Language and Gender" (unpublished paper, University of Sussex, 1977, p. 3).

her own gender as "a painful obstacle or even a debilitating inadequacy." The nineteenth-century woman writer inscribed her own sickness, her madness, her anorexia, her agoraphobia, and her paralysis in her texts; and although Gilbert and Gubar are dealing specifically with the nineteenth century, the range of their allusion and quotation suggests a more general thesis:

> Thus the loneliness of the female artist, her feelings of alienation from male predecessors coupled with her need for sisterly precursors and successors, her urgent sense of her need for a female audience together with her fear of the antagonism of male readers, her culturally conditioned timidity about self-dramatization, her dread of the patriarchal authority of art, her anxiety about the impropriety of female invention—all these phenomena of "inferiorization" mark the woman writer's struggle for artistic self-definition and differentiate her efforts at self-creation from those of her male counterpart. [*Madwoman*, p. 50]

In "Emphasis Added," Miller takes another approach to the problem of negativity in psychoanalytic criticism. Her strategy is to expand Freud's view of female creativity and to show how criticism of women's texts has frequently been unfair because it has been based in Freudian expectations. In his essay "The Relation of the Poet to Daydreaming" (1908), Freud maintained that the unsatisfied dreams and desires of women are chiefly erotic; these are the desires that shape the plots of women's fiction. In contrast, the dominant fantasies behind men's plots are egoistic and ambitious as well as erotic. Miller shows how women's plots have been granted or denied credibility in terms of their conformity to this phallocentric model and that a gynocentric reading reveals a repressed egoistic/ambitious fantasy in women's writing as well as in men's. Women's novels which are centrally concerned with fantasies of romantic love belong to the category disdained by George Eliot and other serious women writers as "silly novels"; the smaller number of women's novels which inscribe a fantasy of power imagine a world for women outside of love, a world, however, made impossible by social boundaries.

There has also been some interesting feminist literary criticism based on alternatives to Freudian psychoanalytic theory: Annis Pratt's Jungian history of female archetypes, Barbara Rigney's Laingian study of the divided self in women's fiction, and Ann Douglas' Eriksonian analysis of inner space in nineteenth-century women's writing.[34] And for the past few years, critics have been thinking about the possibilities of a

34. See Annis Pratt, "The New Feminist Criticisms," in *Beyond Intellectual Sexism*, ed. Joan I. Roberts (New York, 1976); Barbara Rigney, *Madness and Sexual Politics* (Athens, Ohio, 1979); and Ann Douglas, "Mrs. Sigourney and the Sensibility of the Inner Space," *New England Quarterly* 45 (June 1972): 163–81.

new feminist psychoanalysis that does *not* revise Freud but instead emphasizes the development and construction of gender identities.

The most dramatic and promising new work in feminist psychoanalysis looks at the pre-Oedipal phase and at the process of psychosexual differentiation. Nancy Chodorow's *The Reproduction of Mothering: Psychoanalysis and the Sociology of Gender* (1978) has had an enormous influence on women's studies. Chodorow revises traditional psychoanalytic concepts of differentiation, the process by which the child comes to perceive the self as separate and to develop ego and body boundaries. Since differentiation takes place in relation to the mother (the primary caretaker), attitudes toward the mother "emerge in the earliest differentiation of the self"; "the mother, who is a woman, becomes and remains for children of both genders the other, or object."[35] The child develops core gender identity concomitantly with differentiation, but the process is not the same for boys and girls. A boy must learn his gender identity negatively as being not-female, and this difference requires continual reinforcement. In contrast, a girl's core gender identity is positive and built upon sameness, continuity, and identification with the mother. Women's difficulties with feminine identity come after the Oedipal phase, in which male power and cultural hegemony give sex differences a transformed value. Chodorow's work suggests that shared parenting, the involvement of men as primary caretakers of children, will have a profound effect on our sense of sex difference, gender identity, and sexual preference.

But what is the significance of feminist psychoanalysis for literary criticism? One thematic carry-over has been a critical interest in the mother-daughter configuration as a source of female creativity.[36] Elizabeth Abel's bold investigation of female friendship in contemporary women's novels uses Chodorow's theory to show how not only the relationships of women characters but also the relationship of women writers to each other are determined by the psychodynamics of female bonding. Abel too confronts Bloom's paradigm of literary history, but unlike Gilbert and Gubar she sees a "triadic female pattern" in which the Oedipal relation to the male tradition is balanced by the woman writer's pre-Oedipal relation to the female tradition. "As the dynamics of female friendship differ from those of male," Abel concludes, "the dynamics of female literary influence also diverge and deserve a theory of influence attuned to female psychology and to women's dual position in literary history."[37]

35. Nancy Chodorow, "Gender, Relation, and Difference in Psychoanalytic Perspective," in *Future of Difference,* p. 11. See also Chodorow et al., "On *The Reproduction of Mothering:* A Methodological Debate," *Signs* 6 (Spring 1981): 482–514.

36. See, e.g., *The Lost Tradition: Mothers and Daughters in Literature,* ed. Cathy M. Davison and E. M. Broner (New York, 1980); this work is more engaged with myths and images of matrilineage than with redefining female identity.

37. Elizabeth Abel, "(E)Merging Identities: The Dynamics of Female Friendship in Contemporary Fiction by Women," *Signs* 6 (Spring 1981): 434.

Like Gilbert, Gubar, and Miller, Abel brings together women's texts from a variety of national literatures, choosing to emphasize "the constancy of certain emotional dynamics depicted in diverse cultural situations." Yet the privileging of gender implies not only the constancy but also the immutability of these dynamics. Although psychoanalytically based models of feminist criticism can now offer us remarkable and persuasive readings of individual texts and can highlight extraordinary similarities between women writing in a variety of cultural circumstances, they cannot explain historical change, ethnic difference, or the shaping force of generic and economic factors. To consider these issues, we must go beyond psychoanalysis to a more flexible and comprehensive model of women's writing which places it in the maximum context of culture.

6. Women's Writing and Women's Culture

> I consider women's literature as a specific category, not because of biology, but because it is, in a sense, the literature of the colonized.
> —Christiane Rochefort, "The Privilege of Consciousness"

A theory based on a model of women's culture can provide, I believe, a more complete and satisfying way to talk about the specificity and difference of women's writing than theories based in biology, linguistics, or psychoanalysis. Indeed, a theory of culture incorporates ideas about woman's body, language, and psyche but interprets them in relation to the social contexts in which they occur. The ways in which women conceptualize their bodies and their sexual and reproductive functions are intricately linked to their cultural environments. The female psyche can be studied as the product or construction of cultural forces. Language, too, comes back into the picture, as we consider the social dimensions and determinants of language use, the shaping of linguistic behavior by cultural ideals. A cultural theory acknowledges that there are important differences between women as writers: class, race, nationality, and history are literary determinants as significant as gender. Nonetheless, women's culture forms a collective experience within the cultural whole, an experience that binds women writers to each other over time and space. It is in the emphasis on the binding force of women's culture that this approach differs from Marxist theories of cultural hegemony.

Hypotheses of women's culture have been developed over the last decade primarily by anthropologists, sociologists, and social historians in order to get away from masculine systems, hierarchies, and values and to get at the primary and self-defined nature of female cultural experience. In the field of women's history, the concept of women's culture is still controversial, although there is agreement on its significance as a theoretical formulation. Gerda Lerner explains the importance of examining women's experience in its own terms:

> Women have been left out of history not because of the evil conspiracies of men in general or male historians in particular, but because we have considered history only in male-centered terms. We have missed women and their activities, because we have asked questions of history which are inappropriate to women. To rectify this, and to light up areas of historical darkness we must, for a time, focus on a *woman-centered* inquiry, considering the possibility of the existence of a female culture *within* the general culture shared by men and women. History must include an account of the female experience over time and should include the development of feminist consciousness as an essential aspect of women's past. This is the primary task of women's history. The central question it raises is: What would history be like if it were seen through the eyes of women and ordered by values they define?[38]

In defining female culture, historians distinguish between the roles, activities, tastes, and behaviors prescribed and considered appropriate for women and those activities, behaviors, and functions actually generated out of women's lives. In the late-eighteenth and nineteenth centuries, the term "woman's sphere" expressed the Victorian and Jacksonian vision of separate roles for men and women, with little or no overlap and with women subordinate. If we were to diagram it, the Victorian model would look like this:

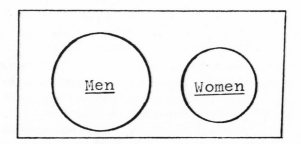

Woman's sphere was defined and maintained by men, but women frequently internalized its precepts in the American "cult of true womanhood" and the English "feminine ideal." Women's culture, however, redefines women's "activities and goals from a woman-centered point of view. . . . The term implies an assertion of equality and an awareness of sisterhood, the communality of women." Women's culture refers to "the broad-based communality of values, institutions, relationships, and

38. Gerda Lerner, "The Challenge of Women's History," *The Majority Finds Its Past* (New York, 1981); all further references to this book, abbreviated *MFP*, will hereafter be included parenthetically in the text.

methods of communication" unifying nineteenth-century female experience, a culture nonetheless with significant variants by class and ethnic group (*MFP*, pp. 52, 54).

Some feminist historians have accepted the model of separate spheres and have seen the movement from woman's sphere to women's culture to women's-rights activism as the consecutive stages of an evolutionary political process. Others see a more complex and perpetual negotiation taking place between women's culture and the general culture. As Lerner has argued:

> It is important to understand that "woman's culture" is not and should not be seen as a subculture. It is hardly possible for the majority to live in a subculture. . . . Women live their social existence within the general culture and, whenever they are confined by patriarchal restraint or segregation into separateness (which always has subordination as its purpose), they transform this restraint into complementarity (asserting the importance of woman's function, even its "superiority") and redefine it. Thus, women live a duality—as members of the general culture and as partakers of women's culture. [*MFP*, p. 52]

Lerner's views are similar to those of some cultural anthropologists. A particularly stimulating analysis of female culture has been carried out by two Oxford anthropologists, Shirley and Edwin Ardener. The Ardeners have tried to outline a model of women's culture which is not historically limited and to provide a terminology for its characteristics. Two essays by Edwin Ardener, "Belief and the Problem of Women" (1972) and "The 'Problem' Revisited" (1975), suggest that women constitute a *muted group,* the boundaries of whose culture and reality overlap, but are not wholly contained by, the *dominant (male) group.* A model of the cultural situation of women is crucial to understanding both how they are perceived by the dominant group and how they perceive themselves and others. Both historians and anthropologists emphasize the incompleteness of androcentric models of history and culture and the inadequacy of such models for the analysis of female experience. In the past, female experience which could not be accommodated by androcentric models was treated as deviant or simply ignored. Observation from an exterior point of view could never be the same as comprehension from within. Ardener's model also has many connections to and implications for current feminist literary theory, since the concepts of perception, silence, and silencing are so central to discussions of women's participation in literary culture.[39]

39. See, e.g., Tillie Olsen, *Silences* (New York, 1978); Sheila Rowbotham, *Woman's Consciousness, Man's World* (Harmondsworth, 1976), pp. 31–37; and Marcia Landy, "The Silent Woman: Towards a Feminist Critique," in *Authority of Experience* (n. 7 above), pp. 16–27.

By the term "muted," Ardener suggests problems both of language and of power. Both muted and dominant groups generate beliefs or ordering ideas of social reality at the unconscious level, but dominant groups control the forms or structures in which consciousness can be articulated. Thus muted groups must mediate their beliefs through the allowable forms of dominant structures. Another way of putting this would be to say that all language is the language of the dominant order, and women, if they speak at all, must speak through it. How then, Ardener asks, "does the symbolic weight of that other mass of persons express itself?" In his view, women's beliefs find expression through ritual and art, expressions which can be deciphered by the ethnographer, either female or male, who is willing to make the effort to perceive beyond the screens of the dominant structure.[40]

Let us now look at Ardener's diagram of the relationship of the dominant and the muted group:

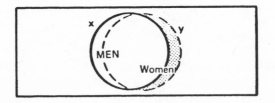

Unlike the Victorian model of complementary spheres, Ardener's groups are represented by intersecting circles. Much of muted circle Y falls within the boundaries of dominant circle X; there is also a crescent of Y which is outside the dominant boundary and therefore (in Ardener's terminology) "wild." We can think of the "wild zone" of women's culture spatially, experientially, or metaphysically. Spatially it stands for an area which is literally no-man's-land, a place forbidden to men, which corresponds to the zone in X which is off limits to women. Experientially it stands for the aspects of the female life-style which are outside of and unlike those of men; again, there is a corresponding zone of male experience alien to women. But if we think of the wild zone metaphysically, or in terms of consciousness, it has no corresponding male space since all of male consciousness is within the circle of the dominant structure and thus accessible to or structured by language. In this sense, the "wild" is always imaginary; from the male point of view, it may simply be the projection of the unconscious. In terms of cultural anthropology, women know what the male crescent is like, even if they have never seen it, because it becomes the subject of legend (like the wilderness). But men do not know what is in the wild.

40. Edwin Ardener, "Belief and the Problem of Women," in *Perceiving Women* (n. 28 above), p. 3.

For some feminist critics, the wild zone, or "female space," must be the address of a genuinely women-centered criticism, theory, and art, whose shared project is to bring into being the symbolic weight of female consciousness, to make the invisible visible, to make the silent speak. French feminist critics would like to make the wild zone the theoretical base of women's difference. In their texts, the wild zone becomes the place for the revolutionary women's language, the language of everything that is repressed, and for the revolutionary women's writing in "white ink." It is the Dark Continent in which Cixous' laughing Medusa and Wittig's *guérillères* reside. Through voluntary entry into the wild zone, other feminist critics tell us, a woman can write her way out of the "cramped confines of patriarchal space."[41] The images of this journey are now familiar in feminist quest fictions and in essays about them. The writer/heroine, often guided by another woman, travels to the "mother country" of liberated desire and female authenticity; crossing to the other side of the mirror, like Alice in Wonderland, is often a symbol of the passage.

Many forms of American radical feminism also romantically assert that women are closer to nature, to the environment, to a matriarchal principle at once biological and ecological. Mary Daly's *Gyn/Ecology* and Margaret Atwood's novel *Surfacing* are texts which create this feminist mythology. In English and American literature, women writers have often imagined Amazon Utopias, cities or countries situated in the wild zone or on its border: Elizabeth Gaskell's gentle *Cranford* is probably an Amazon Utopia; so is Charlotte Perkins Gilman's *Herland* or, to take a recent example, Joanna Russ' *Whileaway*. A few years ago, the feminist publishing house Daughters, Inc. tried to create a business version of the Amazon Utopia; as Lois Gould reported in the *New York Times Magazine* (2 January 1977), "They believe they are building the working models for the critical next stage of feminism: full independence from the control and influence of "male-dominated" institutions—the news media, the health, education, and legal systems, the art, theater, and literary worlds, the banks."

These fantasies of an idyllic enclave represent a phenomenon which feminist criticism must recognize in the history of women's writing. But we must also understand that there can be no writing or criticism totally outside of the dominant structure; no publication is fully independent from the economic and political pressures of the male-dominated society. The concept of a woman's text in the wild zone is a playful abstraction: in the reality to which we must address ourselves as critics, women's writing is a "double-voiced discourse" that always embodies the social, literary, and cultural heritages of both the muted and the dominant.[42]

41. Mari McCarty, "Possessing Female Space: 'The Tender Shoot,' " *Women's Studies* 8 (1981): 368.

42. Susan Lanser and Evelyn Torton Beck, "[Why] Are There No Great Women

And insofar as most feminist critics are also women writing, this precarious heritage is one we share; every step that feminist criticism takes toward defining women's writing is a step toward self-understanding as well; every account of a female literary culture and a female literary tradition has parallel significance for our own place in critical history and critical tradition.

Women writing are not, then, *inside* and *outside* of the male tradition; they are inside two traditions simultaneously, "undercurrents," in Ellen Moers' metaphor, of the mainstream. To mix metaphors again, the literary estate of women, as Myra Jehlen says, "suggests . . . a more fluid imagery of interacting juxtapositions, the point of which would be to represent not so much the territory, as its defining borders. Indeed, the female territory might well be envisioned as one long border, and independence for women, not as a separate country, but as open access to the sea." As Jehlen goes on to explain, an aggressive feminist criticism must poise itself on this border and must see women's writing in its changing historical and cultural relation to that other body of texts identified by feminist criticism not simply as literature but as "men's writing."[43]

The difference of women's writing, then, can only be understood in terms of this complex and historically grounded cultural relation. An important aspect of Ardener's model is that there are muted groups other than women; a dominant structure may determine many muted structures. A black American woman poet, for example, would have her literary identity formed by the dominant (white male) tradition, by a muted women's culture, and by a muted black culture. She would be affected by both sexual and racial politics in a combination unique to her case; at the same time, as Barbara Smith points out, she shares an experience specific to her group: "Black women writers constitute an identifiable literary tradition . . . thematically, stylistically, aesthetically, and conceptually. Black women writers manifest common approaches to the act of creating literature as a direct result of the specific political, social, and economic experience they have been obliged to share."[44] Thus the first task of a gynocentric criticism must be to plot the precise cultural locus of female literary identity and to describe the forces that intersect an individual woman writer's cultural field. A gynocentric criticism would also situate women writers with respect to the variables of literary culture, such as modes of production and distribution, relations

Critics? And What Difference Does It Make?" in *The Prism of Sex: Essays in the Sociology of Knowledge*, ed. Beck and Julia A. Sherman (Madison, Wis., 1979), p. 86.

43. Myra Jehlen, "Archimedes and the Paradox of Feminist Criticism," *Signs* 6 (Autumn 1981): 582.

44. Smith, "Black Feminist Criticism," p. 32. See also Gloria T. Hull, "Afro-American Women Poets: A Bio-Critical Survey," in *Shakespeare's Sisters*, pp. 165–82, and Marks, "Lesbian Intertextuality," in *Homosexualities and French Literature*, ed. Marks and George Stambolian (Ithaca, N.Y., 1979).

of author and audience, relations of high to popular art, and hierarchies of genre.

Insofar as our concepts of literary periodization are based on men's writing, women's writing must be forcibly assimilated to an irrelevant grid; we discuss a Renaissance which is not a renaissance for women, a Romantic period in which women played very little part, a modernism with which women conflict. At the same time, the ongoing history of women's writing has been suppressed, leaving large and mysterious gaps in accounts of the development of genre. Gynocentric criticism is already well on the way to providing us with another perspective on literary history. Margaret Anne Doody, for example, suggests that "the period between the death of Richardson and the appearance of the novels of Scott and Austen" which has "been regarded as a dead period, a dull blank" is in fact the period in which late eighteenth-century women writers were developing "the paradigm for women's fiction of the nineteenth century—something hardly less than the paradigm of the nineteenth-century novel itself."[45] There has also been a feminist re-habilitation of the female gothic, a mutation of a popular genre once believed marginal but now seen as part of the great tradition of the novel.[46] In American literature, the pioneering work of Ann Douglas, Nina Baym, and Jane Tompkins, among others, has given us a new view of the power of women's fiction to feminize nineteenth-century American culture.[47] And feminist critics have made us aware that Woolf belonged to a tradition other than modernism and that this tradition surfaces in her work precisely in those places where criticism has hitherto found obscurities, evasions, implausibilities, and imperfections.[48]

Our current theories of literary influence also need to be tested in terms of women's writing. If a man's text, as Bloom and Edward Said have maintained, is fathered, then a woman's text is not only mothered but parented; it confronts both paternal and maternal precursors and must deal with the problems and advantages of both lines of inheritance. Woolf says in *A Room of One's Own* that "a woman writing thinks back through her mothers." But a woman writing unavoidably thinks back through her fathers as well; only male writers can forget or mute half of their parentage. The dominant culture need not consider the muted, except to rail against "the woman's part" in itself. Thus we need

45. Margaret Anne Doody, "George Eliot and the Eighteenth-Century Novel," *Nineteenth Century Fiction* 35 (December 1980): 267–68.

46. See, e.g., Judith Wilt, *Ghosts of the Gothic: Austen, Eliot, and Lawrence* (Princeton, N.J., 1980).

47. See Douglas, *The Feminization of American Culture* (New York, 1977); Nina Baym, *Woman's Fiction: A Guide to Novels by and about Women in America, 1820–1870* (Ithaca, N.Y., 1978); and Jane Tompkins, "Sentimental Power: *Uncle Tom's Cabin* and the Politics of Literary History," *Glyph* 8 (1981): 79–102.

48. See, e.g., the analysis of Woolf in Gilbert, "Costumes of the Mind: Transvestism as Metaphor in Modern Literature," *Critical Inquiry* 7 (Winter 1980): 391–417.

more subtle and supple accounts of influence, not just to explain women's writing but also to understand how men's writing has resisted the acknowledgment of female precursors.

We must first go beyond the assumption that women writers either imitate their male predecessors or revise them and that this simple dualism is adequate to describe the influences on the woman's text. I. A. Richards once commented that the influence of G. E. Moore had had an enormous negative impact on his work: "I feel like an obverse of him. Where there's a hole in him, there's a bulge in me."[49] Too often women's place in literary tradition is translated into the crude topography of hole and bulge, with Milton, Byron, or Emerson the bulging bogeys on one side and women's literature from Aphra Behn to Adrienne Rich a pocked moon surface of revisionary lacunae on the other. One of the great advantages of the women's-culture model is that it shows how the female tradition can be a positive source of strength and solidarity as well as a negative source of powerlessness; it can generate its own experiences and symbols which are not simply the obverse of the male tradition.

How can a cultural model of women's writing help us to read a woman's text? One implication of this model is that women's fiction can be read as a double-voiced discourse, containing a "dominant" and a "muted" story, what Gilbert and Gubar call a "palimpsest." I have described it elsewhere as an object/field problem in which we must keep two alternative oscillating texts simultaneously in view: "In the purest feminist literary criticism we are . . . presented with a radical alteration of our vision, a demand that we see meaning in what has previously been empty space. The orthodox plot recedes, and another plot, hitherto submerged in the anonymity of the background, stands out in bold relief like a thumbprint." Miller too sees "another text" in women's fiction, "more or less muted from novel to novel" but "always there to be read."[50]

49. I. A. Richards, quoted in John Paul Russo, "A Study in Influence: The Moore-Richards Paradigm," *Critical Inquiry* 5 (Summer 1979): 687.

50. Showalter, "Literary Criticism," p. 435; Miller, "Emphasis Added," p. 47. To take one example, whereas *Jane Eyre* had always been read in relation to an implied "dominant" fictional and social mode and had thus been perceived as flawed, feminist readings foreground its muted symbolic strategies and explore its credibility and coherence in its own terms. Feminist critics revise views like those of Richard Chase, who describes Rochester as castrated thus implying that Jane's neurosis is penis envy, and G. Armour Craig, who sees the novel as Jane's struggle for superiority, to see Jane instead as healthy within her own system, that is, a *women's* society. See Chase, "The Brontës; or, Myth Domesticated," *Jane Eyre* (New York, 1971), pp. 462–71; G. Armour Craig, "The Unpoetic Compromise: On the Relation between Private Vision and Social Order in Nineteenth-Century English Fiction," in *Self and Society,* ed. Mark Schorer (New York, 1956), pp. 30–41; Nancy Pell, "Resistance, Rebellion, and Marriage: The Economics of *Jane Eyre,*" *Nineteenth Century Fiction* 31 (March 1977): 397–420; Helene Moglen, *Charlotte Brontë: The Self Conceived* (New York, 1977); Rich, "*Jane Eyre:* The Temptations of a Motherless Woman," *MS,* October 1973; and Maurianne Adams, "*Jane Eyre:* Woman's Estate," in *Authority of Experience,* pp. 137–59.

Another interpretive strategy for feminist criticism might be the contextual analysis that the cultural anthropologist Clifford Geertz calls "thick description." Geertz calls for descriptions that seek to understand the meaning of cultural phenomena and products by "sorting out the structures of signification . . . and determining their social ground and import."[51] A genuinely "thick" description of women's writing would insist upon gender and upon a female literary tradition among the multiple strata that make up the force of meaning in a text. No description, we must concede, could ever be thick enough to account for all the factors that go into the work of art. But we could work toward completeness, even as an unattainable ideal.

In suggesting that a cultural model of women's writing has considerable usefulness for the enterprise of feminist criticism, I don't mean to replace psychoanalysis with cultural anthropology as the answer to all our theoretical problems or to enthrone Ardener and Geertz as the new white fathers in place of Freud, Lacan, and Bloom. No theory, however suggestive, can be a substitute for the close and extensive knowledge of women's texts which constitutes our essential subject. Cultural anthropology and social history can perhaps offer us a terminology and a diagram of women's cultural situation. But feminist critics must use this concept in relation to what women actually write, not in relation to a theoretical, political, metaphoric, or visionary ideal of what women ought to write.

I began by recalling that a few years ago feminist critics thought we were on a pilgrimage to the promised land in which gender would lose its power, in which all texts would be sexless and equal, like angels. But the more precisely we understand the specificity of women's writing not as a transient by-product of sexism but as a fundamental and continually determining reality, the more clearly we realize that we have misperceived our destination. We may never reach the promised land at all; for when feminist critics see our task as the study of women's writing, we realize that the land promised to us is not the serenely undifferentiated universality of texts but the tumultuous and intriguing wilderness of difference itself.

51. Geertz, *Interpretation of Cultures*, p. 9.

The Question of Language: Men of Maxims and *The Mill on the Floss*

Mary Jacobus

> The first question to pose is therefore: how can women analyze their exploitation, inscribe their claims, within an order prescribed by the masculine? Is a politics of women possible there?
> —LUCE IRIGARAY[1]

To rephrase the question: Can there be (a politics of) women's writing? What does it mean to say that women can analyze their exploitation only "within an order prescribed by the masculine"? And what theory of sexual difference can we turn to when we speak, as feminist critics are wont to do, of a specifically "feminine" practice in writing? Questions like these mark a current impasse in contemporary feminist criticism. Utopian attempts to define the specificity of women's writing—desired or hypothetical, but rarely empirically observed—either founder on the rock of essentialism (the text as body), gesture toward an avant-garde practice which turns out not to be specific to women, or, like Hélène Cixous in "The Laugh of the Medusa," do both.[2] If anatomy is not destiny, still less can it be language.

1. Luce Irigaray: "La première question à poser est donc: comment les femmes peuvent-elles analyser leur exploitation, inscrire leurs revendications, dans un ordre prescrit par le masculin? *Une politique des femmes y est-elle possible?*" ("Pouvoir du discours, subordination du féminin," *Ce sexe qui n'en est pas un* [Paris, 1977], p. 78; my translation, here and elsewhere, unless otherwise indicated).

2. See Hélène Cixous, "The Laugh of the Medusa," trans. Keith and Paula Cohen, *Signs* 1 (Summer 1976): 875–93. The implications of such definitions of *"écriture féminine"* are discussed briefly in my "The Difference of View," in *Women Writing and Writing about Women,* ed. Jacobus (London, 1979), pp. 12–13, and by Nancy K. Miller, "Emphasis

A politics of women's writing, then, if it is not to fall back on a biologically based theory of sexual difference, must address itself, as Luce Irigaray has done in "Pouvoir du discours, subordination du féminin," to the position of mastery held not only by scientific discourse (Freudian theory, for instance), not only by philosophy, "the discourse of discourses," but by the logic of discourse itself. Rather than attempting to identify a specific practice, in other words, such a feminist politics would attempt to relocate sexual difference at the level of the text by undoing the repression of the "feminine" in all systems of representation for which the Other (woman) must be reduced to the economy of the Same (man). In Irigaray's terms, "masculine" systems of representation are those whose self-reflexiveness and specularity disappropriate women of their relation to themselves and to other women; as in Freud's theory of sexual difference (woman equals man-minus), difference is swiftly converted into hierarchy. Femininity comes to signify a role, an image, a value imposed on women by the narcissistic and fundamentally misogynistic logic of such masculine systems. The question then becomes for Irigaray not What is woman? (still less Freud's desperate What does a woman want?) but How is the feminine determined by discourse itself?—determined, that is, as lack or error or as an inverted reproduction of the masculine subject.[3]

Invisible or repressed, the hidden place of the feminine in language is the hypothesis which sustains this model of the textual universe, like ether. We know it must be there because we know ourselves struggling for self-definition in other terms, elsewhere, elsehow. We need it, so we invent it. When such an article of faith doesn't manifest itself as a mere rehearsal of sexual stereotypes, it haunts contemporary feminist criticism in its quest for specificity—whether of language, or literary tradition, or women's culture. After all, why study women's writing at all unless it is "women's writing" in the first place? The answer, I believe, must be a political one, and one whose impulse also fuels that gesture toward an elusive *"écriture féminine"* or specificity. To postulate, as

---

Added: Plots and Plausibilities in Women's Fiction," *PMLA* 96 (January 1981): 37. The present essay owes its existence in part to Miller's stimulating account of *The Mill on the Floss* in the context of the theoretical implications of "women's fiction" in general.

3. See Irigaray, "Pouvoir du discours," pp. 67–82 passim, and her *Speculum, de l'autre femme* (Paris, 1974), pp. 165–82. See also Carolyn Burke, "Introduction to Luce Irigaray's 'When our Lips Speak Together,' " *Signs* 6 (Autumn 1980): 71.

Mary Jacobus is an associate professor of English and of women's studies at Cornell University. She is the author of a book on Wordsworth as well as the editor of a collection of feminist criticism, *Women Writing and Writing about Women.*

Irigaray does, a "work of language" which undoes the repression of the feminine constitutes in itself an attack on the dominant ideology, the very means by which we know what we know and think what we think. So too the emphasis on women's writing politicizes in a flagrant and polemical fashion the "difference" which has traditionally been elided by criticism and by the canon formations of literary history. To label a text as that of a woman, and to write about it for that reason, makes vividly legible what the critical institution has either ignored or acknowledged only under the sign of inferiority. We need the term "women's writing" if only to remind us of the social conditions under which women wrote and still write—to remind us that the conditions of their (re)production are the economic and educational disadvantages, the sexual and material organizations of society, which, rather than biology, form the crucial determinants of women's writing.

Feminist criticism, it seems to me, ultimately has to invoke as its starting-point this underlying political assumption. To base its theory on a specificity of language or literary tradition or culture is already to have moved one step on in the argument, if not already to have begged the question, since by then one is confronted by what Nancy Miller, in a recent essay on women's fiction, has called "the irreducibly complicated relationship women have historically had to the language of the dominant culture."[4] Perhaps that is why, baffled in their attempts to specify the feminine, feminist critics have so often turned to an analysis of this relationship as it is manifested and thematized in writing by and about women. The project is, and can't escape being, an ideological one, concerned, that is, with the functioning and reproduction of sexual ideology in particular—whether in the overtly theoretical terms of a Luce Irigaray or in the fictional terms of, for instance, George Eliot. To quote Miller again, the aim would be to show that "the maxims that pass for the truth of human experience, and the encoding of that experience in literature, are organizations, when they are not fantasies, of the dominant culture."[5]

But Irigaray's "politics of women," her feminist argument, goes beyond ideology criticism in its effort to recover "the place of the feminine" in discourse. The "work of language" which she envisages would undo representation altogether, even to the extent of refusing the linearity of reading. "*Après-coup*," the retroactive effect of a word ending, opens up the structure of language to reveal the repression on which meaning depends; and repression is the place of the feminine. By contrast, the "style" of women—*écriture féminine*—would privilege not the look but the tactile, the simultaneous, the fluid. Yet at the same time, we discover, such a style can't be sustained as a thesis or made the object of a position;

4. Miller, "Emphasis Added," p. 38.
5. Ibid., p. 46.

if not exactly "nothing," it is nonetheless a kind of discursive practice that can't be thought, still less written. Like her style, woman herself is alleged by Irigaray to be an unimaginable concept within the existing order. Elaborating a theory of which woman is either the subject or the object merely reinstalls the feminine within a logic which represses, censors, or misrecognizes it. Within that logic, woman can only signify an excess or a deranging power. Woman for Irigaray is always that "something else" which points to the possibility of another language, asserts that the masculine is not all, does not have a monopoly on value, or, still less, "the abusive privilege of appropriation." She tries to strike through the theoretical machinery itself, suspending its pretension to the production of a single truth, a univocal meaning. Woman would thus find herself on the side of everything in language that is multiple, duplicitous, unreliable, and resistant to the binary oppositions on which theories of sexual difference such as Freud's depend.[6]

Irigaray's argument is seductive precisely because it puts all systems in question, leaving process and fluidity instead of fixity and form. At the same time, it necessarily concedes that women have access to language only by recourse to systems of representation which are masculine. Given the coherence of the systems at work in discourse, whether Freudian or critical, how is the work of language of which she speaks to be undertaken at all? Her answer is "mimetism," the role historically assigned to women—that of reproduction, but deliberately assumed; an acting out or role playing within the text which allows the woman writer the better to know and hence to expose what it is she mimics. Irigaray, in fact, seems to be saying that there is no "outside" of discourse, no alternative practice available to the woman writer apart from the process of undoing itself:

> To play with mimesis, is, therefore, for a woman, to attempt to recover the place of her exploitation by discourse, without letting herself be simply reduced to it. It is to resubmit herself . . . to "ideas," notably about her, elaborated in/by a masculine logic, but in order to make "visible," by an effect of playful repetition, what should have remained hidden: the recovery of a possible operation of the feminine in language. It is also to "unveil" the fact that, if women mime so well, they do not simply reabsorb themselves in this function. *They also remain elsewhere.*[7]

6. See Irigaray, "Pouvoir du discours," pp. 72–77 passim.

7. Irigaray: "Jouer de la mimésis, c'est donc, pour une femme, tenter de retrouver le lieu de son exploitation par le discours, sans s'y laisser simplement réduire. C'est se resoumettre . . . à des 'idées,' notamment d'elle, élaborées dans/par une logique masculine, mais pour faire 'apparaître,' par un effet de répétition ludique, ce qui devait rester occulté: le recouvrement d'une possible opération du féminin dans le langage. C'est aussi 'dévoiler' le fait que, si les femmes miment si bien, c'est qu'elles ne se résorbent pas simplement dans cette fonction. *Elles restent aussi ailleurs*" ("Pouvoir du discours," p. 74).

Within the systems of discourse and representation which repress the feminine, woman can only resubmit herself to them; but by refusing to be reduced by them, she points to the place and manner of her exploitation. "A possible operation of the feminine in language" becomes, then, the revelation of its repression, through an effect of playful rehearsal, rather than a demonstrably feminine linguistic practice.

Irigaray's main usefulness to the feminist critic lies in this half-glimpsed possibility of undoing the ideas about women elaborated in and by masculine logic, a project at once analytic and ideological. Her attack on centrism in general, and phallocentrism in particular, allows the feminist critic to ally herself "otherwise," with the "elsewhere" to which Irigaray gestures, in a stance of dissociation and resistance which typically characterizes that of feminist criticism in its relation to the dominant culture or "order prescribed by the masculine." But like Irigaray herself in "Pouvoir du discours," feminist criticism remains imbricated within the forms of intelligibility—reading and writing, the logic of discourse—against which it pushes. What makes the difference, then? Surely, the direction from which that criticism comes—the elsewhere that it invokes, the putting in question of our social organization of gender; its wishfulness, even, in imagining alternatives. It follows that what pleases the feminist critic most (this one, at any rate) is to light on a text that seems to do her arguing, or some of it, for her—especially a text whose story is the same as hers—hence, perhaps, the drift toward narrative in recent works of feminist criticism such as Sandra Gilbert and Susan Gubar's formidable *Madwoman in the Attic.*[8] What is usually going on in such criticism—perhaps in all feminist criticism—is a specificity of relationship that amounts to a distinctive practice. Criticism takes literature as its object, yes; but here literature in a different sense is likely to become the subject, the feminist critic, the woman writer, woman herself.

This charged and doubled relationship, an almost inescapable aspect of feminist criticism, is at once transgressive and liberating, since what it brings to light is the hidden or unspoken ideological premise of criticism itself. *Engagée* perforce, feminist criticism calls neutrality in question, like other avowedly political analyses of literature. I want now to undertake a "symptomatic" reading of a thematically relevant chapter from Eliot's *The Mill on the Floss* in the hope that this quintessentially critical activity will bring to light if not "a possible operation of the feminine in language" at least one mode of its recovery—language itself. I will return later to the final chapter of Irigaray's *Ce sexe qui n'en est pas un* in which an escape from masculine systems of representation is glimpsed through the metaphors of female desire itself.

8. See Sandra M. Gilbert and Susan Gubar, *The Madwoman in the Attic: The Woman Writer and the Nineteenth-Century Literary Imagination* (New Haven, Conn., 1979).

2

Nancy Miller's "maxims that pass for the truth of human experience" allude to Eliot's remark near the end of *The Mill on the Floss* that "the man of maxims is the popular representative of the minds that are guided in their moral judgment solely by general rules."[9] Miller's concern is the accusation of implausibility leveled at the plots of women's novels: Eliot's concern is the "special case" of Maggie Tulliver—"to lace ourselves up in formulas" is to ignore "the special circumstances that mark the individual lot." An argument for the individual makes itself felt by an argument against generalities. For Eliot herself, as for Dr. Kenn (the repository of her knowledge at this point in the novel), "the mysterious complexity of our life is not to be embraced by maxims" (p. 628). Though the context is the making of moral, not critical, judgments, I think that Eliot, as so often at such moments, is concerned also with both the making and the reading of fiction, with the making of another kind of special case. Though Maggie may be an "exceptional" woman, the ugly duckling of St. Ogg's, her story contravenes the norm, and in that respect it could be said to be all women's story. We recall an earlier moment, that of Tom Tulliver's harsh judgment of his sister (" 'You have not resolution to resist a thing that you know to be wrong' "), and Maggie's rebellious murmuring that her life is "a planless riddle to him" only because he's incapable of feeling the mental needs which impel her, in his eyes, to wrongdoing or absurdity (pp. 504, 505). To Tom, the novel's chief upholder of general rules and patriarchal law (he makes his sister swear obedience to his prohibitions on the family Bible), the planless riddle of Maggie's life is only made sense of by a "Final Rescue" which involves her death: " 'In their death they were not divided' " (p. 657). But the reunion of brother and sister in the floodwaters of the Ripple enacts both reconciliation and revenge, consummation and cataclysm; powerful authorial desires are at work.[10] To simplify this irreducible swirl of contradictory desire in the deluge that "rescues" Maggie as well as her brother would be to salvage a maxim as "jejune" as *"Mors omnibus est communis"* (one of the tags Maggie finds when she dips into her brother's Latin Grammar) stripped of its saving Latin.[11] We

9. Eliot, *The Mill on the Floss*, ed. A. S. Byatt (Harmondsworth, 1979), p. 628; all further references to this work will be included in the text. I am indebted to Byatt's helpful annotations.

10. See Gilbert and Gubar, *The Madwoman in the Attic*, which succinctly states that Maggie seems "at her most monstrous when she tries to turn herself into an angel of renunciation" (p. 491), and Gillian Beer, "Beyond Determinism: George Eliot and Virginia Woolf," in *Women Writing and Writing about Women*, on an ending that "lacks bleakness, is even lubricious" in its realization of "confused and passionate needs" (p. 88).

11. *"Mors omnibus est communis* would have been jejune, only [Maggie] liked to know the Latin" *(The Mill on the Floss,* pp. 217–18); see below.

might go further and say that to substitute a generality for the riddle of Maggie's life and death, or to translate Latin maxims into English commonplaces, would constitute a misreading of the novel as inept as Tom's misconstruction of his sister, or his Latin. Maggie's incomprehensible foreignness, her drift into error or impropriety on the river with Stephen Guest, is a "lapse" understood by the latitudinarian Dr. Kenn. For us, it also involves an understanding that planlessness, riddles, and impropriety—the enigmas, accidents, and incorrectness of language itself—are at odds with the closures of plot (here, the plot of incestuous reunion) and with interpretation itself, as well as with the finality of the maxims denounced by Eliot.

For all its healing of division, *The Mill on the Floss* uncovers the divide between the language or maxims of the dominant culture and the language itself which undoes them. In life, at any rate, they remain divided—indeed, death may be the price of unity—and feminist criticism might be said to install itself in the gap. A frequent move on the part of feminist criticism is to challenge the norms and aesthetic criteria of the dominant culture (as Miller does in defending Eliot), claiming, in effect, that "incorrectness" makes visible what is specific to women's writing. The culturally imposed or assumed "lapses" of women's writing are turned against the system that brings them into being—a system women writers necessarily inhabit. What surfaces in this gesture is the all-important question of women's access to knowledge and culture and to the power that goes with them. In writing by women, the question is often explicitly thematized in terms of education. Eliot's account of Tom's schooling in "School-Time," the opening chapter of book 2, provides just such a thematic treatment—a lesson in antifeminist pedagogy which goes beyond its immediate implications for women's education to raise more far-reaching questions about the functioning of both sexual ideology and language. Take Maggie's puzzlement at one of the many maxims found in the Eton Grammar, a required text for the unfortunate Tom. As often, rules and examples prove hard to tell apart:

> The astronomer who hated women generally caused [Maggie] so much puzzling speculation that she one day asked Mr Stelling if all astronomers hated women, or whether it was only this particular astronomer. But, forestalling his answer, she said,
> "I suppose it's all astronomers: because you know, they live up in high towers, and if the women came there, they might talk and hinder them from looking at the stars."
> Mr Stelling liked her prattle immensely. [P. 220]

What we see here is a text-book example of the way in which individual misogyny becomes generalized—"maximized," as it were—in the form of a patriarchal put down. Maggie may have trouble construing *"ad unam mulieres,*" or "all to a woman," but in essence she has got it right.[12] Just to prove her point, Mr. Stelling (who himself prefers the talk of women to star gazing) likes her "prattle," a term used only of the talk of women and children. Reduced to his idea of her, Maggie can only mimic man's talk.

Inappropriate as he is in other respects for Tom's future career, Mr. Stelling thus proves an excellent schoolmaster to his latent misogyny. His classroom is also an important scene of instruction for Maggie, who learns not only that all astronomers to a man hate women in general but that girls can't learn Latin; that they are quick and shallow, mere imitators ("this small apparatus of shallow quickness," Eliot playfully repeats); and that everybody hates clever women, even if they are amused by the prattle of clever little girls (pp. 214, 221, 216). It is hard not to read with one eye on her creator. Maggie, it emerges, rather fancies herself as a linguist, and Eliot too seems wishfully to imply that she has what one might call a "gift" for languages—a gift, perhaps, for ambiguity too. Women, we learn, don't just talk, they double-talk, like language itself; that's just the trouble for boys like Tom:

> "I know what Latin is very well," said Maggie, confidently. "Latin's a language. There are Latin words in the Dictionary. There's bonus, a gift."
>
> "Now, you're just wrong there, Miss Maggie!" said Tom, secretly astonished. "You think you're very wise! But 'bonus' means 'good,' as it happens—bonus, bona, bonum."
>
> "Well, that's no reason why it shouldn't mean 'gift,' " said Maggie stoutly. "It may mean several things. Almost every word does."
> [P. 214]

And if words may mean several things, general rules or maxims may prove less universal than they claim to be and lose their authority. Perhaps only "this particular astronomer" was a woman hater or hated only one woman in particular. Special cases or particular contexts—"the special circumstances that mark the individual lot" (p. 628)—determine or render indeterminate not only judgment but meaning too. The rules of language itself make Tom's rote learning troublesome to him. How can he hope to construe his sister when her relation to language proves so treacherous—her difference so shifting a play of possibility, like the difference within language itself, destabilizing terms such as "wrong" and "good"?

Maggie, a little parody of her author's procedures in *The Mill on the*

---

12. "*Astronomer: ut*—'as', *astronomus*—'an astronomer', *exosus*—'hating', *mulieres*—'women', *ad unum* [*mulierem*]—'to one' [that is, in general]. (*Eton grammar,* 1831 edition, p. 279)" (*The Mill on the Floss,* p. 676 n.55).

Floss, decides "to skip the rules in the syntax—the examples became so absorbing":

> These mysterious sentences snatched from an unknown context,—like strange horns of beasts and leaves of unknown plants, brought from some far-off region, gave boundless scope to her imagination, and were all the more fascinating because they were in a peculiar tongue of their own, which she could learn to interpret. It was really very interesting—the Latin Grammar that Tom had said no girls could learn: and she was proud because she found it interesting. The most fragmentary examples were her favourites. *Mors omnibus est communis* would have been jejune, only she liked to know the Latin; but the fortunate gentleman whom every one congratulated because he had a son "endowed with *such* a disposition" afforded her a great deal of pleasant conjecture, and she was quite lost in the "thick grove penetrable by no star," when Tom called out,
> "Now, then, Magsie, give us the Grammar!" [Pp. 217–18]

Whereas maxims lace her up in formulas, "these mysterious sentences" give boundless scope to Maggie's imagination; for her, as for her author (who makes them foretell her story), they are whole fictional worlds, alternative realities, transformations of the familiar into the exotic and strange. In their foreignness she finds herself, until roused by Tom's peremptory call, as she is later to be recalled by his voice from the Red Deeps. Here, however, it is Maggie who teaches Tom his most important lesson, that the "dead" languages had once been living: "that there had once been people upon the earth who were so fortunate as to know Latin without learning it through the medium of the Eton Grammar" (p. 221). The idea—or, rather, fantasy—of a language which is innate rather than acquired, native rather than incomprehensibly foreign, is a consoling one for the unbookish miller's son; but it holds out hope for Maggie too, and presumably also for her creator. Though Latin stands in for cultural imperialism and for the outlines of a peculiarly masculine and elitist classical education from which women have traditionally been excluded, Maggie can learn to interpret it. The "peculiar tongue" had once been spoken by women, after all—and they had not needed to learn it from Mr. Stelling or the institutions he perpetuates. Who knows, she might even become an astronomer herself or, like Eliot, a writer who by her pen name had refused the institutionalization of sexual difference as cultural exclusion. Tom and Mr. Stelling tell Maggie that " 'Girls never learn such things' "; " 'They've a great deal of superficial cleverness but they couldn't go far into anything' " (pp. 214, 221). But going far into things—and going far—is the author's prerogative in *The Mill on the Floss.* Though Maggie's quest for knowledge ends in death, as Virginia

Woolf thought Eliot's own had ended,[13] killing off this small apparatus of shallow quickness may have been the necessary sacrifice in order for Eliot herself to become an interpreter of the exotic possibilities contained in mysterious sentences. Maggie—unassimilable, incomprehensible, "fallen"—is her text, a "dead" language which thereby gives all the greater scope to authorial imaginings, making it possible for the writer to come into being.

3

We recognize in "School-Time" Eliot's investment—humorous, affectionate, and rather innocently self-loving—in Maggie's gifts and haphazard acquisition of knowledge. In particular, we recognize a defence of the "irregular" education which until recently had been the lot of most women, if educated at all. Earlier in the same chapter, in the context of Mr. Stelling's teaching methods (that is, his unquestioning reliance on Euclid and the Eton Grammar), Eliot refers whimsically to "Mr Broderip's amiable beaver" which "busied himself as earnestly in constructing a dam, in a room up three pairs of stairs in London, as if he had been laying his foundation in a stream or lake in Upper Canada. It was 'Binny's' function to build" (p. 206). Binny the beaver, a pet from the pages of W. J. Broderip's *Leaves from the Note Book of a Naturalist* (1852), constructed his dam with sweeping-brushes and warming-pans, "hand-brushes, rush-baskets, books, boots, sticks, clothes, dried turf or anything portable."[14] A domesticated *bricoleur,* Binny made do with what he could find. A few lines later, we hear of Mr. Stelling's "educated" condescension toward "the display of various or special knowledge made by irregularly educated people" (p. 207). Mr. Broderip's beaver, it turns out, does double duty as an illustration of Mr. Stelling's "regular" (not to say "rote") mode of instruction—he can do no otherwise, conditioned as he is—and as a defence of Eliot's own display of irregularly acquired "various or special knowledge." Like Maggie's, this is knowledge drawn directly from books, without the aid of a patriarchal pedagogue. Mr. Stelling and the institutions he subscribes to (Aristotle, deaneries, prebends, Great Britain, and Protestantism—the Establishment, in fact) are lined up against the author-as-eager-beaver. Eliot's mischievous impugning of authority and authorities—specifically, cultural authority—becomes increasingly explicit until, a page or so later, culture itself comes under attack. Finding Tom's brain "peculiarly impervious to etymology and demonstrations," Mr. Stelling concludes that it "was peculiarly in

13. See Woolf, "George Eliot," *Collected Essays,* 4 vols. (London, 1966), 1:204: "With every obstacle against her—sex and health and convention—she sought more knowledge and more freedom till the body, weighted with its double burden, sank worn out."

14. See *The Mill on the Floss,* pp. 675–76 n.44.

need of being ploughed and harrowed by these patent implements: it was his favourite metaphor, that the classics and geometry constituted that culture of the mind which prepared it for the reception of any subsequent crop." As Eliot rather wittily observes, the regimen proves "as uncomfortable for Tom Tulliver as if he had been plied with cheese in order to remedy a gastric weakness which prevented him from digesting it" (p. 208). Nor is Eliot only, or simply, being funny. The bonus or gift of language is at work here, translating dead metaphor into organic tract.

Like Maggie herself, the metaphor here is improper, disrespectful of authorities, and, as Tom later complains of his sister, not to be relied on. Developing the implications of changing her metaphor from agriculture to digestion, Eliot drastically undermines the realist illusion of her fictional world, revealing it to be no more than a blank page inscribed with a succession of arbitrary metaphoric substitutions:

> It is astonishing what a different result one gets by changing the metaphor! Once call the brain an intellectual stomach, and one's ingenious conception of the classics and geometry as ploughs and harrows seems to settle nothing. But then, it is open to some one else to follow great authorities and call the mind a sheet of white paper or a mirror, in which case one's knowledge of the digestive process becomes quite irrelevant. It was doubtless an ingenious idea to call the camel the ship of the desert, but it would hardly lead one far in training that useful beast. O Aristotle! if you had had the advantage of being "the freshest modern" instead of the greatest ancient, would you not have mingled your praise of metaphorical speech as a sign of high intelligence, with a lamentation that intelligence so rarely shows itself in speech without metaphor,—that we can so seldom declare what a thing is, except by saying it is something else? [Pp. 208–9]

In the *Poetics* Aristotle says: "It is a great thing to make use of . . . double words and rare words . . . but by far the greatest thing is the use of metaphor. That alone cannot be learned; it is the token of genius. *For the right use of metaphor means an eye for resemblances.*"[15] Of course there's authorial self-congratulation lurking in this passage, as there is in Eliot's affectionate parade of Maggie's gifts. But an eye for resemblances (between Binny and Mr. Stelling, for instance, or brain and stomach) is also here a satiric eye. Culture as (in)digestion makes Euclid and the Eton

---

15. Aristotle *Poetics* 22. 16 (my italics); see *The Mill on the Floss*, p. 676 n.46. J. Hillis Miller notes apropos of this passage that it "is followed almost immediately by an ostentatious and forceful metaphor [that of a shrewmouse imprisoned in a split tree (p. 209)], as if Eliot were compelled . . . to demonstrate that we cannot say what a thing is except by saying it is something else" ("The Worlds of Victorian Fiction," *Harvard English Studies* 6 [1975]: 145 n).

Grammar hard to swallow; Aristotle loses his authority to the author herself. On one level, this is science calling culture in question, making empiricism the order of the day. But there's something unsettling to the mind, or, rather, stomach, in this dizzy progression from culture, digestive tract, and *tabula rasa* to ship of the desert (which sounds like a textbook example of metaphor). The blank page may take what imprint the author chooses to give it. But the price one pays for such freedom is the recognition that language, thus viewed, is endlessly duplicitous rather than single-minded (as Tom would have it be); that metaphor is a kind of impropriety or oxymoronic otherness; and that "we can so seldom declare what a thing is, except by saying it is something else."

Error, then, must creep in where there's a story to tell, especially a woman's story. Maggie's "wrong-doing and absurdity," as the fall of women often does, not only puts her on the side of error in Tom's scheme of things but gives her a history; "the happiest women," Eliot reminds us, "like the happiest nations, have no history" (p. 494). Impropriety and metaphor belong together on the same side as a fall from absolute truth or unitary schemes of knowledge (maxims). Knowledge in *The Mill on the Floss* is guarded by a traditional patriarchal prohibition which, by a curious slippage, makes the fruit itself as indigestible as the ban and its thick rind. The adolescent Maggie, "with her soul's hunger and her illusions of self-flattery," begins "to nibble at this thick-rinded fruit of the tree of knowledge, filling her vacant hours with Latin, geometry, and the forms of the syllogism" (p. 380). But the Latin, Euclid, and Logic, which Maggie imagines "would surely be a considerable step in masculine wisdom," leave her dissatisfied, like a thirsty traveler in a trackless desert. What does Eliot substitute for this mental diet? After Maggie's chance discovery of Thomas à Kempis, we're told that "The old books, Virgil, Euclid, and Aldrich—that wrinkled fruit of the tree of knowledge—had been all laid by" for a doctrine that announces: " 'And if he should attain to all knowledge, he is yet far off' " (pp. 387, 383). Though the fruits of patriarchal knowledge no longer seem worth the eating, can we view Thomas à Kempis as anything more than an opiate for the hunger pains of oppression? Surely not. The morality of submission and renunciation is only a sublimated version of Tom's plain-spoken patriarchal prohibition, as the satanic mocker, Philip Wakem, doesn't fail to point out. Yet in the last resort, Eliot makes her heroine live and die by this inherited morality of female suffering—as if, in the economy of the text, it was necessary for Maggie to die renouncing in order for her author to release the flood of desire that is language itself.[16] Why?

The Mill on the Floss gestures toward a largely unacted error, the

16. See Carol Christ, "Aggression and Providential Death in George Eliot's Fiction," *Novel* (Winter 1976): 130–40, for a somewhat different interpretation.

elopement with Stephen Guest which would have placed Maggie finally outside the laws of St. Ogg's. Instead of this unrealized fall, we are offered a moment of attempted transcendence in the timeless death embrace which abolishes the history of division between brother and sister—"living through again in one supreme moment, the days when they had clasped their little hands in love" (p. 655). What is striking about the novel's ending is its banishing not simply of division but of sexual difference as the origin of that division. The fantasy is of a world where brother and sister might roam together, "indifferently," as it were, without either conflict or hierarchy. We know that their childhood was not like that at all, and we can scarcely avoid concluding that death is a high price to pay for such imaginary union. In another sense, too, the abolition of difference marks the death of desire for Maggie; "The Last Conflict" (the title of the book's closing chapter) is resolved by her final renunciation of Guest, resolved, moreover, with the help of "the little old book that she had long ago learned by heart" (p. 648). Through Thomas à Kempis, Eliot achieves a simultaneous management of both knowledge and desire, evoking an "invisible" or "supreme teacher" within the soul, whose voice promises "entrance into that satisfaction which [Maggie] had so long been craving in vain" (p. 384). Repressing the problematic issue of book learning, this "invisible teacher" is an aspect of the self which one might call the voice of conscience or, alternatively, sublimated maxims. In "the little old book," Maggie finds the authorized version of her own and Eliot's story, "written down by a hand that waited for the heart's prompting . . . the chronicle of a solitary, hidden anguish . . . a lasting record of human needs and human consolations, the voice of a brother who, ages ago, felt and suffered and renounced" (pp. 384–85).

Where might we look for an alternative version or, for that matter, for another model of difference, one that did not merely substitute unity for division and did not pay the price of death or transcendence? Back to the schoolroom, where we find Tom painfully committing to memory the Eton Grammar's "Rules for the Genders of Nouns," the names of trees being feminine, while some birds, animals, and fish *"dicta epicoena . . .* are said to be epicene."[17] In epicene language, as distinct from language imagined as either neutral or androgynous, gender is variable at will, a mere metaphor. The rules for the genders of nouns, like prescriptions about "masculine" or "feminine" species of knowledge, are seen to be entirely arbitrary. Thus the lament of David for Saul and Jonathan can be appropriated as the epitaph of brother and sister (" 'In their death they were not divided' "), and "the voice of a brother who, ages ago, felt and suffered and renounced" can double as the voice of a sister-author, the passionately epicene George Eliot. One answer, then, to my earlier question (Why does Eliot sacrifice her heroine to the

17. See *The Mill on the Floss,* p. 676 n.53.

morality of renunciation?) is that Eliot saw in Thomas à Kempis a language of desire, but desire managed as knowledge is also managed—sublimated not as renunciation but as writing. In such epicene writing, the woman writer finds herself, or finds herself in metaphor.

4

For Irigaray, the price paid by the woman writer for attempting to inscribe the claims of women "within an order prescribed by the masculine" may ultimately be death; the problem as she sees it is this: "[How can we] disengage ourselves, *alive,* from their concepts?"[18] The final, lyrical chapter of *Ce sexe qui n'en est pas un,* "Quand nos lèvres se parlent," is, or tries to be, the alternative she proposes. It begins boldly: "If we continue to speak the same language to each other, we will reproduce the same story."[19] This would be a history of disappropriation, the record of the woman writer's self-loss as, attempting to swallow or incorporate an alien language, she is swallowed up by it in turn:

> On the outside, you attempt to conform to an order which is alien to you. Exiled from yourself, you fuse with everything that you encounter. You mime whatever comes near you. You become whatever you touch. In your hunger to find yourself, you move indefinitely far from yourself, from me. Assuming one model after another, one master after another, changing your face, form, and language according to the power that dominates you. Sundered. By letting yourself be abused, you become an impassive travesty.[20]

This, perhaps, is what Miller means by "a posture of imposture," "the uncomfortable posture of all women writers in our culture, within and without the text."[21] Miming has become absorption to an alien order. One thinks of Maggie, a consumer who is in turn consumed by what she reads, an imitative "apparatus" who, like the alienated women imagined by Irigaray, can only speak their desire as "machines that are spoken, machines that speak." Speaking the same language, spoken in the language of the Same ("If we continue to speak this sameness, if we speak to each other as men have spoken for centuries . . . we will fail each other"), she can only be reproduced as the history of a fall.[22] Eliot herself, of course, never so much as gestures toward Irigaray's jubilant utopian love

18. Irigaray, "When Our Lips Speak Together," trans. Carolyn Burke, *Signs* 6 (Autumn 1980): 75.
19. Ibid., p. 69.
20. Ibid., pp. 73–74.
21. Miller, "Emphasis Added," p. 46.
22. Irigaray, "When Our Lips Speak Together," p. 69.

language between two women—a language of desire whose object *("l'in-differente")* is that internal (in)difference which, in another context, Barbara Johnson calls "not a difference between . . . but a difference within. Far from constituting the text's unique identity, it is that which subverts the very idea of identity." What is destroyed, conceptually, is the "unequivocal domination of one mode of signifying over another."[23] Irigaray's experiment in "Quand nos lèvres se parlent" is of this kind, an attempt to release the subtext of female desire, thereby undoing repression and depriving metalanguage of its claim to truth. "This wearisome labor of doubling and miming" is no longer enough.[24]

But for all Irigaray's experimentalism, the "difference" is not to be located at the level of the sentence, as Miller reminds us.[25] Rather, what we find in "Quand nos lèvres se parlent" is writing designed to indicate the cultural determinants which bind the woman writer and, for Irigaray, deprive her of her most fundamental relationship: her relationship to herself. In fact, what seems most specifically "feminine" about Irigaray's practice is not its experimentalism as such but its dialogue of one/two, its fantasy of the two-in-one: "In *life* they are not divided," to rephrase David's lament. The lips that speak together (the lips of female lovers) are here imagined as initiating a dialogue not of conflict or reunion, like Maggie and Tom's, but of mutuality, lack of boundaries, continuity. If both Irigaray and Eliot kill off the woman engulfed by masculine logic and language, both end also—and need to end—by releasing a swirl of (im)possibility:

> These streams don't flow into one, definitive sea; these rivers have no permanent banks; this body, no fixed borders. This unceasing mobility, this life. Which they might describe as our restlessness, whims, pretenses, or lies. For all this seems so strange to those who claim "solidity" as their foundation.[26]

Is that, finally, why Maggie must be drowned, sacrificed as a mimetic "apparatus," much as the solidity of St. Ogg's is swept away, to the flood whose murmuring waters swell the "low murmur" of Maggie's lips as they repeat the words of Thomas à Kempis? When the praying Maggie feels the flow of water at her knees, the literal seems to have merged with a figural flow; as Eliot writes, "the whole thing had been so rapid—so dreamlike—that the threads of ordinary association were broken" (p. 651). It is surely at this moment in the novel that we move most clearly into the unbounded realm of desire, if not of wish fulfilment. It is at this

23. Barbara Johnson, *The Critical Difference* (Baltimore, 1981), pp. 4, 5.
24. Irigaray, "When Our Lips Speak Together," p. 71.
25. See Miller, "Emphasis Added," p. 38.
26. Irigaray, "When Our Lips Speak Together," pp. 76–77.

moment of inundation, in fact, that the thematics of female desire surface most clearly.[27]

We will look in vain for a specifically feminine linguistic practice in *The Mill on the Floss;* "a possible operation of the feminine in language" is always elsewhere, not yet, not here, unless it simply reinscribes the exclusions, confines, and irregularities of Maggie's education. But what we may find in both Eliot and Irigaray is a critique which gestures beyond cultural boundaries, indicating the perimeters within which their writing is produced. For the astronomer who hates women in general, the feminist critic may wish to substitute an author who vindicates one woman in particular or, like Irigaray, inscribes the claims of all women. In part a critic of ideology, she will also want to uncover the ways in which maxims or *idées reçus* function in the service of institutionalizing and "maximizing" misogyny or simply deny difference. But in the last resort, her practice and her theory come together in Eliot's lament about metaphor—"that we can so seldom declare what a thing is, except by saying it is something else." The necessary utopianism of feminist criticism may be the attempt to declare what is by saying something else— that "something else" which presses both Irigaray and Eliot to conclude their very different works with an imaginative reaching beyond analytic and realistic modes to the metaphors of unbounded female desire in which each finds herself as a woman writing.

27. See Gillian Beer, "Beyond Determinism": "Eliot is fascinated by the unassuageable longings of her heroine. She allows them fulfilment in a form of plot which simply glides out of the channelled sequence of social growth and makes literal the expansion of desire. The river loses its form in the flood" (p. 88).

Eliot, Wordsworth, and the Scenes of the Sisters' Instruction

Margaret Homans

Two of Wordsworth's most important lyrics about the growth of the poet's imagination, "Tintern Abbey" and "Nutting," are also the scenes of a sister's instruction. Different as these two poems are, at the end of each the poet turns unexpectedly to his sister (named either as a sister or, in the case of "Nutting," as "dearest Maiden") who enters the poem not in her own right but in answer to the poet's and the poem's needs. At the end of "Tintern Abbey," the poet exhorts the sister to "remember me" by living out the stages of youth to which he himself cannot return.[1] "Nutting" 's last three lines frame the poet's painfully earned knowledge with the address, "Then, dearest Maiden," so as to turn that knowledge into instructions:

> Then, dearest Maiden, move along these shades
> In gentleness of heart; with gentle hand
> Touch—for there is a spirit in the woods.
>
> [ll. 54–56]

Both sisters exist to receive the brother's wishes, to confirm for him his hope that what he has gained in the course of the poem will find a habitation in a consciousness perhaps more enduring than his own. We

---

1. All quotations from Wordsworth are from *The Poetical Works of William Wordsworth*, ed. E. de Selincourt and Helen Darbishire, 5 vols. (London, 1940–1949), and from *The Prelude*, ed. Selincourt, 2d ed. rev. by Darbishire (London, 1959). Quotations from *The Prelude* are from the 1850 version. All further references to these works will be included in the text.

do not expect to learn anything from her about how she will use the gift contained in the poet's words. Her quietude verifies the power of the poet's performative words: he speaks, and, implicitly, for her to hear his words is to enact them. To ask what this listening might mean to her is perhaps in part a facetious question; yet for George Eliot it is also a real one. What is the female listener (or reader) to do with these words that are intended to help her circumvent the painful experiences that have forged the poet's consciousness? What does it mean to follow instructions given not for the sake of the student but for the sake of the teacher? The poet implies that the sister he addresses will learn to follow his path if she follows his instructions, but how are they to be followed, and with what results? These are not Wordsworth's concerns, but they are Eliot's.

Mary Ann Evans' remarks on reading Wordsworth at the age of twenty suggest that while, like Wordsworth's ideal sister, her feelings are congruent with his, she also experiences some ambivalence about receiving the poet's instructions. "I have been so self-indulgent as to possess myself of Wordsworth at full length. . . . I never before met with so many of my own feelings, expressed just as I could like them."[2] She does wish to be instructed: "to possess myself of" admits to a foreign excellence that must be possessed as different, not simply recognized. Yet simply to accept the poet's words would be, like the sister in the poems, to remain silent. That she describes her reading as "self-indulgent" and as a recognition of "my own feelings" suggests that, even though it is done half-jokingly, she needs to diminish Wordsworth's power of suggestion and to make it clear that any Wordsworthian act or feeling was hers before she learned that it might seem derivative. This tension between the need to respect and the need to deny a powerful influence—the feeling that what she possesses herself of, she had already possessed—is representative of the attitude toward Wordsworth expressed later on in Eliot's works.

Eliot's ambivalence toward Wordsworth's authority has been magnified for modern readers by a certain critical predisposition. Most readers who identify Wordsworthian features in Eliot have simply demonstrated affinity or resemblance without raising the question of derivation, taking Mary Ann Evans' word for it that Eliot's mind converged

2. Letter to Maria Lewis, Griff, 22 Nov. 1839, *The George Eliot Letters,* ed. Gordon S. Haight, 9 vols. (New Haven, Conn., 1954–1978), 1:34.

Margaret Homans, an assistant professor of English at Yale University, is the author of *Women Writers and Poetic Identity: Dorothy Wordsworth, Emily Brontë, and Emily Dickinson.*

spontaneously with Wordsworth's on the same point.³ Had there been no Wordsworth, Eliot would still have discovered for herself what are commonly taken to be their shared beliefs in the value of childhood and of rural life and in the necessity of constant interchange between feeling and knowledge. But while these are freely granted to be Eliot's own beliefs, criticism has nonetheless continued to comment on her Wordsworthian qualities (as it has sought out her Feuerbachian and Comtean qualities). Perhaps this is because believing her philosophic power imitates male originals (like her pseudonym) allows readers to portion out among various male authors some of the respect Eliot commands. It is generally assumed that her Wordsworthianism is pure, oddly, for two opposing reasons: the respect critics feel for "George Eliot" 's originality is so great that they do not think of calling "him" derivative; but their knowledge that "he" is really only Mary Ann Evans prepares them to find a daughterly veneration that would never tamper with literary authority. Criticism's need to find Eliot derivative not only highlights Eliot's own ambivalence but also situates the question of that ambivalence in the question of gender. For we could not possibly have been so concerned to see authority so docilely obeyed if the genders in the case were reversed.

Despite criticism's collusion with Eliot, there are a number of incongruities between Wordsworth's ideas and Eliot's texts that do not seem to be simply differences, scenes and passages that Eliot invites her readers to find Wordsworthian while she indicates a significant pattern of divergence from Wordsworthian prototypes. The brotherly instructions that Eliot is most generally concerned at once to follow and to deny are contained in Wordsworth's wish, in the verse "Prospectus" to *The Recluse,* to see "Paradise, and groves / Elysian" be "A simple produce of the common day" (ll. 47–48, 55). But when she follows this wish literally, her "common day," the intensely social world of her novels, tests far more strenuously the adaptability of the paradisal vision than does anything Wordsworth wrote. The generic incompatibility between a poet's vision and the form of the novel may account for some of the obvious differences, yet, as I will try to suggest later, it may be that Eliot's choice of the realistic novel as the form for her vision is in part an effect, not a cause, of her ambivalent divergences from Wordsworth (for example, a series of her sonnets articulates these concerns as much as do the novels).

3. There are far too many articles and parts of books about Eliot's Wordsworthianism to cite them all here. Among the excellent recent essays are: Henry Auster, "George Eliot and the Modern Temper," in *The Worlds of Victorian Fiction,* ed. Jerome H. Buckley (Cambridge, Mass., 1975); Deborah H. Roazen, "*Middlemarch* and the Wordsworthian Imagination," *English Studies* 58 (Oct. 1977): 411–25; and Jay Clayton, "Visionary Power and Narrative Form: Wordsworth and *Adam Bede,*" *English Literary History* 46 (Winter 1979): 645–72. Of value also is Robert Dunham, "Wordsworthian Themes and Attitudes in George Eliot's Fiction" (Ph.D. diss., Stanford University, 1972).

Often seeming to intend to, Eliot neither wishes nor is able, like the good sisters invented in Wordsworth's poems, always to carry out Wordsworthian instructions verbatim. I will argue that gender difference is the basis of Eliot's ambivalent response to Wordsworth's instructions. To anticipate my argument slightly, it is precisely the literalness of her transposition of Wordsworthian themes—her effort to be a docile student on the model of Wordsworth's implied sister—that constitutes her subversion of them; for the literal is destructive.

The Mill on the Floss is Eliot's "most Wordsworthian novel,"[4] and it is also her novel most concerned both with female education and with the brother-sister relationship. Maggie Tulliver's experience first as a reader and then as a sister may shed light on Eliot's relation to instruction, especially to brotherly instruction. Maggie's existence in the novel is framed by scenes of her reading. She starts out as an accurate reader who distinguishes easily between elucidating a text foreign to her and inventing her own stories (the two kinds of reading that become confused in Eliot's reading of Wordsworth). Having been reprimanded for her very perceptive reading of *The History of the Devil* as "not quite the right book for a little girl" and asked if she has "no prettier book," Maggie defends herself by opposing accurate reading to invention: " 'I know the reading in this book isn't pretty—but I like the pictures, and I make stories to the pictures out of my own head, you know.' "[5] At this point in her story, Maggie feels free both to read independently and to imagine freely, but we see her being chastized as a girl for both processes indifferently. However Maggie reads, " 'a woman's no business wi' being so clever; it'll turn to trouble, I doubt' " (bk. 1, chap. 3).

As Maggie grows up, learning to be feminine, her way of reading changes. As an adolescent in search of spiritual food and guidance, she becomes an overly literal reader of Thomas à Kempis. As the eager pupil of two guides, the author and the "quiet hand" that marked certain passages in her copy, Maggie acts out exactly the text's prescriptions and in so doing radically misreads it in at least two ways. She misconstrues renunciation not as sorrow but as an available form of satisfaction, and, according to Philip Wakem, she misuses her own gifts: " 'What you call self-conquest—blinding and deafening yourself to all but one train of impression—is only the culture of monomania in a nature like yours' " (bk. 5, chap. 4). The general effect of her reading Thomas à Kempis is to contribute to her education in femininity. She has turned to Thomas à Kempis in the first place because her brother Tom won't let "*my* sister"

---

4. Donald D. Stone, *The Romantic Impulse in Victorian Fiction* (Cambridge, Mass., 1980), p. 194.

5. *The Works of George Eliot*, vol. 5, *The Mill on the Floss*, 2 vols. (Edinburgh and London, 1877), 1:22; while I have quoted from this edition throughout, I will hereafter include parenthetically in the text only book and chapter numbers, for the convenience of those using other editions.

work to help pay off the family debt, depriving her of any useful (masculine) occupation. Her docility toward the text, her wish to follow its prescriptions exactly, is repeated both in the self-suppression she learns from the text's preaching and in her willingness to let her mother do with her as she pleases: "Her mother felt the change in her with a sort of puzzled wonder that Maggie should be 'growing up so good'; it was amazing that this once 'contrairy' child was become so submissive, so backward to assert her own will" (bk. 4, chap. 3). Though Maggie does not think of herself as learning how to be feminine—she sees herself as an ascetic—there is a grim joke in the very neat coincidence of her mother's wish for a conventionally "good" daughter and Thomas à Kempis' message of self-denial.

The more literal her reading, the less accurate and the more feminine. Yet when she attempts, as she used to with the pictures in *The History of the Devil,* her own imaginative departures from Scott's *The Pirate,* which she reads at about the same time, she meets with an equal lack of success that is again part of her education in femininity. Philip offers her his copy of *The Pirate* the first time they meet in the Red Deeps. " 'O, I began that once,' " she responds, " 'I read to where Minna is walking with Cleveland, and I could never get to read the rest. I went on with it in my own head, and I made several endings; but they were all unhappy. I could never make a happy ending out of that beginning' " (bk. 5, chap. 1).

Maggie is discovering here the inexorable laws of feminine plotting. It is the same discovery she makes later on when she laments that *Corinne* is merely one more repetition of the law requiring the blonde heroine to triumph over the dark heroine. Her invention of optimistic endings for a love story about a dark-haired girl is limited by the conventions both of plot and of social life. In fact, her endeavor to depart from convention only underscores for her both the heroine's and her own entrapment.[6] Her memory of trying and failing to invent happy endings for *The Pirate* is evoked by the fact that Philip has the book with him because he is studying a scene for a picture. His rationale for offering the book is, " 'I don't want it now. I shall make a picture of you instead—you, among the Scotch firs and the slanting shadows' " (bk. 5, chap. 1). But though she refuses the book, he makes the picture anyway: whether she reads or refuses to read, she will become a static visual object that prefigures her final silence.

Maggie enters the novel as a reader, and in her last scene before the flood carries her toward home, Tom, and death, she is reading again, choosing this time between two texts: the letter from Stephen and the words of Thomas à Kempis that would help her resist Stephen's appeal.

6. I am generally indebted to the recent work of Nancy K. Miller for my understanding of the issue of feminine plotting; see esp. her reading of the *Corinne* scene in "Emphasis Added: Plots and Plausibilities in Women's Fiction," *PMLA* 96 (Jan. 1981): 36–48.

At this last stage in her growth, her reading is only passive reiteration of conflicting texts for which she is simply the medium, providing no original word of her own. (Ironically, the two texts are really only representations of her own feelings, but she feels that they come from outside her.) Stephen's writing is so vivid to her that "she did not *read* the letter: she heard him uttering it, and the voice shook her with its old strange power" (bk. 7, chap. 5). He asks her to " 'Write me one word—say "Come!" In two days I should be with you.' " Her response takes the form of writing to his dictation, a literal repetition of his word provoked by the prospect not of her own joy but of Stephen's sorrow and by her self-doubts, which "made her once start from her seat to reach the pen and paper, and write 'Come!' " Maggie knows that her obedient and selfless literal repetition is wrong, but she is so exhausted emotionally that she can only wait passively "for the light that would surely come again." When it comes, the corrective to the reiteration of Stephen's word is her repetition of another's word: "The words that were marked by the quiet hand in the little old book that she had long ago learned by heart, rushed even to her lips, and found a vent for themselves in a low murmur that was quite lost in the loud driving of the rain against the window." First an unwilling copier of Stephen's word, now a ready voice for the words of Thomas à Kempis, Maggie does at last determine what her own words will be, but they "find no utterance but in a sob," and she defers writing them until the next day, which for her never comes.

Maggie's childhood capacity for original invention and for self-expression has by the end of her story quite vanished. Her adult self is a battleground for conflicting texts; when she takes up a pen or opens her mouth, the words that come forth as if they were her own are not hers. And this state of affairs results from, and in turn reinforces, the self-suppressing submissiveness that is identified throughout as feminine. To learn how to read as a repeater of others' words is feminine, and it is also fatal. Her departures from what she reads as an adolescent (her unintentional departure from Thomas à Kempis, her effort to vary the inexorable plot of *The Pirate*) are signs of her vital resistance (willful or unconscious) to feminine submissiveness, even though her efforts fail. When in the last reading scene Maggie gets her texts right, this final docility is a harbinger of her death: her complete passivity as a reader prefigures her succumbing to the flood the next morning.

When Eliot describes her own reading of Wordsworth as a process of possessing herself of what she already possesses, the ambiguous balance of originality and deference prefigures in compressed form some of the features of Maggie's development as a reader. It may be that Eliot is articulating through Maggie the stages of her own education in feminine readership, in how to be a docile or self-suppressing reader. To submit to others' words in Maggie's case is to submit to the law of cause and effect and therefore to reach the unhappy end predicted for all dark heroines. Eliot thematizes both docility and disobedience to instruction through the relation between Maggie's reading and the pattern of her life: disobedient reading is incompatible with femininity, yet complete feminine docility leads to the self's silence and ultimately to death. I would like to turn now to some instances of that dual reading (in *The Mill on the Floss* and elsewhere) that may suggest how the balance between docility and disobedience that Eliot thematizes in Maggie appears in her reading of Wordsworth. How is it possible to honor Wordsworth's words yet not die, as Maggie does, of the desire to be Wordsworth's sister and follow silently and involuntarily the wishes performed by his words? Carrying out Wordsworth's "remember me" in a way that she asks us to think of as literal (as Maggie's later readings are literal), she nonetheless departs radically from her original in passing from poetic and imaginative vision to the novelist's realistic vision. But the literal reading that for Maggie results in death issues for Eliot in the novelist's originality.

In calling *The Mill on the Floss* Eliot's most Wordsworthian novel, Donald Stone also locates in it "the most serious case of Wordsworthian blight on Eliot's creative imagination" because "the heroine is paralyzed by a myth of the past and a myth of her own childhood."[7] U. C. Knoepflmacher similarly sees "George Eliot's Wordsworthian novel vainly [trying to] enlist the Romantic's power of memory."[8] As he goes on to point out, where Wordsworth restores himself in "Tintern Abbey" through his own memories and through the memory he makes visible in his sister's eyes, Maggie and Tom succumb to the realities of "evil tongues, / Rash judgments," and the "dreary intercourse of daily life" Wordsworth refers to in his poem (ll. 128–29, 131). The question that these acute analyses raise is why the myth of the realistic novelist's growth must diverge so radically from Wordsworth's myth of the poet's growth. "Tintern Abbey" and "Nutting" have only an incidental place for the sister, while the poet's accounts of the growth of the imagination picture a solitary, even narcissistic relation between himself and nature's maternal presence in childhood. At its most powerful, too, the visionary imagination can isolate the self from the ordinary, visible world, as in the "spots of time" and the Simplon Pass passages in *The Prelude*.[9] Eliot's myth of childhood, however, for reasons that I will explore more fully later on, necessarily includes other people and a visible world that can never be occluded. In her revision of the Wordsworthian myth of childhood, Eliot's most autobiographical characters pass through what appear to be Wordsworthian childhoods not to become Romantic poets but to find that their ideal visions originating in childhood are thwarted by

7. Stone, *Romantic Impulse*, p. 194.

8. U. C. Knoepflmacher, *George Eliot's Early Novels: The Limits of Realism* (Berkeley, 1968), p. 175.

9. I am relying here on Thomas F. Weiskel's reading of Wordsworth's imagination: see *The Romantic Sublime* (Baltimore, 1976), pp. 167–204.

circumstances or by social needs. She sets her heroines' insatiable need for love, together with her own narrative commitment to realism, against the antisocial implications of what she represents as the introverting power of the imagination. Her heroines' need for love is insatiable because those who can supply it never love as unconditionally as Wordsworth's nature does, and Eliot schools her heroines to choose a love that represents a turning away from disruptive visionary power. In *The Mill on the Floss* and in the lesser-known sonnet sequence "Brother and Sister" (1869), the heroine gives up visionary aspirations (that are perhaps in any case untenable in the world of the novel) in favor of the love of a usually more practical-minded brother whose love makes childhood last forever and closes off the visionary world. That choice may lead to death, but the loss of vision may also be compensated for by an increase in a wisdom that is ultimately more appropriate to the novel.[10]

This ambivalent relation to Wordsworth stands out in one of the moments considered most Wordsworthian in Eliot, the fishing scene in *The Mill on the Floss* and the narrator's subsequent reflections on the value of memories of a childhood passed in nature (bk. 1, chap. 5). A close look at these passages reveals a willful misreading of the Wordsworthian implications of the scene, and the later consequences of the scene are the opposite of Wordsworthian. Opposing one brother (Tom) to a very different one (Wordsworth, brother of silent sisters), Eliot has Maggie defend against Wordsworth's authority while yet retaining all the forms of a sister's deference.[11]

As Sandra Gilbert and Susan Gubar point out, Maggie and Tom spend most of their precious time together making each other miserable, and while Maggie, Tom, and their narrator cling to the idea that their idyllic fishing expedition is typical of their childhood, the reader must suspect the effort to generalize from this exceptional scene.[12] The children live in a fallen, gendered world in which they can never escape for

10. Almost everything I will have to say about Maggie and the little sister in the sonnets holds true for Dorothea and Mary Garth in *Middlemarch* (though in varying ways; e.g., the brother in *The Mill on the Floss* and the sonnets becomes the brotherly lovers Will and Fred in *Middlemarch*). Due to limitations of space, I have omitted here discussions of these characters.

11. Mary Ann Evans' beloved older brother Isaac seems to have provided the model for many of Eliot's fictive brothers, including their dictatorial distaste for reading and the pleasures of the imagination. Apparently Evans was so anxious, as a child, to please her brother, whose only pleasures were physical, that she learned to read with difficulty and did not become an avid reader until he abandoned her to her own amusements (the story comes from her half-sister, Fanny Houghton, in *George Eliot's Life as Related in Her Letters and Journals*, ed. J. W. Cross, 3 vols. [Edinburgh and London, 1885], 1:15). However, the brothers in Eliot's fiction seem to be generated not so much to immortalize him as to justify the novelist's choice of realism and of the novel, to justify her affirmation of love over the visionary imagination.

12. See Sandra M. Gilbert and Susan Gubar, *The Madwoman in the Attic: The Woman Writer and the Nineteenth-Century Literary Imagination* (New Haven, Conn., 1979), p. 492.

very long the pain produced by their social condition. Fishing harmoniously together at "the old favourite spot," "Maggie thought it would make a very nice heaven to sit by the pool in that way, and never be scolded." But this heaven is brief and contingent on absolute physical and mental seclusion. That it cannot be carried over into the common day of their ordinary lives is underscored by the very precise description of its locale. The "old favourite spot" is a pool of unknown depth and mysterious origin that is also literally obscure, being "framed in with willows and tall reeds, so that the water was only to be seen when you got close to the brink."

Tom supervises the practical business of fishing, while Maggie "had forgotten all about the fish, and was looking dreamily at the glassy water." Hearing Tom's "loud whisper," Maggie is "frightened lest she had been doing something wrong, as usual," and when it turns out instead that she has inadvertently caught a fish, she "was not conscious of unusual merit." Maggie's happiness consists in such accidental absence of wrongdoing and in listening alternately to Tom's whispers and to the "happy whisperings" exchanged between the "light dipping sounds of the rising fish" and the gentle rustling of the willows and reeds. These illusions of reciprocity—for she and Tom communicate no more effectively than the water and the willows—encourage the children's equally illusory idea that their lives will always be like this. The narrator ends her account of Maggie and Tom by generalizing the Wordsworthian principle that the scene has apparently generated: "Life did change for Tom and Maggie; and yet they were not wrong in believing that the thoughts and loves of these first years would always make part of their lives." The narrator then turns to generalize about all human childhoods and finally to speak of her own.

It would seem at this point that "the thoughts and loves of these first years" refers primarily to the children's love for each other, with the mill and the river as setting. But as the passage continues into its larger and explicitly Wordsworthian frame of reference, the reader is given the strange impression that the foregoing scene has instead been solely concerned with the children's love for their natural surroundings.

> We could never have loved the earth so well if we had had no childhood in it,—if it were not the earth where the same flowers come up again every spring that we used to gather with our tiny fingers as we sat lisping to ourselves on the grass. . . . What novelty is worth that sweet monotony where everything is known, and *loved* because it is known?

The child's love of "rural objects" leads here not to deeper, wider kinds of love but simply to a renewed love of those identical objects. Even the expected reference to the endurance of Maggie's love for Tom—for which there would in any case be no place in the Wordsworthian paradigm of a solitary childhood in nature—is replaced by this love of objects. Stressing continuity over growth, the passage suggests how the Wordsworthian features of Maggie's childhood will contribute to narrowing her consciousness, not enlarging it. When, seeing all their old possessions taken away after the bankruptcy, Maggie cries to Tom, "The end of our lives will have nothing in it like the beginning!" (bk. 3, chap. 6), Eliot is presenting us with a version of childhood far more literal than Wordsworth's.

Eliot's ambiguous expression "make part of their lives" suggests, vaguely enough so as not to appear purposely misleading, the Wordsworthian idea that the experiences of childhood seed the ground of character to bear unpredictable fruits, as when Wordsworth's "glad animal movements," remembered later, lead circuitously to the more sober pleasures of the mature poet. He recalls specific incidents from his childhood for their place in his growing awareness, first of nature's presence and then of his own mind's powers. But Maggie's yearnings later are for particular objects—a book, that mill, that river—and in this she is not altogether different from the literal-minded Tom, whose adult energies are devoted solely to repossessing his property, or even from her even more limited mother, whose worship of objects connected with her Dodson past is pathetic and un-Wordsworthian in the extreme. For Maggie, objects loved in childhood remain beloved for their own sakes, or for their place in consecrating her love for her brother, but never for what they teach her about the growth of her own mind. A literal recapitulation of childhood could hardly be further from Wordsworth's aims for himself as poet; he does portray the dangers of obsessive fixation to a particular spot, but only in characters like Margaret in *The Excursion,* never in images of himself.

The Mill on the Floss' largest plot patterns turn on Maggie's need continually to reaffirm her ties to home. Her conflicting loves for Tom and for Philip are almost equally strong, having taken root in kindnesses conferred in childhood. Among her first sensations on "waking" from "the great temptation" is the urgent need to go home, where she may affirm her identity as a child needing discipline and protection from her wilder impulses and her adult self. The feature of childhood she wishes to repeat is not its illusion of Edenic peace but its pain: "in her anguish at the injury she had inflicted—she almost desired to endure the severity of Tom's reproof, to submit in patient silence to that harsh disapproving judgment against which she had so often rebelled" (bk. 7, chap. 1). She craves and believes she can return to a pattern, established in childhood by incidents like those with Tom's rabbits or the jam puffs, of harsh judgment, confession, and forgiveness. " 'I will endure anything. I want to be kept from doing wrong again.' " Tom, refusing her home and forgiveness, refuses to let her be a child again. But her final attempt to return to the mill (on the flood) does succeed in achieving a restoration both of childhood ties and of cathartic pain. Her death in returning home is thus doubly insured: by the fact that what she wants from childhood is its pain and by the fact that wishing to turn backward to childhood is itself a death wish.

For Wordsworth the natural objects to which the child feels bonded are always subordinate to the bond itself and to the wider sense of connectedness and vitality engendered by that bond; but Maggie's loyalty does not shift from those primary objects themselves. Wordsworth grows past his love for his mother and even for nature's maternal presence, but Maggie never transcends her love for Tom. Wordsworth's memories of childhood in *The Prelude* even include "the impressive discipline of fear" (1. 603) brought by nature's "Severer interventions, ministry / More palpable" (1. 355–56). But where Wordsworth's memory transforms that pain into imaginative power, Maggie seeks a literal recapitulation of the identical pain (inflicted in the same home by the same person) in Tom's punishment. The huge fragments of machinery that overtake Maggie and Tom are literalization itself: the failure of a life's worth of experiences to transcend themselves, remaining instead an agglomeration of things—the very literalness of the novel's revision of the Wordsworthian pattern. The narrator's conclusion to the fishing episode, speaking of "the sweet monotony" of a well-known landscape and of the return of the seasons, offers a seductively beautiful version of the narrative pattern of Maggie's life. In both, what might be self-transcendent turns out to be a return to particularity. Maggie's repetitions transform the beautiful "sweet monotony" into something more dangerous, since to repeat in human life is to go backward, not to stay the same.

To answer the question of why neither Maggie nor her narrative can go beyond the literal, it may be useful at this point to suggest the relationship between Maggie's education in feminine reading and her literalizing life. Along with her regressive wishes, her reading prefigures, if it does not actually insure, her death. When Maggie cries out "the end of our lives will have nothing in it like the beginning," her immediate reference is to the copy of *The Pilgrim's Progress* that she interpreted so acutely for Mr. Riley in her first reading scene. " 'Our dear old Pilgrim's Progress that you coloured with your little paints; and that picture of Pilgrim with a mantle on, looking just like a turtle—oh dear!' Maggie went on, half sobbing as she turned over the few books. 'I thought we should never part with that while we lived' " (bk. 3, chap. 6). Pilgrim "looking just like a turtle" reminds us that this book symbolizes her independent way in childhood of "making stories to the pictures out of my own head," a way of reading that is now lost to her. When the book is sold off with all the other books, it is converted into the chief symbol, among the objects that Maggie misses, of her literalized version of the

Wordsworthian sense of the past and thus of the kind of literal reading she has now fallen into. Furthermore, it is Maggie's sorrow over the loss of the book that indirectly leads her to become a more and more literal reader: it is because of witnessing her sorrow that Bob Jakin later brings Maggie the gift of assorted books among which she finds the Thomas à Kempis. Her docile feminine repetitions, first of Stephen's "Come!" and then of the memorized text of Thomas à Kempis, echo and confirm her desire literally to repeat her childhood by returning home to Tom and the mill, first after she has left Stephen and finally during the flood, a passive repetition that overdetermines her death. These repetitions of texts represent an abandonment of self that signals the approach of death; and that the repetition is literal prefigures the particular shape that death will take—her literally being overtaken by the huge mass of machinery on the flood. The reading acts do not themselves cause her death, but they identify the thematics of return with rhetorical repetition and the thematics of death with the lack of one's own word. And as specifically feminine reading acts, they identify learned feminine behavior with return, literal repetition, death, and silence.

Maggie's docility and final silence connect her, then, to the figure of Wordsworth's silent, listening sister. Yet her kind of education is also linked to Wordsworth's own: the sonnet sequence "Brother and Sister" presents another version of Maggie's kind of education, one which displays some verbal similarity to a Wordsworthian scene of the poet's instruction. Drawn from the same stock of Eliot's own experience as the dreamy little sister of a practical-minded older brother, the sonnet sequence shares with the fishing scene in *The Mill on the Floss* both its general contours of plot and characterization and its ostensible aim, to assert that "the thoughts and loves of these first years would always make part of their lives."[13] The sonnet sequence also revises the rowing episode from book 1 of *The Prelude,* which Eliot had reread at least two years previous to composing the sonnets and perhaps more recently than that.[14] In order to find a paradigm more suitable than that of the silent sister, Eliot considers that of the future poet; yet she cannot go so far as to portray herself as a brother. Remaining a sister, she makes it clear what limits gender places on what it is possible for a heroine to do or to be.

13. "Brother and Sister" and *The Mill on the Floss* have always been taken to be generally autobiographical, but it is of course both impossible and unnecessary to tell how accurately they record the actual events of Eliot's early life. It is possible that these works have been taken, tautologically, as the source of biographical information. See Ruby Redinger, *George Eliot: The Emergent Self* (New York, 1975), pp. 44–65, for an extensive reading of "Brother and Sister" as autobiography; see also Haight, *George Eliot: A Biography* (New York, 1968), pp. 5–6 and 421.

14. See Thomas Pinney, "George Eliot's Reading of Wordsworth: The Record," *Victorian Newsletter* 24 (Fall 1963): 20–22.

Like the Round Pool, the canal setting of the sonnets' fishing episode literalizes the sublime. Where the Round Pool is literally profound and obscure, "Our brown canal was endless to my thought," and barges float into view around "a grassy hill to me sublime / With some Unknown beyond it."[15] While the brother and sister fish together in the canal, the sister tells us that "One day my brother left me in high charge, / To mind the rod while he went seeking bait" (7), with instructions to pull the line out of the way of oncoming barges. Like Maggie fishing in the Round Pool, the little sister's attention lapses,

> Till sky and earth took on a strange new light
> And seemed a dream-world floating on some tide—
>
> A fair pavilioned boat for me alone
> Bearing me onward through the vast unknown.
>
> [7]

Her "dreamy peace" is broken by the arrival of a barge and by the sounds of her brother's anger, but the unhappy situation is turned around when it appears that the line she lifts out at the last minute has a fish on it, so that "My guilt that won the prey" is "Now turned to merit" (8). This scene replays very closely Maggie's fishing scene, in which she, too, felt "she had been doing something wrong, as usual," but has instead by pure chance caught a fish. Like Maggie, the little sister here, accidentally rewarded for doing wrong, learns from this event only that "luck was with glory wed." Morally ambiguous, these scenes teach Maggie and the little sister the insignificance of their actions relative to material coincidence.

Like the two fishing scenes, Wordsworth's rowing episode in *The Prelude* concerns a child's transgression, but Wordsworth's "act of stealth / And troubled pleasure" (1. 361–62) clearly deserves and as clearly receives punishment, unlike the ambiguous moral situations in which the two little girls find themselves. Having stolen a rowboat, Wordsworth's child enjoys a brief period of wonder that may be identified with what Coleridge and Wordsworth call "fancy." The "elfin pinnace" moves on,

> Leaving behind her still, on either side,
> Small circles glittering idly in the moon,
> Until they melted all into one track
> Of sparking light.
>
> [1. 364–67]

15. Eliot, "Brother and Sister," *The Legend of Jubal and Other Poems, Old and New* (Edinburgh and London, 1874), sonnet 6, p. 202; all further references to the sonnets will be included in the text, with sonnet number in parentheses.

This part of the episode corresponds to the "dreamy peace" that appears sublime for the sister in the sonnets, a remembered state that includes a vision of "The wondrous watery rings that died too soon" (7), and corresponds also to the moment of transgression before transgression is recognized as such, when "sky and earth took on a strange new light / And seemed a dream-world." The scene turns sinister for Wordsworth's child when, as he rows away from the shore, the "nothing but the stars and the grey sky" beyond the ridge is replaced by "a huge peak, black and huge" that "As if with voluntary power instinct / Upreared its head" and that appears to grow larger and to stride after him as the boy tries to escape it (1. 378–80). This huge and animated peak corresponds to the sonnets' "barge's pitch-black prow" (8) appearing around the hill that—like Wordsworth's ridge, beyond which is only the sky—has previously screened a sublime vacancy.

Despite the similarity of the two situations, the moral outcome is entirely different for each child. Where Wordsworth senses that nature has arranged this spectacle for his instruction, the looming object is for Eliot an accidental occurrence, not the product of a moral design. The actual barge might be the literalization of the little girl's dream of the "fair pavilioned boat," so that its frightening arrival would be the self-inflicted punishment for daydreaming, as Wordsworth's "huge peak, black and huge" seems to embody the boy's guilt. But the barge in the sonnets is pursuing its own independent, commercial course—unknown to the girl but not therefore a product of her imagination—and does not "stride after her" in the manner of the purposeful "grim shape" of Wordsworth's story. Its arrival is simply bad luck, just as the appearance of the fish on her line at the critical moment is simply good luck. Both are material accidents occurring independently of the girl's psychic growth. Significantly, Eliot's child is stationary on the canal bank, imagining herself in a "fair pavilioned boat" but about to be threatened by the arrival of a real one, while Wordsworth's child is himself in the real boat, the performer of the action, not the object of it. Like Maggie, the girl finds herself to be a passive spectator in a world of powerful things that are governed by chance. Of course, if we look at what "really" happens in Wordsworth, the appearance of the peak on the horizon is sheer accident too; what is important is that while the girl knows that she is subject to luck, the boy never deviates from his certainly that, because nature regulates her actions according to the needs of his education, nature has in this instance acted for him.

Had the girl been punished for daydreaming, by losing the line, say, she would have received an amply ambiguous moral lesson against imaginative, rather than immoral (as for Wordsworth), actions; as it is, she is even more confusingly rewarded for doing something that is considered wrong, but not being punished. Out of this confusion, if there is any lesson for her, it is that daydreaming is inefficacious and irrelevant, too trivial to be either punished or rewarded. Yet it is precisely at this point in his story that Wordsworth's child's imagination is made to grow. One of nature's "severer interventions" on his behalf issues first and almost incidentally in a moral lesson that is both clear and just, a lesson that is, however, subordinate to the deep and troubling indeterminacy he feels in response to his discovery of nature's ministrations:

> my brain
> Worked with a dim and undetermined sense
> Of unknown modes of being; o'er my thoughts
> There hung a darkness, call it solitude
> Or blank desertion.
>
> [1. 391–95]

This "blank desertion" suspends and restructures the boy's total relation to the world around him. Lacking nature's active ministry, Eliot's child learns both to fear and to discount her imagination.

Following the fishing episode, the little sister completes her conversion from dreaming by entering into her brother's exclusively physical pleasures, such as knocking apples out of trees and playing with marbles and tops.

> Grasped by such fellowship my vagrant thought
> Ceased with dream-fruit dream-wishes to fulfill;
> My aëry-picturing fantasy was taught
> Subjection to the harder, truer skill
>
> That seeks with deeds to grave a thought-tracked
>   line,
> And by "What is," "What will be" to define.
>
> [10]

This conversion to the principles of linear plot and realism is presented as a good, supported by and reinforcing the myth of George Eliot as a contentedly realistic novelist, even though the examples of realistic behavior she adduces are not very persuasive. The next (and final) sonnet's sketch of the two children's futures confirms the realist's patterning of " 'What will be' " on " 'What is,' " when "the dire years whose awful name is Change" "pitiless" shapes their souls "in two forms that range / Two elements which sever their life's course"(11). Eliot is formulating here in terms that seem applicable to herself as a realistic novelist the same discovery that Maggie makes when she tries to invent alternate endings for *The Pirate*. "I could never make a happy ending out of that beginning" is Maggie's recognition that, like Minna, she will succumb to the inexorable laws of cause and effect of realistic plotting.

The sonnets' commitment to linear plotting reverses Wordsworth's conclusion to the rowing scene. Moving from the actual "huge peak, black and huge" to the "huge and mighty forms" of the mind, Wordsworth concludes with a disruption between the familiar past and any possible future, a cleavage that is the signature of the imagination:

> No familiar shapes
> Remained, no pleasant images of trees,
> Of sea or sky, no colours of green fields;
> But huge and mighty forms, that do not live
> Like living men, moved slowly through the mind
> By day, and were a trouble to my dreams.
>   [1. 395–400]

Wordsworth does value familiar shapes and rural images, but ultimately because they aid in forming and sustaining the affections of the heart, which then can survive independently of shapes and images. The imagination casts off, if painfully, precisely those things that both Maggie and the narrator of *The Mill on the Floss* cling to and affirm to be of highest value in themselves. The sonnets' turn to realism and the asserted determination of the future by the present reiterates both Maggie's suffocating repetitions of the literal past and the way in which the novel's narrator, moving at the close of the fishing scene, like Maggie, not from the finite to the sublime but from particular to particular, recalls and celebrates the literal repetition of exactly those "familiar shapes," those "pleasant images of trees, / Of sea or sky," those "colours of green fields," that Wordsworth's young imagination in its most powerful activity discards. For the narrator, love of a natural scene moves beautifully but statically to love of the same natural scene:

> These familiar flowers, these well-remembered bird-notes, this sky, with its fitful brightness, these furrowed and grassy fields, each with a sort of personality given to it by the capricious hedgerows— such things as these are the mother tongue of our imagination, the language that is laden with all the subtle inextricable associations the fleeting hours of our childhood left behind them. Our delight in the sunshine on the deep-bladed grass to-day, might be no more than the faint perception of wearied souls, if it were not for the sunshine and the grass in the far-off years which still live in us, and transform our perception into love. [Bk. 1, chap. 5]

The allusion to the imagination is problematic here, since this love, rich as it is, is not what Wordsworth, whose presence is so clearly invoked, would call the imagination. Human relatedness stands in the place of Wordsworth's solitary perception of nature as the central formative influence on the growing child. Prefatory to the series of related incidents that culminates in the rowing episode, Wordsworth writes: "Fair seed-time had my soul and I grew up / Fostered alike by beauty and by fear" (1. 301–2). In a comparable position prefatory to the fishing incident, Eliot recalls Wordsworth's lines, but with a crucial difference:

> Thus rambling we were schooled in deepest lore,
> And learned the meanings that give words a soul,
> The fear, the love, the primal passionate store,
> . . . .
>
> Those hours were seed to all my after good.
>
> [5]

Wordsworth's beauty and fear are nature's ministries, devoted gratuitously and unconditionally to the growing boy, while for Eliot "The fear, the love" are purely human: the love is between the sister and the brother, and the fear is merely of its loss (and also of a gypsy glimpsed in the sonnet preceding these lines). Just as throughout *The Mill on the Floss* Maggie's "need of love had triumphed over her pride, . . . it is a wonderful subduer, this need of love" (bk. 1, chap. 5), the little sister's allegiance to realism results from a kind of emotional blackmail through which her other needs as an individual are subordinated to the one overwhelming craving to be loved. The sister purchases love through acknowledging the preeminence of the objects that the brother loves; the transformation of perception into love defines the imagination as a binding love (of things and of the brother inextricably) that for Maggie will become obsessive and constricting and that for Wordsworth is antithetical to the imagination.

That "things" should have so privileged a relation to the imagination is troubling, but that things should be "the mother tongue of our imagination" is more problematic still, as the phrase ironically illuminates one source of Eliot's heroines' exclusive need to choose love over the world of imagination. A "mother tongue" in Wordsworth might signify feminized nature's fostering of imaginative growth in passages such as the rowing episode. But the nature for which Eliot's narrator expresses her enduring love is not at all Wordsworth's maternal nature but rather the nature of objects that signify the brother's realism and the sister's devotion to it. Because of the girl's differing place in and experience of the family configuration, it would be impossible for any female character in Eliot ever plausibly to imagine herself in the same relation to the idea of maternal nature that Wordsworth is privileged to feel. Mrs. Tulliver's restrictiveness toward Maggie, her partiality to Tom, and her preoccupation with domestic objects reappear in the mother in "Brother and Sister," whose loving overprotectiveness the children try to escape: "Our mother bade us keep the trodden ways," while "the benediction of her gaze / Clung to us lessening, and pursued us still" (3). In a social world in which mothers are not "presences" but socially conditioned beings, these inappropriately mothered little sisters are unable to assume maternal love and guidance in the way that Wordsworth's young self can.

Wordsworth's introduction to the rowing episode, "One summer evening (led by her)" (1. 357), emphasizes the theme of nature's purposive moral instruction. Introducing her comparable story in "Brother and Sister," Eliot writes, "One day my brother left me in high charge." It is under the brother's responsibility that the girl experiences the moral confusion of luck. The brother can hardly regulate circumstances as nature can, and he cannot be expected to direct the event toward his sister's moral growth. His love, like almost any human love after the myth of maternal love, is conditional, almost as accidental as the motions of barges and fish, and can never be taken for granted by his sister. Lacking the unconditional devotion of the Wordsworthian mother, daughters in Eliot seek for the imagination a *brother* tongue. But because of the brother's fixation on objects that seal him, together with the sister who accepts his values, away from the imaginary, that brother tongue is unobtainable. The transformation of perception into love prevents the transformation of perception into the Wordsworthian, visionary imagination.

In the rowing episode, the boy must violate the law in order to learn of nature's ceaseless attention to his actions, just as in "Nutting" the boy must ravage the virgin bower before he can discover that "there is a spirit in the woods." Such experiences are necessary to the boy's moral and imaginative education, and they are never final because maternal nature always forgives. It is these experiences from which Wordsworth as a brother would protect his sister. Eliot's young sisters are just as much protected from experiencing such enlarging transgressions, by their fear of losing the brother's love. The two kinds of brothers (Wordsworth; Tom and the brother of the sonnets) share this trait of mediating, or attempting to, between their younger sisters and the sublime. They are linked only in this regard, standing otherwise for opposing values, but this connection suggests the significance of their opposition in Eliot's alignment of them.

Eliot's comments about reading Wordsworth, we have seen, like the change in Maggie's reading, reflect an ambivalent response to the authority of a text that seems both to foster and to subvert her originality. The temptation to silence or rote repetition is an especially feminine one, a temptation to docility and self-suppression. Thus though Eliot might like to write in congruence with a revered male authority, conforming as Wordsworth's silent sister might do, or as Maggie does in devoutly repeating the words of Thomas à Kempis, she cannot and does not want to do so in these gendered matters. To defend against being Wordsworth's sister (and perhaps in part also because Mary Ann Evans had such a brother), Eliot represents her heroines as sisters of explicitly anti-Wordsworthian brothers, so that to follow the authority of one is necessarily to contravene that of the other. Excluded from the Wordsworthian paradigm for continuity between a childhood spent with a guiding maternal nature and visionary imagination, Eliot and her female characters seek approval in brothers. But they find that the brother's approval is earned only by turning away from what that other brother, Wordsworth, would approve, the solitary world of the imagination, toward a world governed by the law of cause and effect. When Eliot's heroines are torn between the imaginary world and the practical world of the brother, they thematize the tension between Eliot's desire to listen silently or repeat Wordsworth and her desire to show that what she reads in his authoritative texts was originally her own. To have the heroine enter fully into the world of imagination would be to concur that there are no truths beyond Wordsworth's, while to have her wholly allied with the brother would be, for Eliot, to deny altogether the values she shares with Wordsworth. Defending herself from one powerful male authority by inventing (or investing) another, Eliot finds a way to be at once original and deferential.

To repeat Wordsworth literally would in any case be a contradiction in terms. Eliot exploits this contradiction fully: to pay proper homage to Wordsworth would be to have' him speak through her, as Maggie lets Thomas à Kempis speak through her; but to do so is necessarily to get Wordsworth wrong and thus to fail to pay proper homage. The more literally Maggie repeats the texts authoritative for her, and the more literally Eliot has her live out what seem to be Wordsworthian notions (in her repetitions of childhood experiences and in her desire for the home objects), the closer she comes both to perfect femininity and to death. But the more literal the repetition, the more divergent from Wordsworth's aims, for to read Wordsworth literally in a female context is to become a realist. Where the Wordsworthian imagination interrupts or would interrupt between " 'What is' " and " 'What will be,' " between material cause and effect, and between the introduction of a dark heroine and the certainty that her end will be unhappy, Eliot's heroines, in submitting to these laws, define a realistic fictional world. The literalizing that characterizes Maggie's adult feelings and actions (her love of the home objects, her desire for literal repetitions of her early life, and her repetitions of texts) is paralleled by Eliot's general turn toward what she persuades us is realism. For Maggie, literalization leads to her death, but it leads for Eliot to something definitively her own—her identity as a novelist of real life, which she establishes under cover of seeming to be a docile, feminine reader of her beloved Wordsworth. It is in fact Maggie's death that consolidates Eliot's vital independence from Wordsworth: she dies of choosing social bonds over the self's needs. The scenes of Maggie's reading and instruction are also the scenes of Eliot's reading and instruction; but while Maggie fatally learns the lesson of feminine readership, Eliot fortunately fails.

"The Blank Page" and the Issues of Female Creativity

Susan Gubar

> When the "Mona Lisa" was stolen from the Louvre in Paris in 1911 and was missing for two years, more people went to stare at the blank space than had gone to look at the masterpiece in the 12 previous years.
> —BARBARA CARTLAND, *Book of Useless Information*

> "The female genital, like the blank page anticipating the poem, is an absence, a not me, which I occupy."
> —SANDRA MCPHERSON, "Sentience," *The Year of Our Birth*

Consider for a moment Ovid's story of Pygmalion: a king, shocked at the vices of the female disposition, creates a beautiful statue, significantly an ivory statue white as snow, with which he falls in love. Pygmalion brings his lovely statue presents, dresses it, bedecks it with jewels, fondles its curves, takes it to bed, and prays to Venus that his wife be (or be like) his "ivory girl." When he feels the ivory under his fingers soften, "as wax grows soft in sunshine, made pliable by handling," Pygmalion is astonished with joy: "It is a body!"[1] Not only has he created life, he has created female life as he would like it to be—pliable, responsive, purely physical. Most important, he has evaded the humiliation, shared by many men, of acknowledging that it is *he* who is really created out of and from the *female* body.

I am indebted to Sandra M. Gilbert for her insights and encouragement on this paper.

1. Ovid, *Metamorphoses,* trans. Rolfe Humphries (Bloomington, Ind., 1955), pp. 241–43.

Our culture is steeped in such myths of male primacy in theological, artistic, and scientific creativity. Christianity, as feminist theologians have shown us, is based on the power of God the Father, who creates the natural world of generation out of nothing.[2] Literary men like Coleridge, Shelley, Keats, and Ruskin describe the author as priest, prophet, warrior, legislator, or emperor, reinforcing the idea most lucidly articulated by Gerard Manley Hopkins that "the male quality is the creative gift."[3] The example of scientific overreachers from the Faust of Marlowe and Goethe and Mann to the most recent DNA biologists implies that scientific ingenuity also seeks to usurp the generative powers of the womb, even as it tries to re-create the female in the male's image. But if the creator is a man, the creation itself is the female, who, like Pygmalion's ivory girl, has no name or identity or voice of her own. Margaret Atwood's prose poem about two boys who construct a woman out of mud ("She began at the neck and ended at the knees and elbows: they stuck to essentials") seems far removed from Ovid's ivory girl. Yet the boys continually "repair her, making her hips more spacious, enlarging her breasts with their stone nipples," as they make use of "her brown wormy flesh" ("They would take turns, they were not jealous, she preferred them both"):[4] both the ivory girl and the mud woman are products of the male imagination, objects created for the use of men. As Simone de Beauvoir has demonstrated in *The Second Sex,* the phallus as the transcendent incarnate turns woman's self into an object, an other.[5]

Woman is not simply an object, however. If we think in terms of the production of culture, she is an art object: she is the ivory carving or mud replica, an icon or doll, but she is not the sculptor. Lest this seem fanciful, we should remember that until very recently women have been barred from art schools as students yet have always been acceptable as

2. See Mary Daly, *Beyond God the Father* (Boston, 1973), and *Womanspirit Rising: A Feminist Reader in Religion,* ed. Carol P. Christ and Judith Plaskow (San Francisco, 1979).

3. Hopkins, letter to Richard Watson Dixon, 30 June 1896, *The Correspondence of Gerard Manley Hopkins and Richard Watson Dixon,* ed. C. C. Abbott (London, 1935), p. 133. For a fuller discussion of the identification of paternity and creativity, see Sandra M. Gilbert and Gubar, *The Madwoman in the Attic: The Woman Writer and the Nineteenth-Century Literary Imagination* (New Haven, Conn., 1979), pp. 3–44.

4. Margaret Atwood, untitled poem in the Circle/Mud sequence, *You Are Happy* (New York, 1974), p. 61.

5. See Simone de Beauvoir, *The Second Sex,* trans. H. M. Parshley (New York, 1970).

Susan Gubar, associate professor of English at Indiana University, is coauthor of *The Madwoman in the Attic: The Woman Writer and the Nineteenth-Century Literary Imagination* and coeditor of *Shakespeare's Sisters: Feminist Essays on Women Poets,* both with Sandra M. Gilbert.

models. Both Laura and Beatrice were turned into characters by the poems they inspired. A poet as sensitive as Chaucer to this reification of the female allowed Criseyde to recognize and lament her own dilemma: "Allas, of me, unto the worldes ende, / Shall neyther ben ywriten nor ysonge / No good word; for these bokes wol me shende" (bk. 5, st. 152). Like the words written about her, she fears she will be "rolled on many a tongue!"[6] Shakespeare also studied this entrapment of the woman: looking at Desdemona, whom he imagines dishonest, Othello asks, "Was this fair paper, this most goodly book, / Made to write 'whore' upon?" (4. 2. 71–72).[7] The appropriation of the female "read" or "written" into textuality makes one wonder about many another heroine's fate. On more than one occasion, Dorothea Brooke in *Middlemarch* bemoans her inability to become a poet; how much of a comfort is Will Ladislaw's assurance to her that "You *are* a poem"?[8] Ezra Pound quotes a similar line to the poet H. D.: "You are a poem, though your poem's naught."[9] When the metaphors of literary creativity are filtered through a sexual lens, female sexuality is often identified with textuality.

We can see this clearly in Henry James' *Portrait of a Lady*, where the ideal *jeune fille* is described as "a sheet of blank paper." So "fair and smooth a page would be covered with an edifying text," we are told, whereas the experienced woman who is "written over in a variety of hands" has a "number of unmistakable blots" upon her surface.[10] In *To the Lighthouse*, egotistical Mr. Ramsay sees his wife in a window "as an illustration, a confirmation of something on the printed page to which one returns, fortified and satisfied."[11] In Conrad's *Victory*, Axel Heyst saves a girl called Lena (after the seductress Magdalena) from "murdering silence" in an all-female orchestra by renaming her Alma (soul). Converted from artist to accompanist to accomplice, she seems "like a script in an unknown language" or "like any writing to an illiterate." Looking at her Heyst feels like a "man looking this way and that on a piece of writing which he was unable to decipher, but which may be big

6. I am indebted for this view of Criseyde to Marcelle Thiebaux's "Foucault's Fantasia for Feminists: The Woman Reading" (paper delivered at the MMLA Convention, Indianapolis, 8 November 1979).

7. The symbolic value of the "handkerchief / Spotted with strawberries" (3.3.434–45) is closely identified with Othello's fear that his "lust-stained" bedsheets must "with lust's blood be spotted." For a brilliant discussion of male sexual anxiety in *Othello*, see Stephen J. Greenblatt, "Improvisation and Power," in *Literature and Society: Selected Papers from the English Institute*, ed. Edward W. Said (Baltimore, 1980), pp. 57–99.

8. George Eliot, *Middlemarch* (Boston, 1968), p. 166.

9. Pound, quoted by H. D., *End To Torment* (New York, 1979), p. 12.

10. Henry James, *The Portrait of a Lady* (New York, 1978), pp. 238, 268. It is interesting to compare this view of the blank female text with the horror Margaret Laurence's heroine, Morag, feels at the dying, fat, and servile stepmother whose "face is as blank as a sheet of white paper upon which nothing will ever now be written" (*The Diviners* [Toronto, 1978], p. 250).

11. Virginia Woolf, *To the Lighthouse* (New York, 1955), p. 53.

with some revelation."[12] From *The Waste Land,* in which a woman's hair "glow[s] into words," to *The Great Gatsby,* in which the "black rivulets" of mascara on a weeping woman lead to the "humorous suggestion . . . that she sing the notes on her face," the female body has been feared for its power to articulate itself.[13] More recently, Ishmael Reed describes sex in this way: "He got good into her Book tongued her every passage thumbing her leaf and rubbing his hands all over her binding."[14] And John Berryman sums up the implications of this metaphor when he concludes a sequence of sonnets written to his mistress with the emphatic admission, "You are the text."[15]

In fact contemporary critics not infrequently write about the act of reading in sexual terms. A "passage" of a text is a way of knowing a "corpus" or "body" of material that should lead us on, tease us—but not too obviously. "Knowing" a book is not unlike sexual knowing, as Roland Barthes has demonstrated in *The Pleasure of the Text,* his erotics of reading.[16] Not only do we experience gratification orally as we "devour" books voraciously, we also respond subliminally to the "rhythms" of the plot, looking forward to a "climax." Furthermore, Claude Lévi-Strauss implies that the female must be identified with language used by men in the perpetuation of culture when he explains in *Structural Anthropology* that women are "*circulated* between clans, lineages, or families, in place of *the words of the group,* which are *circulated* between individuals."[17] Similarly, William Gass argues that "ordinary language ought to be like the gray inaudible wife who services the great man: an ideal engine, utterly self-effacing, devoted without remainder to its task; but when language is used as an art it is no longer used merely to communicate. It demands to be treated as a thing, inert and voiceless."[18] The connection between women and words is less explicit but just as significant in David Lodge's

12. Joseph Conrad, *Victory* (Garden City, N.Y., 1957), p. 183.

13. T. S. Eliot, *The Waste Land and Other Poems* (New York, 1962), sec. 2, l. 110; see also sec. 5, ll. 378–90: "A woman drew her long black hair out tight / And fiddled whispered music on those strings." F. Scott Fitzgerald, *The Great Gatsby* (New York, 1953), p. 34; see also p. 119 where Jordan Baker is described as "a good illustration."

14. Ishmael Reed, *Mumbo Jumbo* (New York, 1978), p. 208–9.

15. John Berryman, *Berryman's Sonnets* (New York, 1967), p. 114. Russell Baker recently compared women to books, bemoaning the fact that "it is common nowadays to find yourself confronting a woman no thicker than a slim volume of poetry while buying a book wider than a piano" ("Sunday Observer," *New York Times Magazine,* 2 December 1979, p. 28).

16. See Roland Barthes, *The Pleasure of the Text,* trans. Richard Miller (New York, 1975), p. 32: "There are those who want a text (an art, a painting) without a shadow, without the 'dominant ideology'; but this is to want a text without fecundity, without productivity, a sterile text (see the myth of the Woman without a Shadow)." Barthes' next book, *A Lover's Discourse,* makes the connection explicit by moving directly from the eroticism of texts to the eroticism of bodies.

17. Claude Lévi-Strauss, *Structural Anthropology,* trans. Claire Jacobson and Brooke Grundfest Schoepf (New York, 1963), p. 61.

18. William H. Gass, *Fiction and the Figures of Life* (New York, 1971), p. 93.

Language of Fiction. Lodge asserts that the medium of fiction "is never virgin: words come to the writer already violated by other men. . . ."[19] This corrupt lexicon presumably can be redeemed by the semantics of the text, for its seminal meaning is almost always closely associated with the seed or semen of the author's mind brooding on the repository of the page that bodies this meaning forth: Pound, for example, describes ideal creativity as a result of "the balance of the ejector [male] and retentive media [female]."[20] And in an effort to criticize what he calls phallocentrism, Jacques Derrida describes the literary process in terms of the identification of the pen with the penis, the hymen with the page. As Gayatri Spivak explains in her introduction to *Of Grammatology*, "The hymen is the always folded . . . space in which the pen writes its dissemination."[21]

This model of the pen-penis writing on the virgin page participates in a long tradition identifying the author as a male who is primary and the female as his passive creation—a secondary object lacking autonomy, endowed with often contradictory meaning but denied intentionality. Clearly this tradition excludes woman from the creation of culture, even as it reifies her as an artifact within culture. It is therefore particularly problematic for those women who want to appropriate the pen by becoming writers. Especially in the nineteenth-century, women writers, who feared their attempts at the pen were presumptuous, castrating, or even monstrous, engaged in a variety of strategies to deal with their anxiety about authorship. Sandra M. Gilbert and I discuss some of these strategies in *The Madwoman in the Attic.* But just as important as the anxiety the male pen produces in the would-be woman writer is the horror she experiences at having been defined as his creation. Indeed, this problem seems to explain the coherence of nineteenth- and twentieth-century writing by women. Isak Dinesen's short story "The Blank Page" addresses this question with brilliant clarity.[22] This story can be used to illustrate how woman's image of herself as text and artifact has affected her attitudes toward her physicality and how these attitudes in turn shape the metaphors through which she imagines her creativity.

Briefly, the story of "The Blank Page" centers on the sisters of a

19. David Lodge, *Language of Fiction* (New York, 1966), p. 47.

20. Pound's postscript to his translation of Remy de Gourmont's *Natural Philosophy of Love* is discussed and quoted by Lawrence S. Dembo in *Conceptions of Reality in Modern American Poetry* (Berkeley, 1966), p. 158.

21. Gayatri Chakravorty Spivak, introduction to Derrida, *Of Grammatology* (Baltimore, 1976), pp. lxv–lxvi. See also Derrida's discussion of how "woman is (her own) writing" in *Spurs: Nietzsche's Style/Eperons: Les Styles de Nietzsche* (Chicago, 1979), p. 57.

22. Isak Dinesen, "The Blank Page," *Last Tales* (New York, 1957), pp. 99–105. Because of the frequent quotations and the brevity of the fable, I have omitted page numbers entirely. For useful criticism of this story, see Thomas R. Whissen, *Isak Dinesen's Aesthetics* (Port Washington, N.Y., 1973), pp. 101–6; Robert Langbaum, *Isak Dinesen's Art: The Gayety of Vision* (Chicago, 1975), p. 219; and Florence C. Lewis, "Isak Dinesen and Feminist Criticism," *The North American Review* 264 (Spring 1979): 62–72.

Carmelite order of nuns who grow flax to manufacture the most exquisite linen in Portugal. This linen is so fine that it is used for the bridal sheets of all the neighboring royal houses. After the wedding night, it is solemnly and publicly displayed to attest to the virginity of the princess and is then reclaimed by the convent where the central piece of the stained sheet "which bore witness to the honor of a royal bride" is mounted, framed, and hung in a long gallery with a plate identifying the name of the princess. These "faded markings" on the sheets are of special interest to female pilgrims who journey to the remote country convent, for "each separate canvas with its coroneted name-plate has a story to tell, and each has been set up in loyalty to the story." But pilgrims and sisters alike are especially fascinated by the framed canvas over the one nameless plate which displays the blank, snow-white sheet that gives the story its title.

Before approaching the mysterious promise of this blank page, let us consider the framed, bloodied sheets in the convent gallery, which is both a museum of women's paintings (each sheet displays a unique, abstract design and is mounted in a heavy frame) and a library of women's literary works (the bloodstains are the ink on these woven sheets of paper). Collected and cherished by a female community that has seen better days, a kind of paradigmatic women's studies department, these bloodstained marks illustrate at least two points about female anatomy and creativity: first, many women experience their own bodies as the only available medium for their art, with the result that the distance between the woman artist and her art is often radically diminished; second, one of the primary and most resonant metaphors provided by the female body is blood, and cultural forms of creativity are often experienced as a painful wounding. Although I will deal with each point separately, they are clearly related, for the woman artist who experiences herself as killed into art may also experience herself as bleeding into print.

As to my first point, the objects of art in "The Blank Page" are quite literally made out of the bodies of the royal princesses whose internal fluids are the print and the paint. Not only are artist and art object physically linked but also the canvases in the nuns' gallery are a direct response to the princesses' private lives. Royal ladies and highborn spinsters would proceed "on a pilgrimage which was by nature both sacred and secretly gay" to read the canvas bearing the name of a princess they had once served and to review the bride's life as a wife and mother. The stained pages are therefore biographical remnants of otherwise mute existences, a result of and response to life rather than an effort at producing an independent aesthetic object. Indeed, were the female community less sensitive to the significance of these signs, such stained sheets would hardly be considered art at all. Dinesen implies that woman's use of her own body in the creation of art results in forms of expression devalued or totally invisible to eyes trained by traditional aesthetic standards. She also seems to imply that, within the life of domesticity assigned the royal princess from birth, the body is the only accessible medium for self-expression.

Certainly women's limited options—expressed in the parable by the fact that all royal (privileged) women marry while all single women are nuns—have shaped the art they create. Unable to train themselves as painters, unable to obtain the space or income to become sculptors, gifted women in these areas have had to work in private, using the only materials at hand—their bodies, their selves. If, as Dinesen implies, female creativity has had to express itself within the confines of domesticity (in part because of the emphasis on the personal in female socialization), women could at the least paint their own faces, shape their own bodies, and modulate their own vocal tones to become the glass of fashion and the mold of form. To make up, for such women, means not only making up stories but making up faces. In terms of the Pygmalion myth with which I began, the woman who cannot become an artist can nevertheless turn herself into an artistic object.

Nowhere is this better illustrated than in the novels of George Eliot, in which many female characters squander their creativity on efforts to reconstruct their own images. From Hetty Sorrel in *Adam Bede* (1859), who peers at her earrings and ribbons in a blotched mirror as she sits at a dressing table where the brass handles hurt her knees, to Gwendolen Harleth in *Daniel Deronda* (1876), who poses as Saint Cecilia in a glass exquisitely framed in black and gold, Eliot analyzes the ways in which women's creativity has been deformed by being channeled into self-destructive narcissism. Eliot criticizes the idea that beauty is an index of moral integrity by demonstrating how narcissism infantilizes the female, turning her from an autonomous person into a character in search of an author (or a page in search of a pen, to keep up the metaphor with which I began). Such a woman is always and only "becoming"—that is, she is beautiful but she is also always imagining some future identity that she is unable to realize by herself.

Hetty, for example, is like a hopeful child waiting to be adopted and adapted by Arthur Donnithorne. Gwendolen's case is even clearer. After arranging at a party a series of *tableaux vivants* to gain the admiration of prospective suitors, she chooses to represent herself imitating a character who looks like a statue. Instead of turning back to life on cue, Gwendolen is terrified by a picture of a dead face that unexpectedly springs out of a movable panel before her eyes; when she returns to herself, she looks "like a statue into which a soul of Fear had entered: her pallid lips were parted; her eyes, usually narrowed under their long lashes, were dilated and fixed."[23] The dead face, Eliot implies, is Gwen-

23. Eliot, *Daniel Deronda* (Baltimore, 1967), p. 91.

dolen's own. For in the process of turning herself into an artistic object, she makes herself autistic. Increasingly enmeshed in dreadful hallucinatory visions of her own distress, Gwendolen eventually is impelled to desire the death of her husband and her own death. Eliot's conviction that female creativity has been perverted (here as female narcissism and elsewhere in Eliot's fiction as enthrallment to male authority) helps us understand why she never wrote a *Kunstlerroman*.

Many female modernists have studied the deflection of female creativity from the production of art to the re-creation of the body,[24] but Edith Wharton, especially in *The House of Mirth* (1905), was most clearly influenced by Eliot. Cynthia Griffin Wolff has already brilliantly shown how Wharton's first title, "A Moment's Ornament," captures "the decorative imperative of that aspect of femininity that Lily embodies and the ultimate fragility of a self that has grown out of that imperative."[25] Lily Bart's gracefulness, her stylish clothing, her belief in the power of her own beauty to do good, her use of furniture and nature as backdrop scenery, even the lines on her face she traces with dismay in the mirror justify Diana Trilling's view that "Lily herself possesses the quality of a fine work of art."[26] Because financially she cannot afford to maintain herself as a work of art without the money of a man, Lily's artful presentation resembles Gwendolen's; she too must attract a husband. Furthermore, the only man in the novel who could possibly save her from becoming a commodity on the marriage market is himself incapable of viewing her as anything but a collectable in the aesthetic market: "As a spectator, Lawrence Selden had always enjoyed Lily Bart," making "use of the 'argument from design,' " for he knows that "she must have cost a great deal to make" (p. 3). In fact, he believes that "even her weeping was an art" (p. 69). While he is correct that her self-presentation empties her of spontaneity and makes her relationships duplicitous, Selden only further imprisons her in this ornamental behavior by characterizing it as so uniquely her own.

24. Elinor Wylie (herself a beautiful woman) wrote a series of poems and novels about the "firing" of girls into porcelain artifacts. For a fuller discussion of Wylie's attraction to formal perfection, see Céleste Turner Wright, "Elinor Wylie: The Glass Chimaera and the Minotaur," *Women's Studies* 7, nos. 1 and 2 (1980): 159–70 (special issue on women poets, ed. Gilbert and Gubar).

25. Cynthia Griffin Wolff, *A Feast of Words: The Triumph of Edith Wharton* (New York and Oxford, 1977), p. 109; all further references to Wharton's *The House of Mirth*, ed. R. W. B. Lewis (New York, 1977), will be included in the text. Wharton's second provisional title, "The Year of the Rose," points up the ways in which the Jew Rosedale is a double for Lily, in part because his Semitism allows him to glimpse the sordid economic realities behind the veneer of culture, much as Wharton's feminism did for her. For a useful consideration of Wharton's debt to Eliot, see Constance Rooke, "Beauty in Distress: *Daniel Deronda* and *The House of Mirth*," *Women and Literature* 4, no. 2 (Fall 1976): 28–39.

26. Diana Trilling, "*The House of Mirth* Revisited," in *Edith Wharton*, ed. Irving Howe (Englewood Cliffs, N.J., 1962), p. 109.

Although Lily's art does not procure her security in the form of a husband, and although she is quite destitute on her deathbed at thirty years of age, Lily seems to triumph at the end of *The House of Mirth,* for her death is the logical extension of her life. Having turned herself into an artistic object, she now literally kills herself into art. Significantly, before taking the overdose that lulls her to sleep and death, Lily goes through her wardrobe of dresses which "still kept the long unerring lines, the sweep and amplitude of the great artist's stroke, and as she spread them out on the bed the scenes in which they had been worn rose vividly before her" (p. 211). She remembers specifically the party at which she, like Gwendolen, participated in *tableaux vivants;* when Lily turned herself into Reynolds' portrait of "Mrs. Lloyd," she looked "as though she had stepped, not out of, but into, Reynolds' canvas" (p. 131), thereby demonstrating to Selden and the other onlookers "the touch of poetry in her beauty" (p. 131).

While Lily waits in bed for the drug to bring oblivion, she thinks that there is "some word she had found" to tell Selden that would make everything well (p. 317). On entering her room, Selden sees "a narrow bed along the wall, and on the bed, with motionless hands and calm, unrecognizing face, the semblance of Lily Bart." He kneels by this semblance for a final moment, "drain[ing] their last moment to the lees; and in the silence there passed between them the word which made all clear" (p. 323). This word is Lily's dead body; for she is now converted completely into a script for his edification, a text not unlike the letters and checks she has left behind to vindicate her life. She submits to being thus defined, although she liberates her lover from such a degradation by destroying his letters. Lily's history, then, illustrates the terrors not of the word made flesh but of the flesh made word. In this respect, she illuminates the problems Wharton must have faced in her own efforts to create rather than be created—efforts not always successful, if we can trust the reported comments of as important a contemporary critic as Percy Lubbock who, in comparing her to Henry James, quipped: "She was herself a novel of his, no doubt in his earliest manner."[27]

Like Kafka's victim in "The Penal Colony," women have had to experience cultural scripts in their lives by suffering them in their bodies. This is why Maxine Hong Kingston writes so movingly about her resemblance to the mythic woman warrior who went into battle scarred by the thin blades which her parents literally used to write fine lines of script on her body.[28] For the artist, this sense that she is herself the text means that there is little distance between her life and her art. The attraction of women writers to personal forms of expression like letters, autobiog-

27. Lubbock, quoted in Millicent Bell, *Edith Wharton and Henry James: The Story of Their Friendship* (New York, 1965), p. 21.
28. See Maxine Hong Kingston, *The Woman Warrior: Memoirs of a Girlhood among Ghosts* (New York, 1977), pp. 41–42 and 62–63.

raphies, confessional poetry, diaries, and journals points up the effect of a life experienced as an art or an art experienced as a kind of life, as does women's traditional interest in cosmetics, fashion, and interior decorating. Many books by women writers (like Dorothy Richardson's *Pilgrimage* and Olive Schreiner's *From Man to Man*) cannot be finished because they are as ongoing and open-ended as the lives of their authors. The mythic lives of women artists from Emily Dickinson (who played out the Gothic fiction of the white-dressed maiden imprisoned in daddy's house) to Isadora Duncan (whose costumes and affairs and death express her creed as well as her autobiography does) also reveal the close identification experienced between the female artist and her art. Duncan's medium, dance, has always been acceptable for women, I suspect, because the body of the dancer becomes an instrument or icon on stage.

Not a few of the most exciting experiments of women artists, moreover, grow out of a self-conscious attempt to obliterate aesthetic distance. The insistence that the domestic is artistic is illustrated, for example, by Katherine Mansfield, who writes lovingly about the ways in which a kitchen is decorated with utensils and food.[29] It finds a kind of culmination in the performative art of Mierle Laderman Ukeles, whose "Maintenance Art Activity" consists in washing museum floors with a damp mop, over and over again, and even more to the purpose here, Carolee Schneemann, who reads from a long scroll she removes from her vagina in her performance of *Up To and Including Her Limits* (1975).[30] Writing about Eleanor Antin's videotape in which she applies makeup to the "canvas" of her face and her photo sequence in which she documents "carving" ten pounds off her body, Arlene Raven and Deborah Marrow explain that "Antin's work is of the verb rather than the object" in its effort to illuminate how "in this culture women themselves are the art product."[31] Judy Chicago's *The Dinner Party* celebrates creative women who, refusing conventional definitions of the female, are in a privileged position to question the definitions of art that our culture accepts.[32] But *The Dinner Party* plates also imply that women, who have served, have been served up and consumed. They therefore remind us of the sacrificial nature of the body "dressed" as art. Indeed, in *The House of Mirth*

29. Domestic artistry is repeatedly celebrated in Mansfield's stories, most especially in the figure of Mrs. Fairfield in "Prelude" (*The Short Stories of Katherine Mansfield*, ed. John Middleton Murry [New York, 1976]), but also throughout the letters in which Mansfield writes about the culinary skills of a maid or the interior decorating she herself performs on a hotel room.

30. For a photograph of Mierle Laderman Ukeles performing her *Washing, Tracks, Maintenance: Maintenance Art Activity III* (22 July 1973), see Lucy R. Lippard, *From the Center: Feminist Essays on Women's Art* (New York, 1976), p. 60; for her discussion of Carolee Schneemann, see p. 126.

31. Arlene Raven and Deborah Marrow, "Eleanor Antin: What's Your Story," *Chrysalis* 8 (Summer 1979): 43–51.

32. See Judy Chicago, *Through the Flower: My Struggle as a Woman Artist* (New York, 1975) and her book on the work, *The Dinner Party* (Garden City, N.Y., 1979).

the fashion plate often lifts a face "like an empty plate held up to be filled" (p. 45); Lily's beauty is described as a "glaze," (pp. 3 and 51), reminding us of the fragility and vulnerability of Chicago's "service."

The stain that darkens the reputation of a girl like Lily and the stains of vaginal imagery at the center of the porcelain plates turn us to my second point, the centrality of blood as a symbol furnished by the female body. Luce Irigaray has argued recently that women are made vulnerable by their inability to express their delirium: "Women do not manage to articulate their madness: they suffer it directly in their body."[33] In "The Blank Page," the sacrificial suffering of the inarticulate female body is revealed in the bloody ink print, which is the result of the hymen's penetration and which is so valued by the community; the high steward to the royal house proclaims, "*Virginem eam tenemus*—'we declare her to have been a virgin.' " While bloodstains can be a certification of freedom from pregnancy or the mark of entrance into puberty, in the Dinesen story they call to mind the more tragic associations of blood for women, especially for women writers. Unlike the blood of menstruation which presumably defiles like a curse or the blood of childbirth which is also taboo, the blood on the royal sheets is holy, for it certifies purity. By making the sheets into objects as sacred as altar cloths, the nuns sanctify the sacrifice of the virgin, and by reading the stains as if they were hieroglyphs, they imply that we must come to terms with the fact of blood before we can understand the nature of female art.

Lest this seem too gothic a pronouncement, let me point to as pious and proper a poet as Christina Rossetti, for this Victorian conspicuously offers her song as a virginal blood sacrifice.[34] At least part of Rossetti's plan came from her sense that she was the model, not the painter, the character, not the author. She has been represented, moreover, "Not as she is, but as she fills his dream" ("In an Artist's Study"). Rossetti therefore experiences herself as "Dead before Death," to quote the title of a characteristic poem. In "From the Antique" she is explicit about her life's being "Doubly blank in a woman's lot." As in Dinesen's tale of the convent, Rossetti's speaker on the doorstep of "The Convent Threshold" feels caught between sexuality and chastity. Choosing to become a nun because there is mysterious "blood" between her lover and herself, she looks down to see her lily feet "soiled with mud, / With *scarlet* mud *which tells a tale*" [my italics]. The same identification of bleeding with telling or singing appears in the vision of the suffering woman poet in "From House to Home." Beginning with a sense of sinfulness, of being stained, Rossetti transforms herself in a number of religious poems into the bride of Christ and into a female Christ (she had modelled for a painting of the Virgin Mary). Imitating his blood sacrifice, she testifies repeatedly

33. Irigaray, quoted by Diana Adlam and Couze Venn in "Women's Exile: Interview with Luce Irigaray," *Ideology and Consciousness* (Summer 1978): 74.

34. See *The Complete Poems of Christina Rossetti*, ed. R. W. Crump (Baton Rouge, La., 1979).

to the "mark of blood" that distinguishes her door ("Despised and Rejected"). But this sign also recalls the tokens of virginity on the cloth brought before the elders of the city to redeem the honor of a slandered bride, as described and prescribed in Deuteronomy.[35]

The blood sacrifice of the royal princesses in Dinesen's story represents the sacrifice of virginity not through martyrdom but through marriage, although the stained sheets also seem to imply that marriage may be a martyrdom. The blood on the royal sheets is considered holy because it proves that the bride is a valuable property, given by father to husband for the production of sons. In other words, before the sheet is collected by the convent sisters and assumes the status of art, the bloodstains are a testimony to the woman's function as a silent token of exchange. But this blood wedding transforms the marriage bed into a kind of coffin in which the virgin is sacrificed. Dinesen may have considered her own marriage deathly because she believed her many illnesses in later life were related to the syphilis she unwittingly contracted from her husband, but she implies that many women in a patriarchy experience a dread of heterosexuality. The storyteller of "The Blank Page," who has told "one more than a thousand" tales, is thereby associated with Scheherazade, who told stories in the night to circumvent the death awaiting her after sexual initiation in the bridal chamber.[36] Not only a surrogate for her own body, her stories save the daughters of the land who have been threatened with penetration and execution by the misogynist king who is enraged by the infidelity of women.

The framed stained sheets imply, then, that all the royal princesses have been "framed" into telling the same story, namely, the story of their acquiescence as objects of exchange. The American poet H. D. treats this confinement as a primary plot (conspiracy) against women and an effective plot (burial mound) for women.[37] She has therefore dedicated

---

35. See Deut. 22:13–24. I am indebted to Stephen Booth for pointing out the relevance of this biblical passage. The issue of blood and sacrifice is a complicated one in the Catholic tradition, as this quotation from Charles Williams illustrates: "There is also, of course, that other great natural bloodshed common to half the human race—menstruation. That was unclean. But it is not impossible that that is an image, naturally, of the great bloodshed on Calvary, and perhaps, supernaturally, in relation to it. Women share the victimization of the blood; it is why, being the sacrifice so, they cannot be the priests. They are mothers, and, in that special sense, victims; witnesses, in the body, to the suffering of the body, and the method of Redemption" (*The Forgiveness of Sins* [London, 1950], p. 138).

36. Scheherazade is an important model of the female storyteller for Dinesen. See the conclusion of "The Deluge at Norderney," *Seven Gothic Tales* (New York, 1972), p. 79, and Hannah Arendt's foreword, "Isak Dinesen, 1885–1962," to Dinesen's *Daguerreotypes* (Chicago, 1979), p. xiv. See also Gilbert's poem "Scheherazade," *Poetry Northwest* 19, no. 2 (Summer 1978): 43.

37. On women's entrapment in erotic plots, see Elizabeth Hardwick, *Seduction and Betrayal: Women and Literature* (New York, 1974), pp. 175–208, and Joanna Russ, "What Can a Heroine Do; or, Why Women Can't Write," in *Images of Women in Fiction: Feminist Perspectives*, ed. Susan Koppelman Cornillon (Bowling Green, Ohio, 1972), pp. 3–20.

her late poems to excavating the female by creating alternative scripts, as she explains in *Trilogy* (1944–46), where her muse carries "the blank pages / of the unwritten volume of the new."[38] In *Helen in Egypt* (1961), H. D. begins with a character who is a phantom because she has barely survived being turned into a heroine. Basing her epic on a seventh-century palinode by Stesichorus that claims Helen never got any further than Egypt—it was merely an image of Helen that accompanied Paris to Troy to give the pretext for war—H. D. shows us a Helen haunted by stories told about the war, specifically, the blame heaped on her for presumably causing it and the role allotted to her as an object of exchange: war booty, gift, ransom.[39] Helen realizes at the beginning of H. D.'s revisionary epic that her own imagined role in the war was a sacrifice inflicted on her, that "the script was a snare" (p. 220). But it is terribly difficult for her to evade this snare or escape it, because, like Eliot's and Wharton's heroines and Dinesen's royal princesses, she feels that "*She herself is the writing*" (p. 91). She tries to rescue herself by considering other stories of growing up female, but these turn out to be the same story of the blood sacrifice of daughters and virgins: Iphigenia, Polyxena, Chryseis, Cassandra, and Persephone.

"Helen returns constantly to this theme of sacrifice" (p. 84) because the daughters "were all sacrificed in one way or another" (p. 173). Inside this blood factory, she mourns the "bridal pledge at the altar" as a "pledge to Death" (p. 73). Her blood consciousness harkens back to the mythic female artist, Philomela: raped by Tereus who cut out her tongue, Philomela took her revenge by weaving her story for all to see with "purple / On a white background."[40] In addition, Helen's blood consciousness also reaches forward to contemporary poems (by writers like May Swensen and Marge Piercy) in which the phallus is a weapon. The desecrated female body that feels like the self of the poet bleeds into print.[41] Anne Sexton therefore associates her female anatomy with the absence of control: in her female revision of *The Waste Land,* "Hurry Up Please It's Time," she identifies herself with Eliot's wasted, working-class women, for she knows "I have ink but no pen." As a result, Sexton feels that her poems "leak" from her "like a miscarriage."[42] Likewise, Frida Kahlo, who

38. H. D., *Trilogy* (New York, 1973), p. 103.

39. H. D., *Helen in Egypt* (New York, 1961); all further references to this poem will be included in the text.

40. Ovid, *Metamorphoses,* trans. Humphries, pp. 148–51. Significantly, once Procne reads Philomela's story, she kills her own son and cooks him up for Tereus who is made to eat him. The sisters are transformed into birds, "And even so the red marks of the murder / Stayed on their breasts; the feathers were blood-colored."

41. See May Swenson, "Cut," *Iconographs* (New York, 1970), p. 13, and Marge Piercy, "I Still Feel You," in *Psyche: The Feminine Poetic Consciousness,* ed. Barbara Segnitz and Carol Rainey (New York, 1973), pp. 187–88.

42. Anne Sexton, "Hurry Up Please It's Time," *The Death Notebooks* (Boston, 1974), p. 62; "The Silence," *Book of Folly* (Boston, 1972), p. 32.

presents herself as bound by red cords that are not only her veins and her roots but also her paint, is a painter whose tragic physical problems contributed to her feeling wounded, pierced and bleeding.[43]

Mired in stories of our own destruction, stories which we confuse with ourselves, how can women experience creativity? In Dinesen's story, the creation of female art feels like the destruction of the female body. Because of the forms of self-expression available to women, artistic creation often feels like a violation, a belated reaction to male penetration rather than a possessing and controlling. Not an ejaculation of pleasure but a reaction to rending, the blood on the royal marriage sheets seems to imply that women's paint and ink are produced through a painful wounding, a literal influence of male authority. If artistic creativity is likened to biological creativity, the terror of inspiration for women is experienced quite literally as the terror of being entered, deflowered, possessed, taken, had, broken, ravished—all words which illustrate the pain of the passive self whose boundaries are being violated. In fact, like their nineteenth-century foremothers, twentieth-century women often describe the emergence of their talent as an infusion from a male master rather than inspiration from or sexual commerce with a female muse. This phallic master causes the woman writer to feel her words are being expressed from her rather than by her. Like Mary Elizabeth Coleridge who sees her lips as a silent wound, or Charlotte Brontë who suffers from a "secret, inward wound" at the moment she feels the "pulse of Ambition," or Emily Dickinson who is bandaged as the empress of Calvary in some poems and as the wounded deer in others, women writers often dread the emergence of their own talents.[44]

If writing feels as if "the ink was pouring on to the sheets like blood," as it does for the heroine of Margaret Drabble's *The Waterfall,* then the poet can easily become frightened by her sense of victimization: "I was unnaturally aware of my own helpless subjugation to my gifts, my total inability to make a poem at will," Drabble's poet explains. "I resented this helplessness as I resented a woman's helplessness with a man."[45] The twentieth-century prototype of this anxious sense that poetry comes from being possessed and wounded is, of course, Sylvia Plath. Like Drabble's heroine, whose creativity is released by giving birth to a second child, Plath begins *Ariel* with a relatively cheerful poem about childbirth that seems to promise a more positive way of imagining creativity for women.

43. See Joyce Kozloff, "Frida Kahlo," *Women's Studies* 7 (1978): 43–58.

44. See Mary Elizabeth Coleridge, "The Other Side of a Mirror," *The World Split Open: Four Centuries of Women Poets in England and America, 1552–1950,* ed. Louise Bernikow (New York, 1974), p. 137; Charlotte Brontë, *The Professor* (New York, 1964), p. 195; and the discussion of Emily Dickinson in Gilbert and Gubar, *The Madwoman in the Attic,* pp. 581–650.

45. Margaret Drabble, *The Waterfall* (New York, 1977), pp. 114–15.

But even here in "Morning Song," the new birth of morning seems converted into grief and mourning, for the child is a "New statue" and the parents "stand round blankly as walls." This statue, confined by blank walls, is transformed into the far more terrible wife of "The Applicant": "Naked as paper to start," she is "A living doll." Like Pygmalion's ivory girl, Atwood's mud woman, Eliot's living statues, Lily Bart who really is a living doll, or Sexton who is her own dead doll, Plath's wife is a kind of automaton in the clutches of someone else's will. Plath herself is not infrequently filled with a "thin / Papery feeling" which helps explain the thousands of paper dolls she played with as a child, and her poems lend sinister insight into Mansfield's perception that "Female dolls in their nakedness are the most female things on earth."[46] From Maggie Tulliver, who tortures her doll in the attic in *The Mill on the Floss,* to Pecola Breedlove in Toni Morrison's *The Bluest Eye,* who tortures herself because she cannot look like her doll, the heroines of women's fiction have played with dolls to define themselves.

Plath can only escape the dread that she has been created as an object (as she says in "Lady Lazarus," "I am your opus") by self-inflicted violence, by watching the bloodstain darkening the bandages, proving she is alive. A sense of helplessness seems inextricably related to the emergence of her voice: "By the roots of my hair some god got hold of me," Plath exclaims in "The Hanging Man"; "I sizzled in his blue volts like a desert prophet." As terrible as her muse is, however, her pain at his violation also proves she is alive. But the jolting words snapped out by these electric charges mean that the poetry Plath creates will kill her: "The blood jet is poetry, / There is no stopping it" ("Kindness"). She has had the blood sucked out of her by "Daddy," who "Bit [her] pretty red heart in two." While she has killed "The vampire who said he was you / And drank my blood for a year," she is still haunted by the black bat airs, and, having been bitten, she has herself become a bloodsucker, for "The blood flood is the flood of love" ("The Munich Mannequins"). The redness of the "Tulips" in her hospital bed therefore "talks to [her] wound, it corresponds." If she sees herself as "flat, ridiculous, a cut-paper shadow / Between the eye of the sun and the eyes of the tulips," she knows she will eventually fly into these eyes which are, of course, "the red / Eye, the cauldron of morning" ("Ariel"). The only way to escape papery perfection in "Stings" is to become the "red / Scar in the sky." At the end of *Ariel,* she is finally perfected into a statue: "The illusion of a Greek necessity / Flows in the scrolls of her toga" as she accepts her role as heroine in the tragedy that is not only her art but her life ("Edge"). The

46. Katherine Mansfield to Violet Schiff, October 1921, *Letters,* ed. Murry (New York, 1932), pp. 405–6. It is significant in this regard that both Mansfield and H. D. can only imagine the reeducation and redemption of boys in terms of their learning to play with dolls.

dialectic between perfection and blood destruction means finally that Plath's "Words" are "Axes" from whose rhythmic strokes she will never recover.[47]

Adrienne Rich also identifies blood with the female body: "Some-times every / aperture of my body / leaks blood. I don't know whether / to pretend that this is natural." In other words, Rich is aware that even her most intimate attitudes toward her own blood have been defined by male voices:

> You worship the blood
> you call it hysterical bleeding
> you want to drink it like milk
> you dip your finger into it and write
> you faint at the smell of it
> you dream of dumping me into the sea.[48]

Rich seeks a way of experiencing the blood through her own sensibilities. In "Women," she sees three Fates who seem to represent her sense of women's progress in history: the first sister is sewing a costume for her role as Transparent Lady when "all her nerves will be visible"; the second is sewing "at the seam over her heart which has never healed entirely"; and the third is gazing "at a dark-red crust spreading westward far out on the sea."[49] Her beauty and her vision promise a time when women can authentically deny that our "wounds come from the same source as [our] power."[50] Refusing a poetry that implies performance, competition, or virtuosity, Rich strives in her most recent volume for "the musings of a mind / one with her body," within

> . . . the many-lived, unending
> forms in which she finds herself,
> becoming now the sherd of broken glass
> slicing light in a corner, dangerous
> to flesh, now the plentiful, soft leaf
> that wrapped round the throbbing finger, soothes the wound.[51]

Rich's promise returns us to Dinesen's story, for the snow-white sheet of the nameless princess also seems to promise a breakthrough into new beginnings for new stories that can soothe the wound. The single and singular blank sheet that so fascinates pilgrims and nuns alike in the convent library-museum seems an alternative to the bloody sheets

47. See Sylvia Plath, *Ariel* (New York, 1965). Plath's paper doll collection can be seen in the Lilly Library at Indiana University.

48. Adrienne Rich, "Waking in the Dark," *Adrienne Rich's Poetry,* ed. Barbara Charlesworth Gelpi and Albert Gelpi (New York, 1975), p. 61.

49. Rich, "Women," in *Psyche,* ed. Segnitz and Rainey, p. 152.

50. Rich, "Power," *The Dream of a Common Language* (New York, 1978), p. 3.

51. Rich, "Transcendental Etude," ibid., p. 77.

that surround it. Thus, in terms of the patriarchal identification of women with blankness and passivity with which we began, Dinesen's blank page becomes radically subversive, the result of one woman's defiance which must have cost either her life or her honor. Not a sign of innocence or purity or passivity, this blank page is a mysterious but potent act of resistance. The showing of the sheet, moreover, proves that the anonymous princess has forced some sort of acknowledgment or accommodation in the public realm. On a literal level, the blank sheet may mean any number of alternative scripts for women: Was this anonymous royal princess not a virgin on her wedding night? Did she, perhaps, run away from the marriage bed and thereby retain her virginity intact? Did she, like Scheherazade, spend her time in bed telling stories so as to escape the fate of her predecessors? Or again, maybe the snow-white sheet above the nameless plate tells the story of a young woman who met up with an impotent husband, or of a woman who learned other erotic arts, or of a woman who consecrated herself to the nun's vow of chastity but within marriage. Indeed, the interpretation of this sheet seems as impenetrable as the anonymous princess herself. Yet Dinesen's old storyteller, who learned her art from her grandmother much as her grandmother learned it from her own mother's mother, advises her audience to "look at this page, and recognize the wisdom of my grandmother and of all storytelling women!"

The storyteller says this, I think, first of all because the blank page contains all stories in no story, just as silence contains all potential sound and white contains all color. Tillie Olsen's *Silences* and Rich's *On Lies, Secrets, and Silences* teach us about the centrality of silence in women's culture, specifically the ways in which women's voices have gone unheard. While male writers like Mallarmé and Melville also explored their creative dilemmas through the trope of the blank page, female authors exploit it to expose how woman has been defined symbolically in the patriarchy as a tabula rasa, a lack, a negation, an absence. But blankness here is an act of defiance, a dangerous and risky refusal to certify purity. The resistance of the princess allows for self-expression, for she makes her statement by not writing what she is expected to write. Not to be written on is, in other words, the condition of new sorts of writing for women. The nuns and the storyteller recognize wisdom in the place where the uninitiated see nothing, in part by removing their attention from the traditional foreground to what is usually relegated to background, much as we might radically revise our understanding of the 1,001 blank days during which Scheherazade silently bore the king three sons whose surprise appearance at the end of the 1,001 nights wins her a reprieve from the death sentence. But the old crone also praises the blank sheet because it is the "material" out of which "art" is produced. Women's creativity, in other words, is prior to literacy: the sisterhood produces the blank sheets needed to accomplish writing.

Olive Schreiner, the great feminist theorist, explains what this implies about English culture when one of her heroines holds up a book
and theorizes about literary history:

> When I hold these paper leaves between my fingers, far off across
> the countless ages I hear the sound of women beating out the fibres
> of hemp and flax to shape the first garment, and, above the roar
> of the wheels and spinnies in the factory, I hear the whirr of the
> world's first spinning wheel and the voice of the woman singing to
> herself as she sits beside it, and know that without the labor of
> those first women kneeling over the fibres and beating them swiftly
> out, and without the hum of those early spinning wheels, neither
> factory nor paper pulp would ever have come into existence. . . .
> This little book!—it has got its roots down, down, deep in the life
> of man on earth; it grows from there.[52]

If we take Schreiner's claim seriously, no woman is a blank page: every
woman is author of the page and author of the page's author. The art
of producing essentials—children, food, cloth—is woman's ultimate creativity. If it is taken as absence in the context of patriarchal culture, it is
celebrated within the female community by the matrilineal traditions of
oral storytelling. The veiled, brown, illiterate old woman who sits outside
the city gates in Dinesen's tale therefore represents her grandmother
and her grandmother's grandmother: "they and I have become one."
Existing before man-made books, their stories let us "hear the voice of
silence."

The blank page is created in Dinesen's story through the silent act
of "sowing" the flax seed and "sewing" the linen, acts traditionally performed by the female community. This is the subversive voice of silence,
and we can associate it with the silent sound of Philomela's shuttle. The
process whereby "the seed is skillfully sown out by labor-hardened virginal hands" and the "delicate thread is spun, and the linen woven" is
the secret of Dinesen's society of convent spin-sters. For the nuns who
have raised the production of flax into art, then, the blank page is a
tribute to what has been devalued as mere craft or service. The nuns
refuse to relegate the domestic or the decorative to a category outside
the realm of true creativity. At the same time, moreover, they sanctify
their own creative efforts; for the germ of the story, the first seed of the
flax, comes from the holy land of the daughter Achsah who sought and
received a blessing—specifically, the blessing of springs of water. When
the flax blooms, we are told, the valley becomes "the very color of the
apron which the blessed virgin put on to go out and collect eggs within
St. Anne's poultry yard, the moment before the Archangel Gabriel in
mighty wing-strokes lowered himself onto the threshold of the house,

52. Olive Schreiner, *From Man to Man* (Chicago, 1977), p. 409.

and while high, high up a dove, neck-feathers raised and wings vibrating, stood like a small clear silver star in the sky."

Members of this "blithe sisterhood" thus preserve the history of lesser lives in the blood markings and glorify the blank page as a sacred space consecrated to female creativity, thereby pulling heaven down to earth. While the bloodstained sheets resemble the true icon of suffering divinity as seen on Veronica's veil, the virgin-blue flax blossoms remind us of Mary at the moment before the Annunciation—Mary waiting, about to become pregnant with divinity.[53] In her readiness for rapture, she represents the female community, and its blank page is therefore hers. The convent in Dinesen's story is a Carmelite order, the order which propagates a special devotion to our Lady; indeed, in the Middle Ages, Carmelite theologians were among the earliest defenders of the Immaculate Conception, the doctrine that Mary was conceived without original sin. But the Carmelites have also produced the greatest Christian mystics, most importantly Saint Theresa, who inspired Dorothea Brooke's, and George Eliot's, quest for a life of significant action. Like Mary, whose sanctity is hidden in the ordinary, Theresa's mysticism was grounded in the everyday. The vows of poverty, chastity, and obedience taken by the Carmelite nuns are strenuous attempts to aid contemplation, to achieve Theresa's ordinary mysticism. Not martyrs who suffer death but prophets who suffer inspiration, the convent virgins spend much time in silence, seeking to duplicate Mary's receptivity to bearing and giving birth to the Incarnate Word.[54] Thus, the blank place, a female inner space, represents readiness for inspiration and creation, the self conceived and dedicated to its own potential divinity.

Many of the late-Victorian and twentieth-century women writers whom I have mentioned were involved in the creation of a revisionary theology that allowed them to reappropriate and valorize metaphors of uniquely female creativity and primacy. I have space here only for a few examples. Florence Nightingale in *Cassandra* (1852), pronounced her audacious belief that "the next Christ will perhaps be a female Christ."[55]

53. I am indebted to Mary Jo Weaver for informing me that the image on Veronica's headcloth has been associated by the gnostics with the woman cursed by blood in Matt. 9:20–22.

54. See Thomas Merton, *Disputed Questions* (New York, 1960), pp. 222x and 227. For a feminist discussion of the usefulness of the figure of the Virgin Mary to Catholic women, see Elisabeth Schussler Fiorenza, "Feminist Spirituality, Christian Identity, and Catholic Vision," in *Womanspirit Rising*, ed. Christ and Plaskow, pp. 138–39, and Drid Williams, "The Brides of Christ," in *Perceiving Women*, ed. Shirley Ardener (London, 1975), pp. 105–26. The most important feminist analysis of how the Virgin Mary is exalted for virtues men would like women to exhibit is Marina Warner, *Alone of All Her Sex: The Myth of the Virgin Mary* (New York, 1976). While I agree that Mary has been used against women who cannot be virgin and mother, I am arguing here that women have reclaimed her image in positive ways.

55. Florence Nightingale, *Cassandra* (Old Westbury, N.Y., 1979), p. 53.

Schreiner claimed by extension that God is female when she argued that "the desire to incarnate" in the true artist "is almost like the necessity of a woman to give birth to her child."[56] From the blessed Lady who carries the new Bible of blank pages in H. D.'s *Trilogy* to Gertrude Stein's liturgical drama in praise of *The Mother of Us All,* modernist texts by women appear to corroborate the contemporary French feminist Hélène Cixous' sentiment that the woman writer sanctifies herself when she gives birth to "an amniotic flow of words that reiterates the contractual rhythms of labor."[57] Margaret Anderson and Jane Heap's desire for a radically new kind of art is brilliantly illustrated by the *Little Review* volume that consisted of sixty-four blank pages.[58] The substitution of the female divinity for the male god, the womb for the penis, as the model of creativity was so pronounced by the turn of the century that it posed a real problem for such male modernists as T. S. Eliot, Lawrence, and Joyce. But of course, many women writers remained sensitive to the fact that such a mother-goddess myth was compensatory and that— unless freed from any biological imperative—it could entrap women in destructive stereotypes. To celebrate uniquely female powers of creativity without perpetuating destructive feminine socialization is the task confronted by writers as dissimilar as George Eliot, Rossetti, Schreiner, Wharton, H. D., and Mansfield, all of whom are involved in efforts to sanctify the female through symbols of female divinity, myths of female origin, metaphors of female creativity, and rituals of female power. "The Blank Page" is only one of many parables in an ongoing revisionary female theology.[59]

Since I have here persistently and perhaps perversely ignored history, I feel it is only fair to conclude by acknowledging that certain historical factors helped make this modulation in valuation possible. The shift in metaphors from the primacy of the pen to the primacy of the page is a late nineteenth-century phenomenon. The Romantic movement in poetry, the suffrage movement in politics, the rise of anthropology with its interest in fertility gods and goddesses, the myth of Mother Right coming at a time when the infant mortality rate was significantly lowered and birth control became more widely available, and finally World War I—all of these need to be studied, for we are only just beginning to read the patterns and trace the figures in what all too recently has been viewed as nothing but the blank pages of women's cultural and literary history.

56. Schreiner, *From Man to Man,* p. 453.

57. Hélène Cixous, quoted by Verena Andermatt, "Hélène Cixous and The Uncovery of a Feminine Language," *Women and Literature* 7 (Winter 1979): 42.

58. See Margaret Anderson, *The Unknowable Gurdjieff* (London, 1962), p. 75.

59. Gilbert's two brilliant papers, "Potent Griselda: D. H. Lawrence's *Ladybird* and Literary Maternity" and "Soldier's Heart: Literary Men, Literary Women, and the Great War" (both unpublished), document the importance to women of rising anthropological theories of mother right and the significance of World War I to women writers.

Denise Levertov expresses my own sense of excitement at engaging in such a task, even as she reminds us how attentive and patient we must be before the blank page to perceive genuinely new and sustaining scripts. Like Dinesen, moreover, Levertov seeks to consecrate her own repeated efforts to contribute to the blank pages of our future history. Recognizing that strenuous and risky readiness at the moment before conception is itself an art, a kind of balancing act, Levertov praises the discipline that allows the poet to stand firm on "one leg that aches" while upholding "the round table" of the "blank page." Such diligence receives its just reward when the round table of the blank page is transformed into living wood that sighs and sings like a tree in the wind. This attitude toward creativity substitutes for the artistic object an act or process. Furthermore, just as sexuality was previously identified with textuality, the text itself now becomes infused with potent sexual energy, or so Levertov claims in what we can now recognize as a decidedly female vision:

> One at a time
> books, when their hour is come
> step out of the shelves.
> Heavily step (once more, dusty, fingermarked,
>   but pristine!)
> to give birth:
>
> each poem's passion
> ends in an Easter,
> a new life.
>   The books of the dead
> shake their leaves,
> word-seeds fly and
> lodge in the black earth.[60]

---

60. Denise Levertov, "Growth of a Poet," *The Freeing of the Dust* (New York, 1975), pp. 83, 78–79. See also Susan Fromberg Schaeffer, "The Nature of Genres," *Granite Lady* (New York, 1974), p. 136.

Diana Described: Scattered Woman and Scattered Rhyme

Nancy J. Vickers

The import of Petrarch's description of Laura extends well beyond the confines of his own poetic age; in subsequent times, his portrayal of feminine beauty became authoritative. As a primary canonical text, the *Rime sparse* consolidated and disseminated a Renaissance mode. Petrarch absorbed a complex network of descriptive strategies and then presented a single, transformed model. In this sense his role in the history of the interpretation and the internalization of woman's "image" by both men and women can scarcely be overemphasized. When late-Renaissance theorists, poets, and painters represented woman's body, Petrarch's verse justified their aesthetic choices. His authority, moreover, extended beyond scholarly consideration to courtly conversation, beyond the treatise on beauty to the after-dinner game in celebration of it. The descriptive codes of others, both ancients and contemporaries, were, of course, not ignored, but the "scattered rhymes" undeniably enjoyed a privileged status: they informed the Renaissance norm of a beautiful woman.[1]

An early version of this paper was shared with the University Seminar on Feminist Inquiry at Dartmouth College; I sincerely appreciate the time, attention, and suggestions of its members. I am particularly indebted to Richard Corum, Jonathan Goldberg, Katherine Hayles, Marianne Hirsch, David Kastan, Stephen Orgel, Esther Rashkin, Christian Wolff and Holly Wolff for their contributions.

1. On this "thoroughly self-conscious fashion," see Elizabeth Cropper, "On Beautiful Women, Parmigianino, *Petrarchismo,* and the Vernacular Style," *Art Bulletin* 58 (1976): 374–94. Cropper shares many of the observations on Petrarchan descriptive technique outlined in the following paragraph (see pp. 385–86). I am indebted to David Quint for bringing this excellent essay to my attention.

We never see in the *Rime sparse* a complete picture of Laura. This would not be exceptional if we were considering a single "song" or even a restricted lyric corpus; gothic top-to-toe enumeration is, after all, more appropriate to narrative, more adapted to the "objective" observations of a third-person narrator than to those of a speaker who ostensibly loves, and perhaps even addresses, the image he describes. But given an entire volume devoted to a single lady, the absence of a coherent, comprehensive portrait is significant.[2] Laura is always presented as a part or parts of a woman. When more than one part figures in a single poem, a sequential, inclusive ordering is never stressed. Her textures are those of metals and stones; her image is that of a collection of exquisitely beautiful disassociated objects.[3] Singled out among them are hair, hand, foot and eyes: golden hair trapped and bound the speaker; an ivory hand took his heart away; a marble foot imprinted the grass and flowers; starry eyes directed him in his wandering.[4] In terms of qualitative attributes (blondness, whiteness, sparkle), little here is innovative. More specifically Petrarchan, however, is the obsessive insistence on the particular, an insistence that would in turn generate multiple texts on individual fragments of the body or on the beauties of woman.

When the sixteenth-century poet Joachim Du Bellay chose to attack the French propensity for Italianizing, his offensive gesture against the Petrarchans (among whose number he had once prominently figured) culminated in just this awareness: in his final verses he proposed to substitute the unified celebration of female beauty for the witty clichés of Petrarchan particularization:

> De voz *beautez* je diray seulement,
> Que si mon oeil ne juge folement,

2. Description is, of course, always fragmentary in that it is by nature enumerative. Petrarch, however, systematically avoids those structures that would mask fragmentation. On enumeration and the descriptive text, see Roland Barthes, *S/Z* (Paris, 1970), pp. 120–22.

3. For lengthy discussions of these qualities of Petrarchan descriptions, see Robert Durling, "Petrarch's 'Giovene donna sotto un verde lauro,' " *Modern Language Notes* 86 (1971): 1–20, and John Freccero, "The Fig Tree and the Laurel: Petrarch's Poetics," *Diacritics* 5 (Spring 1975): 34–40.

4. On Petrarch's role in the popularization of this *topos*, see James V. Mirollo, "In Praise of '*La bella mano*': Aspects of Late Renaissance Lyricism," *Comparative Literature Studies* 9 (1972): 31–43. See also James Villas, "The Petrarchan Topos 'Bel piede': Generative Footsteps," *Romance Notes* 11 (1969): 167–73.

Nancy J. Vickers, an associate professor of French and Italian at Dartmouth College, has published articles on Dante and Petrarch. The present essay is part of a recently completed book on anatomical blazon.

Vostre *beauté* est joincte egalement
A vostre bonne grace:
. . . .

Si toutefois Petrarque vous plaist mieux,
. . . .
Je choisiray cent mille nouveautez,
Dont je peindray voz plus grandes *beautez*
    Sur la plus belle Idee.
        ["Contre les Petrarquistes," ll. 193–96, 201, 206–8]

> Of your *beauties* I will only say that, if my eye does not mistakenly judge, your *beauty* is perfectly joined to your good grace: . . . But if you still like Petrarch better . . . I will choose a hundred thousand new ways to paint your greatest *beauties* according to the most beautiful Idea.[5]

Du Bellay's opposition of "beauties" and "beauty" suggests the idiosyncratic nature of Petrarch's depiction of woman as a composite of details. It would surely seem that to Petrarch Laura's whole body was at times less than some of its parts; and that to his imitators the strategy of describing her through the isolation of those parts presented an attractive basis for imitation, extension, and, ultimately, distortion. I will redefine that strategy here in terms of a myth to which both the *Rime* and the Renaissance obsessively return, a myth complex in its interpretation although simple in its staging. As a privileged mode of signifying, the recounting of a mythical tale within a literary text reveals concerns, whether conscious or unconscious, which are basic to that text.[6] It is only logical, then, to examine Petrarch's use of a myth about seeing woman in order to reexamine his description of a woman seen. The story of Actaeon's encounter with the goddess Diana is particularly suited to this purpose, for it is a story not only of confrontation with forbidden naked deity but also with forbidden naked femininity.

   In the twenty-third *canzone*, the *canzone* of the metamorphoses, Petrarch's "I" narrates a history of changes: he was Daphne (a laurel), Cygnus (a swan), Battus (a stone), Byblis (a fountain), Echo (a voice), he will never be Jove (a golden raincloud), and he is Actaeon (a stag). He has passed through a series of painful frustrations, now experiences a highly specific one, and will never be granted the sexual fulfillment of a god capable of transforming himself into a golden shower and inseminating the object of his desire. His use of the present in the last full stanza, the Actaeon stanza, is telling, for it centers this *canzone* on the

5. Italics and translation mine.
6. For a recent summary and bibliography of the place of myth in the Renaissance text, see Leonard Barkan, "Diana and Actaeon: The Myth as Synthesis," *English Literary Renaissance* 10 (1980).

juxtaposition of what the speaker was and what he now is: "Alas, what am I? What was I? The end crowns the life, the evening the day."[7] The end also crowns the song, and this song paradoxically abandons its speaker in the form of a man so transmuted that he cannot speak:

> I' segui' tanto avanti il mio desire
> ch' un dì, cacciando sì com' io solea,
> mi mossi, e quella fera bella et cruda
> in una fonte ignuda
> si stava, quando 'l sol più forte ardea.
> Io perché d'altra vista non m'appago
> stetti a mirarla, ond' ella ebbe vergogna
> et per farne vendetta o per celarse
> l'acqua nel viso co le man mi sparse.
> Vero dirò; forse e' parrà menzogna:
> ch'i' senti' trarmi de la propria imago
> et in un cervo solitario et vago
> di selva in selva ratto mi trasformo,
> et ancor de' miei can fuggo lo stormo.
>
> [*RS*, 23. 147–60]

I followed so far my desire that one day, hunting as I was wont, I went forth, and that lovely cruel wild creature was in a spring naked when the sun burned most strongly. I, who am not appeased by any other sight, stood to gaze on her, whence she felt shame and, to take revenge or to hide herself, sprinkled water in my face with her hand. I shall speak the truth, perhaps it will appear a lie, for I felt myself drawn from my own image and into a solitary wandering stag from wood to wood quickly I am transformed and still I flee the belling of my hounds.

Petrarch's account of Actaeon's story closely follows the subtext that obviously subtends the entire *canzone*—Ovid's *Metamorphoses*. Actaeon is, as usual, hunting with friends. At noon, he stumbles upon a grove where he sees Diana, chaste goddess of the hunt and of the moon, bathing nude in a pool.[8] In the *Metamorphoses* she is surrounded by protective nymphs, but Petrarch makes no mention of either her company or of Actaeon's.

7. *Petrarch's Lyric Poems: The "Rime sparse" and Other Lyrics,* trans. and ed. Robert M. Durling (Cambridge, Mass., 1976), *canzone* 23, ll. 30–31; all further references to the *Rime sparse* will be included in the text with poem and line number in parentheses and with Durling's translation. For recent analyses of *Rime sparse* 23, see Dennis Dutschke, *Francesco Petrarca: Canzone XXIII from First to Final Version* (Ravenna, 1977), and Albert J. Rivero, "Petrarch's 'Nel dolce tempo de la prima etade,'" *Modern Language Notes* 94 (1979): 92–112.

8. For an extremely useful comparison of the Ovidian and Petrarchan narrations of this scene, see Dutschke, *Francesco Petrarca,* pp. 200–209. On the relationship between midday and sexuality in this myth, see Nicolas J. Perella, *Midday in Italian Literature: Variations on an Archetypal Theme* (Princeton, N.J., 1979), pp. 8–9.

He thus focuses the exchange on its principal players. Actaeon is trans-fixed (a stance Petrarch exaggerates), and Diana, both in shame and anger, sprinkles ("spargens") his face ("vultum") and hair ("comas") with water. Although in the *Rime sparse* Diana is significantly silenced, in the *Metamorphoses* she utters, "Now you can tell ["narres . . . licet"] that you have seen me unveiled ["posito velamine"]—that is, if you can tell ["si poteris narrare"]."[9] Diana's pronouncement simultaneously posits telling (description) as the probable outcome of Actaeon's glance and negates the possibility of that telling. Her vengeful baptism triggers a metamor-phosis: it transforms Actaeon from horn to hoof into a voiceless, fearful stag (*Metamorphoses* 3. 193–98). It is at this moment that Petrarch, with his characteristic use of an iterative present, situates his speaker: No other sight appeases me; "I am transformed"; "I flee."[10] The speaker *is* Actaeon, but, more important, he is a self-conscious Actaeon: he knows his own story; he has read his own text; he is defined by it and even echoes it in articulating his suffering. What awaits him is annihilation through dismemberment, attack unto death by his own hounds goaded on by his own devoted friends.

Seeing and bodily disintegration, then, are related poles in the Ovidian context that Petrarch brings to his text; they also are poles Ovid conjoins elsewhere. Actaeon's mythological antitypes in dismember-ment, Pentheus and Orpheus, are both textually and experientially linked to his story.[11] His is the subtext to their suffering; he is the figure for their pain. In *Metamorphoses* 3. 708–33, Pentheus gapes with "profane eyes" upon the female celebrants of the sacred rites of Bacchus, and they, urged by his mother (the woman who sees him), tear his body limb from limb: "Let the ghost of Actaeon move your heart," he pleads, but "she [his mother] knows not who Actaeon is, and tears the suppliant's right arm away." In *Metamorphoses* 11. 26–27, Orpheus is so grief stricken at having irrevocably lost Eurydice by turning back to look at her that he shuns other women; falling victim to an explosion of female jealousy, he is dismembered and scattered, "as when in the amphitheatre . . . the doomed stag is the prey of dogs."

All three men, then, transgress, see women who are not to be seen, and are torn to bits. But the Orpheus-Actaeon analogy is particularly suggestive, for in the case of Orpheus, seeing and dismemberment are discrete events in time. The hiatus between them, the extended reprieve,

9. Ovid, *Metamorphoses*, ed. and trans. Frank J. Miller, 2 vols. (1921; London, 1971), bk. 3, ll. 192–93; all further references to the *Metamorphoses* will be included in the text with book and line number in parentheses. The quotations from this work are based upon but do not entirely reproduce Miller's edition.

10. On the use of the present tense in relation to Actaeon, see Durling's introduction to *Petrarch's Lyric Poems*, p. 28.

11. On the association of Actaeon and Orpheus, see ibid., p. 29. On Actaeon and Pentheus, see Norman O. Brown, "Metamorphoses II: Actaeon," *American Poetry Review* 1 (November/December 1972): 38.

is a span of exquisite though threatened poetry, of songs of absence and loss. Petrarch's "modern" Actaeon is in that median time: he is fearful of the price of seeing, yet to be paid, but still pleased by what he saw. The remembered image is the source of all joy and pain, peace and anxiety, love and hate: "Living is such heavy and long pain, that I call out for the end in my great desire to see her again whom it would have been better not to have seen at all" (*RS*, 312. 12–14). Thus he must both perpetuate her image and forget it: he must "cry out in silence," cry out "with paper and ink," that is to say, write (*RS*, 71. 6, 23. 99).

It is especially important to note that the productive paralysis born of this ambivalence determines a normative stance for countless lovesick poets of the Petrarchan generations. As Leonard Barkan has recently shown, "From that source [Petrarch] Actaeon's story becomes throughout the Renaissance a means of investigating the complicated psychology of love."[12] When Shakespeare, for example, lends a critical ear to Orsino in his opening scene to *Twelfth Night,* we hear what was by 1600 the worn-out plaint of a languishing lover caught precisely in Actaeon's double bind:

> CURIO: Will you go to hunt, my lord?
> ORSINO: What, Curio?
> CURIO: The hart.
> ORSINO: Why, so I do, the noblest that I have.
> O, when mine eyes did see Olivia first,
> Methought she purg'd the air of pestilence!
> That instant was I turn'd into a hart,
> And my desires, like fell and cruel hounds,
> E'er since pursue me.
>   [Act 1, sc. 1, ll. 16–23]

Subsequent imitation, no matter how creative or how wooden, bears witness to the reader's awareness of and the writer's engagement in the practice of "speaking" in Actaeon's voice. A reassessment of Petrarch's use of Actaeon's fate to represent the status of his speaking subject, then, constitutes a reassessment of not just one poetic stance but of many. When we step back from the Petrarchans to Petrarch, the casting of the poet in this role (and, by extension, the beloved in that of Diana) is less a cliché than a construct that can be used to explain both the scattering of woman and of rhyme in his vernacular lyric. Here the "metaphor of appearance," so central to the volume, is paired with the myth of ap-

---

12. Barkan, "Diana and Actaeon," p. 335. On the use of this myth in medieval lyric, see Stephen G. Nichols, Jr., "Rhetorical Metamorphosis in the Troubadour Lyric," in *Mélanges de langue et de littérature médiévales offerts à Pierre Le Gentil, Professeur à la Sorbonne, par ses collègues, ses élèves, et ses amis,* ed. Jean Dufournet and Daniel Poirion (Paris, 1973), pp. 569–85.

pearance: the fateful first perception of Laura—an image obsessively remembered, reworked, and repeated—assumes a mythical analogue and mythical proportion.[13] What the reader must then ask is why that remembrance, like the rhyme ("rimembra" / "membra" [remember / members]) that invokes it, is one of parts: "Clear, fresh, sweet waters, where she who alone seems lady to me rested her lovely body ["membra"], gentle branch where it pleased her (with sighing I remember)" (*RS*, 126. 1–5).[14]

Although traces of Diana are subtly woven into much of the imagistic texture that progressively reveals the composite of Laura, only one text refers to her by name:

> Non al suo amante più Diana piacque
> quando per tal ventura tutta ignuda
> la vide in mezzo de le gelide acque,
>
> ch' a me la pastorella alpestra et cruda
> posta a bagnar un leggiadretto velo
> ch' a l'aura il vago et biondo capel chiuda;
>
> tal che mi fece, or quand' egli arde 'l cielo,
> tutto tremar d'un amoroso gielo.
>
> [*RS*, 52]

Not so much did Diana please her lover when, by a similar chance, he saw her all naked amid the icy waters,

as did the cruel mountain shepherdess please me, set to wash a pretty veil that keeps her lovely blond head from the breeze;

so that she made me, even now when the sky is burning, all tremble with a chill of love.

This simple madrigal based on the straightforward equation of the speaker's pleasure at seeing Laura's veil and Actaeon's pleasure at seeing Diana's body has, of late, received lengthy and suggestive comment. Giuseppe Mazzotta, in an analysis centered on Petrarch's "language of the self," reads it in relation to a reversibility of "subject and object."[15] John Freccero places Petrarch's use of the "veil covering a radiant face" motif within its traditional context (Saint Paul to Dante), that of a "figure

---

13. See Giuseppe Mazzotta, "The *Canzoniere* and the Language of the Self," *Studies in Philology* 75 (1978): 277.

14. The connection between these verses and the Diana /Actaeon myth is noted by Durling, *The Figure of the Poet in Renaissance Epic* (Cambridge, Mass., 1965), p. 73. See also my "Re-membering Dante: Petrarch's 'Chiare, fresche et dolci acque,'" *Modern Language Notes* 96 (1981): 8–9

15. See Mazzotta, "The *Canzoniere*," pp. 282–84.

for the relationship of the sign to its referent." He concludes that Laura's "veil, bathed in the water like the naked goddess seen by Acteon, functions as a fetish, an erotic signifier of a referent whose absence the lover refuses to acknowledge." That act of substituting the veil for the body, previously linked by Freccero to the Augustinian definition of idolatry, ultimately associates the fragmentation of Laura's body and the "non-referentiality" of Petrarch's sequence:

> One of the consequences of treating a signifier as an absolute is that its integrity cannot be maintained. Without a principle of intelligibility, an interpretant, a collection of signs threatens to break down into its component parts. . . . So it is with Laura. Her virtues and her beauties are scattered like the objects of fetish worship: her eyes and hair are like gold and topaz on the snow, while the outline of her face is lost; . . . Like the poetry that celebrates her, she gains immortality at the price of vitality and historicity. Each part of her has the significance of her entire person; it remains the task of the reader to string together her gemlike qualities into an idealized unity.[16]

Freccero's analysis departs from a position shared by many contemporary Petrarch critics—that of the centrality of a dialectic between the scattered and the gathered, the integrated and the disintegrated.[17] In defining Petrarch's "poetics of fragmentation," these same critics have consistently identified as its primary figure the particularizing descriptive strategy adopted to evoke Laura.[18] If the speaker's "self " (his text, his "corpus") is to be unified, it would seem to require the repetition of her dismembered image. "Woman remains," as Josette Féral has commented in another context, "the instrument by which man attains unity, and she pays for it at the price of her own dispersion."[19]

Returning to *Rime sparse* 52, some obvious points must be made: first, this text is read as an emblem of Petrarchan fragmentation; and second, it turns on a highly specific analogy ("I am pleased by Laura's veil as Actaeon was pleased by Diana's nakedness"; "My fetish equals Diana's body"). It is the analogy itself that poses an additional problem. While the enunciation of "I" 's fetishistic pleasure through comparison with Actaeon's voyeuristic pleasure might appear incongruous, it is both appropriate and revealing.

16. Freccero, "The Fig Tree," pp. 38–39.

17. See, e.g., Durling, introduction to *Petrarch's Lyric Poems;* Freccero, "The Fig Tree"; and Mazzotta, "The *Canzoniere.*"

18. For the phrase "poetics of fragmentation," see Mazzotta, "The *Canzoniere,*" p. 274.

19. Josette Féral, "Antigone or *The Irony of the Tribe,*" trans. Alice Jardine and Tom Gora, *Diacritics* 8 (Fall 1978): 7. I am indebted to Elizabeth Abel for calling this quotation to my attention. See also Durling, introduction to *Petrarch's Lyric Poems,* p. 21, and Mazzotta, "The *Canzoniere,*" p. 273.

The Actaeon-Diana story is one of identification and reversal: Actaeon hunts; Diana hunts; and their encounter reduces him to the status of the hunted.[20] This fated meeting, this instant of midday recognition, is one of fascination and repulsion: it is a confrontation with difference where similarity might have been desired or even expected. It is a glance into a mirror—witness the repeated pairing of this myth with that of Narcissus (*Metamorphoses* 3. 344–510)—that produces an unlike and deeply threatening image.[21] Perceiving that image is, of course, prohibited; such a transgression violates proscriptions imposed on powerless humans in their relation to powerful divinities. Similarly, such a transgression violates proscriptions imposed upon powerless men (male children) in relation to powerful women (mothers):[22] "This is thought," writes Howard Daniel, "to be one of many myths relating to the incest mechanism—punishment for an even accidental look at something forbidden."[23] The Actaeon-Diana encounter read in this perspective reenacts a scene fundamental to theorizing about fetishistic perversion: the troubling encounter of a male child with intolerable female nudity, with a body lacking parts present in his own, with a body that suggests the possibility of dismemberment. Woman's body, albeit divine, is displayed to Actaeon, and his body, as a consequence, is literally taken apart. Petrarch's Actaeon, having read his Ovid, realizes what will ensue: his response to the threat of imminent dismemberment is the neutralization, through descriptive dismemberment, of the threat. He transforms the visible totality into scattered words, the body into signs; his description, at one remove from his experience, safely permits and perpetuates his fascination.

The verb in the *Rime sparse* that places this double dismemberment in the foreground is determinant for the entire sequence—*spargere*, "to scatter." It appears in some form (most frequently that of the past-participial adjective "*sparso, -i, -a, -e*") forty-three times; nineteen apply specifically to Laura's body and its emanations (the light from her eyes, the generative capacity of her footsteps) and thirteen to the speaker's

20. See Barkan, "Diana and Actaeon," pp. 320–22, and Brown, "Metamorphoses II," p. 40.

21. See Barkan, "Diana and Actaeon," pp. 321, 343; Brown, "Metamorphoses II," p. 39; Durling, introduction to *Petrarch's Lyric Poems*, p. 31; and Mazzotta, "The *Canzoniere*," pp. 274, 282.

22. This myth has often been used to point to relationships of power through play on the words *cervus/servus, cerf/serf* (stag/slave); see Barkan "Diana and Actaeon," p. 328. The identification of Diana with women in political power is perhaps best exemplified by the frequent representation of Elizabeth I as Diana; see Barkan, pp. 332–35.

23. Howard Daniel, *Encyclopedia of Themes and Subjects in Painting*, s.v. "Actaeon" (London, 1971). Daniel's point is, of course, supported by the tradition identifying Actaeon's hounds with the Law, with his conscience: "Remorse, the bite of a mad dog. Conscience, the superego, the introjected father or animal: now eating us even as we ate him" (Brown, "Metamorphoses II," p. 39); see also Perella, *Midday in Italian Literature*, p. 42. On Actaeon as "unmanned" or castrated, see Barkan, "Diana and Actaeon," pp. 350–51.

mental state and its expression (tears, voice, rhymes, sighs, thoughts, praises, prayers, hopes). The uses of *spargere* thus markedly gravitate toward "I" and Laura. The etymological roots of the term, moreover, virtually generate Laura's metaphoric codes: "I" knows that the outcome of seeing her body is the scattering of his; hence he projects scattering onto her through a process of fetishistic overdetermination, figuring those part-objects in terms of the connotations of "scattering": *spargere,* from the Latin *spargere,* with cognates in the English "sprinkle" and "sparkle" and in the Greek σπείρω—"I disseminate." Laura's eyes, as in the sequence of three *canzoni* devoted exclusively to them (*RS,* 71–73), are generative sparks emanating from the stars; they sow the seeds of poetry in the "untilled soil" of the poet (*RS,* 71. 102–5), and they sprinkle glistening drops like clear waters. Her body parts metaphorically inseminate; his do not: "Song, I was never the cloud of gold that once descended in a precious rain so that it partially quenched the fire of Jove; but I have certainly been a flame lit by a lovely glance and I have been the bird that rises highest in the air raising her whom in my words I honor" (*RS,* 23. 161–66). Desire directed in vain at a forbidden, distant goddess is soon sublimated desire that spends itself in song. That song is, in turn, the celebration and the violation of that goddess: it would re-produce her vulnerability; it would re-present her nakedness to a (male) reader who will enter into collusion with, even become, yet another Actaeon.[24]

Within the context of Petrarch's extended poetic sequence, the lady is corporeally scattered; the lover is emotionally scattered and will be corporeally scattered, and thus the relation between the two is one of mirroring. "I," striking Actaeon's pose, tells us that he stood fixed to see but also to mirror Diana-Laura ("mirarla").[25] He offers to eliminate the only source of sadness for the "lovely eyes," their inability to see themselves, by mirroring them (*RS,* 71. 57–60). And he transforms the coloration of the lady's flesh into roses scattered in snow in which he mirrors himself (*RS,* 146. 5–6). The specular nature of this exchange explains, in large part, the disconcerting interchangeability of its participants. Even the key rhyme "rimembra/membra" reflects a doubling: twice the *membra* are his (*RS,* 15 and 23); once those of the lost heroes of a disintegrating body politic, a dissolving mother country (*RS,* 53); and twice hers (*RS,* 126 and 127). In reading the Diana-veil madrigal cited

24. See Daniel, "Actaeon." On the casting of the male spectator (reader) in the role of the voyeur, see also John Berger, *Ways of Seeing* (New York, 1977), pp. 45–64, and Laura Mulvey, "Visual Pleasure and Narrative Cinema," *Screen* 16 (Autumn 1975): 6–18. On women conditioned by patriarchal culture to see themselves as "sights," see Jessica Benjamin, "The Bonds of Love: Rational Violence and Erotic Domination," in *The Future of Difference,* ed. Hester Eisenstein and Alice Jardine (Boston, 1980), p. 52, and Berger, *Ways of Seeing,* pp. 46–51.

25. I am, of course, alluding to the etymological associations and not the definition of the verb *mirare* ("to stare").

above, Mazzotta demonstrates this textual commingling, pointing out that Diana's body, in the first tercet, is completely naked ("tutta ignuda") in a pool of icy waters ("gelide acque") but, by the last line, her observer's body is all atremble ("tutto tremar") with a chill of love ("un amoroso gielo"). Mazzotta goes on to note that male/female roles often alternate in Petrarch's figurations of the speaker/Laura relationship: he is Echo to her Narcissus, Narcissus to her Echo; she is Apollo to his Daphne, Daphne to his Apollo, and so on.[26] The space of that alternation is a median one—a space of looks, mirrors, and texts.

Actaeon sees Diana, Diana sees Actaeon, and seeing is traumatic for both. She is ashamed, tries to hide her body (her secret), and thus communicates her sense of violation. Her observer consequently knows that pleasure in the sight before him constitutes transgression; he deduces that transgression, although thrilling (arousing), is threatening (castrating). Their initial communication is a self-conscious look; the following scenario fills the gap between them: "I . . . stood to gaze on her, whence she felt shame and, to take revenge or to hide herself, sprinkled water ["mi sparse"—cf. Ovid, "spargens"] in my face with her hand[s]. I shall speak the truth" (*RS*, 23. 153–56). She defends herself and assaults him with scattered water; he responds with scattered words: "You who hear in scattered rhymes the sound of those sighs with which I nourished my heart during my first youthful error, when I was in part another man from what I am now" (*RS*, 1. 1–4). Water and words, then, pass between them; hands and transparent drops cannot conceal her but do precipitate a metamorphosis, preventing a full sounding of what was momentarily seen. Threatened rhymes try to iterate a precious, fleeting image, to transmute it into an idol that can be forever possessed, that will be forever present.

But description is ultimately no more than a collection of imperfect signs, signs that, like fetishes, affirm absence by their presence. Painting Laura in poetry is but a twice-removed, scripted rendering of a lost woman (body → introjected image of the body → textual body), an enterprise by definition fragmentary. "I" speaks his anxiety in the hope of finding repose through enunciation, of re-membering the lost body, of effecting an inverse incarnation—her flesh made word. At the level of the fictive experience which he describes, successes are ephemeral, and failures become a way of life.

> Quella per cui con Sorga ò cangiato Arno,
> con franca povertà serve ricchezze,
> volse in amaro sue sante dolcezze
> ond' io già vissi, or me ne struggo et scarno.

---

26. Mazzotta, "The *Canzoniere*," pp. 282–84. See also Durling, introduction to *Petrarch's Lyric Poems*, pp. 31–32.

Da poi più volte ò riprovato indarno
al secol che verrà l'alte bellezze
pinger cantando, a ciò che l'ame et prezze,
né col mio stile il suo bel viso incarno.

Le lode, mai non d'altra et proprie sue,
che 'n lei fur come stelle in cielo sparte,
pur ardisco ombreggiare, or una or due;

ma poi ch' i' giungo a la divina parte,
ch' un chiaro et breve sole al mondo fue[,]
ivi manca l'ardir, l'ingegno et l'arte.

[*RS*, 308]

She for whom I exchanged Arno for Sorgue and slavish riches
for free poverty, turned her holy sweetness[es], on which I once
lived, into bitterness, by which now I am destroyed and
disfleshed [I destroy and disflesh myself].

Since then I have often tried in vain to depict in song for the age
to come her high beauties, that it may love and prize them, nor
with my style can I incarnate her lovely face.

Still now and again I dare to adumbrate one or two of the praises
that were always hers, never any other's, that were as many as
the stars spread [scattered] across the sky;

but when I come to her divine part, which was a bright, brief sun
to the world, there fails my daring, my wit, and my art.

This text organizes itself upon a sequence of oppositions which contrast
fullness (presence) with emptiness (absence). The speaker has exchanged Arno (Florence, mother country) for Sorgue (Vaucluse, exile);
riches (although slavish) for poverty (albeit free); sweetness for bitterness; a body for dismemberment; and union for separation. The
speaker's rhymes point to a past place (a body of water, "Arno") and to
two present, though fruitless ("indarno"), activities—he is at once
stripped of flesh ("me ne . . . scarno") and would give flesh to her
("incarno"). He acknowledges his inability to re-create Laura's absent
face, and yet he maintains that he still tries, "now and again." Her praises
(that is, his poems) are but images he "dare[s] to adumbrate," shadows
"scattered," like their source, across the sky. Daring, wit, and art cannot
re-present her to him, but they can evoke her parts "one by one" and
thus generate an exquisite sequence of verse (*RS*, 127. 85–91 and 273. 6).
For it is in fact the loss, at the fictional level, of Laura's body that constitutes the intolerable absence, creates a reason to speak, and permits a

poetic "corpus." As Petrarch's readers have consistently recognized, Laura and *lauro,* the laurel to crown a poet laureate, are one.[27]

Petrarch's poetry is a poetry of tension, of flux, of alternation between the scattered and the gathered. Laura's many parts would point to a unity, however elusive, named Laura; the speaker's ambivalent emotions are spoken by a grammatically constant "io." In the space of exchange, the only space the reader is given, permutation is possible; each part of her body can produce each aspect of his positive/negative reactions. A given text can expand any combination; infinite variety spawns infinite verse. Petrarch's particularizing mode of figuring that body, the product of a male-viewer/female-object exchange that extends the Actaeon/Diana exchange, thus reveals a textual strategy subtending his entire volume: it goes to the heart of his lyric program and understandably becomes the lyric stance of generations of imitators.

And yet such praise carries condemnation with it because it implies at least two interdependent consequences. First, Petrarch's figuration of Laura informs a decisive stage in the development of a code of beauty, a code that causes us to view the fetishized body as a norm and encourages us to seek, or to seek to be, "ideal types, beautiful monsters composed of every individual perfection."[28] Petrarch's text, of course, did not constitute the first example of particularizing description, but it did popularize that strategy by coming into fashion during the privileged early years of printing, the first century of the widespread diffusion of both words and images. It is in this context that Petrarch left us his legacy of fragmentation. And second, bodies fetishized by a poetic voice logically do not have a voice of their own; the world of making words, of making texts, is not theirs. The status of Laura's voice, however, resists easy or schematic characterization. Once dead, it should be noted, she can often address her sleeping, disconsolate lover; while she is alive, direct discourse from her is extremely rare. Her speech, moreover, undergoes a treatment similar to that of her body in that it ranks high on the list of her exquisitely reified parts: "and her speech and her lovely face and her locks pleased me so that I have her before my eyes and shall always have wherever I am, on slope or shore" (*RS*, 30. 4–6).

Rime sparse 23, the *canzone* of the metamorphoses, strikingly dramatizes the complexity of both citing and stifling Laura's voice. Although each of its transformations repeats an Ovidian model, only three stress the active participation of the Lady. In the first she lifts the

27. For recent analyses of the play on Laura /*lauro,* see François Rigolot, "Nature and Function of Paronomasia in the *Canzoniere,*" *Italian Quarterly* 18 (Summer 1974): 29–36, and Marga Cottino-Jones, "The Myth of Apollo and Daphne in Petrarch's *Canzoniere:* The Dynamics and Literary Function of Transformation," in *Francis Petrarch, Six Centuries Later: A Symposium,* ed. Aldo Scaglione (Chapel Hill, N.C., 1975), pp. 152–76.

28. Cropper, "On Beautiful Women," p. 376.

speaker's heart out of his chest, utters two exceptional sentences, and ultimately turns him (like Battus) into a stone; next, she reduces him (like Echo) into a repetitive voice; and finally, she transforms him (like Actaeon) into a stag. The Ovidian models are telling in that they all either limit or negate a voice: Mercury says to Battus, "Whoever you are, my man, if anyone should ask you about some cattle, say that you have not seen them" (*Metamorphoses* 2. 692–94); Juno says to Echo, "That tongue by which I have been tricked shall have its power curtailed and enjoy the briefest use of speech" (*Metamorphoses* 3. 366–67); and Diana says to Actaeon, "Now you are free to tell ["narres . . . licet"] that you have seen me unveiled—if you can tell ["narrare"]" (*Metamorphoses* 3. 192–93).[29]

The first model permits speech, but insists that it not be true, and, when disobeyed, denies it; the second, by reducing speech to repetition, eliminates its generative capacity; and the third, through irony, does away with it altogether. In Ovid's retelling of that third encounter, Diana is the only person to speak once Actaeon has had his first glimpse of her: "*narrare*" is her word; she pronounces it; she even repeats it. Although she cannot (would not?) prevent him from seeing, she can prevent him from telling. Consequently, that Petrarch erases both her speech and the verbal object of her interdiction (*narrare*) from his own narration is significant. A review of the evolution of the Diana/Actaeon sequence of *Rime sparse* 23, a text at many points explicit in its verbal echoing of Ovid, shows that "I shall speak ["dirò"] the truth" initiates the primary and final versions of line 156: two intermediate variants read "I tell ["narro"] the truth."[30] What that rejected present, *narro*, affirms, in a mode perhaps too obvious to be acceptable even to Petrarch, is that his speaker as Actaeon does precisely what Diana forbids: " 'Make no word of this,' " said the "powerful Lady" of a preceding stanza (*RS*, 23. 74, 35). Not only does Petrarch's Actaeon thus nullify Diana's act, he repeats her admonition in so doing; by the time we arrive at the end that "crowns" his song, her speech has been written out and his has been written in. To the measure that he continues to praise her beauties, he persists in inverting the traditional economy of the mythical exchange; he persists in offending her: "Not that I do not see how much my praise injures you [the eyes]; but I cannot resist the great desire that is in me since I saw what no thought can equal, let alone speech, mine or others' " (*RS*, 71. 16–21).

Silencing Diana is an emblematic gesture; it suppresses a voice, and it casts generations of would-be Lauras in a role predicated upon the

---

29. On the Diana/Actaeon myth and "the danger of losing the poetic voice," see Mazzotta, "The *Canzoniere*," p. 278; see also Durling, introduction to *Petrarch's Lyric Poems*, p. 28.

30. See Dutschke, *Francesco Petrarca*, pp. 196–98.

muteness of its player.[31] A modern Actaeon affirming himself as poet cannot permit Ovid's angry goddess to speak her displeasure and deny his voice; his speech requires her silence. Similarly, he cannot allow her to dismember his body; instead he repeatedly, although reverently, scatters hers throughout his scattered rhymes.

31. For the problem of women writing within the constraints of the Petarchan tradition, see Ann R. Jones, "Assimilation with a Difference: Renaissance Women Poets and Literary Influence," *Yale French Studies* no. 62 (October 1981); on the impact of another masculine lyric tradition on women poets, see Margaret Homans, *Women Writers and Poetic Identity: Dorothy Wordsworth, Emily Brontë and Emily Dickinson* (Princeton, N.J., 1980), pp. 12–40.

Laura Mulvey comments on the silencing of women in her rereading of a different medium, film: "Woman then stands in patriarchal culture as signifier for the male other, bound by a symbolic order in which man can live out his phantasies and obsessions through linguistic command by imposing them on the silent image of woman still tied to her place as bearer of meaning, not maker of meaning" ("Visual Pleasure," p. 7).

Magi and Maidens: The Romance of the Victorian Freud

Nina Auerbach

It is commonly assumed that Victorian patriarchs disposed of their women by making myths of them; but then as now social mythology had an unpredictable life of its own, slyly empowering the subjects it seemed to reduce. It also penetrated unexpected sanctuaries. If we examine the unsettling impact upon Sigmund Freud of a popular mythic configuration of the 1890s, we witness a rich, covert collaboration between documents of romance and the romance of science. Fueling this entanglement between the clinician's proud objectivity and the compelling images of popular belief is the imaginative power of that much-loved, much-feared, and much-lied-about creature, the Victorian woman.

Until recently, feminist criticism has depreciated this interaction between myths of womanhood, science, and history, seeing in social mythology only a male mystification which dehumanizes women: the myth of womanhood was thought to be no more than manufactured fantasies about woman's nature (inferior brain weight, educated women's tendency to brain fever, a ubiquitous maternal instinct, raging hormonal imbalance) meant to shackle female experience to male convenience.[1] As feminist criticism gains authority, however, its new sense

I would like to thank the Guggenheim Foundation for their generous support during the research and writing of this essay. I would also like to thank Sharon Bassett, Rachel Blau DuPlessis, and Lee Sterrenburg for their bibliographical and intellectual generosity in our discussions of Freud and H. D., though all errors and eccentricities are solely my own.

1. Kate Millett (*Sexual Politics* [New York, 1970]) sees myth exclusively as a male assault upon women. Elizabeth Janeway offers more subtle and sophisticated denunciations in *Man's World, Women's Place: A Study in Social Mythology* (New York, 1971) and *Between Myth and Morning: Women Awakening* (New York, 1975), though recently even

of power has resulted in an impulse toward rather than a denial of mythology.[2]

As we fabricate new mythologies commensurate with a growing belief in our strength, the time seems right to explore the mythologies of the past as well: they can tell us much about the blend of anger and awe men feel in our culture and much too about the secret victories of apparent female victims. When properly understood, the angel in the house, along with her still more passive and supine Victorian sisters, is too strong and interesting a creature for us to kill.

The myth I will look at here flourishes most obviously in popular literature of the 1890s, though its roots extend before and beyond that eccentric decade: the deliberate freakishness of nineties imagery illuminates both earlier ideals of respectability and later conventions of advanced thought.[3] A rich instance is the alluring conjunction of women and corpses, which has a resonance beyond both the titillating sadomasochistic vogue Mario Praz perceives and Frank Kermode's Romantic metaphor of art's self-contained detachment.[4] The female life-in-death figure may indeed be a metaphor for higher, or at least other, concerns, but if we look at her simply as a literal woman, her recurrent fits of vampirism, somnambulism, mesmerism, or hysterical

---

Janeway has cautiously hoped for a new mythos; see her "Who Is Sylvia?: On the Loss of Sexual Paradigms," *Signs* 5 (Summer 1980): 589.

2. Sandra M. Gilbert and Susan Gubar's *The Madwoman in the Attic: The Woman Writer and the Nineteenth-Century Literary Imagination* (New Haven, Conn., 1979), a compendious anatomy of the wounded rage of nineteenth-century women writers, begins by echoing Virginia Woolf's exhortation that we kill the male projections of angel and monster, but it ends half in love with its antagonist's images, weaving them into a rhapsodic and sibylline myth of its own: woman's freedom is no longer simply initiation into historical integrity but the rebirth of mythic potential. Following this new impulse, two recent feminist critics appropriate to their own uses Erich Neumann's celebration of the mythic Psyche, on whom they project their own revisionist images of heroic womanhood; see Rachel Blau DuPlessis, "Psyche, or Wholeness," *The Massachusetts Review* 20 (Spring 1979): 77–96, and Lee R. Edwards, "The Labors of Psyche: Toward a Theory of Female Heroism," *Critical Inquiry* 6 (Autumn 1979): 33–49. Carolyn G. Heilbrun's *Reinventing Womanhood* (New York, 1979) is a call for an expanded female mythos incorporating characteristics that had been reserved for male heroes alone.

3. For a wonderful anatomy of the complex ethos of the 1890s, see Linda Dowling, "The Decadent and the New Woman in the 1890s," *Nineteenth-Century Fiction* 33 (March 1979): 434–53.

4. See Mario Praz, *The Romantic Agony* (Oxford, 1933), and Frank Kermode, *Romantic Image* (New York, 1957), pp. 49–91.

Nina Auerbach, associate professor of English at the University of Pennsylvania, is the author of *Communities of Women: An Idea in Fiction* as well as articles on Victorian women and culture. The present essay is an excerpt from her book, *Woman and the Demon: The Life of a Victorian Myth,* a mythography of Victorian womanhood.

paralysis illuminate powers that were somewhat fancifully, somewhat wistfully, and somewhat fearfully imagined in women throughout the century. The passage of our own century has not entirely dispelled the vision of these powers. Let us look at three of woman's best-known incarnations, both for the shapes they take on in the nineties and for their revelations about imagined womanhood in general.

In a key tableau of the nineties, we see first, as we often do, not women but men: three men lean hungrily over three mesmerized and apparently characterless women, whose wills are suspended by those of the magus/masters. The looming men are Svengali, Dracula, and Freud; the lushly helpless women are Trilby O'Ferrall, Lucy Westenra, and (as Freud calls her) "Frau Emmy von N., age 40, from Livonia." It seems as if no men could be more culturally and inherently potent than these, no women more powerless to resist. Svengali is not only a master mesmerist and musician—the vocal genius with which he endows Trilby is his alone, her mouth its mere monumental repository—but he brings with him incalculable inherited lore from his birthplace in "the mysterious East! The poisonous East—birthplace and home of an ill wind that blows nobody good."[5]

The master-mesmerist Dracula seems derived from Svengali, with his powers still further extended over time and space. The spell he casts on women—we never see him mesmerizing a man, though he captures several—includes the animal kingdom, whose power he draws to himself at will, and at times the elements as well. As he tells his relentlessly up-to-date antagonists, who destroy him with the modern weapons of committee meetings and shorthand minutes, his monstrous immortality aligns his power with time's: his memory encompasses not merely the primeval lore of the vampire but the military and political strategies of Hungarian nationalism through the centuries. Svengali and Dracula, then, are endowed with a magic beyond their own: they possess the secret traditions of their culture, while the women they captivate seem not merely enfeebled but culturally naked.

As a mere mortal and historical figure, Freud might seem out of place in this preternatural company, but in his case history of Frau Emmy von N., his first contribution to *Studies on Hysteria* (1893–1895), written with Josef Breuer, there is delicious magic in his use of hypnosis, which he had not yet abandoned. After boasting that with hypnosis he can regulate Frau Emmy's menstrual periods, he revels in a psychic appropriation that is quite Svengali-like:

> I made it impossible for her to see any of those melancholy things again, not only by wiping out her memories of them in their *plastic* form but by removing her whole recollection of them, as though they had never been present in her mind. I promised her that this

5. George du Maurier, *Trilby* (1894; New York, 1977), p. 337; all further references to this work will be included in the text.

would lead to her being freed from the expectation of misfortune which perpetually tormented her and from the pains all over the body, of which she had been complaining precisely during her narrative, after we had heard nothing of them for several days.[6]

In fact Freud's promise was too sanguine, but the virtually limitless powers he arrogates to himself in this initial amalgam of science, myth, and magic give him access to our mythic pantheon in a manner A. C. Bradley had already foreseen in a prescient essay on the rise of social mythologies: "Is not the popularisation of that science which is the most active dissolvent of old mythology, itself thoroughly mythological?"[7]

In these two popular romances and in the romantic beginnings of modern science, we seem to see the image of prone womanhood at its most dispiriting. Personal and cultural disinheritance, we feel, could go no further than these *tabulae rasae,* all selfhood suspended as these women are invaded by the hyperconscious and culturally fraught male/master/monster. But when we actually read *Trilby, Dracula,* or *Studies on Hysteria,* what strikes us is the kinds of powers that are granted to the women: the victim of paralysis possesses seemingly infinite capacities of regenerative being that turn on her triumphant mesmerizer and paralyze him in turn. Dispossessed and seemingly empty, the women reveal a sort of infinitely unfolding magic that is quite different from the formulaic spells of the men.

The put-upon heroine of George du Maurier's *Trilby* is not fragile, as her role in the plot would lead one to assume, but a virtual giantess. Her size is so great, in fact, that she can be parcelled into fragments with a self-contained and totemistic value of their own, such as her majestic (but not Cinderella-like) foot or the awesomely cavernous roof of her mouth. Like George Eliot's noble, outsize heroines, Trilby seems crammed by the very setting and action of her story; underlying her sacrificial destiny (like Camille, Trilby repudiates her true love at the instigation of his snobbish parent, and thus she falls under Svengali's fatal power) is the hint that the novel's world is simply too small for her to live in. Du Maurier's illustrations reinforce our sense of her stature: in all, Trilby towers helplessly over her interlocutors, like Lewis Carroll's Alice. None of the illustrations reflects the paradigm of prone victim and omnipotent devourer, though this tableau does appear in the text. When under Svengali's spell, the Trilby of the illustrations looms so monumentally over him that she seems about to swoop down and crush him (see fig. 1).

Reinforcing Trilby's size is her seemingly boundless capacity for

6. Josef Breuer and Sigmund Freud, *Studies on Hysteria,* trans. and ed. James Strachey (1895; New York, 1957). p. 61; all further references to this work will be included in the text.

7. A. C. Bradley, "Old Mythology in Modern Poetry," *Macmillan's Magazine* 44 (May 1881): 29.

mutability. The great singer she becomes when mesmerized is only an index of her endlessly changing nature. From the beginning, her three adorers, Taffy, the laird, and Little Billee, see that she is a different woman in English and in French—as she will later have a tone-deaf and a singing self—and they await with awe each "new incarnation of Trilbyness." Falling in love is yet another metamorphosis, leading her to renounce all three men with the odd declaration: "You have changed me into another person—you [Taffy] and Sandy and Little Billee" (p. 156). She does not need Svengali to incite her to new incarnations; her power of metamorphosis defines her character.

When she becomes a great singer under Svengali's spell, Trilby's metamorphic power enervates her master (he dies of a heart attack while trying to mesmerize her to new heights of genius) but takes possession of the novel. The essence of her singing lies in its seemingly endless variations. What dazzles is her "slight, subtle changes in the quality of the

"AU CLAIR DE LA LUNE"

Fig. 1

sound—too quick and elusive to be taken count of, but to be felt with, oh what poignant sympathy!" (p. 250). These perpetual changes are not Svengali's endowment but Trilby's maddening essence. As simultaneous siren and angel, she haunts Little Billee as an image of infinite change: "And little innocent, pathetic, ineffable, well-remembered sweetness of her changing face kept painting themselves on his retina; and incomparable tones of this new thing, her voice, her infinite voice, went ringing in his head, till he all but shrieked aloud in his agony" (p. 264). Even before this most dramatic of metamorphoses, however, Trilby's love for Little Billee was only one component of a comradely *mariage à quatre* that included Taffy and the laird. Her endowed voice is an accidental index of the multiplicity which allows her always to be a new incarnation of herself.

Finally, the role of magus and mythmaker passes to her. Her ability under hypnosis to ring endless variations upon familiar tunes is the power of her character to transform itself endlessly and, in so doing, to renew endlessly the world around her. Her exquisitely lingering death licenses her to marry all three of the artists who love her: she bequeathes to each a wedding ring for his future wife. The myth at the heart of the novel comes not from Svengali's lore but from the capacious, regenerating mystery of its heroine, which awes and destroys both hero and villain: though Little Billee is supposed to be a great artist and Svengali a great musician, their artistry loses all meaning before the transforming bounty of Trilby's familiar presence. In drawing on ideals of the alluring vacuum of the uncultured woman waiting for the artist-male to fill her, du Maurier imagines powers that dwarf male gestures toward redemption and damnation.

The potent essence of each "incarnation of Trilbyness," counterpointing her passive and stupefied role in the plot, is repeated in the characteristic patterns of du Maurier's drawings. In an illustration of one of the few episodes in which Trilby does not figure, captioned "Darlings, Old or Young" (fig. 2), the composition is such that she might as well be present: two giant, bedecked women tower over a huddled-up Little Billee, suggesting that the overpowering Trilby is not an anomaly but the quintessence of womanhood. The same pattern governs du Maurier's society cartoons in *Punch*. Typically, a bevy of large-bustled society women sweeps up and down the picture plane, taking to itself all available motion, while a few rigid young men stand immobilized and isolated. In the typical configuration of "The Tables Turned" (fig. 3), though the women are saying stupid and enfeebled things, the force of their numbers and their costumes and the dynamic and multitudinous lines with which they are drawn make them the generators of the illustration's activity. Du Maurier's women observe the proprieties with more demure compliance, less swelling fierceness, than those of his contempo-

"DARLINGS, OLD OR YOUNG"

FIG. 2

THE TABLES TURNED

TIRED DAUGHTERS.—"Don't you think we might *go* now, mamma? It's three o'clock."
FESTIVE MAMMA.—"Oh, that's not so *very* late, darlings. . . . Mayn't I have *one* more dance?"

FIG. 3.—George du Maurier, *English Society Sketches* (New York, 1897). Courtesy of Lilly Library, Indiana University, Bloomington, Indiana.

rary, Aubrey Beardsley, but like Beardsley's women, du Maurier's appropriate all available vitality, whatever the demands of the ostensible context.

Moreover, du Maurier uses the contemporary fashion of tight lacing and bustle for a significant reversal of physical fact. Though in actuality corsets and bustles transformed a woman's body to a construction of rigid, almost Japanese, angularity, as any fashion plate from the 1880s illustrates, du Maurier's women are creatures of active, curving lines. Their characteristic motion is a ceaseless, elegant swoop, while the men in their freer attire seem mysteriously hampered and inhibited. Du Maurier reverses the actualities of a Victorian ballroom to accord with the sexual dynamics we have seen in his novel: in both, despite the demands of probability and the plot, the women are free, mobile, and flexible, while the men appear by nature corseted and strangulated.

Despite the dominance of the wicked old count in the popular folklore Bram Stoker's novel inspired, in *Dracula,* too, women secretively take the novel away from the villain.[8] Early on in his traumatic visit to Dracula's castle, Jonathan Harker realizes that the sinister count is less terrifying than his three hungry brides—"If I be sane, then surely it is maddening to think that of all the foul things that lurk in this hateful place, the Count is the least dreadful to me"[9]—and once the novel reaches England, it focuses on the vampiristic mutations Mina and Lucy undergo, of which the count is reduced to an increasingly immobilized catalyst.

Like Trilby, Lucy Westenra has two selves. She is all silly sweetness in the daylight, but as Dracula's powers invade her, she becomes a florid predator at night. Like Trilby, too, she longs to marry three men but can accept only one of them until death grants her wish: as Trilby bequeathed a wedding ring to each suitor, so the blood transfusions in which each suitor in turn pours himself into the dying Lucy provide the most convincing epithalamia in the novel (p. 158). Though Lucy does not meet the usual fate of English belles, she is not an aberration in nineties visions of femininity. Her fluctuations between virginal purity and bloody attacks link her to Thomas Hardy's dual-natured Tess Durbeyfield as well as to Trilby, and her penchant for somnambulism, trance, and strange physical and mental alterations, even before Dracula's arrival, would find her a place in either a romantic sonnet by Wilde or in Breuer and Freud's garland of female hysterics.

8. Recent vampire films are beginning to incorporate this underlying dynamic in Stoker's novel. In the most recent Hollywood *Dracula* (1979), directed by John Bodham, Frank Langella's count quite pales before the aggressive ardor of Kate Nelligan's Mina. In Werner Herzog's *Nosferatu, the Vampyre* (1979), Isabelle Adjani's Lucy takes the entire story into her hands, overriding the inscrutable passivity of hero and villain alike.

9. Bram Stoker, *Dracula,* ed. Leonard Wolf (1897; New York, 1975), p. 38; all further references to this work will be included in the text.

Stoker might conceivably have known of Freud's work. In 1893, F. W. H. Meyers reported enthusiastically on Breuer and Freud's "Preliminary Communication" to *Studies on Hysteria* at a general meeting of the Society for Psychical Research in London. Stoker's alienist Dr. Seward, indefatigably recording bizarre manifestations of vampirism, mentions the mesmerist Charcot, Freud's early teacher; Dr. Seward's relentless attempt to make sense of his patient Renfield's "zoophagy" is a weird forecast of the later Freud rationalizing the obsessions of his Wolf Man and Rat Man. Dr. Seward's meticulous case histories of Renfield, Lucy, and Dracula's other victims introduce into the Gothic genre a form that Freud would raise to a novelistic art; his anguished clinician's record makes of Lucy both the early heroine of a case history and an ineffable romantic image of *fin de siècle* womanhood.

The word "change," sometimes modified by "strange" and "terrible," almost always accompanies Lucy in the text; along with "beloved," it is her epithet. After her first transfusion, "she looked a different being from what she had been before the operation" (p. 119), and in her fluctuations between passivity and prowling, consciousness and dreaming, innocence and experience, pallor and ruddiness, she can be said to be "a different being" every time she appears. Though Dracula supposedly instigates her capacity for perpetual self-incarnation, he appears only in shadowy glimpses as Lucy passes into life-in-death. In fact, as women gain primacy, he withdraws increasingly except for intermittent stagy boasts; though he is the object of pursuit, Lucy, and then the vampirized Mina, are the objects of attention. His threat to turn London into a city of vampires is never as real as Van Helsing's ominous confidence to Dr. Seward: "Madam Mina, our poor, dear, Madam Mina, is changing" (p. 285).

By this time, we have learned that, unlike Lucy's and Mina's unpredictable changes, Dracula's powers of change are limited to noon, sunrise, and sunset. Moreover, as Mina's mind expands under hypnosis to meet Dracula's, his world contracts into the box of earth within which he is paralyzed. As the novel draws to a close, its "good brave men" become more aimless and confused than ever. Heroes and villains recede as the metamorphosed Mina appropriates the qualities of all groups. As Van Helsing says of her: ". . . we want all her great brain which is trained like man's brain, but is of sweet woman and have a special power which the Count give her, and which he may not take away altogether" (p. 298). In Stoker's influential literary myth, the apparently helpless woman assumes male, female, and preternatural powers, taking away from the now paralyzed Dracula the magus' potency.

It is fashionable to perceive Dracula as an emanation of Victorian sexual repression. Despite Mina's pious disclaimer that she has anything in common with the New Woman, it seems more plausible to read the novel as a nineties myth of newly empowered womanhood, whose two heroines are violently transformed from victims to instigators of their story. Aggrandized by her ambiguous transformations, Mina, and by implication womanhood itself, grows into the incarnation of irresistible Truth: "And I have read your diary that you have so goodly written for me, and which breaths out truth in every line. . . . Oh, Madam Mina, good women tell all their lives, and by day and by hour and by minute, such things that angels can read" (p. 167). In her many incarnations, Trilby also embodied Truth to her audience of reverent men: "Truth looked out of her eyes, as it had always done—truth was in every line of her face" (p. 309).[10] By the end, these seemingly supine women assume the authority of personifications, the guiding spirits of their novels' action. The power of Dracula himself narrows to the dimensions of his vulnerable coffin, for, despite his ambitious designs on the human race, he seems to be the world's last surviving male vampire. Neither Renfield nor the Russian sailors Dracula attacked at sea are transformed after death; only his three thirsty brides, Lucy, and Mina rise into the Undead. Had Dracula survived the end of the novel, this army of women might indeed have devoured the human race under his generalship, for as far as we see, his greatest power lies in his ability to catalyze the awesome changes potential in womanhood, in those modest personifications of divine and human truth.

The implicit primacy of women in *Dracula* becomes explicit in Stoker's later romances, *The Lady of the Shroud* (1909), *The Lair of the White Worm* (1911), and *The Jewel of Seven Stars* (1912). These novels contain sketchy and desultory recapitulations of the myth that in *Dracula* is painstakingly and elaborately documented, but in all of them, the Dracula figure himself is missing: like a vestigial organ of waning patriarchal divinity, he is displaced by a larger-than-life woman of a "strange dual nature." In *The Lady of the Shroud,* Stoker's one Radcliffian denial of the supernatural, the brave daughter of a Voivode nationalist disguises herself as an Undead. Before she reveals her mortal nature, the hero, obsessed with her as a lamialike vision, marries her in a secret ceremony. In this slight story, a woman takes over Dracula's role as Voivode nationalist with the powers of the Undead to transform and possess, but the rationalistic political context alchemizes male demonism into female heroism.

In contrast, *The Lair of the White Worm* is Stoker's darkest myth of womanhood. The book's Dracula figure, Lady Arabella March of Diana's Grove, is in her true self a giant white worm older than mankind, living at the bottom of a deep and fetid well that crawls with the repulsive vitality of vermin, insects, and worms. From the mythic associations of

10. Alexander Welsh ("The Allegory of Truth in English Fiction," *Victorian Studies* 9 [September 1965]: 7–28) discusses at length the hallowed iconographical tradition wherein Truth is represented as a woman. My own interest lies in the subversive implications within this conventional emblem.

her estate to the vaginal potency of her true lair, Lady Arabella's metamorphic power seems darkly intrinsic to womanhood itself. Lilla, the pure heroine, is so passive and susceptible as to be virtually nonexistent. Though she is recurrently mesmerized, she has no capacity for transformation, suggesting that Lucy's and Mina's powers are becoming divided: here the acceptable, womanly woman has renounced access to the powers of womanhood. *Dracula's* women were poised between angelic service and vampiristic mutation; here the lovable domestic woman loses her strength, while the dark outcast woman alone is equated with primal, self-transforming truth.

The Jewel of Seven Stars is a still more blatantly unresolved allegory of female power. Its Dracula figure is the ancient-Egyptian queen Tera, passionate and intellectual as Rider Haggard's mighty She-Who-Must-Be-Obeyed. We see Queen Tera only through mysterious signs indicating that she is about to be reincarnated in our strapping heroine, Margaret Trelawny. The story builds ominously toward Margaret's amalgamation with her potent and ancient double, but at the designated moment the queen fails to appear: Stoker can no longer accommodate his noble Victorian wives-to-be with his vision of primordial, transfigured womanhood. Reigning without need of Dracula's catalyzing powers, Stoker's later magus-women hover outside the gates, but they are blocked from invading modern London. Efficient contemporaneity may defeat an immortal foreign count, but it could not withstand the assault of these dark and brilliant women.

The maimed females of Breuer and Freud's *Studies on Hysteria* seem incapable of asserting power over their age. Like Dr. Seward's possessed inamorata, though, they are presented to us through that new medium of portraiture, the case history; like that of Dr. Seward himself, the documentary rationalism of Freud's new science will be insufficient to conquer Dracula, a Dracula sleeping in himself as well as in his patients.

Freud knew himself to be a believer in the myth of womanhood; Haggard's She haunted his dreams as "the eternal feminine, the immortality of our emotions." For Freud, however, myths bestow timeless order on the confusions of the present; as Philip Rieff perceives, "[h]is notion of myth is . . . basically anti-historical," giving glimpses of a deeper truth than history's.[11] Unlike Stoker's, then, Freud's female hysterics are not directly associated with the assaults on family life that were current in the nineties; he seems to have insulated his turbulent consulting room from its adjacent, ordered, domestic kingdom. But though Freud allows no topical validity to his female hysterics, he accepts as wholeheartedly as du Maurier did the absolute authority of performing

11. Philip Rieff, *Freud: The Mind of the Moralist* (New York, 1967), p. 181. For a provocative analysis of the congruence between Haggard and Freud, see Norman A. Etherington, "Rider Haggard, Imperialism, and the Layered Personality," *Victorian Studies* 22 (Autumn 1978): 71–87.

womanhood. He wrote of Sarah Bernhardt in the 1880s: "But how that Sarah plays! After the first words of her vibrant lovely voice I felt I had known her for years. Nothing she said could have surprised me; I believed at once everything she said."[12] This faith in "Sarah" is a surprising reversal of Freud's skepticism toward virtually all the assertions of his female patients; his characteristic professional stance is to translate their helpless deceit into his own impregnable truth. It seems that only the controlled self-transformation of performance, rather than the involuntary mutations of illness, could move Freud to believe, as novelists did, that women and truth were one.

Though Freud's patients lack the immediate authority of du Maurier's and Stoker's creations, they too are vehicles of incessant metamorphosis. Their symptoms twist them into bizarre shapes: like Mina and Lucy, they are prone to somnambulism, inability to eat or to stay awake through the day; like Trilby, they divide into magnified totemistic parts of themselves, as with "Miss Lucy R., age 30," who is troubled by a smell of burnt pudding so overwhelming that she begins to disappear into her own nasal cavity, or "Katharina," whose anxiety attacks throw each part of her body into vivid relief:

> "It comes over me all at once. First of all it's like something pressing on my eyes. My head gets so heavy, there's a dreadful buzzing, and I feel so giddy that I almost fall over. Then there's something crushing my chest so that I can't get my breath."
> "And you don't notice anything in your throat?"
> "My throat's squeezed together as though I were going to choke."
> "Does anything else happen in your head?"
> "Yes, there's a hammering, enough to burst it." [*Hysteria,* p. 126]

Freud's prompting forces our awareness of the hallucinatory consciousness that invades parts of her body in turn. He shows the same anatomical fascination with the hysterical pains of "Fraulein Elisabeth Von R.," which he locates precisely in a "fairly large, ill-defined area of the anterior surface of the right thigh" (*Hysteria,* p. 135). Like the discovery of Lucy's newly prominent teeth, these revelations that parts of a woman's body can become thus preternaturally animated make the reader uneasily aware of undiscovered powers.

Though Freud presents himself as a stabilizing presence, his actual task resembles that of Svengali, Dracula, and Van Helsing in that he strives to effect a further metamorphosis in his mobile victim. Katharina's cure is apparent in her speaking transformation, of which

12. Freud, quoted in Ernest Jones, *The Life and Work of Sigmund Freud: The Formative Years and the Great Discoveries, 1856–1900,* 3 vols. (New York, 1953), 1:177–78.

his interpretation is only a shadow: "At the end of these two sets of memories she came to a stop. She was like someone transformed. The sulky, unhappy face had grown lively, her eyes were bright, she was lightened and exalted. Meanwhile, the understanding of her case had become clear to me" (*Hysteria,* p. 131). Changing womanhood is the vessel of scientific, as it was of supernatural, power.

Freud reminds us with some pride of the likeness of his case histories to short stories, and, as with so much contemporary fiction, the true theme of *Studies on Hysteria* is woman's capacity for amazing and empowering transformations. Here, though, Freud as narrator/healer/magus/master is always in control, as if to galvanize in anticipation the feeble magic of Svengali and Little Billee, Dracula and Van Helsing. Freud's own amalgam of mythic art and science, religion and iconoclasm, austerity and eroticism, combines the tools of all the men in romances who want to save and subdue mutable womanhood. The popularity of *The Seven Per Cent Solution* has allowed us to pair Freud and Sherlock Holmes instinctively in our imagination of the nineties. It may be more difficult for some to associate him with these darker, more complex literary figures, though Freud himself might not have repudiated the role of hero/villain in a quintessentially British romance. Like Svengali, Dracula, and Van Helsing, he was deeply drawn to the apparent rationalism of Victorian British civilization: in the last months of his life, he played out their role of exiled foreign wizard in his imaginative homeland. British romantic mythology was one of the staunchest loves in his life, but in his role as dark magician, evoking and controlling the secrets of womanhood, creation was sometimes at war with human reality. When a patient, now famous as "Dora," wanted to take her life from the master's possession, the result was Freud's anguished account of a failed myth that also became a failed case history.

Unfortunately, the woman Dora cannot be separated in our imagination from the resonant name Freud gave her, her ever changing repertoire of hysterical illnesses, the verdict of one anonymous doctor that she was "one of the most repulsive hysterics" he had ever met, and her stiff-necked persistence in saying "no" to Freud. Despite his attempt to orchestrate her unconscious into agreement with his consciousness—at one difficult point, he invents a consoling aphorism of her infinite, if inaudible, acquiescence: "there is no such thing at all as an unconscious 'No' "[13]—Dora met Freud's interpretations with a perfect symphony of nos until, on the last day of the year, she abruptly terminated treatment altogether. For me, at least, the facts of Dora's life and Freud's constructions explain her resistance perfectly: hedged by the pressure of authoritative men, she seems to have been fighting for her life.

13. Freud, *Dora: An Analysis of a Case of Hysteria,* trans. Strachey (1905; New York, 1963), p. 75; all further references to this work will be included in the text.

Dora's parents were unhappily married. In writing of the family, Freud lays much weight on the mother's "housewife's psychosis," or compulsive domesticity, a disease he diagnoses more portentously than he does the syphilis Dora's father brought with him to the marriage. The father soon began a long-standing affair with one "Frau K.," who had befriended Dora as well; when Dora was fourteen, "Herr K." began to make violently sexual lunges at her. When she accused him, her father insisted that she had imagined these attacks, but her protests continued: as Dora saw the situation, her acceptance of Herr K. was meant to sanction her father's liaison with Frau K. It was then that her self-mortifying series of symptoms and depressions began and her father "handed her over" to Freud.

Freud overrode Dora's father by accepting the truth of his patient's story. Incredibly, though, he insisted that any healthy young woman would become the sexual pawn her elders were trying to make of her. For Freud, her illness and her resistance were one: by his definition, her unconscious could not but respond to Herr K. Though Dora's resistance to a coercive father and a loathsome suitor was of the pattern of a British heroine Freud might have admired—her model could have been Richardson's Clarissa—he insisted that Herr K. was "prepossessing" and her feelings aberrant: "This was surely just the situation to call up a distinct feeling of sexual excitement in a girl of fourteen who had never before been approached. But Dora had at that moment [of Herr K.'s sudden embrace] a violent feeling of disgust, tore herself free from the man, and hurried past him to the staircase and from there to the street door" (*Dora*, p. 43). Surely, not only Victorian morality but the psychology and physiology of fourteen-year-old girls everywhere explain Dora's revulsion and fear. Yet Freud was so relentless in hammering at her repressed desire for Herr K. that even his most sympathetic commentators grow uneasy.[14]

As Freud writes about it, the case is reduced to a series of skirmishes in which Dora, refusing to transform herself under his touch as had Frau Emmy, Katharina, and the rest, meets his interpretative assaults as she did Herr K.'s: with a recurrent "no." The integrity of Freud's account lies not in his interpretations but in his fidelity to the intransigence of his experience with Dora and the Bartleby-like drama of her recurrent refusals. Freud's pained definition of the case as "a fragment of an analysis" makes it for Steven Marcus a quintessentially modern document, great in its dogged truth to the impossibility of solution. For Marcus, Dora's desertion of the great man is sufficiently punished by the fact that all her psychiatrists found her "an unlikable person," though he does implicate Freud in a telling, if unexplored, insight: "Above all, he

14. See Rieff's introduction to *Dora*, ibid., pp. 15–18, as well as his more general remarks on Freud's ideas of womanhood in *The Mind of the Moralist*, pp. 178–81.

doesn't like her inability to surrender herself to him."[15] For Freud, though, the loss of Dora seems to have inflicted a pain beyond modern malaise and personal dislike. What is lost, one feels, is the female capacity for metamorphosis without which male magic has no meaning.

The interpretations Freud thrusts at Dora are a pageant of symbolic transformations she will not enact. Not only are the objects and events in her dreams amenable to a boundless process of becoming something else but in Freud's vision her emotions are constantly mutating. He begins with her suppressed love for Herr K., then goes on to insist that she is in love with (of course) her father, with Freud himself, with the suitor disguised in her second dream, and finally and fundamentally, with Frau K.— in short, it seems, with everybody but her mother. Not only is Dora's inner life capable of seemingly limitless expansion but her very costume is alive with significant transformations. Her commonplace reticule becomes a speaking symbolic narrative: "The reproaches against her father for having made her ill, together with the self-reproach underlying them, the leucorrhoea, the playing with the reticule, the bedwetting after her sixth year, the secret which she would not allow the physicians to tear from her—the circumstantial evidence of her having masturbated in childhood seems to me complete and without a flaw" (*Dora,* p. 97). Freud's gratingly censorious tone here is typical, but, as with Svengali and Dracula, his disdain for the woman he has captured is at war with his need for the gifts she brings.

Of all the predatory men in this story, it is Freud whose lust for Dora is fiercest, but despite the pyrotechnical transformation of her reticule into a vagina, her sexuality is incidental to him. The sexual connotations of a woman's reticule, which Freud was not needed to translate, were familiar comic staples of Victorian art and pornography;[16] the metamorphosis of the reticule is as commonplace as the linguistic metamorphoses scattered throughout the German text, in which such household objects as "mother's jewel-case" or a "box for keeping pictures in" translate themselves into crude symbols of female genitalia. A more valuable attribute than Dora's reticule or her "jewel-case" is her capacity for boundlessly suggestive dreams, the essence of her transforming power which she withholds from Freud by leaving. Dora's case history, which was originally to be called *Dreams and Hysteria* and to be published as an outgrowth of Freud's *Interpretation of Dreams* (1900), is organized around two central visitations: "The First Dream" and "The Second Dream." Like Trilby's voice, like Lucy's and Mina's telepathic perceptions, Dora's dreams function in this case history as a token of a transforming power that enervates her increasingly paralyzed master. The

15. Steven Marcus, "Freud and Dora: Story, History, Case History," *Representations: Essays on Literature and Society* (New York, 1975), p. 309.

16. See Elaine Showalter, "Guilt, Authority, and the Shadows of *Little Dorrit*," *Nineteenth-Century Fiction* 34 (June 1979): 38–39.

note of frustration, of radical incompletion, pervading Freud's story seems less to signal Marcus' ache of modernism than the ache caused by loss of Dora and the powers she inadvertently brings. The central emotion of the case history is not Dora's "penis envy," as a vulgarizer of Freud might have it, nor, in Karen Horney's feminist inversion, Freud's "womb envy," but the teller's affliction, like that of an emotionally eroded Jamesian narrator, with what might be called "dream envy."[17]

Since in this case an imaginative myth played itself out in a real consulting room, Dora's story could not end satisfactorily. Freud makes several tentative and contradictory suggestions that she married, but these do not provide closure so much as further stabs in the dark. Later Freudians assert that she lived an appropriately miserable life,[18] but in fact Dora seems to have died querulously at a ripe age without any violent emotional or psychic upheavals. Life does not usually round things out: there was no last cry of "*Svengali . . . Svengali . . . Svengali,*" nor did anybody need to drive a stake through her heart. But in reading the transcript of her case history, where Freud obsessively explains her but where she is never allowed to explain herself, she seems as much a product of the mythmaking mind as were the popular romance heroines I have discussed, though as a real woman she was reluctant to the end. Insofar as Dora "refused to be a character in the story that Freud was composing for her, and wanted to finish it herself " she both repudiated his projection and attempted to exercise the powers it allowed her.[19] Though she escaped Freud as she had her father and Herr K., she never wrested the role of magus from her possessive master. For us, at least, she is inextricably entangled in the myth Freud wanted to make of her; his mythmaking imagination took its final revenge when he imposed upon his recreant patient the name of Dickens' most fatally pliable and infantilized heroine. As with a character in a novel whose fate is muddied, we wonder how Dora would have named herself.

Freud's mythic and literary affinities are usually applauded, but their complex impact on his treatment of actual women has not yet been analyzed. From the beginning of his life to the end, though, his clinical work with women was intensely affected by an essentially literary

17. On the face of it, Freud's actual achievements in these years are our clearest reminder that the myth is not true: his eleven-week analysis of Dora took place in 1900, by which time he had completed his laborious self-analysis and his seminal *Interpretation of Dreams,* using his own dreams as the primary source of both. But if we consider his ensuing drained depression, not to mention (dare one say it?) his essentially masturbatory role as both dreamer and interpreter, the anguished undercurrent of his failure with Dora, as well as his gleeful harping on her childhood masturbation, gain emotional if not objective coherence.

18. See, for instance, Marcus, "Freud and Dora," p. 306, and Felix Deutsch, "A Footnote to Freud's Fragment of an Analysis of a Case of Hysteria," *Psychoanalytic Quarterly* 26 (1957): 159–67.

19. Marcus, "Freud and Dora," p. 306.

mythology. As a young man studying with Charcot, he was so profoundly moved by a lithograph of Charcot in his clinic that he kept a
copy all his life (fig 4). The lithograph depicts a rigidly upright Charcot
supporting a seductively supine patient, a tableau closer to the popular
image of Svengali and Trilby than du Maurier's illustrations are. One
suspects that the constant presence of this picture told more to and about
Freud than he knew.

Freud's powerful mythic urge proved a professional triumph, however, in his treatment of a woman who shared his dream. Late in life,
Freud analyzed the American poet Hilda Doolittle ("H. D."). The analysis
must have been successful, for H. D. wrote a rhapsodically affectionate
tribute to her master (though his art collection seems to have impressed
her more vividly than his interpretations). Since H. D. was not a desperate young girl but a successful poet in lifelong pursuit of her transfigured self, she approached Freud in the right occult spirit;

> "By chance or intention," I started these notes on September 19th.
> Consulting my "Mysteries of the Ancients" calendar, I find Dr.
> W. B. Crow has assigned this date to Thoth, Egyptian form of Mer-
> cury. Bearer of the Scales of Justice. *St. Januarius.* And we know of
> *Janus* the old Roman guardian of gates and doors, patron of the
> month of January which was sacred to him, with all "beginnings."[20]

Most Freudian analysts today would gleefully untangle these exuberant
oracular connections, but Freud apparently let them stand. Whether or
not he feared that Jungianism had tainted H. D.'s correspondences, they
seem to have been at one in their central aim: to metamorphose the
woman's selfhood into an infinitely shifting myth. In his foreword to
H. D.'s *Tribute to Freud,* Norman Holmes Pearson quotes H. D.'s mythic
creed: " 'For me, it was so important,' she wrote, repeating, 'it was so
important, my own LEGEND. Yes, my own LEGEND. Then, to get well and
re-create it.' She used 'legend' multiply—as a story, a history, an account,
a thing for reading, her own myth."[21] Though by the time of H. D.'s visit
Freud was as surrounded by artifacts of old religions as "a curator in
a museum," living as far as possible in a timeless atmosphere, one suspects that his central if unacknowledged faith belonged to the age that
bred him. Long before, he had accepted with resignation that "one still
remains a child of one's own age, even with something one had thought
was one's very own."[22] As a child of his own age, he apparently ap-

---

20. H. D., *Tribute to Freud* (with *Writing on the Wall* and *Advent*) (1956; Boston, 1974),
p. 100.

21. Ibid., p. vii.

22. Freud, letter to Wilhelm Fliess, Vienna, 5 November 1897, *The Origins of
Psychoanalysis, Letters to Wilhelm Fliess, Drafts and Notes: 1887–1902,* trans. Eric Mosbacher
and Strachey (New York, 1954), p. 228.

FIG. 4.

proached H. D. with the same mixture of awe, horror, and reverence that infused Van Helsing's words: "Madam Mina, our poor, dear, Madam Mina, is changing." For in Freud's imagination, as in the fiction written during his life, the power of the magus is less than the self-creations of his prey.[23]

Realizing this dream in our own century, H. D. translated her analysis into an instrument of mythic self-creation. Her long autobiographical parable, *Helen in Egypt,* casts Freud in the ancillary role of the nurturing Theseus who enables the fleeing Helen to embrace her own grandeur. Though at first she shuns her transfigured self, asserting "I am not nor mean to be / the Daemon they made of me," Helen is soothed into power by Theseus' "solution": "All myth, the one reality dwells here." H. D.'s narrative gloss makes it plain that the "postanalytic" Helen is reborn into magic, not mere humanity: "Was Helen stronger than Achilles even 'as the arrows fell'? That could not be, but he recognised in her some power other than her legendary beauty."[24] Like du Maurier's Trilby and like Stoker's Lucy and Mina, H. D. in her mythic awakening as Helen accepts possession by the magus as the crucible for her mighty self-apotheosis. In Victorian romances, in psychoanalytic documents, and in a modern poet's spiritual autobiography, the myth of the entranced woman is as covertly inspiring as it seems superficially enfeebling. The writers we have looked at and the readers who believe their visions imagine a Sleeping Beauty who only seems asleep, for her powers are secretly superior to those of the wicked witch who subdued her and the handsome prince who aroused her.

23. Freud's psychic recasting of ancient mythology lies at the heart of his "new science," but we are just gaining perspective on his responsiveness to the mythologies latent in his own culture. Lee Sterrenburg's "Psychoanalysis and the Iconography of Revolution" (*Victorian Studies* 19 [December 1975]: 241–64) traces Freud's appropriation of "a nineteenth-century myth of our cannibalistic and revolutionary origins" which now "lives on in the guise of psychoanalytic discourse" (p. 264). More recently, Frank J. Sulloway's *Freud: Biologist of the Mind* (New York, 1979) analyzes the degree to which Freud's interest in magic and mythmaking has affected our understanding of his role in the history of science. Like Sterrenburg's intellectual tapestry of science, myth, and magic, Sulloway's conclusion that "myth rules history with an iron grip" (p. 503) recovers A. C. Bradley's apprehension in 1881 that mythmaking lies at the heart of scientific modernism.

24. H. D., *Helen in Egypt* (New York, 1961), pp. 113, 161, 260.

Travesties of Gender and Genre in Aristophanes' *Thesmophoriazousae*

Froma I. Zeitlin

Three of Aristophanes' eleven extant comedies use the typical comic device of role reversal to imagine worlds in which women are "on top."[1] Freed from the social constraints which keep them enclosed within the house and silent in the public realms of discourse and action, women are given a field and context on the comic stage. They issue forth to lay their plans, concoct their plots, and exercise their power over men.

The *Lysistrata* and the *Ecclesiazousae* stage the intrusion of women into the public spaces of Athens—the Acropolis and Agora, respectively—as an intrusion into the political and economic life of the city. The *Thesmophoriazousae,* however, resituates the battle of the sexes in another domain—that of aesthetics and, more precisely, that of the theater itself. Instead of the collective confrontation of men and women, the play directs the women's actions against a single male target—the tragic poet, Euripides. Like the better-known *Lysistrata,* performed in the same year (411 B.C.), the *Thesmophoriazousae* (or the *Women at the Festival of the Thesmophoria)* is set on the Acropolis; this time it is not appropriated by the women as a novel and outrageous strategy but is granted to them in accordance with the rules of their annual festival, which reserved this sacred space for their exclusive use in the fertility rites dedicated to Demeter and Persephone.

1. For this term, see Natalie Davis, "Women on Top," *Society and Culture in Early Modern France* (Stanford, Calif., 1975), pp. 124–51. I am indebted to the members of the Aristophanes seminar at Princeton University, spring 1980, who contributed more to this essay than I can acknowledge here. A longer and more detailed version of this essay appears in *Reflections of Women in Antiquity,* ed. Helene Foley (London, 1981).

Criticism has not been generous to this play. Studies of role inversion, even in recent feminist perspectives, have focused on *Lysistrata* and *Ecclesiazousae* because of their implications for Athens' political and economic problems.[2] Similarly, with regard to literary questions, the *Frogs* has claimed almost exclusive attention, both because of its formal contest between Aeschylus and Euripides and because of its emphasis on the role of the poet as teacher and "savior" of the city.[3] While the *Thesmophoriazousae* has been admired for its ingenuity and wit, generally it has been dismissed as merely a "parody play," a trifling interlude in the comic poet's more significant and enduring dialogue with the city and its institutions. Some critics look for simplistic equivalences between the play's transvestism, effeminacy, and Euripides' newer forms of tragedy, and all find difficulties with the plot, especially with Euripides' apparently sudden reconciliation with the women at the end.[4]

But the *Thesmophoriazousae* is a far more complex and more inte-

2. See the studies of Michèle Rosellini, Suzanne Said, and Danièle Auger in *Les Cahiers de Fontenay* 17 (December 1979): 11–32, 33–70, 71–102, respectively. See also Nicole Loraux, "L'Acropole comique," *Les Enfants d'Athéna: Idées athéniennes sur la citoyenneté et la division des sexes* (Paris, 1981), and Helene Foley, "The Female Intruder Reconsidered: Women in Aristophanes' *Lysistrata* and *Ecclesiazousae*" (forthcoming in *Classical Philology*). For a historian's view, see Edmond Lévy, "Les Femmes chez Aristophane," *Ktema* 1 (1976): 99–112.

3. For example, Rosemary Harriott (*Poetry and Criticism before Plato* [London, 1969]) devotes only half a page to one passage from the *Thesmophoriazousae*, while Bruno Snell makes no mention of the play at all in "Aristophanes and Aesthetic Criticism," *The Discovery of the Mind: The Greek Origins of European Thought*, trans. T. G. Rosenmeyer (Cambridge, Mass., 1953), pp. 113–35.

4. There is virtually no extended treatment of this play as a play. Cedric Whitman comes the closest in *Aristophanes and the Comic Hero* ([Cambridge, Mass., 1964], pp. 216–27), which takes a rather negative view of the play: "The parody here is without venom, and the plot, or fantasy, is without reference to very much beyond its own inconsequential proposition. . . . The art of tragedy is shown to be on the wane, but any deeper implications that might have been involved in that fact are saved for the *Frogs*" (p. 217). For him, the play has "little of the theme of fertility or life"; "somehow," he continues, "femininity, whether real or assumed, is under a somewhat morbid cloud; by contrast, there is something genuinely refreshing about the masculinity of Mnesilochus, however coarse, and of the Scythian archer, whose main male attribute plays an unblushing role in the solution of the play" (pp. 216, 224). Hardy Hansen ("Aristophanes' *Thesmophoriazousae*: Theme Structure and Production," *Philologus* 120 [1976]: 165–85) follows Whitman's interpretation but concentrates on theatrical problems.

Froma I. Zeitlin, an associate professor of classics at Princeton University, is the author of several articles on Greek tragedy and on the ancient novel, and also of a monograph, *Under the Sign of the Shield: Language, Structure, and the Son of Oedipus in Aeschylus' "Seven against Thebes."*

grated play. It is located at the intersection of a number of relations: between male and female; between tragedy and comedy; between theater (tragedy and comedy) and festival (ritual and myth); between festival (the Thesmophoria) and festival (the Dionysiac, which provides the occasion for its performance and which determines its comic essence); and, finally, between bounded forms (myth, ritual, and drama) and the more fluid "realities" of everyday life. All these relations are unstable and reversible: they cross boundaries and invade each other's territories; they erase and reinstate hierarchical distances to reflect ironically upon each other and themselves.

I intend to take another look at this play from the joint perspectives of the theme of "women on top" and that of the self-reflectiveness of art concerned with the status of its own mimetic representation. However satirically the play may represent Euripides' "unnatural" and "unmanly" concern with *eros* and with women, with female sexuality and with female psyche, it poses a more intrinsic connection between the ambiguities of the feminine and those of art, linked together in various ways in Greek notions of poetics from their earliest formulations. The setting of the play and the progress of the plot are constructed not only to make the most of the perennial comic value of female impersonation but also to use the notions of gender in posing questions of genre and to draw attention to the problematics of imitation and representation which connect transvestism of costume with mimetic parody of texts. Transvestism works on the visual level, parody on the verbal. Together they expose the interrelationship of the crossing of genres and the crossing of genders; together they exemplify the equivalence of intertextuality and intersexuality.

1. Mimesis: Gender and Genre

In this brilliant and ingenious play, the contest between the genders must share the spotlight with the contest between the genres, comedy and tragedy. Along with the parody of other serious forms of discourse within the city (judicial, ritual, political, poetic), *paratragodia,* or the parody of tragedy, is a consistent feature of Aristophanic comedy. The effect of making a tragic poet the comic protagonist in a comic plot and of elevating parody to the dominant discourse of the play shifts the contest between the sexes onto another level, one that not only reflects the tensions between the social roles of men and women but also focuses on their theatrical representation as tragic and comic personae.

In the privacy of their ritual enclosure, the women have determined to exact vengeance from the tragic poet, Euripides, whom they charge with the offenses of misogyny and slander in his dramatic portrayal of women. He has made their lives intolerable, they complain. Their husbands come home from the theater, all fired up with suspicion at their every gesture and movement, and lock them up in the house. Euripides himself appears at the opening of the play to devise his counterplot and to rescue himself from this present danger which will determine this day whether he will live or die. Euripides first tries and fails to persuade the effeminate tragic poet, Agathon, to go in woman's dress to infiltrate the women's rites and argue in his defense. Hence, he must finally send his own kinsman. Dressed as a woman with a costume and accessories from Agathon's own wardrobe, shaved and depilated on stage, the kinsman Mnesilochus makes his way to the Acropolis to mingle unnoticed with the other women and to carry out the mandates of the master plotter. He is ultimately unmasked and his true sex is revealed both by the nature of his defense of Euripides and by the information of Cleisthenes, the effeminate politician and the friend of women, who comes to warn them of the interloper in their midst. While Cleisthenes goes off to bring back the Scythian policeman to remove the malefactor, the poor kinsman has recourse to elaborate parodies of Euripidean drama. He tries one tragic role after another in his efforts to save himself, finally bringing Euripides on stage, not once but twice, to impersonate those of his own characters who might rescue the kinsman. When this strategy fails, Euripides, at last, reconciles himself with the women, and dressed now as an old procuress, he succeeds in diverting the policeman with a comic, not a tragic, ploy—the perennial dancing girl—so that he and the kinsman can make their escape.

The meeting of the poet and the women complicates both the *topos* of "women in charge" and the role and stance of the comic hero himself. The launching of the great comic idea, which is the heart and soul of the comic plot, is divided between the women who have determined to prosecute Euripides before the play actually begins and the poet/hero, who cannot now initiate the action in the service of his own imaginative vision of the world. Instead, as comic protagonist, the wily man of many turns must employ all his professional techniques to extricate himself from a situation in which he is not only hero but also potential victim.

Similarly, the device of staging the women's presence on the Acropolis has a double edge. On one level, the women's occupation of civic space maintains the transgression which their presence upon the public stage implies, and the ritual regulations which put women in charge offer rich comic possibilities for women's use and misuse of male language in their imitation of the typical male institutions of tribunal and assembly. Moreover, the *topos* of role inversion gives the women, as always, an opportunity to redress the social imbalances between male and female in an open comic competition with men for superior status, as the parabasis of this play demonstrates best. But on another level, their legitimate presence at their own private ritual also reverses the direction of the transgression; now men are forced to trespass on forbidden space, and they penetrate the secret world of women for the purpose of spying upon them and disclosing their secrets.

Another paradox is evident as a result of the confrontation of the poet and the women. The scandal of Euripides' theater lies in his exhibition of erotic heroines upon the tragic stage—women who openly solicit men, like the unhappy Phaedra with her Hippolytus and the wanton Sthenoboia, who, like Potiphar's wife, shamelessly tempted the young Bellerophon. The kinsman's defense, however, claims that Euripides exercised restraint; he could have told other stories worse than these. Penelopes don't exist any more, the kinsman declares, all are Phaedras and Melanippes.[5] His charge of misdoing leveled against all women incurs the women's anger at their supposed betrayal by one of their very own. Yet the anecdotes he tells of adultery and supposititious babies come straight out of the typical male discourse of the comic theater (476–519). The women he depicts as overly fond of wine and sex conform to the portrait of the comic woman, who displays her unruly Dionysiac self, even in this play, in the spirit of carnival and misrule. As the comic male character in the comic play, the kinsman is only playing true to form. And if he defends the tragic poet in the comic way, he makes "unspeakable" what comedy has always claimed as its right to speak. Is tragedy taking the fall for comedy? Is the kinsman's defense, in fact, the defense mounted by comedy against the trespass on its ground by Euripidean tragedy?

The speech in which the kinsman corroborates Euripides' intimate familiarity with women's secrets replicates Euripides' transgression of tragic decorum. This transgression is also spatialized in dramatic form as the violation itself of the sacred enclosure reserved for women at their ritual. Having penetrated earlier into a world he was forbidden to enter, Euripides now penetrates it again through the kinsman's infiltration of the Thesmophoria, an act which therefore profanes the pieties yet again. In comedy, these revelations of women's "nature" cause laughter rather than indignation among the spectators. It is rather in the tragic theater that the mimetic effects of representation work with such realism and persuasiveness that drama overtakes and invades the real world, sending husbands away, wild with anxiety, to look to their womenfolk at home.

At the heart of this repeated violation is the transgression of the distance which normally maintains the fiction of theater's relation to the "real" world. Tragedy, as Aristotle tells us, is "the imitation of a serious action." Designated as the genre which holds up a more heroic and mythic mirror to the society of its spectators, tragedy must depend for its effects upon the integrity of its fictions within its own theatrical con-

---

5. See Aristophanes, *Thesmophoriazousae,* ed. Victor Coulon, vol. 4, Budé text (Paris, 1954), ll. 549–50; all further references to this work will be included with line numbers in the text.

ventions and generic norms. In the *Thesmophoriazousae,* the violation of
that integrity is focused on the issue which for the society of men bears
the greatest psychological charge—namely, the integrity of their house-
holds and, above all, of their women. The violation of women's sexual
secrets serves, then, not only as the actual subject for complaint but as the
metaphorical representation in social terms of the poet's trespass of
aesthetic modes.

At stake in this theatrical tug-of-war between tragedy and comedy is
the nature of mimesis itself. The *Thesmophoriazousae* wants it all ways: it
dramatizes and exploits to their furthest extremes the confusions which
the notion of imitation suggests—whether art is a mimesis of *reality* or a
mimesis of reality; whether it conceals its art by its verisimilitude or
exposes its fictions in the staging and testing of its own illusions. Consider the complications of the mimetic process when character and poet
are conflated in the personage of Euripides, when the comic character,
the kinsman, is designated as the actor who is to carry out the plot which
Euripides has devised within the comic play. Once his "true" identity is
revealed, the kinsman must then transform himself into the theatrical
actor of the Euripidean parodies whose lines he now self-consciously and
incongruously renders with reference to his comic role.

Moreover, the play, as a whole, takes its cue from and sets as the
condition of its plot the offense of Euripides in having tilted his dramas
too far in the direction of a mimesis which exceeds the boundaries of the
theater. For, given the comic stage as the ground of reality in the play,
the "real" women, who resent being "characters" in Euripides' drama,
put him in a "real" situation in which he must live out for himself the
consequences of his own mimetic plots. As others have noticed,
Euripides is not a character in a typical comic scenario; rather, he plays
the hero/victim in a parodic version of his favorite type of tragic
drama—the intrigue-rescue play which often includes a recognition of a
lost loved one. The hero/heroine from the beginning faces overwhelming danger and only reaches the desired salvation through a series of
ingenious stratagems.[6] What better comic version of tragic justice than to
turn the tables on Euripides? Yet, what better stage than this for
Euripides, the man of a thousand plots (927), upon which to display all
his *méchanai* and to turn, at last, from victim to savior of himself and his
kinsman? He plays first in the tragic mode, then in the comic mode,

---

6. On connections of the plot with Euripidean patterns, see Carlos Ferdinando Russo,
Aristofane, autore di teatro (Florence, 1962), p. 297, Peter Rau, *Paratragodia: Untersuchung
einer kömischen Form des Aristophanes* (Munich, 1967), p. 50, and Rau, "Das Tragödienspiel in
den 'Thesmophoriazusen,'" in *Aristophanes und die alte Komödie, Wege der Forschung,* ed. Hans
Joachim Newiger, vol. 265 (Darmstadt, 1975), p. 349. On the motif of salvation in Euripidean drama, see Antonio Garzya, *Pensiero e technical drammatica in Euripide: Saggio sul motivo
della salvazione* (Naples, 1962).

when Aristophanes, cleverer than he, puts him squarely on the "real" ground of the comic play.

From the beginning, Euripides must act the part of the playwright-within-the-play to devise his own plot, to direct the actor to play his appointed part, then to furnish him with the scripts from which to read, and, eventually, to intervene as actor in the parodies of two plays which he has already composed. The comedy can never, therefore, escape the metatheatrical implications of the play within the play within the play and all the variations and permutations of the device. As the comedy progresses, as the kinsman's own improvisations founder and he is "unmasked," the temple and the altar of the Thesmophorion conveniently serve as the "theatrical space" within the play on which to stage those parodies of Euripidean theater.[7] By the last paratragic scene, the comedy draws upon all its theatrical resources, from within and without. The Scythian policeman's fastening of the kinsman to the punishment plank suggests the cast, the setting, and the props for Euripides' poor Andromeda, bound to the rock in far-off Ethiopia, awaiting her fate from the sea monster who is to devour her. But then Euripides himself as Perseus flies by on the "real" theatrical device of the *mēchanē* ("the crane") and cues the kinsman as to the role he intends to play. Thus, as the play moves on to the end, as Euripides, in fact, assumes not only one but two parts in the *Andromeda,* the *Thesmophoriazousae* exposes more and more the obvious inconcinnities between theater and "reality," to the apparent detriment of the former, even as it implicitly conspires, as we shall see, to validate those same dramatic fictions.

2. *Mimesis: Transvestism*

The theme of mimesis is specifically set in the prologue of the play; in fact, this is the first attested techincal use of the word "mimesis" and the first demonstration, albeit ludicrous, of the mimetic theory of art which will later figure so largely in the aesthetic theories of Plato and Aristotle.[8] Agathon, the tragic poet for whom Euripides is searching, is wheeled out of the house on the *ekkyklema,* the stage device used to bring an interior scene outside, singing sensuous hymns that send the kinsman into an erotic swoon (130–33). Androgynous in appearance, Agathon

7. See Russo, *Aristofane, autore di teatro,* p. 297.
8. For a discussion and bibliography of mimesis in antiquity, see Göran Sorböm, *Mimesis and Art* (Uppsala, 1966). See also Jean-Pierre Vernant, "Image et apparence dans la théorie platonicienne de la mimésis," *Journal de Psychologie* 2 (1975): 133–60; rpt. as "Naissances d'images" in his *Religions, histoires, raisons* (Paris, 1979), pp. 103–37. For useful surveys of aesthetic theory and criticism before Plato, see Harriott, *Poetry and Criticism before Plato,* and T. B. L. Webster, "Greek Theories of Art and Literature down to 400 B.C.," *Classical Quarterly* 33 (1939):166–79.

wears women's clothing and carries an incongruous assortment of accessories (134–40). In reply to the kinsman's questions as to his identity and his gender, Agathon now replies:

> I wear my garb according to my thought.
> The poet, you see, must shape his ways
> in accordance with the plays to be composed.
> If someone is composing women's plays,
> his body must needs share in women's ways.
> If plays of men, he has already what it takes.
> Whatever we don't have, we must capture by mimesis.
>
> [146–52]

So far, so good. The poet is a versatile fellow who must dress the dramatic roles he creates. But Agathon then declares that a beautiful poet wears beautiful clothes and writes beautiful dramas—and vice versa for the ugly poet. One must compose in accordance with one's nature (159–72).

The clue to this apparent confusion between mimesis as impersonation, as investiture, and mimesis as a harmony of body, soul, and poetry lies in the comic fact that Agathon is indeed by nature an effeminate man, just the type whom Aristophanes always loves to mock.[9] Hence, what Agathon imitates (female appearance) is indeed harmonious with his nature and his ways. And this is precisely the reason why he must refuse to go as a spy among the women—because he fits the role too well. As a poet, he is second only to Euripides (187); as a "woman," he claims he would be unfair competition for the other women at the Thesmophoria (204–5); the sample of his poesy, the choral hymns he sings, involving female deities, are all too much in tune. In short, he is the unnatural "natural" for the part, the pathic well adapted for tragic pathos, as the kinsman wryly observes (199–201). How could Agathon defend Euripides against the charges which are leveled against his fellow poet? He is as much or more a friend to women, their kindred spirit, as the effeminate Cleisthenes declares of himself when he enters the women's festival to denounce the male imposter in their midst (574–76). No, Mnesilochus, the hirsute kinsman, all male, must go instead; he must be dressed on stage in a woman's costume; he must be shaved of his beard

9. Critics miss the point of this confusion, especially Raffaele Cantarella ("Agatone e il prologo della 'Tesmoforiazuse,' " *Komoidotragemata* [Amsterdam, 1967], pp. 7–15), who is most often cited on this prologue and who imagines that, since Agathon is effeminate, he is somehow no longer a male.

It should be noted that poets, beginning with Thespis, did, in fact, act in their own plays in the earlier years of the Greek theater before acting became a more professional specialty. Aeschylus most probably did so and Sophocles too in the beginning of his career. See Sir Arthur Pickard-Cambridge, *The Dramatic Festivals of Athens,* 2d ed., rev. J. Gould and D. M. Lewis (Oxford, 1968), pp. 93–94.

and raise his rump in full view of the audience to have it singed with a flame, as women do when they depilate their genitals in accordance with Greek standards of female beauty.

With the interchange between Agathon and Mnesilochus in this prologue scene, Aristophanes has accomplished a real *coup de théâtre*. He has managed with artful economy to introduce his *topos* of "women on top" in a way which exposes its implications to the naked eye. Making Mnesilochus into a woman exactly reproduces in advance the inevitable result of the inversion of gender roles—when women are in a position to rule men, men must become women. In the miniature reversal played out between Agathon and Mnesilochus, Mnesilochus, as the comic character, first indulges in all the witty obscenities to which he is entitled at the expense of the effeminate poet. But the transfer of Agathon's persona to him returns against the kinsman the full measure of that social shame which the breach of gender norms poses to identity, manhood, and power. Comedy's scandalous privilege to expose those parts and functions of the body which decorum keeps hidden—physically, in the padded leather phallus which the comic actor wears, verbally, in the obscenities and sexual jokes which are licensed by the Dionysiac festival—takes on a double twist here. For in exposing the lusty comic male only in the process of becoming a woman, the comedy is playing with the extreme limit of its own promiscuous premises where all can now converge in the ambiguities of intersexuality.

But transvestism in the theater and especially in this scene has yet another function in addition to exposing the natural facts of the body which the social conventions normally keep offstage; that is, to expose the secret artifices which theatrical conventions keep offstage to maintain its mimetic fictions. Mnesilochus is, after all, dressing as a woman because he is to play the part of a woman, carrying out the clever stratagem of Euripides.

In this theatrical perspective, taking the role of the opposite sex invests the wearer with the power of appropriation, of supplement, not only loss. Androgynous myths and transvestite rites speak to this increased charge in symbolic terms, even as androgyny and transvestism incur the shame of deviance within the social code. Thus the depilation of Mnesilochus is balanced by the putting on of women's clothing, for in this ambivalent game of genders, the female is not only a "not" but also an "other."[10] When the women in the parabasis examine the comic contradictions of misogyny and put the superiority of men to the test, they joke in terms of attributes common to each: we women have still kept safe at home our weaving rod *(kanōn)* and our sunshade *(skiadeion)*, while

10. See the excellent distinctions made by Sandra M. Gilbert, "Costumes of the Mind: Transvestism as Metaphor in Modern Literature," *Critical Inquiry* 7 (Winter 1980): 391–417.

you men have lost your spear shaft *(kanōn)* and your shield *(skiadeion)* (824–27). The play with castration is appropriate enough to the inversion of roles, but the ambiguities of role playing involve both this loss and gain, even for Mnesilochus who plays so ill, and by his misplaying exposes, when the women expose him, the limits of mimesis.

Since all female roles in the Greek theater were played by men, the exhibitionist donning of female costume focuses the problem of mimesis at its most ambiguous and most sensitive spot, where social and artistic rules are in greatest conflict with each other. Impersonation affects the whole creative process—from the poet to the actor—and determines its aesthetic success. But feminization attracts all the scorn and abuse which the culture—and comedy—can muster. Just so in this play, Aristophanes mocks Euripides at the end by finally putting a female dress on him but yet grants him the stage on which to display, with ultimate impunity, the repertory of his mimetic range.

The contradictions inherent in the mimetic process, as adumbrated by Agathon, between what you play and what you are, are tested again and again from within the play itself, as it uncovers the dissonances between the fictive theatrical device and the comic ground of "reality." Twice Mnesilochus is put up against a "true" effeminate, once with Agathon and once with Cleisthenes, as if to pose a theatrical distance between one actor in women's clothes and another (and let us not forget that the women of the Thesmophoria are, of course, played by men). Mnesilochus himself, in the instability of his dual roles, in his male discomfort with his female parts, is best suited to reflect ironically upon his position during the course of the play. Still disguised, he indignantly asks Cleisthenes, "What man would be such a fool as to allow himself to be depilated?" (592–94). Yet when his first two theatrical parodies of Euripides fail, parodies in which he plays male roles in female costume (another inversion), he has a new and happy idea: "Why, I'll play Helen, the new version—I've got the female dress I need" (850–51). Still, in the next stage, when the magistrate whom Cleisthenes has summoned comes and orders the poor Mnesilochus to be bound to the punishment plank for breaking the city's laws and invading the secret rites of women, he begs: "At least, undress me and bind me naked to the plank. Please don't leave me dressed up in feminine fripperies. I don't want to give the crows a good laugh as well as a good dinner" (939–42). Now that the masculine world of authority has intruded into the play, Mnesilochus expresses well the full reversal from mastery to subjugation his position as a male has taken. When the magistrate reports the council's decree that it is precisely in woman's costume that he is to be bound to the plank, in order to exhibit his villainy to all as an imposter, this is the point where the helpless kinsman most fits the role of the pitiful Andromeda which he now will play. Yet, at the same time, he offers the last and best incongruity between himself, an ugly old man, and his theatrical persona of the beautiful maiden.

3. Mimesis: Parody

Just as the comic actor's discrepancies between character and costume threaten his mimetic integrity, so does parody address the questions of mimesis in the service of a fictive reality. The transvestite actor might succeed in concealing the telltale sign that marks him as an imitation with a difference, but parody is the literary device that openly declares its status as imitation with a difference. In the rhetorical logic of the play, the exposure of the kinsman's intersexual game appropriately brings parody fully out of hiding to play its intertextual game with comedy and tragedy. In the thematic logic of the piece, the first defense of Euripides, misconducted by the kinsman in the comic mode, is properly transferred to the parodies of the plays themselves, which will eventually bring Euripides on stage to play the tragic roles he has composed. It is also consonant with the narrative logic of the plot that the kinsman now have recourse to Euripidean parodies. For with the peripeteia in his comic situation, he is now truly imitating the typical Euripidean plot of danger-recognition-intrigue-rescue.

The parodies function as the new intrigues of the kinsman (and later of Euripides), which he invokes each time in response to each new exigency of his plight. But these are also intrigues on the aesthetic plane, whose comic success depends upon their ability as specimens of tragic art to deceive their comic audience within the play with their mimetic credibility. Read as successive intrusions into the text, the parodies function like metatheatrical variants of the series of different imposters who come to threaten the comic hero's imaginative world and which, like those figures, must be deflated and driven out. If we read the parodies as a sequence, however, we see that the kinsman must move further and further into the high art of mimesis with increasing complications and confusions; at the same time, the comic spectators within the play whom he would entice into performing his dramas move further and further down the scale of comprehension, ending with the barbarian policeman, who speaks only a pidgin Greek. In the course of their development, the parodies play again with notions of gender and genre, with costume and character, with comic and tragic, and orchestrate a medley of variations on the theme of mimesis itself.

Some have judged these parodies as opportunistic displays of Aristophanic skill which take over the play and consign the conflict of the women and Euripides to the sidelines. Others respond to the shifts from one text to another as signs of the continuing failure of Euripidean tragedy to maintain the necessary mimetic illusion which would effect the kinsman's rescue. The success, in turn, of Euripides' last ploy, a comic not a tragic strategy, only confirms this opinion. Certainly, Euripides' scandalous innovations lend themselves as targets for the satirist's brush. It is also true that, on the surface, comedy seems to be indulging its license to dispense with strict rules of dramatic coherence. But such judgments overlook the fundamental ambiguities which arise from the "taking in and taking over" of another's text to generate a "poetics of contradiction" (at what price imitation?).[11] And they do not perceive that comedy can exploit its looser structure to work through paratactic arrangements which imply rather than state. The parodies, I would suggest, can serve double and discrepant purposes—as framed disruptions of narrative continuity and as integral and integrating elements of the entire plot. The outer and inner surfaces of the text play off each other, with and against each other, as sequence and/or juxtaposition. Furthermore, each parody has a double allegiance—to its present comic context and to the tragic context of the original. Thus each parodic scene conveys multiple messages, including each time some reflection of its status as a theatrical artifact.

The four parodies are artfully arranged into a significant composition. The first two are parodies of male roles which the kinsman plays (from the *Telephus* and the *Palamedes*) true to his gender but at odds with his female costume. The kinsman first attempts to save himself by playing the role of Telephus, the Mysian king disguised as a beggar at the court of Agamemnon, by taking a baby as a hostage—not the infant Orestes, as in the original, but a baby girl held by one of the women nearby. This ploy fails to produce the desired results—the women will not set him free, and the baby turns out to be a wineskin—and the kinsman then determines to summon Euripides to his aid. This time he imitates Oiax, Palamedes' brother, who, after Palamedes' unjust trial and condemnation for treason in the Greek camp at Troy, sends the news to their father which he writes on an oar and casts into the sea.[12] In the next two parodies, the relation between gender and costume is reversed. The kinsman now takes advantage of his theatrical persona to play female characters, the titular protagonists of their respective plays *(Helen, An-*

---

11. For the formulation of "taking in a⸱ᵈ taking over," I am indebted to Susan Stewart, *Nonsense: Aspects of Intertexuality in Folklore and Literature* (Baltimore, 1979), p. 20. I have profited from her work more than I can indicate in this essay. I have borrowed "poetics of contradiction" from Margaret A. Rose, *Parody/Metafiction* (London, 1979), p. 185. In addition to Rose and Stewart, a very useful treatment of parody can be found in Claude Abastado, "Situation de la parodie," *Cahiers du 20ᵉ siècle* 6 (1976): 9–37.

12. On the use of the *Telephus* in this play, see H. W. Miller, "Euripides' *Telephus* and the *Thesmophoriazousae* of Aristophanes," *Classical Philology* 43 (1948): 174–83; Rau, *Paratragodia,* pp. 42–50, and "Tragödienspiel," pp. 344–46. For the parodic treatment of the *Palamedes,* see Rau, *Paratragodia,* pp. 51–53, and "Tragödienspiel," pp. 347–48. Both plays are known to us only through fragments and testimonia.

dromeda). Moreover, these two parodies set the stage for the entrance of Euripides, first to play Menelaus to the kinsman's Helen and then to assume two parts for his Andromeda—the nymph Echo and, finally, the hero Perseus.

These two sets of parodies are formally separated by the parabasis, the convention peculiar to Old Comedy which allows the chorus an opportunity to step forward to address the audience directly. This parabasis not only marks the division between male and female roles but serves as the shifter from one to the other. Here the women defend themselves against the slanders heaped upon them and prove their worth, this time in public and political terms. They speak to the illogic of misogyny: If we are such a bane, why lock us up and not let us out of your sight? If we are such an evil, why do those of you outside always try to get a peek at us (785–89)? And through the etymologies of their names, they comically prove themselves the superiors of men: no man can compete with Nausimache (battle at sea), Aristomache (best in battle), Stratonike (victory of the army), and Euboule (good counsel).

As space does not permit detailed analyses of these texts, I reserve my comments here for the two most elaborate and significant parodies, those of the *Helen* and the *Andromeda,* both produced the year before (412 B.C.), and both demanding from the kinsman that he "live through" female experience to gain his rescue. The *Helen* holds the center of the play; it is carefully framed on one side by the parabasis and, on the other, by the brief removal of the imposter from the stage for the first time in the play, an event which leads the women to reinaugurate their festive dance and song. The parody of the *Helen* is the last direct appeal to the women of the Thesmophoria, for the *Andromeda* is addressed to a new audience—the barbarian Scythian archer.

The new Helen whom the kinsman will play refers not only to the recent production of the play but to the new representation of Helen in a new role as the chaste and virtuous wife. In this version, which has precedents in the mythological tradition, the true Helen never went to Troy but was transported to Egypt, and an *eidolon,* a cloudlike imitation of her, was sent in her stead. She has remained for ten years in isolation, faithful to her husband and her ideals of purity, while the phantom Helen remained at the center of the hostilities at Troy. In Euripides' play, the old king Proteus, who had protected her, has died, and his impious son Theoclymenus is determined to impose a forcible marriage on her. Menelaus is returning home after the war with his crew and the phantom Helen whom he assumes is his real wife. Storm and shipwreck drive him to Egypt where he confronts the "real" Helen. Once their complicated recognition is accomplished, the reunited couple plan their escape with two false stories. The success of their fictions depends upon the cooperation of the prophetess, Theonoe, the virgin sister of the king, whose purity of intellect and spirit makes her the opposite of her violent brother. No synopsis can do justice to this brilliant romantic play which combines the themes of *eros* and *thanatos* with a philosophical testing of the categories of illusion and reality, name and fact, name and body, mind and body, and truth and falsehood. For our purposes, however, Aristophanes' parody is particularly significant in two respects.

First, the audience in the comic parody is Critylla, the woman guarding Mnesilochus, to whom the part of Theonoe is also assigned. To Critylla, whose comic realism insists on literal readings, there is no Helen, only the scoundrel kinsman: Have you become a woman again, before you have paid the penalty for that other womanization of yours (863–64)? For Critylla, the stranger who has entered the scene is the innocent outsider whom she must enlighten; that is, until she recognizes their Egyptian intrigue for what it is and identifies the stranger/ Menelaus as a coconspirator who must be driven off.[13] In this brief and absurd scene, all the issues which characterized the novelty of the original play are present but wonderfully deflected through the comic travesty as a dissonance between the two levels of reference—the comic fiction of the play and the paratragic rendition. In the counterpoint of the text which sets the recognition scene from the *Helen* against Critylla's misrecognition of the identity of the parody, the questions of illusion and reality, of truth and falsehood, and of mimesis and deception are reframed in metatheatrical terms.

From this point of view, the problem of the name as a guide to identity is transposed exactly in reverse to its Euripidean model. In the *Helen,* the epistemological confusion lies in the possibility that the same name may be allotted to more than one (e.g., two Helens). But in the parody, the theatrical confusion lies in the refusal to allow the same character/actor to bear more than one name or, to be sure, more than one gender. The costume can never conceal what the naked truth has revealed and serves here as the focal point at which to test the mimetic premises of the theater in general and the premises of this romantic play in particular. The *eidolon* of Helen, not seen or mentioned in the parody, best personifies illusion itself and, as such, hovers over the scene.[14]

In the split perspective in which the incongruities of the comic and tragic fictions are made most evident, the failure of the tragic parody to persuade lies as much with the comic spectator, who entertains no illusions, as it does with those characters who are trying to create them. And in the relation of the parody to its larger comic matrix, we can note another set of reversals—both thematic and theatrical—which come into

13. On the parody of the *Helen,* see the technical analysis of Rau, *Paratragodia,* pp. 53–65, and "Tragödienspiel," pp. 348–50. See also the useful discussion in Frances Muecke, "Playing with the Play: Theatrical Self-Consciousness in Aristophanes," *Antichthon* 11 (1977): 64–67.

14. Rau, in both his analyses, assumes that all these significant motifs have dropped out of the parody and concludes that Aristophanes is just playing for laughs.

play through the silent juxtaposition of different texts. We may remember that the original basis of the women's complaint was the hyperrealism of Euripidean drama, its failure to create the proper distance between fiction and life. Now we see the opposite—a play whose plot places it directly in the mode of the fabulous and exotic, in short, a mimesis in the service of theater itself. And instead of the "bad" woman whom Euripides has put upon the stage, he has portrayed a woman who, against all odds (and credence), has never betrayed her husband but has waited long and faithfully for him. When the women earlier asked the kinsman why Euripides had never put any Penelopes on the stage, he replied that Penelopes no longer existed (547–50). Yet here he stages the myth of another Penelope, who like her is besieged with importunate suitor(s). Best of all, Helen is not Penelope but, in the normative tradition, her exact opposite, the adulterous woman who ran off with another man. Helen, in fact, is the "baddest" of women who, through the poet's art, is re-created as the best of them. By reversing the myth of Helen, Euripides has reversed the terms. In playing the part of Menelaus in the parody, he has turned from the maligner of women to their potential redeemer, a role which he will play once again, in even better form, as Perseus to the kinsman's Andromeda.

The *Helen* and the *Andromeda* are doublets of each other. Both imagine similar situations—an exotic locale (Egypt/Ethiopia), a woman in captivity and in danger, a dramatic rescue. But in the *Andromeda,* the situation is more extreme. No reunions or recognitions for her but rather a handsome stranger, Perseus, who, flying by with the Gorgon's head tucked into his pouch, falls in love with the beautiful maiden at first sight. This play, unfortunately lost to us except for fragments, was famous in antiquity for the seductiveness of its erotic fantasy.[15] In the *Frogs,* Dionysus, who is in the Underworld to bring Euripides back to Athens, claims as the reason for his mission the sudden desire, the overwhelming passion, which struck at his heart while he was reading the *Andromeda,* a passion not for a woman but for the clever poet, Euripides (51–56, 59). Euripides' Helen, then, rehabilitated and "revirginized," stands as the middle term between the "whores," who were his Phaedras and his Sthenoboias, and this purest of all virgins, Andromeda. If the *Thesmophoriazousae,* in a sense, traces out the career of Euripides as it progresses from one extreme to the other, from hyperrealism to seductive fantasy, the women in Helen's two faces (i.e., carnal sexuality and romantic eroticism) serve not only as the subject of his dramas but also as the essential metaphor for the art of mimesis as it is represented in its two modes.

The parody of the *Andromeda* is addressed to two different audi-

15. On the parody of the *Andromeda,* see Rau, *Paratragodia,* pp. 66–89, and "Tragödienspiel," pp. 353–56. Rau finds this parody redundant of the *Helen,* motivated solely by comic opportunism, not by dramaturgical necessity.

ences and provokes two different reactions. On the theatrical level, the *Andromeda* is not a critical success, for the policeman/spectator can hardly understand a word of what is going on. But the parody might well have been a thematic success with the women. The ensuing choral song that begins with the invocation to Pallas Athena, the unyoked virgin maiden (1139), and ends with the two goddesses of the Thesmophoria (1148–59) might only refer to the chorus' joy at the triumph of the policeman over the violator of their ritual. But it cannot only be a coincidence that, immediately after, Euripides offers terms of peace to the women in return for the rescue of the kinsman, that never again will he slander women (1162). The women willingly accept the offer, but the male world has taken matters out of their hands. Euripides must persuade the barbarian too and meet him on his terms (1170–71).

The Scythian archer, like all barbarians and others with outlandish language, gestures, and costumes, belongs fully to the conventions of the comic theater. In the *Helen,* the comic already intrudes more directly in the intervention of Critylla, but in the *Andromeda,* the parody takes on a double focus by playing to the tragic as well as the comic; the parody exploits the props and scenery for its tragic setting and the intrinsic properties of the comic barbarian.

"Double exposure" rules this last and grandest finale where the perplexities of gender and genre reach their furthest extremes. Once Euripides, flying by, has given the cue, the kinsman plays two roles (himself and Andromeda) and in two modes (solo and duet). His opening monody of lament is a wonderful mixture of the details of his own comic situation with those tragic ones of Andromeda (1015–55). Euripides himself plays two roles—the female Echo and the male Perseus. What is more, as Echo, Euripides plays a double role, first tormenting the kinsman with his abusive repetitions and then the Scythian policeman.

Echo itself is the doubling of another's voice; it is also the purest representation of mimesis as an imitation of another's words. Retrospectively, the two preceding parodies each bear this metatheatrical charge—the *Palamedes,* in the art of writing which imitates speech (Palamedes himself is the inventor of this skill), and the *Helen,* in its intimations of the *eidolon* which imitates the human form and now Echo as the mimesis of the voice. Even the parabasis, with its comic etymologies of women's names, contributes to the same theme, for in reduced and absurd form it adumbrates the theory of imitation which Cratylus will make famous in Plato's dialogue, according to which names mimetically represent the natures of those who bear them.

What distinguishes Echo from the others is its paradoxical status as both nature and artifice. As the one example of mimesis in nature itself, Echo's mimetic representation on stage translates the imitation of nature into an artificial theatrical effect. In turning his parodic skills on Echo,

Aristophanes, in fact, singles out the most radical innovation in Euripidean art and succeeds in exposing it as the highest example of mimetic illusion. But it is also significant for the theme of mimesis in general that Echo, its mythic figuration, is not an "it" but a "she." She is the voice that imitates in both her myths, one that relates her to Narcissus (Ovid *Metamorphoses* 3. 356–40) and the other to Pan (e.g., Longus *Daphnis and Chloe* 3. 23). Echo, as the embodiment (or, better, the disembodied voice) of mimesis, is also the focal point for the concept of the feminine as the one who can never be grasped as primary and original but can only be the one who is imitated or the one who imitates; yet as such, she is therefore empowered as the mistress of mimesis.

Although I will return to this point later, it is important to note here that the exposure of Echo, as played by Euripides who brings her out from behind the scene, turns the tragic to comic, that is, mixes the tragic with the comic. Echo, in fact, might stand as the mediating figure between tragedy and comedy; she is divided between them and yet brings the genres together, as the artful device of the original and as the slapstick cliché of the comic theater. If this is no longer a true contest between the women and Euripides, it is now at last one between the comic poet and his rival whom the comic poet imitates.[16] Imitation retains to the end its ambiguous status, its "poetics of contradictions," as to who is imitating whom. For in his last theatrical act, Euripides turns finally and fully to the comic stage. Dressed as an old procuress, he offers the Scythian policeman a dancing girl to distract him while he hustles the kinsman and himself off the stage. The play began with one tragic poet in drag (Agathon) and ends with another (Euripides); or does it? Is Euripides brought down to the comic level, or is he, with this ploy, the expert ending to a comic play, led to imitate his imitator but, by that imitation, allowed to take over the comic stage? Yet on the grounds of the comic plot, the end, abbreviated as it is, also means that the play of "women on top" has brought the female back to her normal place.

Yet this motif of "women on top" has not altogether disappeared; it is distilled and defused in the name Euripides adopts as the old procuress—Artemisia, the Carian queen, who "manned" a ship during the Persian Wars and put up a brilliant fight, to the Greeks' undying shame that they had to do battle with a woman who was the equal of a man. In his accommodation to a comic ending, one that saves him and his kinsman, Euripides has reverted back to the purely sexual mode. But he has kept his promise to the women—displacing as far as possible from

16. This rivalry is, in fact, attested in ancient texts. A fragment of Aristophanes' older contemporary, Cratinos, reads: "And who are you? some clever theater-goer may ask: some subtle quibbler, an idea-chaser, a euripidaristophanizer?" (Theodorus Kock, *Comicorum Atticorum Fragmenta*, 3 vols. [Leipzig, 1880], 1:307); and the scholiast who quotes these lines observes: "Aristophanes was satirized for imitating Euripides through his mockery of him."

the world of the married women of the Thesmophoria the open sexuality which the dancing girl represents and which the comic world of sexual exuberance demands as its program. Yet the Thesmophoria too is a festival and it too has as its program a renewal of fertility. Thus when the play draws to a close, comedy, tragedy, and festival have all converged for a common purpose.

Euripides, by his inventiveness, has rescued the kinsman and has redeemed himself of his impiety more directly than we have recognized. For Euripides, despite his innovations on this stage and his own, has not invented everything himself. He has perhaps reinvented, realigned his plots with more traditional paradigms. There are two "secrets" embedded in the text which integrate the ritual and aesthetic elements of the play and which explain still more cogently the women's willingness to accept Euripides' tender of peace. If, on one level, the parodies display their status as "mere" fictions which pretend to represent reality and to cause an effect in the real world, on another level these fictions are essential to the revitalizing properties of myth and poetry and to the effects of comic and tragic alike. The sottish Scythian policeman mistakes the name of the Gorgon, which Perseus/Euripides carries, as that of Gorgias, the fifth century Sophist,[17] whose statement on the theater might best express this paradox: "Tragedy deceives by myths and the display of various passions; and whereas the tragic poet who deceives is juster than he who does not, the deceived is also wiser than the one who is not deceived." The figure of Helen is the clue to both "secrets"; due to limitations of space, I must omit the discussion of the first, which pertains to the festivals and myths of Dionysus and Demeter, and pass to the second, which belongs to the domain of art and the literary tradition.

4. Mimesis: Art and the Literary Tradition

The kinsman's impersonation of the "new" Helen, as I have suggested, introduces a new role for women in Euripides' plays which serves implicitly to counteract the charges of slander which the women have brought against the poet. A new positive version of the feminine is offered in place of the old, and its representation forecasts the renunciation Euripides is to make of his earlier errant ways. In this respect, the *Helen* functions within the thematic terms of the comedy as Euripides' palinode, the song that "takes everything back." More precisely, that reversal is located within the *Helen* itself, since Euripides' play offers a revised version of the traditional Helen. In this Euripides is not

17. "Gorgo the Scribe" may refer to another contemporary and not to the famous Sophist. But Aristophanes mentions Gorgias several times in his comedies, and Plato contains a word-play between Gorgias and Gorgon (*Symposium* 198c). See B. B. Rogers, *The Thesmophoriazousae of Aristophanes* (London, 1904), p. 119.

the inventor of the "new" plot of the *Helen* but follows another earlier poet of the sixth century, Stesichorus, who was the first to compose a palinode. The subject of that palinode was Helen herself, and it introduced the original motif of the *eidolon*. The story goes that Stesichorus, having slandered Helen, was blinded for his blasphemy, but he composed another song which denied that Helen went to Troy, and thus regained his sight (Plato *Phaedrus* 243b).

The story has been interpreted as a reflection of the double and contradictory role of Helen—as goddess, daughter of Zeus, and as woman, the adulterous wife. The case of Stesichorus has been referred to the violation of the cultic norms of Sparta where Helen was indeed worshipped as a goddess. The palinode, in its creation of the *eidolon,* therefore unequivocally confirmed her divine status. Generally, in the mythic tradition, the *eidolon,* the cloud image, is appropriately the creation of Zeus, the cloud gatherer, and is most often used as a substitute for a goddess whom a mortal man has attempted to ravish, as in the myth of Ixion who grasped at Hera but found Nephele (cloud) instead.[18]

The *Thesmophoriazousae* suggests a model of the female which oscillates between the profane ("bad" woman) and the sacred ("pure virgin"), but Stesichorus' diptych of ode and palinode seems to propose a more radical division between the two categories of the female, separated by the fine but firm line which divides mortal and immortal. But if we look back at Stesichorus, now in the light of the *Thesmophoriazousae,* the question of the two Helens might be posed differently. The fault for Stesichorus may not lie with the received myth of Helen itself (i.e., that Helen went to Troy) but rather in its mode of poetic representation which violated Helen by violating the norms of poetic decorum.

Having revealed too much of the mortal Helen, that is, her sexuality, Stesichorus turns in repentance to the other extreme—untainted erotic beauty, which is preserved through the figure of the pure Helen, who never went to Troy, and her imitation, who played her traditional part.[19] With his palinode, Stesichorus now avoids altogether the problem

18. On Stesichorus (and esp. in relation to Euripides' *Helen*), see Richard Kannicht's introduction to *Euripides: Helena,* 2 vols. (Heidelberg, 1969): 1:26–41. Some recently discovered papyri suggest the possibility of a second palinode, but Kannicht persuasively argues for one.

19. We learn from ancient testimony that in Stesichorus' version, Tyndareus, the father of Helen and Clytemnestra, had forgotten to sacrifice to Aphrodite while giving worship to other gods. The goddess, angered by his neglect, predicted that his daughters would be twice wedded (*digamoi*) and thrice wedded (*trigamoi*); that is, they would experience an excess of Aphrodite to compensate for their father's underestimation of the goddess and her power. The slander of Helen, then, perhaps, lay in the lubricious sexuality attributed to her, a trait which now belonged to her by "nature," as it were, rather than to the circumstantial facts of the myth itself. See also Kannicht, ibid., 1:39–41.

Euripides himself may be said to have composed a palinode when he offered a second version of the *Hippolytus* in circumstances which resembled those of Stesichorus. The first *Hippolytus* (known to us from fragments and other evidence) caused a scandal in Athens

of the woman as morally "good" (respectable) or "bad" (shameless) but rather raises another question with regard to the feminine. This new *eros* that Helen incarnates divides itself from within to establish another set of opposites—the false illusory *eidolon* and the true figure of the divine—opposites which, however, are now both equally unattainable. One is a false imitation of the other, which itself (as divine) can never be grasped by mortals in a "real" state but only in the empty form which is inevitably substituted for the original. Helen, as the darling of Aphrodite, always embodies in herself the irresistible principle of the erotic. But Stesichorus' story also suggests that *eros* is not divided from poetics. The poet slandered Helen, and to atone he fabricated a fictive *eidolon* in her place and openly declared the original version as a fiction. Helen, whose "true," that is, traditional, myth may be denied as a fiction, may also therefore personify poetics even as she embodies *eros*. For as fictive *eidolon,* Stesichorus' Helen acquires the capacity to impersonate herself and to draw attention to the notion of imitation as a conscious poetic creation.

Stesichorus uses Helen, as it were, to assert his role as a poet. Working within a received tradition which he alters in two different ways (the "blasphemy" in the first version and the recantation in the second), he raises the notion of fictionality as a possible attribute of mythic texts in order to account for his own innovations, and in the process, he invents a new generic form—the palinode. As a result, he inaugurates a new tradition, establishes a new paradigm upon which Aristophanes can draw in constructing his own piece in which the Helen of Euripides can serve to exonerate that poet from the charge of blaspheming against women. And this paradigm, reproduced in the Euripidean play itself, can serve at the same time to raise these questions of fictionality and imitation. Others have noted that Euripides' play itself shows a consciousness of its status as a piece for the theater, that Helen and Menelaus, when they contrive their fictions for escape, also strive *not* to imitate the clichés of other tragic plots. In satirizing Euripides' theatrical innovations in the *Helen* and in presenting a parody with metatheatrical dimensions, Aristophanes reaffirms, as it were, through the tradition that goes back go Stesichorus, the perennial utility of Helen as the figure upon whom can be focused the poetic problems of imitation itself.

One might call Stesichorus' *eidolon* a prototheatrical and protomimetic representation insofar as the poet precedes the fifth-century

---

because of its shameless Phaedra, to whom Aristophanes, in fact, refers in the *Thesmophoriazousae* and in the *Frogs*, where she is called a *pornē*, a whore (1043). In response, Euripides changed his representation of Phaedra to that of a noble woman who struggles heroically to suppress the fatal passion with which Aphrodite has afflicted her.

Stesichorus' blindness may be a "sacralized" version of Euripides' violation of literary decorum. Blindness is a punishment for mortal men who mingle with goddesses or who view them naked at their bath, but blindness is also an attribute of poets and prophets.

developments of the theater and of theories of mimesis. Yet although Stesichorus invented the *eidolon* of Helen, he is not the first to associate Helen with questions of imitation. A longer tradition stands behind her; it begins with her first appearance in Greek epic and is worth exploring briefly in order to understand better the paradigmatic value of Helen for the particular aesthetic problems which are posed in the time of Aristophanes and Euripides. I turn, then, to my final area of concern—the categories of Greek thought which connect the feminine with mimesis.

5. Mimesis: Eros and Art

Already in the *Iliad*, Helen, as the erotic center of the poem, is connected with the art of poetry when she weaves a tapestry depicting the contests of Greeks and Trojans which they suffered on account of her, as if she was "weaving the very fabric of heroic epic."[20] Better still, in the fourth book of the *Odyssey*, when Telemachus visits Sparta and finds Helen and Menelaus at home, they each tell a tale of Helen and Odysseus from the days when she was still at Troy. In her story, Odysseus, disguised as a beggar, comes secretly into the city as a spy. She alone recognizes him and does not betray him but cares for him and rejoices that her homecoming will soon be at hand (4. 240–64). Menelaus, on the other hand, tells another story of Helen: on the night in which the Trojan horse stood within the gates of the city, Helen, now the wife of Paris' brother, came down, and, by imitating all the different voices of their wives, tempted the Greeks who were hidden inside to betray their presence, a ruse which would have succeeded had it not been for Odysseus' discerning prudence (4. 266–89). Two stories are juxtaposed; each offers the same characterization of Odysseus but a different version of Helen. She is the mistress of many voices, linked in both stories to secrecy, disguise, and deception. She is the mistress of mimesis, like the nymph Echo, even more, like the Delian maidens in the Homeric hymn to Appolo (156–64), who can imitate the tongues of all humankind (*anthropoi*) and their chattering speech.

Even more, Helen is the mistress of ceremonies, who stages the mood of the tales, when, to counteract the grief which their sad memories of Odysseus had aroused, she casts a drug into their wine, a *pharmakon* (from Egypt), which takes away pain and brings forgetfulness of sorrows. She bids them to delight themselves with stories (*mythoi*), which she herself will begin, narrating a plausible/appropriate tale (4. 220–39). These *pharmaka* belong to the poetics of enchantment, which

20. L. L. Clader, *Helen: The Evolution from Divine to Heroic in Greek Epic Tradition* (Leiden, 1976), p. 8.

seduce the hearer with tales of deception, of impersonation in costume and speech. As tales of Helen, they are told without comment, memories of a past that seems to have been forgiven, transmuted into a play of symmetrical reversals that charm instead of dismay.[21]

Yet the ordering of the two stories also makes clear that the second story is also an implicit comment on the first story, a second version, which, like a protopalinode (but in reverse), revises the first. Menelaus' tale operates on two levels: on the first, it undermines the fidelity of Helen's earlier version which represents her fidelity to the Greeks in favor of a version which shows she can imitate many voices, each time with the intention to seduce and betray; on the second level, the story functions as a self-reflective comment on the nature of fiction and mimesis which Helen embodies. Menelaus' story thus intimates the status of Helen's earlier story as fiction and suggests in the process that Helen and storytelling might be the same thing—the imitation of many voices in the service of seduction and enchantment. Helen is the figure who therefore links *eros* and poetics together under the rubric of mimesis. And this mimesis is appropriately divined as a fiction from within this story of Menelaus by the master storyteller himself, Odysseus—the man of many turns.

Menelaus' story can only hint at the difference between fiction and truth. But the story Menelaus recalls the next day, that of his experience with Proteus after he left Troy and came with Helen to Egypt, is more precise in this regard. Proteus is the master of lies and truth; better still, he is the figure of the shifting nature of truth, which Menelaus can grasp as one and true only if he grasps Proteus himself, who will change his shape from one creature to another until, under Menelaus' unremitting grip, he will return to his single original form. Menelaus' success depends upon the advice of a female, Proteus' daughter, and note how she fulfills her feminine role: she *betrays* the existence of Proteus and the *secrets* of his power and also the means of overcoming him—a *mimetic disguise* and a *secret ambush* among the seals (351–570). The story of the mimesis practiced by Helen can never escape the ambiguities of its telling, but the mimetic repertoire of Proteus has a limit which will end in the revelation of an absolute truth. Here, that truth is the future of Menelaus—his homecoming and his ultimate fate—not death, but eternal sojourn in the Elysian Fields, "because Helen is yours and you are therefore son-in-law to Zeus" (561–70). Helen in the end rules both tales of mimesis—as divinity, connected through her genealogy to truth (and immortality) beyond the reaches of fiction, and earlier, as mortal, skilled in the arts of deception and seduction.

21. For two different treatments of these stories, see Reselyne Dupont-Roc and Alain Le Boulluec, "Le Charme du récit," *Ecriture et théorie poétiques* (Paris, 1976), pp. 30–39, and A. L. T. Bergren, "Helen's 'Good Drug': Odyssey IV 1–305," *University of Ottawa Quarterly* 50 (July and October 1980): 517–30.

For the *Odyssey*, this ultimate "truth," whether the translation of Menelaus to the permanence of the Elysian Fields or the "truth" of the recognition between Odysseus and Penelope, grounded in the fact that Penelope has truly been "true" to him, suggests the alternatives to the ambiguities of poetics and erotics which the two stories of Helen and Menelaus propose. In the light of this future reunion on Ithaca, these ambiguities not only recall a past which belongs to Helen and Menelaus but potentially forecast the future for Penelope. This future depends upon Penelope's choice of one of the two possible roles which the two stories offer her—that of the faithful woman who receives the beggar in disguise and welcomes him or that of the woman who, surrounded by men (read "suitors" for "Greeks"), practices the wiles of seduction, although another man's wife. Penelope is no teller of stories—quite the contrary. She is worn out with hearing the false tales of Odysseus which travelers have brought to her over the years and with meeting the false imposters of Odysseus himself, and she has become skilled at testing the fictions of another's words which have not power to seduce her. Yet she is the mistress of one fiction—and that to preserve her "true" self for Odysseus—one "story" which she tells again and again and never finishes, weaving and unweaving the fabric of Laertes' shroud, until Helen's story of herself, not that of Menelaus, becomes her own.

The *Odyssey*, by virtue of its Penelope, can afford its Circes, Calypsos, Sirens, and Helens, whom Odysseus encounters in various ways. But the *Odyssey*, as the repertory of all fictions, adumbrates even in the ambiguities of Odysseus himself the ambivalence which Greek thought will manifest with increasing articulation toward the mimetic powers of the verbal and visual arts to persuade with the truths of their fictions. This ambivalence is not incongruent, at some level, with the increasing ambivalence with which the city's male ideology views its other gender, an attitude which links the feminine still more closely with art and artifice.[22]

Thus the two Helens, the daughter of Zeus and the fictive *eidolon*, might exemplify in the erotic sphere the hesitation in the aesthetic domain between an art that is divinely inspired and a craft that makes counterfeits of the real.[23] But while the *eidolon* can be separated from the

22. Space does not permit a more detailed discussion of the ambiguities of persuasion and the *logos* in connection with the feminine and *eros*. See further, Pedro Laín Entralgo, *The Therapy of the Word in Classical Antiquity*, ed. and trans. L. J. Rather and J. M. Sharp (New Haven, Conn., 1970), pp. 51–69; Marcel Detienne, *Les Maîtres de vérité dans la Grèce archaïque* (Paris, 1973), pp. 51–80; and Laurence Kahn, *Hermès; ou, Les Ambiguïtés de la communication* (Paris, 1978), pp. 119–64. For art and literature, see also Jesper Svenbro, *La Parole et le marbre: Aux origines de la poétique grecque* (Lund, 1976), and Zoé Petre, "Un âge de la représentation: Artifice et image dans la pensée grecque du VIᵉ Av. N.E.," *Revue roumaine d'histoire* 2 (1979): 245–57.

23. The more pejorative notion of art as a counterfeit imitation of the real owes more, of course, to Platonic aesthetic theories. Craft includes and even gives first priority to

real Helen as an insubstantial likeness of herself, a figment of the imagination, the *eidolon* as a seductive *objet d'art* cannot be separated from the generic image of the feminine. The "real" woman, in fact, could be defined as a "real" *eidolon*, created as such from the beginning in the person of the first woman, Pandora.

Fashioned at the orders of Zeus as punishment for Prometheus' deceptive theft of celestial fire for man, the female is the first imitation, who, replying to the first deception, embodies now for all time the principle of deception. She imitates both divine and bestial traits, endowed by the gods with an exterior of wondrous beauty and adornment that conceals the thievish and greedy nature of her interior. Artifact and artifice herself, Pandora installs the woman as *eidolon* in the frame of human culture, equipped by her "unnatural" nature to delight and deceive. More specifically, as has been argued, the origin of Pandora coincides in the text with the origin of language: "Because of her symbolic function and, literally, because of her ornaments and her flowers, her glamor and her scheming mind, Pandora emblematizes the beginning of rhetoric; but at the same time, she also stands for the rhetoric of the beginning. For she is both the 'figure' of the origin and the origin of the 'figure'—the first being invested with symbolic referential elements."[24] This reading of Pandora can only be suggested by the implicit terms of the text, for rhetoric in Hesiod's time (c. 700 B.C.) had not yet been invented. But his negative view of Pandora, which arises naturally from his peasant's instrumental view of nature and culture, can still serve as a preview of later philosophical thought which, in testing the world of physical appearances, finds it deceptive precisely in the spheres of physical *eros* and of artistic mimesis, specifically, in fact, in the art of rhetoric itself.

It should therefore not surprise us that Gorgias, the historical figure most closely identified with the development of rhetorical theory in fifth-century Athens, should, in fact, have composed an encomium on Helen which is as much a defense of his art of the *logos* as it is a defense of Helen. I invoke this last example to return to the text and context of Aristophanes, since Gorgias is very much present, I suspect, in the *Thesmophoriazousae,* and not only as the possible garbled reference to him by the barbarian policeman who confuses Gorgon and Gorgias. For the *Palamedes* and the *Helen,* while they serve, of course, as parodies of

---

artisanal skill. But this is a category which is not without its ambiguities for Greek thought in which the artistic product is far more admired than the artist who produces it. Poetry claimed a higher status than representational art, but greater consciousness of the poet as *poiētēs* ("maker") introduces comparisons with artisanal activity. The *Thesmophoriazousae* itself, in fact, offers the two opposing notions of poetic composition in its comic presentation of Agathon, where the sacred (e.g., the hymn he sings) is juxtaposed with technical terms drawn from the more homely méitiers (52–57).

24. Piero Pucci, *Hesiod and the Language of Poetry* (Baltimore, 1977), pp. 100–101.

Euripides' plays, are also titles of two specimens of Gorgias' epideictic oratory. More broadly, Gorgias' theories owe much to the theater—to the psychological effects it produces in the spectators and in the aesthetic effects which it employs.

Gorgias, having accepted the premise that the phenomenal world cannot be grasped as real, is free to embrace the shifting world of appearances, of *doxa* ("opinion"), in its deceptions and its fictions; hence, he is also in a position to embrace Helen. The mastery of the world can only come about through the installation of the *logos* as its master, which, through the techniques of persuasion, manipulates the sense impressions and emotions of its auditors. For Plato, who is to stand directly on the other side of the divide, Gorgias (as the other Sophists) will, like a painter, "make imitations which have the same names as the real things and which can deceive . . . at a distance." The Sophists can "exhibit spoken images [*eidola*] of all things, so as to make it seem that they are true and that the speaker is the wisest of all men in all things" (Plato *Sophist* 234b–c).

For Gorgias, the *logos* is real, akin to a physical substance and possessing the magico-medical quality of the *pharmakon*. Hence its power *(dynamis)*, like that of the incantation, mingles together with the *doxa* ("opinion") of the psyche and charms, persuades, and changes it by enchantment. The force of persuasion, when added to the *psyche*, can make an impression, can put a stamp *(typos)* on the *psyche*, which responds, in turn, to its manipulation with the appropriate emotions. Similarly, sight *(opsis)* affects the *psyche* of the one who sees, "stamping [*typos*] it with its sensations of objects," "engraving in the mind the images of the things one sees," if fearful, causing fear, if beautiful, bringing pleasure, "like the sculpting of statues and production of images which afford the eyes divine delight; thus some things naturally please or pain the sight, and many things produce in many men love and desire for many actions or bodies."[25]

Gorgias' defense of Helen reverses the image of the seductive and deceptive woman by portraying a Helen overmastered by irresistible forces—whether by the gods, by physical violence, by the persuasion of the *logos*, or by the power of *eros*. It is here that *opsis* enters into the discourse in order to propose a theory of *eros*, and Gorgias can therefore query: "If Helen's eye was so entranced by Paris' body, and she delivered up her soul to an eager contest of love, what is so strange in that?" Since

25. Citations from Gorgias' *Encomium of Helen* are in Diels-Kranz, *Die Fragmente der Vorsokratiker*, vol. 2 (Dublin and Zurich, 1966), pp. 288–94; my translations. Relevant work on Gorgias includes Mario Untersteiner, *The Sophists*, trans. Kathleen Freeman (Oxford, 1954), pp. 101–201; Thomas Rosenmeyer, "Gorgias, Aeschylus, and *Apatē* (Deceit)," *American Journal of Philology* 76 (1955): 225–60; Charles Segal, "Gorgias and the Psychology of the Logos," *Harvard Studies in Classical Philology* 66 (1962): 99–155; and the relevant sections in Entralgo, *Therapy of the Word in Classical Antiquity*, and Detienne, *Les Maîtres de vérité*.

the entire discourse is a *logos* which is meant to persuade, the demonstration within the piece of the persuasive power of the *logos* assures it the dominant position in the piece. As the *megas dynastēs,* the *logos* even proves to overmaster the other categories whose indisputable claims to power it appropriates for itself.

Stesichorus' and Euripides' excuse of the *eidolon* has, of course, no place in Gorgias' argument. But the aesthetics of the image remain, now interiorized within the body as the *psyche* which *logos* or *opsis* molds, as an artist shapes and molds his product. The *psyche,* in turn, responds to the physical body whose visual impressions it receives, as a spectator who gazes upon an object of art. By treating the *psyche* as a corporeal entity and in endowing *opsis* and *logos* with physical properties, Gorgias introduces a set of tactile relations that somatizes psychology as it psychologizes aesthetics. *Opsis* is already invoked in the cause of *eros,* but *logos* behaves like *eros,* which takes possession of another's body to penetrate its interior and to work its effects. The relation between rhetor and auditor, therefore, is not unlike that between a man and a woman, even as the writing tablet, as Artemidorus tells us, signifies a woman to the dreamer, "since it receives the imprints [*typoi*] of all kinds of letters" (*Oneirocritica* 2. 45). Thus if Helen is the subject of the discourse, she is also the object within it. She is the auditor who, seduced and persuaded by the deceptive rhetoric of Paris, is reseduced (and therefore exonerated) by the rhetoric of Gorgias, who claims as the truth of his discourse the demonstration of the power of rhetoric to seduce and deceive. For the outside auditor, the artful beauty of the text, with its persuasive *logos* about persuasion, operates as the rhetorical equivalent of the godlike beauty of Helen, which Gorgias mentions at the beginning of the text, in order to describe its irresistible erotic effect upon the suitors who came to her from all parts of Greece.

Moreover, the seduction of this *logos* works a double pleasure of the text—for the auditors it masters within and without the discourse and for Gorgias himself, which he acknowledges when he concludes that "This speech is a plaything [*paignion*] for me, but an encomium for Helen," who, in his terms, is worthy not only of defense but also of praise. This ending explains best of all, perhaps, the choice of Helen for his discourse, beyond that of an unpopular case which he wishes to win by his rhetorical skill. Helen, as the paradigm of the feminine, is the ideal subject/object of the discourse; first, in sexual terms, as the passive partner to be mastered by masculine rhetorical persuasion, and second, in aesthetic terms. Helen, as the mistress of mimesis and also its object, is a fitting participant in the world of make-believe, the antiworld which reverses the terms in mimetic display and reserves the right under the name of play to take everything back. Seduction, like rhetoric, is a game, a *paignion,* and both *eros* and *logos* are now invested with a new power that is precisely the power of play, a delight in the aesthetic capacity to seduce and deceive. This point of view, I suggest, must inevitably invoke and rehabilitate the feminine whom Greek thought represents as the subject/object of *eros* (nature) and artifice (culture). In her corporeal essence, she functions both as the psychological subject and as the aesthetic object, and the artist needs her to substantiate his own conception of his art.

Thus, for both Gorgias and Euripides, the woman has a place, a place that the end of the fifth century makes for her more and more to Aristophanes' seeming comic chagrin, and this from two points of view. First, she is in the domain of art itself, which is discovering a sense of its capacities for mimesis as an explicit category of the fictive, the make-believe. This discovery takes place in the various verbal arts which, in turn, are influenced by the earlier advances in illusionist painting and in the other plastic arts. In this development, theater too played no small role, as Aristophanes' play itself attests. Second, she is in the social world. As the war dragged on to its unhappy close, attention began to shift away from masculine values of politics to the private sphere—to the domestic milieu at home, to the internal workings of the psyche, and to a new validation of *eros,* all of which the feminine as a cultural category best exemplifies. This new focus will receive further emphasis in the next century with the emergence in sculpture of the female nude as an art form and in the literary genres of New Comedy, mime, romance, and pastoral. Old Comedy comes to an end with Aristophanes, whose last productions already make the transition to Middle Comedy, while Euripides, who scandalized his Athenian audience again and again, winning only four first prizes in his lifetime, will become the theatrical favorite of the next era and thereafter.

In this "feminization" of Greek culture, Euripides was, above all, a pioneer, and so Aristophanes perhaps correctly perceived that Euripides' place was indeed with the women (as that of Socrates in the *Clouds* was with the men). In a second *Thesmophoriazousae,* which is lost to us except for a few fragments and testimonia, the same cast of characters (more or less) seem to have been involved. This time, our information, which comes from an ancient life of Euripides and which seems to refer to this piece, states explicitly that the women, because of the censures he passed on them in his plays, attacked him at the Thesmophoria with murderous intent; but they spare him, first because of the (his) Muses, and second because he promises never to abuse them again. These Muses are perhaps still to be found in the play we have, hidden behind the noisy laughter of Aristophanic parody.

Turning the Lens on "The Panther Captivity": A Feminist Exercise in Practical Criticism

Annette Kolodny

I sometimes hear from colleagues unfamiliar with feminist literary criticism that it offers nothing more than just another turn of the lens. Certain features of a text may be put into sharper focus, they allow, but only at the expense of others which are permitted to blur or even disappear altogether. My standard response to such baiting is to point out that all interpretive strategies are partial and incomplete. In asking different questions of, or in bringing different analytical methodologies to, any text, different literary critics necessarily report different gleanings or discover different meanings, meanings which reflect not so much the *text qua text* but *the text as shaped by* the particular questions or analyses applied to it. By concentrating more on developing a wide-ranging area of concerns rather than establishing formulaic methods of procedure, feminist literary criticism has, by and large, escaped the inevitable narrowing of vision implied by so many other "ists" and "isms." The feminist critic, in other words, is free to employ or refine whatever schools or methods suit her present purposes, and her readings thereby benefit from the sheer audacity of her infinite critical variety. Moreover, because feminist criticism essentially adds a vital new perspective to all that has gone before, rather than taking anything away, it enjoys at least the possibility of enhancing and enlarging our appreciation of what is comprised by any specific literary text.

Research for this essay was undertaken during time made available to me by a grant from the John Simon Guggenheim Memorial Foundation, to which I remain continuously grateful. Of inestimable value as I pursued the ideas and materials discussed here have been the comments and critiques of Norman S. Grabo.

To demonstrate the fullness of that possibility, I will offer a reading of one of the most popular of the fictional captivity narratives to appear in the United States at the close of the Revolution.[1] I choose a captivity narrative for this exercise not only because it represents possibly *the* most enduringly popular narrative form in American literary history but also because it, along with the Indian War narrative, has long been appreciated by Americanists as an ongoing literary vehicle through which successive generations of Americans played out the symbolic dramas of westward migration. In recent years, Leslie Fiedler and Richard Slotkin have turned to the capitivity narrative as a resource for discovering and following the developing mythology of the frontier West. In one late eighteenth-century narrative, for example, Fiedler saw the mythopoetic prototype of the white man's fantasied intimacy with the red, as unwilling captivity turned into compliant adoption. It is a fantasy, he insists, "to which our greatest writers have compulsively returned, telling over and over again the story of that sacred-heathen love between White man and colored man in a world without women."[2] Taking his cue from Fiedler but attempting a far more comprehensive study, Richard Slotkin has identified in both the captivity and the Indian War narrative that progressive mythologizing by which Americans came to displace the Indian with the figure of the Indianized white man as the proper hero of the American wilderness.[3]

1. A captivity narrative generally records a white Euro-American's forced confinement among (and, usually, successful escape or ransom from) Indians. Although some narratives exist which record the capture of blacks by Indians, these are relatively rare. The first Puritan captivity narratives from late seventeenth-century New England were authentic, but, by the eighteenth century, fictionalized narratives began to appear. Soon, authentic narratives, sensationalized redactions of earlier narratives, and altogether fictional narratives competed with one another for popularity all across the colonies and in all regions of the early republic.

2. Leslie A. Fiedler, *The Return of the Vanishing American* (London, 1968), p. 119; all further citations to this work will be included in the text.

3. See Richard Slotkin, *Regeneration through Violence: The Mythology of the American Frontier, 1600–1860* (Middletown, Conn., 1973); all citations to this work will be included in the text.

Annette Kolodny, the author of *The Lay of the Land: Metaphor as Experience and History in American Life and Letters,* has recently completed the first volume of *Westering Women,* a projected multivolume analysis of women's imaginative responses to the successive American frontiers.

My purpose here, then, is to reexamine a form which has already attracted considerable attention and, more particularly, by utilizing precisely that same mythopoetic analytic grid established by Fiedler and Slotkin to reread one of its most popular incarnations—only adding to it a feminist perspective. My reading will thus avoid the unacknowledged and unexamined assumption which marks their work: the assumption of gender. Nonfeminist critics, after all, tend to ignore the fact (and significance) of women as readers as much as they tend to ignore the potentially symbolic significations of gender within a text. Fiedler, for example, obviously focuses on a male audience when he asserts that "westering, in America, means leaving the domain of the female" (p. 60). And Slotkin, in making the same mistake, ignores the fact that women, too, required imaginative constructs through which to accommodate themselves to the often harsh realities of the western wilderness. Thus, he insists that "the figure of Daniel Boone, the solitary, Indian-like hunter of the deep woods," stands as "the most significant, most emotionally compelling myth-hero of the early republic," but he looks for no corresponding figure that might have served women's fantasies (p. 21). I will not, however, be discarding such readings. Instead, by asking additional questions which identify feminist approaches, I hope to uncover symbolic resonances that Fiedler and Slotkin, in their overriding concern for exclusively male fantasy structures, necessarily overlooked. In so doing, I also hope to enhance a modern reader's appreciation of a text that has previously intrigued but baffled critics, its symbolic patterns heretofore unavailable to full explication, the longevity of its popular success eluding satisfying explanation.

In 1787, *Bickerstaff's almanack, for the year of our Lord, 1788* printed "A Surprising account of the Discovery of a Lady who was taken by the Indians in the year 1777, and after making her escape, She retired to a lonely Cave, where She lived nine years."[4] Composed as a letter from Abraham Panther to an unnamed correspondent, the pseudonymous narrative has come to be known as "The Panther Capitivity" and has even been reprinted under that title. As the letter opens, the writer is apparently responding to his correspondent's request for some account of a recent journey into "the Western wilderness." Perhaps intentionally echoing John Filson's successful 1784 narrative of *The Adventures of Col. Daniel Boone,* the writer here explains that he and a companion, "Mr. Isaac Camber," were "determin[ed] to penetrate the Western wilderness

4. Abraham Panther, "A Surprising account . . . ," *Bickerstaff's almanack, for the year of our Lord, 1788* (Norwich, Conn., 1787), unpaged; all quotes are from this edition. This first edition, along with a later reprinting, has been included in Wilcomb E. Washburn, comp., *The Garland Library of Narratives of North American Indian Captivities,* vol. 17 (New York, 1978); since these are facsimile reprints, texts are separately paginated.

as far as prudence and safety would permit" and, in the course of that journey, "travelled for thirteen days in a westerly direction."[5] Again echoing Boone's enthusiasm for the fertility and beauty of the Kentucky landscape, combined with his pleasure at the abundance of game, Panther notes that he and Camber found the land "exceeding rich and fertile," emphasizing "the very great variety of birds and wild beasts, which would frequently start before us." "As we had our muskets," he adds, these "contributed not a little to our amusement and support."

"On the 14th day of our travels," the two men are enjoying a particularly "agreeable picturesque prospect" when they are "surprised at the sound of a voice which seemed at no great distance." "Uncertain whether the voice was a human one, or that of some bird," they decide "to proceed up the hill, from whence we judged the sound to come." Daniel Boone, too, had described "gain[ing] the summit of a commanding ridge"; what he encountered there, to his "astonishing delight," were "the ample plains, [and] the beauteous tracts" that later drew him to resettle in Kentucky.[6] By contrast, what Panther and Camber discover as they mount their own "high hill" is the palpable symbolization of what remains just below the surface in Boone, even as that mythic hero recounts his virtual seduction by "the beauties of nature I found here."[7] Following "a small foot path" to "the top of the hill," the letter writer and his companion "passed round a large rock, then through a thicket of bushes at the end of which was a large opening." And there, "to our inexpressible amazement," Panther writes, "we beheld a most beautiful young LADY sitting near the mouth of a cave."

As they approach the lady, who is not yet aware of their presence, they are halted by the barking of "a dog which we had not before observed." Now alarmed, the lady "started up and seeing us, gave a scream and swooned away." Upon her recovery, the two men quiet her apprehensions and, "having convinced her of our peaceable dispositions," are invited into the cave where "she refreshed us with some ground nuts, a kind of apples, some Indian cake and excellent water. We found her to be an agreeable, sensible lady," the letter continues, "and after some

---

5. Boone states that in 1769, along with some male companions, he first "wander[ed] through the wilderness of America, in quest of the country of Kentucke," proceeding "through a mountainous wilderness, in a westward direction"; in addition to the "myriads of trees, some gay with blossoms, others rich with fruits," Boone reports that he and his companions "were diverted with innumerable animals presenting themselves perpetually to our view," and he repeatedly details his hunting expeditions (see John Filson, *The Discovery, Settlement, and Present State of Kentucke . . . To Which is Added an Appendix Containing, The Adventures of Col. Daniel Boon, One of the First Settlers, Comprehending Every Important Occurrence in the Political History of that Province* [Wilmington, Del., 1784], pp. 50–51, 52).

6. Ibid., p. 55.

7. Ibid., p. 56.

conversation we requested to know who she was and how she came to this place." At this point, the text swerves from a Boone-like narrative of masculine adventure in the wilderness to a surprising version of the by-now familiar female captivity narrative. What is surprising about this lady's story is not that she has spent relatively little time in captivity nor that she has subdued at least her second captor—there were already precedents for these in earlier narratives—[8]but that her sojourn in the woods, following upon her escape, has reduced her neither to "a mere skeleton" nor to the "forlorn creature" that characterized so many other escaped female captives.[9] And, more surprising still, she has managed to sustain herself in the wilderness and survive there, on her own, for nine years. As such, her first-person narrative, embedded within the Panther letter and thereby interrupting the masculine hunting story which it would otherwise recount, suggests a subtle readjustment in Americans' imaginative vision of the place and person of the white woman in the wilderness.

"I was born near Albany in the year 1760," the lady begins, the only child of "a man of some consequence and of considerable estate." At age fifteen she fell in love with a young clerk whom her father had recently introduced into the household. The growing attachment between the two had to be concealed, however, because her father, being "excessively eager in pursuit of riches," could not be expected to "countenance our loves or consent to my marriage with a man destitute of fortune." Nonetheless, the father one day discovers the couple together and "with an angry countenance upbraided my lover . . . and after calling him many hard names, dismissed him with peremptory order never again to enter his house." By means of a secret correspondence, the young lovers manage to remain in contact, finally devising a plan to "retire into the country, to a little hut." Her father, "enraged at my elopement," sub-

---

8. See, e.g., "A Narrative of the Captivity and Escape of Mrs. Francis Scott, an Inhabitant of Washington County, Virginia," in *The Adventures of Colonel Daniel Boon, One of the first Settlers at Kentucke . . . To Which are Added a Narrative of the Captivity, and Extraordinary Escape of Mrs. Francis Scott An Inhabitant of Washington-County Virginia; Who after the Murder of her Husband and Children, by the Indians, was Taken Prisoner by Them; on the 19th of June, 1785*, ed. John Trumbull (Norwich, Conn., 1786), pp. 16–24. Scott spent only eleven days in captivity before escaping, and so the major portion of her narrative is devoted to detailing her four weeks of wandering in the wilderness, "being without any provisions, having no kind of weapon or tool to assist her in getting any, and being almost destitute of cloathing . . . and she almost as ignorant as a child of the method of steering through the woods" (pp. 19–20). See also Cotton Mather's *Humiliations Follow'd with Deliverances. A Brief Discourse on the Matter and Method, of that Humiliation which would be an Hopeful Symptom of our Deliverance from Calamity. Accompanied and Accommodated with a Narrative, of a Notable Deliverance Lately Received by Some English Captives, from the Hands of Cruel Indians* (Boston, 1697), wherein Mather details how Hannah Dustan slew and scalped the members of an Indian family which held her captive (pp. 46–57).

9. See "A Narrative of the Captivity and Escape of Mrs. Francis Scott," p. 22.

sequently hires "several men" to pursue the couple and so drives them "further back in the country . . . there to wait till time should calm my father's rage, or effectually cool his resentments."

By traveling deeper into the wilderness, the couple evades the father's hired men, only to fall captive to Indians. The young man is "barbarously murdered," at the sight of which the girl "fainted away and lay some time motionless on the ground." When she regains consciousness, she discovers that her Indian guard has joined his fellows in "singing and dancing," and so she takes the opportunity to withdraw "by degrees into the bushes." Now safely escaped from her Indian captors, she nonetheless feels herself "surrounded, as I supposed, on all sides by danger. . . . without a guide to direct, or friend to protect me." Most previous narratives at this juncture emphasized the woman's lack of woodcraft, detailing her sense of being lost in the wilderness and her inability to find sufficient food to stave off starvation. In "The Panther Captivity," however, while the lady acknowledges that she "wandered about for 14 days without knowing whether I went," the text also insists that raw nature provided at least a modicum of adequate food and shelter: "By day the spontaneous produce of the earth supplied me with food, by night the ground was my couch, and the canopy of heaven my only covering."

"In the afternoon of the fifteenth day," her narrative continues, she is "surprized" by "a man of gigantic figure walking towards me." Concluding escape to be impossible, she allows the man to overtake and then lead her to the cave she now inhabits. Here, her captor first feeds her, "after which he stretched himself out upon a long stone covered with skins which he used as a bed, and several times motioned to me to lay myself beside him." When the girl declines "his offer," the giant fetches his "sword and hatchet. . . . motion[ing] to me that I must either accept of his bed or expect death for my obstinacy." Still she declines, insisting that "I . . . was resolved to die rather than comply with his desire." At that, the giant binds her, "insinuating that he left me till next morning to consider his proposal." While he sleeps, the girl chews away at her bark bindings, frees herself, and, despairing of eluding "him by flight," she determines instead to kill her captor:

> I did not long deliberate, but took up the hatchet he had brought, and summoning resolution I with three blows effectually put an end to his existence. I then cut off his head, and next day having cut him into quarters drew him out of the cave about half a mile distance, when after covering him with leaves and bushes I returned to this place. I now found myself alone in possession of this cave in which are several apartments. I found here a kind of Indian corn which I planted, and have yearly raised a small quantity, here I contented myself as well as I my wretched situation would permit—here have I existed for nine long years, in all which time

this faithful dog which I found in the cave has been my only companion, and you are the only human beings who ever heard me tell my tale.

With that, the young woman's "narration" is completed, accompanied by "a plentiful shower of tears."

The voice of the letter writer then resumes the narrative, detailing the next day's tour of the cave's four compartments (which contain "a spring of excellent water"; a cache of "four skulls," presumed to be those of "persons murdered by the [former] owner of the cave"; a supply of weapons, including "three hatchets, four bows and several arrows, one large tinder box, one sword, one old gun"; and a number of animal skins "and a few cloathes"). "After continuing in the cave five days" more, so Panther writes his correspondent, he and his companion "proposed returning home and requested the lady to accompany us." "At first she refused to quit her cave," he continues, "but after some persuasion she consented." He then briefly summarizes the homeward journey, expanding only on accompanying "the lady, agreeable to her desire, to her father's house." By this time the old man is quite ill and "did not at first recognize his daughter." "But being told who she was," he revives briefly "and then tenderly embraced her crying O! my child, my long lost child." He faints and is again revived—this time sufficiently long enough to hear his daughter's story, to acknowledge that "he had been unjustly cruel to her," and, at the last, to ask "her forgiveness." Once more, then, the old man loses consciousness, but now all efforts to revive him fail. His death brings his daughter "a handsome fortune," and she, in her turn, "notwithstanding his cruelty," is "deeply affected at his sudden death." So ends both the letter and its writer's recounting of "this adventure the most singular and extraordinary of my life."

Even so cursory a summary should alert readers to the disparate generic sources underpinning "The Panther Captivity"—these include the male adventure narrative, the captivity narrative, the sentimental romance, and Indian fertility myths. In the course of the letter, however, the original meaning or intent of each of these is either quietly subverted or altogether superseded. The male wilderness adventure (precursor of the later Western tale) is displaced by a narrative of female adventure; the now standard narrative of female captivity turns instead—and for the first time in American literary history—toward acculturation and accommodation to the wild; the passive, languishing heroine of sentimental romance demonstrates her capacity to survive on her own in the woods; and the story of the slaying of the corn god here makes possible not a tribe's but a white woman's continued existence. Clearly, each generic alteration moves in the direction of projecting an image of a white *lady's* (and I use the word purposefully) capacity to survive and sustain herself in the American wilderness. At the end of the eighteenth century, with Americans energetically renewing their push westward on the roads earlier built to transport opposing armies, this was no idle theme.

The anxiety attendant upon such relocations rested not only on an appreciation of the physical dangers and hardships involved but, as well, on a far deeper fear of the loss of civilization itself. Many eighteenth-century observers believed the savagery of the woods and of their native inhabitants would inevitably make savages of the whites who tried to remove there. Despairing at what he had himself seen of the northeastern "back settlers," J. Hector St. John de Crèvecoeur made his fictional Farmer James insist that "there is something in the proximity of the woods, which is very singular." "By living in or near the woods," James averred, settlers' "actions are regulated by the wildness of the neighborhood."[10] The Anglican minister, Charles Woodmason, traveling in the Carolina backcountry in the years just before the Revolution, confided similar concerns to his journal when he noted that he found the Flat Creek settlers "as rude in their Manners as the Common Savages, and hardly a degree removed from them."[11] At least in part, the phenomenal popularity of Filson's Boone narrative may have been due to the fact that it effectively quieted such fears by substituting for them the heroic myth of white-male conquest of the wilderness. By demonstrating all the woodcraft and hunting skills of the Indian while, at the same time, firmly associating himself with agricultural settlement, Filson's Boone responded to those like Crèvecoeur who, above all, feared that, near the woods, men might abandon the plow and "degenerate altogether into the hunting state."[12] Boone the hunter, after all, was also the protector of the fledgling Kentucky settlements, declaring himself, in Filson's text, "an instrument ordained to settle the wilderness."[13]

Until the appearance of "The Panther Captivity," however, fears for the fate of white *women* in the wilderness could be quieted by no corresponding myth.[14] And these fears were, if possible, even more virulent in their expression. Woodmason, for example, deplored his encounters with the "barefooted and Bare legged" women of the Carolina backcountry, all of them, in his view, "Quite in a State of Nature." Particularly distressing to the good preacher was the women's habit of "Rubbing

10. J. Hector St. John de Crèvecoeur, *Letters from an American Farmer* (1782; New York, 1957), p. 47.

11. Charles Woodmason, quoted in Page Smith, *Daughters of the Promised Land: Women in American History* (Boston, 1970), p. 222.

12. Crèvecoeur, *Letters from an American Farmer*, p. 49.

13. Filson, *The Discovery, Settlement, and Present State of Kentucke*, p. 81.

14. Boone's wife and daughters are rather shadowy figures in the Filson text, and, in printer John Trumbull's 1786 editing of that text (see n. 8), their presence was even further diminished. As a result, not until the nineteenth century did Rebecca Bryan Boone emerge as a figure with symbolic resonances corresponding to those of her husband.

themselves and their Hair with Bears Oil and tying it up behind in a Bunch like the Indians."[15] Somewhat more restrained in his *Letters from an American Farmer,* Crèvecoeur nonetheless also noted the pernicious influence of the woods on the wives and children of those who chose to settle there. "Their wives and children live in sloth and inactivity," he wrote, the parents raising only "a mongrel breed, half civilized, half savage."[16] Indeed, throughout the century, much though they wanted to, Americans seemed incapable of imagining a frontier woman who "will carry a gunn in the woods" and yet display herself "a very civil woman . . . [with] nothing of ruggedness or Immodesty in her carriage." We have ample evidence that such women existed in the journals and diaries of the men who encountered them. Nonetheless, what so consistently marks these entries is a tone of surprise and sometimes even defensiveness. When Philip Ludwell helped survey the westernmost boundary between Virginia and the Carolinas in 1710, for example, he and his party came upon the frontier cabin of a Mrs. Jones. Subsequently, Ludwell somewhat unbelievingly recorded in his journal that "It is said of this Mrs. Jones . . . that she is a very civil woman and shews nothing of ruggedness or Immodesty in her carriage, yett she will carry a gunn in the woods and kill deer, turkeys, &c., shoot down wild cattle, catch and tye hoggs, knock down beeves with an ax and perform the most manfull Exercises as well as most men in those parts."[17] The muted disbelief betrayed by Ludwell's transitional "yett" springs from contemporary notions that a woman simply could not master the skills requisite for survival at the edge of the frontier without becoming either masculinized or Indianized.

It was precisely such notions to which "The Panther Captivity" responded, offering a character who, despite her nine-year isolated sojourn in the woods, still displayed the unmistakable features of a middle-class, stereotypic heroine from the sentimental romance tradition. She swoons and cries copiously and, despite the limitations of her circumstances, is a gracious hostess to her unexpected guests. Like many well-bred young ladies of the period, she has a small dog for her pet. And her singing, while it harmonizes so perfectly with her surroundings that the hunters cannot distinguish it from birdsong, also functions to suggest the more civilized musical adornments in which middle-class young ladies, both in novels and in life, were trained. In other words, the lady of "The Panther Captivity" is decidedly "feminine" in all the ways that contemporary readers would have recognized.

What dramatizes that identification, ironically, is the one act which seems so singularly out of keeping with her sentimental origins: her murder and dismemberment of her giant captor. But when we recall

15. Woodmason, quoted in Smith, *Daughters of the Promised Land,* p. 222.
16. Crèvecoeur, *Letters from an American Farmer,* p. 48.
17. Philip Ludwell, quoted in Mary Sumner Benson, *Women in Eighteenth-Century America: A Study of Opinion and Social Usage* (1935; New York, 1976), p. 284.

that what is being protected in that act is the lady's chastity, we appreciate the ingenuity with which the author of "The Panther Captivity"
managed to bend the outlines of an Indian fertility myth to the requirements of sentimental fiction. For the act not only assures the white
woman's survival—since she now possesses the corn which will sustain
her—but marks as well the white *lady's* survival—since what has been
overcome is not merely the threat of sexual violation but the threat of
being given over to the inherent brutality of the wilderness itself. Apparently because the man inhabits a cave and speaks a language the lady
cannot understand, most commentators have simply assumed that this
second captor is also an Indian. In fact, the text never identifies him one
way or another, and his cave is said to contain the implements of both the
red man and the white. Insofar as he is left so carefully *un*identified, the
"man of a gigantic figure" easily takes on the period's imagined conceptions of the very wilderness he seems to master: overpowering, potentially brutal and brutalizing, essentially promiscuous, and wholly uncivilized. And it is to this—the symbolization of the uncivilized brutality
of the wilderness—as much as it is to his physical body that the heroine
of "The Panther Captivity" successfully refuses to surrender.

To the modern reader, of course, the story is preposterous. To the
contemporary reader, for whom only the "forlorn," starving, and pathetic heroines of earlier captivities had been available, it offered at least the
fantasied possibility that a woman might, indeed, resist Crèvecoeur's dire
prediction that to live "in or near the woods" was inevitably to be "regulated by the wildness of the neighborhood." Moreover, the way in
which "The Panther Captivity" attempted to project women's experience
in the wilderness was not, after all, so far off the mark. If the heroine's
nine-year isolation here is extreme, it nonetheless honors the very real
loneliness of the housebound woman, often separated from her nearest
frontier neighbor by many miles. That the lady survives by yearly plant-
ing a crop of Indian corn echoes the fact that the first crop planted for
survival in those days *was* corn—planted by the women and children
between the stumps of the trees newly felled by their husbands and
fathers. And, further, like most women who entered the wilderness at
the end of the eighteenth century, this lady does not go there on her
own; she follows a man's lead into the forest.

By the time of its last known printing in 1814, "The Panther Captivity" had been followed by other texts which similarly sought to project
positive images of the white woman in the wilderness. Until its appearance in 1787, however, the available captivity literature had exclusively
projected images of the white woman's vulnerability there. But historical
circumstances clearly demanded something other than cringing
heroines and forlorn Eves. By utilizing the trappings of familiar genres
and yoking these to elements taken from Indian legend, "The Panther
Captivity" effectively carried its readers into the realm of myth and there

fulfilled the new fantasy requirement, mirroring back, with symbolic exemplariness, the hopes and anxieties attendant upon American women's increasing removal to the frontier.

That no previous reader, to my knowledge, has commented on this aspect of the tale has always surprised me. Given the historical context in which "The Panther Captivity" is embedded, it seems to me an obvious reading; but that may be because among those practices which mark me as a feminist critic—and necessarily distinguish the readings I generate—is my habit of consciously, purposefully, and consistently seeking out the significance of the presence of women (as readers, writers, and as societal participants) whenever I speak of the historical context for any given literary text. As a result, I am often, but not always, able to detect patterns which respond (either directly or indirectly) to the needs, fears of, or contemporary concerns about women—patterns which readers who assume an exclusively male audience must necessarily overlook.

At the same time, in addition to my abiding concern for *woman as person,* I look also for the *symbolic significance of gender.* This constitutes a second crucial aspect of feminist literary criticism as now practiced in the American academy. I say crucial because it acknowledges the often subtle distinction between the depiction of male or female characters for their recognizable gender behaviors and the manipulation of gender for symbolic purposes that may have only incidental relation to actual contemporary sex roles. Pursuing this second concern thus sometimes reveals little about the authentic reality of men and women but much about the symbolic terms through which a given cultural group struggles to define the meaning of its most perplexing dilemmas. My discussion of "The Panther Captivity" so far has concentrated on establishing the historical context for its more obvious handling of the anxieties attendant upon real-life women as they turned westward at the close of the Revolutionary War. The rest of my discussion will focus upon the ways in which "The Panther Captivity" utilized gender symbolically in such a way as to play out, or at least comment upon, the various crises of identity facing the new nation.

In concentrating on its generic roots, Richard Slotkin detects within the narrative a "tension between the traditional captivity pattern, which emphasizes filial reconciliation, and the fertility-myth pattern, which emphasizes the preparation of the new generation to destroy and replace the old" (pp. 258–59). This "tension," he avers, "expresses the dilemma of all men coming of age, inheriting their parents' world, and replacing their sires as the shapers of that world" (p. 259). Interesting and intelligent as this reading is, it nonetheless ignores one crucial fact: the inheritor here is a woman. Were either "filial reconciliation" or the replacement of the "sires" the only issue, a male protagonist would better have served the narrative's symbolic purposes. The fact that a female displaces both the giant in the wilderness and her own "blood father in the civilized world" clearly marks those chains of inheritance as radically altered (p. 259). For what the lady of "The Panther Captivity" represents, both by virtue of her gender and her experience within the tale, is an order of existence altogether different from those which she displaces. As a result, her story held up a mirror to contemporary reality. The wilderness was, after all, being claimed by those who pushed the agricultural frontier westward; and, both symbolically and historically, this implied the presence of women. At the same time, the mercantile commercial interests of the recent colonial past, it was hoped, were to be replaced by the more benign economic organization of a nation of cultivators; and, insofar as men function as hunters in the narrative, only the lady, as the sole white cultivator, thus stands as the appropriate heir to her father's "considerable estate."

Indeed, the narrative's careful concern to date and place itself suggests that such ecopolitical implications were not wholly unintentional. The lady tells the hunters that she "was born near Albany in the year 1760" and describes her father as "a man of some consequence and of considerable estate in the place where he lived." At the time of her birth, Albany was the central base for British fur-trading interests, competing with the French at Montreal for control over that trade. The counting houses at Albany made fortunes for the merchants who traded with the Iroquois, even as they harnessed English dreams of empire in the Northwest to an economy based on hunting and allied to mercantile interests. No contemporary reader would have been ignorant of these facts; and, for such a reader, the conclusion that the girl's father had amassed his wealth through the fur trade would have been probable, if not inescapable.

By the time the girl falls in love "with a man destitute of fortune," she is fifteen; the year is 1775. Colonial relations with the kinds of mercantile interests that dominated Albany were now strained to the limit. By the time she is forced into the woods because of her greedy father's disapproval of the match, it is 1776; the next year, pursued by her father's hired men, she is first captured by Indians. In these same years a newly independent nation challenged the authority of what it perceived to be the unconscionable greed of George III. Eschewing commercial interests, at least in their public rhetoric, more radical and avowedly idealistic elements within the Revolution broke from the protections of a parent nation and sought to project the image of an independent republic of yeoman farmers. In gross outline, if not in detail, the lady's adventures coincide with these historical events. In rejecting her imperious and greedy father, she is forced into a new relationship with the American wilderness, depending upon its cultivation for her survival. As a result, it is with her nine-year experience as a cultivator behind her that she eventually displaces her father (just as it is as a civilized white *lady* that she had earlier displaced her wilderness captor). I do not mean to suggest that "The Panther Captivity" was consciously composed as an allegory of the birth of the nation; but I do mean to suggest the ways in which the story's purposeful assignment of gender inevitably called forth for contemporary readers that cluster of political associations surrounding the symbol of a resplendent Lady Columbia, sheathing her sword and turning from deeds of war to the peaceful pursuit of agriculture. Pictured with a laden cornucopia or with sheaves of native corn, that female symbol of the new nation often called forth the virtues of agriculture over the exploitive interests of commerce.

Because the lady's story, by allowing for a final reconciliation between father and daughter, adheres to the requirements of both the captivity narrative and the sentimental romance, it invites the illusion that the narrative's competing elements—the wilderness versus civilization, agriculture versus hunting and commerce—have been similarly reconciled. But such is not the case. For once the lady's story is reinserted back into the frame of the Panther letter (with its own store of telling information), the drama reemerges a second time—this time, in the shape of a confrontation that denies even the possibility of reconciliation.

They key to this aspect of the drama has been identified by Leslie Fiedler, even though Fiedler has never actually commented on this particular text. In Fiedler's view, "The Panther Captivity" would be read in the shadow of Hannah Dustan, for him the avatar of all females who come unbidden into the "Dream Garden," signaling that "Second Paradise [which] was lost when White women entered the American woods that are forever hostile to them to scalp the woodland sleepers" (p. 108).[18] To be sure, the heroine here does hatchet to death (if not scalp) a "woodland sleeper." But the more significant pattern to which Fiedler is most directly pointing—that is, the white woman's intrusion into the wilderness paradise of the male—is also the very structure of the narrative: the opening story of masculine adventure in "the Western wilderness" gets interrupted by the embedded account of the "beautiful young LADY." And "the Western wilderness" that Panther and Camber had "imagined totally unfrequented" has become, instead, a white woman's cultivated garden. The turn of the lens that Fiedler's mythopoesis cannot accommodate, however, is the fact that while the lady's presence interrupts the young men's adventure, so too the appearance of the hunters necessarily disrupts—and finally destroys—the lady's wilderness idyll. In these oppositions reside the symbols for the ideological conflict which is at the heart of the narrative's fascination.

18. For the original source of the Hannah Dustan (also spelled Dustin and Duston) story, see n. 8.

Although the style of his letter establishes Abraham Panther as a gentleman, within its story he and his companion, Camber, function essentially as hunter-adventurers, much in the tradition of Daniel Boone. "Determining to penetrate the Western wilderness" for their amusement and curiosity, as Boone had first ventured into Kentucky, they boast that "our muskets contributed not a little to our amusement and support." Again like their prototype, they too encounter a "beautiful," "rich and fertile" landscape which affords them a "very comfortable living." Part of what comprises the beauty and contributes to their comfort is perhaps suggested by the decidedly sexual contours of the topography through which they move when approaching the lady's cave. After ascending a hill, the two men "passed round a large rock, then through a thicket of bushes at the end of which was a large opening." The quality of penetration implied here, however, leads not to further intimacy with the landscape, as it had for Boone, but, instead, to the discovery of a human female who has already appropriated that landscape for herself. And precisely at this point—with the lady's presence making all too palpable the unacknowledged male fantasy and, at the same time, annihilating its possibility—the male adventure narrative gives way to the female's. Little wonder that the two hunters later urge the lady to return with them to civilization. For what she has introduced into the wilderness is not only the fleshly symbolization of the male fantasy projection but, as well, a way of relating to that wilderness which is altogether different from the men's—and, potentially, a threat to it.

For her part, the lady's responses suggest that she, too, perceives something vaguely threatening in her visitors. Their first appearance causes her to scream and faint away; and, as Panther himself admits, it was only with some effort that he and his companion "convinced her of our peaceable dispositions." When the two men "proposed returning home," the lady is at first reluctant to accompany them. "At first she refused to quit her cave," Panther reports, "but after some persuasion she consented." The lady's history, of course, supplies ample justification for her reactions. The suddenness of the men's appearance evokes her father's earlier intrusion into "a little garden adjoining our house," the trysting place for her and her lover. Their very presence suggests the "several men" hired by her father "to search the country in pursuit of us." And her giant captor, whose cave contained a store of weapons, may also perhaps be divined in their shadow. That Panther is, in fact, appropriately to be associated with such figures is strongly implied by his decision to return to civilization with a selection of the cave's contents, "which," he informs his correspondent, "are now in my possession." These include "the bows, some arrows, the sword and one hatchet." Since the information serves in no obvious way to forward the action of the story, we must assume that the author of "The Panther Captivity" included it as a clue to his larger thematic concerns. At the very least,

Panther's decision to take possession of the weaponry reinforces his identification as a hunter, even as it marks him as another in the story's chain of males who either commands or wields the instruments of bloodshed.[19] The lady, by contrast, makes no further mention of using the cave's implements once she has dispatched its owner.

When, however reluctantly, the lady allows herself to be persuaded to quit her cave and return to civilization, she entrusts herself to the care of those who collect and carry weapons—weapons which may later be used by them in the very forest retreats where she had cultivated her yearly corn crop. In that act, one fantasy possibility is terminated and another restored. The woman's autonomous and harmonious accommodation to the landscape, based on agriculture, now ceases, and the wilderness once more becomes the exclusive domain of the male hunter.

Which brings us to my final turn of the lens.

Where Fiedler would ask us to see yet another mythic intrusion of the white woman into the wilderness "Dream Garden" of the male, and where Slotkin detects "the alternatives open to the American generations" (that is, whether "to be reconciled with Europe" and more civilized antecedents or "to acculturate, to adapt to the Indians' wilderness" [p. 259]), the feminist turn of the lens sees all this—and something more. From the lady's perspective, it is *she* who has suffered recurrent intrusions: her father invaded her trysting garden; his hired men pursued her and her lover into the woods in which they take refuge; the Indians violate that refuge and kill her lover; and, finally, her giant captor attempts to invade her person. Here, briefly, the pattern is broken. The lady for once dispatches and then displaces the intrusive male by using his weapons against him; and then, unlike him, settles into her own wilderness idyll. But this, too, is finally intruded upon—and terminated—by the appearance of the two hunter-adventurers. Male figures of greed and violence thus repeatedly breach, or attempt to breach, the precincts of the lady's various Dream Gardens, her romantic trysting place, her person, and, at the last, her wilderness abode.

Within that particular symbolic drama, the oppositions are not so much between civilized European associations and the Indianized wilderness as they are between different ways of being in and relating to the vast American landscape. At stake, in short, was the new nation's choice

19. I use the term "command" here so as to include the lady's father who, while never depicted with a weapon of his own in the narrative, is nonetheless at least indirectly responsible for their use: if he was, in fact, an Albany merchant, then his fur-trading investments certainly benefited from the activities of hunters; moreover, he hires (presumably armed) men to pursue his eloped daughter. The single exception to the chain of males wielding weaponry is, of course, the young clerk, of whom the lady is enamored; but, within the story, he seems less a character in his own right and more a pretext for precipitating the lady out into the wilderness.

of a defining fantasy. Was the republic to establish for itself the heroic mythology of the hunter (with its complex of associations from both the wilderness and the counting houses) or attempt some hybridized romance of the wilderness cultivator? Clearly, it could not be committed to both. For, in fantasy as in life, if the wilderness was to be possessed by the cultivators, then it could be no place for the hunters; and if by the hunters, then however appealing their gardens, the cultivators would nonetheless have to barred. Slotkin argues that "The Panther Captivity" "expresses . . . alternatives" but "chooses neither" (p. 259). But in fact it does choose, if only by making clear the vulnerability of one fantasy structure in the face of the other.

While historically the wilderness was given over, frontier by frontier, to the cultivators, in fantasy it remained the domain of the male hunter-adventurer (albeit stripped of his commercial interests). Daniel Boone emerged from his original incarnation as a brooding, meditative protector of the settlements to become Boone the isolate white male hunter, companion to the Indian, and, in Slotkin's words, "the version of the American myth that attained the widest currency" (p. 259).[20] Nonetheless, "The Panther Captivity" rivaled in popularity the proliferating Boone reprintings.[21] And, for a time, it held its audience precisely because it delineated what all the Boone narratives evaded—that is, the symbolic terms of the then competing fantasy possibilities. I emphasize *symbolic* here because I do not mean to suggest that "The Panther Captivity" defines agriculture as a female activity. Clearly, most Americans recognized that both hunting and farming were essentially masculine pursuits, the wooden plow of the eighteenth-century farmer being too heavy for most women to guide, though we know some did. The gender markings here are important not for the real-life behaviors they imply but for the different potential symbolic contents they might hold for contemporary audiences or with which they could effectively be invested. And, at the heart of those symbolic contents, as I suggested earlier, was the significance of women's increasing advance onto the frontier. For coincident with their arrival, agriculture began to displace hunting, both for sustenance and for peltry, as the means of survival.

20. For a discussion in the way in which the Norwich, Connecticut printer John Trumbull (n. 8) edited John Filson's original Boone narrative (n. 5) in such a way as to delete the original "passages of melancholy or philosophical meditation . . . leaving only the image of an Edenic Kentucky and an adventurous, uncontemplative Daniel Boone," see Slotkin, *Regeneration through Violence,* p. 324. Finally, as Slotkin points out, Trumbull's version outstripped Filson's in popularity, his "pirated version of Filson's Boone narrative . . . copied and reprinted in popular periodicals, pamphlets, and anthologies for the next fifty years" (p. 323).

21. "The Panther Captivity," sometimes in slightly altered versions, ran through twenty-five known editions, comprising pamphlets of sometimes less than a dozen pages. It is impossible to know how many more times it was reprinted in magazines, broadsides, and almanacs between its initial appearance in 1787 and its last known reprinting in 1814.

Gender as symbol and gender as authentic sex-role behavior are not unrelated, then, but they are not necessarily identical either. Thus, while "The Panther Captivity" undoubtedly helped ease contemporary anxieties by projecting a positive image of the woman in the wilderness, at the same time it retained that wilderness as the exclusive precinct of the white male hunter.

I have now finished turning my lens. Unlike the lady of "The Panther Captivity," I hope I have not *wholly* displaced Fiedler's and Slotkin's adventures with my own. Instead, it has been my aim to sharpen their focus where possible, refine their images where fuzzy, and correct their perspective when necessary. I have not, I remind my reader, changed cameras. In other words, I have not introduced any radically different methodology.[22] I have simply invested an already established approach with two questions which, up until now, have been the special concern of the feminist critic only: (1) How do contemporary women's lives, women's concerns, or concerns about women constitute part of the historical context for this work? and (2) What is the symbolic significance of gender in this text? If my reading has been at all persuasive, however, it should have persuaded all critics—feminist and nonfeminist alike—of the value of including such questions in their own investigations. When that happy day comes about, we shall see not only the triumph of feminist literary criticism but, more important, the exhilarating clarity of a lens opened at last to its widest possible angle of vision.

22. This is not to suggest that feminist literary criticism can generate no new methods or analytical procedures; indeed, I think this is already beginning to happen. Nonetheless, the emphasis of most work to date—at least in the United States—has been on refining and correcting the tools and methods already available.

On Female Identity and Writing by Women

Judith Kegan Gardiner

Men who are sure they have them fear other men are losing theirs; women with the authority of possession urge other women to seek and find. "Identity" is a central concept for much contemporary cultural and literary criticism, which, along with its even vaguer terminological twin, the "self," has become a cliché without becoming clear. The word "identity" is paradoxical in itself, meaning both sameness and distinctiveness, and its contradictions proliferate when it is applied to women. Carolyn Heilbrun's brave book, *Reinventing Womanhood,* inadvertently illustrates some current confusions about female identity and literature. For example, she claims that successful women are "male-identified" but that it is a "failure" for a "woman to take her identity from her man."[1] Women never form a self because they "need never undergo an identity crisis," yet they have an identity to lose: "the price of wifehood is abandonment of self" (pp. 103, 178). And fictional women are worse off than real ones: women's "search for identity has been even less successful within the world of fiction than outside it" (p. 72). Sandra Gilbert and Susan Gubar find "the woman's quest for self-definition" the underlying plot of nineteenth-century writing by women, while Elaine Showalter sees "self-discovery," "a search for identity," as the main theme of women's literature since 1920.[2] In a recent anthology of feminist criticism, one scholar claims that "a feminist critique . . . is helping women to

1. Carolyn G. Heilbrun, *Reinventing Womanhood* (New York, 1979), pp. 46, 40; all further references to this work will be included in the text.
2. Sandra M. Gilbert and Susan Gubar, *The Madwoman in the Attic: The Woman Writer and the Nineteenth-Century Literary Imagination* (New Haven, Conn., 1979), p. 76; Elaine Showalter, *A Literature of Their Own* (Princeton, N.J., 1977), p. 13.

recognize themselves"; a second says that fiction by women reveals "a fear of losing . . . one's unique identity"; a third believes "feminist poets" equate "consciousness of oppression; consciousness of identity."[3] Thus the quest for female identity seems to be a soap opera, endless and never advancing, that plays the matinées of women's souls. A central question of feminist literary criticism is, Who is there when a woman says, "I am"? I offer here some notes toward defining the answer to that question.

During the past few years, feminist critics have approached writing by women with an "abiding commitment to discover what, if anything, makes women's writing different from men's" and a tendency to feel that some significant differences do exist.[4] The most common answer is that women's experiences differ from men's in profound and regular ways. Critics using this approach find recurrent imagery and distinctive content in writing by women, for example, imagery of confinement and unsentimental descriptions of child care. The other main explanation of female difference posits a "female consciousness" that produces styles and structures innately different from those of the "masculine mind." The argument from experience is plausible but limited in its applications; the argument from a separate consciousness is subject to mystification and circular evidence. In both cases, scholars tend to list a few characteristics of writing by women without connecting or explaining them.

Feminist psychology can help us through this impasse: the concept of female identity provides a key to understanding the special qualities of contemporary writing by women. Because the concept of identity includes a number of variables, it can explain the diverse ways in which writing by women differs from writing by men more fully than can a theory that poses any single opposition as the explanation. In order to reach a theory of female identity, however, we must first adapt identity theory as it is now constituted by male theorists who assume a male paradigm for human experience. Erik Erikson is the architect of modern identity theory: his ideas are popularly cited, analytically endorsed, and

3. Margret Andersen, "Feminism as a Criterion of the Literary Critic"; Annis Pratt, "The New Feminist Criticism"; Suzanne Juhasz, "The Feminist Poet"; all in *Feminist Criticism,* ed. Cheryl L. Brown and Karen Olson (Metuchen, N.J., 1978), pp. 8, 11, 161.

4. Annette Kolodny, "Some Notes on Defining a 'Feminist Literary Criticism,' " *Critical Inquiry* 2 (Autumn 1975): 78.

Judith Kegan Gardiner is an associate professor of English and a member of the women's studies program at the University of Illinois at Chicago Circle, and author of *Craftsmanship in Context: The Development of Ben Jonson's Poetry* as well as articles on Robert Burton, feminist literary criticism, and contemporary women writers.

incorporated into the critical vocabulary. The only other identity theorist who has significantly influenced literary criticism is the psychoanalyst Heinz Lichtenstein, chiefly through the partisanship of critic Norman Holland. I review the work of these three men in order to establish what identity theory currently means to the literary community. Their theories do not apply specifically to women; there is no separate female identity theory. By extending feminist Nancy Chodorow's psychoanalytic insights about the differences between male and female personality structures into identity theory, however, we discover that for every aspect of identity as men define it, female experience varies from the male model.

I propose the preliminary metaphor "female identity is a process" for the most fundamental of these differences. The hypothesis of the processual nature of female identity illuminates diverse traits of writing by women, particularly its defiance of conventional generic boundaries and of conventional characterization. Female identity formation is dependent on the mother-daughter bond. Because of the primacy of this relationship, I posit my second metaphor, "the hero is her author's daughter."[5] This formulation indicates the way in which I explore literary identifications. The maternal metaphor of female authorship clarifies the woman writer's distinctive engagement with her characters and indicates an analogous relationship between woman reader and character. We thus return to women's "personal" closeness to literature from a new perspective. This perspective, in turn, helps us analyze some typical narrative strategies of women writers—the manipulation of identifications between narrator, author, and reader and the representation of memory.

Heilbrun and other critics refer to Erikson's theories about identity as cultural commonplaces relevant to women as writers and as literary characters. Twenty-five years ago, in *Identity and the Life Cycle,* Erikson popularized the idea of the "identity crisis" through which perplexed youth passes on its way to adulthood.[6] The resolution of the identity crisis leads to "final self-definition, to irreversible role patterns, and thus to commitments 'for life'" (p. 111). The person with a successfully achieved sense of individual identity feels unique, whole, and coherent, although in pathological cases identity formation may fail and the person suffer from "identity diffusion." Identity as Erikson conceives it is both formed and manifested through social relationships. The concept

5. I used a variant on this phrase in "The Heroine as Her Author's Daughter," in *Feminist Criticism,* ed. Brown and Olson, pp. 344–53.

6. See Erik Erikson, *Identity and the Life Cycle* (New York, 1959); all further references to this work will be included in the text. See also his *Childhood and Society* (New York, 1950); "Inner and Outer Space," *Daedalus* 93 (1964): 582–606; *Identity, Youth, and Crisis* (New York, 1968); and *Dimensions of a New Identity* (New York, 1974).

includes both a core configuration of personal character and one's consciousness of that configuration. The concept integrates "constitutional givens, idiosyncratic libidinal needs, favored capacities, significant identifications, effective defenses, successful sublimations, and consistent roles" (p. 116). Although Erikson believes that both sexes pass through the same stages on their way to maturity, he also believes in basic biological and psychosocial differences between the sexes. In his theory, the paradigmatic individual achieving a mature identity is male, whereas the female has a specialized role as childbearer. Her biological structure, her unique "inner space," is congruent with this role, and she seeks to fill and to protect this inner space rather than forge into outward accomplishments. Therefore a young woman spends adolescence looking for the man through whom she will fulfill herself, and the maturational stages of identity and intimacy are conflated for her.

Erikson's terms and concepts are respected by other analysts, and they are often invoked by writers as well. Lichtenstein's more idiosyncratic theories on "human identity" have been less widely accepted by the analytic community, but they have had a significant impact on recent literary criticism. Lichtenstein believes that each child very early forms a "primary identity" in response to the expectations implicitly expressed by its first caretaker, usually the mother. This core identity sets the pattern according to which the person thereafter relates to other people and to the world. "Out of the infinite potentialities within the human infant, the specific stimulus emanating from the individual mother 're-leases' one and only one concrete way of being this organism, this instrument."[7] The self is defined by "the total potential range of all possible variations of the individual which are compatible" with its primary identity, and a person may risk death rather than give up identity (p. 119).

According to Lichtenstein, society depends on the stable identities of individuals. When the cultural storehouse of available roles fails to fit the identity themes of enough people, the mismatched persons may suffer identity crises and the culture suffer catastrophic change. Thus, though everyone has an invariant, early formed identity, it is nonetheless potentially fragile: "loss of identity is a specifically human danger, and maintenance of identity a specifically human necessity" (p. 77). Lichtenstein's frequent use of the adjective "human" implies that identity is an existential and moral imperative as well as a psychologically descriptive category. It also implies that his concept works equally well for all of humanity and is therefore a genderless generic. Lichtenstein believes that both sexes form their primary identities similarly, but in

7. Heinz Lichtenstein, *The Dilemma of Human Identity* (New York, 1977), p. 78; all further references to this work will be included in the text. Some criticisms of Lichtenstein's concepts appear in D. W. Winnicott, *Playing and Reality* (New York, 1971), pp. 79–80, and Sander Abend, "Problems of Identity," *Psychoanalytic Quarterly* 43 (1974): 613.

fact he, too, assumes a male paradigm. He mentions female development only rarely, and then it obtrudes as exceptional to the male norm.

Holland, one of the most influential of psychoanalytic literary critics, makes Lichtenstein's identity theory the cornerstone of his recent criticism. Holland claims his "scientific" literary criticism allows us to "talk rigorously about human uniqueness."[8] Each person has a distinctive identity "theme," like a musical theme with variations. "Identity refers to the whole pattern of sameness within change which is a human life. . . . There remains a continuing me who is the style that permeates all those changes" (p. 452). Using this theory, the critic can explain "everything a person does," because an author's writings exhibit the same identity theme as other forms of behavior, like dreams, habits, speech, and sexual acts. The critic can analyze an author in the same way that one explicates a literary text, looking for a single unifying theme. Like each author, each reader has a unique identity theme and encounters every text only in ways congruent with this theme. Holland believes that this theory unlocks the "personal role" in reading, writing, teaching, popular arts, political choice, jokes, and psychological experience. Each self possesses and competes with the text, using what it wants and needs, discarding, even distorting, the rest. The identity themes of the author and author's text rarely overlap with those of the reader and reader's text. Therefore the fundamental critical problem is achieving common ground among the diverse personal re-creations of any text. In some ways, this literary theory echoes popular humanistic psychology in suggesting that if you do your thing and I do mine, we may be able to savor without pressure the rare pleasures of congruence.

Neither Holland, Lichtenstein, nor Erikson uses gender as a significant variable in his basic theory; none offers a theory of female identity as distinct from male identity. Their models may help us understand aspects of personality and of writing that are similar for the two sexes, but they give us no help with the special understanding of female identity. Recently feminist theorists have evolved reasonable and comprehensive psychoanalytic explanations of gender difference. Chodorow's explanation of personality differences between the sexes has gained widespread acceptance. She seeks to "move beyond descriptive generalizations about sexism, patriarchy, or male supremacy to analysis of how sexual asymmetry and inequality are constituted, reproduced, and changed." Such an analysis, she believes, must focus on "social structurally induced psychological processes" rather than on biol-

---

8. Norman N. Holland, "Human Identity," *Critical Inquiry* 4 (Spring 1978): 451; all further references to this essay will be included in the text. See also his *Poems in Persons* (New York, 1973); *Five Readers Reading* (New Haven, Conn., 1975); "Unity Identity Text Self," *PMLA* 90 (1975): 813–22; "Literary Interpretation and Three Phases of Psychoanalysis," *Critical Inquiry* 3 (Winter 1976): 221–33; "Identity," *Language and Society* 10 (1977): 199–209; and "Why Ellen Laughed," *Critical Inquiry* 7 (Winter 1980): 345–71.

ogy or intentional role training.[9] Being social rather than biological, her analysis implies that personality differences between the sexes are historically variable. Because she does not formulate her explanation of these differences in terms of identity theories which ignore women, her insights may contribute usefully to a theory of female identity pertinent to the analysis of writing by women.

Chodorow argues that a boy defines himself as a male negatively—by differentiation from his first caretaker, the mother. He achieves autonomy as he outgrows the mother-child symbiosis, and his Oedipus complex seals his separation from the mother and his adoption of the role of the father. Thereafter he perceives himself as active, independent, individual, and valued by his family and by society. Thus Chodorow's model of male personality corresponds roughly to Lichtenstein's and Holland's model of the person of either sex who has developed a primary identity.

According to Chodorow, girls' personalities take shape differently. First, a girl forms her gender identity positively, in becoming like the mother with whom she begins life in a symbiotic merger. Second, she must develop in such a way that she can pleasurably re-create the mother-infant symbiosis when she herself becomes a mother. As a result, women develop capacities for nurturance, dependence, and empathy more easily than men do and are less threatened by these qualities, whereas independence and autonomy are typically harder for women to attain. Throughout women's lives, the self is defined through social relationships; issues of fusion and merger of the self with others are significant, and ego and body boundaries remain flexible.

The male identity theorists assume that stability and constancy are desirable goals for human personality. Both Erikson and Lichtenstein occasionally describe identity as an "evolving configuration," but they see the *process* of identity formation as a developmental *progress* toward the achievement of a desired product, the autonomous individual, the paradigm for which is male.[10] Erikson describes this progress through distinct stages that have a biological base. In contrast, Chodorow portrays female personality as relational and fluidly defined, starting with infancy and continuing throughout womanhood. Her argument is sociological and historical, not biological, and she does not see female personality formation as a predetermined progress. She believes women are socialized so that mothers can regress to earlier stages of development in the service of maternal nurturance. Thus her model of female personality formation is cyclical as well as progressive. I extend her insights into identity theory with the formula "female identity is a pro-

9. Nancy Chodorow, *The Reproduction of Mothering* (Berkeley, 1978), pp. 6–7. See also "Feminism and Difference," *Socialist Review* 46 (July–Aug. 1979): 51–69. For one extension of Chodorow's ideas, see Sara Ruddick, "Maternal Thinking," *Feminist Studies* 6 (Summer 1980): 342–67.

10. See Erikson, *Identity and the Life Cycle*, p. 116.

cess." Thus I picture female identity as typically less fixed, less unitary, and more flexible than male individuality, both in its primary core and in the entire maturational complex developed from this core.[11] These traits have far-reaching consequences for the distinctive nature of writing by women.

In current usage, many aspects of this maturational complex bear confusingly similar labels. Before we can proceed to develop a female identity theory and to apply it to writing by women, we must clarify these terms, showing the differences by gender within each concept. The most common terms for which we find a significant difference by gender are primary identity, gender identity, infantile identification, social role, the identity crisis, and self-concept. The first five of these terms correspond approximately to the developmental sequence of individual identity, according to the male identity theorists. Primary identity is a hypothesis about one's permanent essence or way of being. It is Lichtenstein's central concept, and he places its formation in early infancy. Gender identity is established next. It means knowing to which sex one is socially assigned. This ascription is typically stable and irreversible by the age of three, although the maintenance of gender identity appears to be more problematic for boys than for girls.[12] Female infantile identifications seem more problematic than male ones. In classical psychoanalytic theory, a boy's Oedipal phase is considered resolved when he identifies with his father, becoming like him in order to have what the father has, that is, adult power and sexual access to women like his mother. Classical theory has been less definitive about how girls identify with their parents. Chodorow posits an oscillating triangular relationship between the little girl, her mother, and her father.

Thus primary identity, gender identity, and infantile identification are all components of adult identity that form early in childhood. However, the process of identity formation continues later. Children and adolescents learn various social roles and group identifications around which their sense of their identity, that is, their self-concept, con-

11. The declaration that "female identity is a process" necessitates an immediate theoretical proviso against binary polarization. Male identity is not a static product either. The analogy of physical difference may make clearer the scope of the psychological differences discussed here: much of the time we can tell whether a face in a photograph belongs to a man or to a woman—but we would be hard pressed to tabulate our clues in terms of distinctive characteristics. My discussion attempts to describe some of the "faces" of female identity, especially as they express themselves in contemporary writing by women. My generalizations are derived principally from the work of heterosexual, white, middle-class, English-speaking women. Other patterns may be more salient for women of other cultures.

12. See John Money and Anke A. Ehrhardt, *Man and Woman, Boy and Girl* (Baltimore, 1972); Mabel Blake Cohen, "Personal Identity and Sexual Identity," in *Psychoanalysis and Women,* ed. Jean Baker Miller (Baltimore, 1973), pp. 156–82; Frank A. Beach, ed., *Human Sexuality in Four Perspectives* (Baltimore, 1977); Helen Block Lewis, "Gender Identity," *Bulletin of the Menninger Clinic* 43 (1979): 145–60; and Ethyl Spector Person, "Sexuality as the Mainstay of Identity: Psychoanalytic Perspectives," *Signs* 5 (Summer 1980): 605–30.

solidates. These social roles are highly polarized by gender, with a broader variety of acceptable options available to boys than to girls. The two main roles available to women are those of wife and of mother. They assume occupational status as well as denoting personal relationships. These roles then become confused and conflated with the girl's infantile identification with her mother, since being properly female in a society usually involves both doing the sorts of things mother does and being the sort of woman she is. Moreover, female roles often imply the possession of specific personality traits, like passivity and nurturance, that are deemed appropriate for their smooth functioning.[13] For a boy, the adolescent identity crisis tests the accreted components of his individual identity. At its conclusion, he accepts a place in his society roughly congruent with society's view of him. The girl, however, achieves her socially accepted roles through marriage and motherhood, social and biological events that can occur independently of a personal identity crisis and that do not require its resolution.

To summarize, female identity is a process, and primary identity for women is more flexible and relational than for men. Female gender identity is more stable than male gender identity. Female infantile identifications are less predictable than male ones. Female social roles are more rigid and less varied than men's. And the female counterpart of the male identity crisis may occur more diffusely, at a different stage, or not at all. Cumulatively, we see a complex interplay between women's experiences of identity and men's paradigms for the human experience. It is not surprising, therefore, that the area of self-concept is especially troubled for women and that contemporary writing by women reflects these dissonances.

Twentieth-century women writers express the experience of their own identity in what and how they write, often with a sense of urgency and excitement in the communication of truths just understood. Often they communicate a consciousness of their identity through paradoxes of sameness and difference—from other women, especially their mothers; from men; and from social injunctions for what women should be, including those inscribed in the literary canon.

13. The confusing terms "male-identified" and "woman-identified" woman may be mentioned at this point. These terms are used in political controversy and in literary criticism but not in analytic theory. They are not parallel terms, and there are no comparable names for men. Both the male-identified and the woman-identified woman know that they are women. In radical feminist ideology, the woman-identified woman has fought patriarchal cultural conditioning so that she values herself and is loyal to other women. In contrast, male-identified is a term of abuse applied to one's outgrown past or to other women who cast their "social, political, and intellectual allegiances with men" (Adrienne Rich, "Compulsory Heterosexuality and Lesbian Existence," *Signs* 5 [Summer 1980]: 645). Radical feminist thought differs from Freudian orthodoxy in seeing the male-identified woman as heterosexual and the properly woman-identified woman as consciously lesbian. See Rich, "Compulsory Heterosexuality," p. 659; Heilbrun, *Reinventing Womanhood,* p. 202; and Mary Daly *Gyn/Ecology* (Boston, 1978).

The formulation that female identity is a process stresses the fluid and flexible aspects of women's primary identities. One reflection of this fluidity is that women's writing often does not conform to the generic prescriptions of the male canon. Recent scholars conclude that autobiographies by women tend to be less linear, unified, and chronological than men's autobiographies.[14] Women's novels are often called autobiographical, women's autobiographies, novelistic—like Mary McCarthy's *Memories of a Catholic Girlhood* or Maxine Hong Kingston's *Memoirs of a Woman Warrior.* Because of the continual crossing of self and other, women's writing may blur the public and private and defy completion. Thus we have writers like Dorothy Richardson and Anaïs Nin, whose lives, journals, letters, and fiction become nearly coterminous. Another manifestation of this tendency is the autobiographical critical essay as practiced by Virginia Woolf, Adrienne Rich, Louise Bernikow, and Carolyn Heilbrun. Many women critics tell women readers how to read women writers; and they tell women writers how to write for women readers. The implied relationship between the self and what one reads and writes is personal and intense. Margaret Drabble generalizes from her response to Doris Lessing, the "mother and seer" who reports in new ways about the lives of women, that "most of us read books with this question in our mind: what does this say about my life?"[15]

Feminist literary historians are now defining the contribution of women to modernism, concentrating on the fluidity and interiority of Woolf, Richardson, and Gertrude Stein. Recent scholarship chronicles the breakdown in twentieth-century literature of the integrated characters in nineteenth-century fiction. While this is true of fiction by both men and women, male fiction often splits characters into disjunct fragments, while female characters in novels by women tend to dissolve and merge into each other. The model of the integrated individual was predominantly male, and women writers show that this model of characterization is inappropriate to their experience. Heilbrun complains about the woman writer who "projects upon a male character the identity and experience for which she searches" (p. 73). She says that women novelists assume "only a man can stand for the full range of human experience, moving through action and quest to achievement or failure" (p. 88). Her model of the "full range of human experience," however, is the linear male quest, and since this model is hardly "full," women do not always fill it. Not that women's imaginations fail; rather, women writers re-create female experience in different forms.[16] This would seem to be a direct result of their different developmental experience.

14. See Heilbrun, *Reinventing Womanhood,* p. 134, and Estelle C. Jelinek, *Women's Autobiographies* (Bloomington, Ind., 1980).

15. Margaret Drabble, *Saturday Review,* 27 May 1978, pp. 54–56.

16. E.g., Joanna Russ' science fiction *The Female Man* (New York, 1975) demonstrates how the female self is shaped by its times and circumstances by making all the main characters avatars of one woman, superimposed on one another in alternate futures and

Male identity theorists, we have seen, believe that an individual's primary identity, formed in early childhood, is enacted and confirmed through infantile identifications and the acquisition of appropriate social roles. In this male paradigm, the boy becomes a separate, autonomous individual, like his father. In Chodorow's theory, the fluid and processual nature of female personality arises specifically from the mother's relationship with her daughter. The daughter acquires empathy and the capacity for symbiotic merger through her infantile identification with her mother. Discussions of female identity thus inevitably return to the special nature of the mother-daughter bond. The current, rapidly proliferating literature about motherhood stresses that the daughter's identification with and separation from the mother is crucial to the daughter's mature female identity. Often there is a conflict between a "personal identification" with the admirable aspects of the mother and a rejection of "positional identification" with the mother as victim.[17] This conflict is reinforced in terms of roles: the mother as individually experienced is separated both from the ideally loving mother and from the devalued occupation of motherhood. Current writing by women reflects this emphasis on the mother-daughter relationship.[18]

According to Chodorow, the young girl must identify with her mother and also separate from her. To mother maturely, a woman must develop an identity sufficiently flexible that she can merge empathically with her child and still retain an adult sense of herself as nurturing yet independent. This maternal stage of female identity bears special relevance to women's empathic literary identifications, particularly the author's relationship to her character, for which I have proposed the analogy, "the hero is her author's daughter." Psychoanalytic theorists distinguish superficial transient adult identifications, which include literary identifications, from the infantile identifications with parental figures that structure the child's mind. Nonetheless, literary identifications apparently derive some of their undoubted power from analogy to earlier

---

presents, like a multiply exposed film. These characters are not split personalities; rather, they are potential parts of a yet unformed and unmelded whole woman. The freedom of full selfhood lies in the future.

17. The distinction between personal and positional identifications is made by Philip Slater in *Footholds*, ed. Wendy Slater Palmer (New York, 1977), pp. 20–27.

18. Whereas male writers' stereotypes of women polarize around sexual access— women are either virgins or whores—women stereotype their male characters around access to power—they are either wimps or brutes. Women's stereotypes of men seem, however, to be somewhat removed from the most intimate of female fears, that is, from direct threats to women's primary identities and self-concepts. Thus the most disturbing villain in recent women's fiction is not the selfish or oppressive male but instead the bad mother. This mother-villain is so frightening because she is what the daughter fears to become and what her infantile identifications predispose her to become. One way in which the author may dispose of this fear is by rendering the mother so repulsive or ridiculous that the reader must reject her as her fictional daughter does. Another tactic is for the author to kill the mother in the course of the narrative. See my "A Wake for Mother," *Feminist Studies* 4 (June 1978): 145–65.

mental states. David Beres and Jacob Arlow link literary identifications with Heinz Kohut's description of empathy as "vicarious introspection."[19]

I suggest that women writers and readers tend to approach texts differently from men. Instead of guessing at and corroborating a stable identity pattern in a text or author, as Holland does, we can approach a text with the hypothesis that its female author is engaged in a process of testing and defining various aspects of identity chosen from many imaginative possibilities. That is, the woman writer uses her text, particularly one centering on a female hero, as part of a continuing process involving her own self-definition and her empathic identification with her character. Thus the text and its female hero begin as narcissistic extensions of the author. The author exercises magical control over her character, creating her from representations of herself and her ideals. Yet she must allow her text a limited autonomy. The character's "taking on a life of her own" can mean that the author shapes her character according to literary convention and social reality as well as according to projections of her representations of herself. The author judges how such a character would behave in the settings the author provides her, what would be an exciting way of revealing the character's secrets to the reader, and so on. As a result, novels by women often shift through first, second, and third persons and into reverse.[20] Thus the author may define herself through the text while creating her female hero. This can be a positive, therapeutic relationship, like learning to be a mother, that is, learning to experience oneself as one's own cared-for child and as one's own caring mother while simultaneously learning to experience one's creation as other, as separate from the self.

Presumably the woman reader goes through a somewhat analogous process in her empathic identifications, identifying particularly with female characters closely bonded to their authors. Often encouraged by the author's shifting persons and perspectives, the reader shifts her empathic identifications and her sense of immersion in and separation from the text as she reads. Both writer and reader can relate to the text as

19. See David Beres and Jacob Arlow, "Fantasy and Identification in Empathy," *Psychoanalytic Quarterly* 43 (1974): 33 and 46; Heinz Kohut, "Introspection, Empathy, and Psychoanalysis" (1957) and "Creativeness, Charisma, Group Psychology" (1976), in *The Search for the Self,* ed. Paul H. Ornstein, 2 vols. (New York, 1978), 1:205–32, 2:793–843. Psychoanalytic studies of literary identification include Roy R. Grinker, "On Identification," *International Journal of Psychoanalysis* 38 (1957): 379–90; Stanley A. Leavy, "John Keats' Psychology of Creative Imagination," *Psychoanalytic Quarterly* 39 (1970): 173–97. See also Holland, *The Dynamics of Literary Response* (New York, 1968); Murray M. Schwartz, "Where Is Literature?" *College English* 36 (1975): 736–65; Arthur F. Marotti, "Countertransference, the Communication Process, and the Dimensions of Psychoanalytic Criticism," *Critical Inquiry* 4 (Spring 1978): 471–89.

20. Sometimes the clutch slips. For example, Joan Didion says she discovered that her authorial voice had changed into that of another character while she was writing *A Book of Common Prayer;* see Sara Davidson, "A Visit with Joan Didion," *New York Times Book Review,* 3 April 1977, p. 37.

though it were a person with whom one might alternatively be merged empathically or from whom one might be separated and individuated. The complex composite of female identity shimmers between the figure and the ground of character. Many recent women's novels portray the growth of women's self-awareness in the characters' minds and also work to create that awareness. Through the relationship between the narrator and the reader, such fictions re-create the ambivalent experiences of ego violation and mutual identification that occur between mother and daughter. The woman writer allies herself intimately with her female reader through this identification. Together they explore what is public and what is private, what they reject and what they reflect.

Some examples of how these concepts work in twentieth-century writing by women will be helpful. The works of Jean Rhys and Doris Lessing provide good illustrations of two ways in which women writers control empathic identification: by a defensive narrative strategy and by the representation of memory. Jean Rhys' heroes criticize the active male quest through their submissiveness. They repel many readers by their passivity, particularly since they are always considered autobiographical. These characters seem to reflect an oppressed, early stage of female self-awareness. They are poor, improvident, economically dependent, sexually humiliated. They drink. They are losing their looks. They want love they never get. Yet these sad women are not "failures of imagination"; they are complex triumphs in the management of readers' feelings. Although we readers do not want to be like these women, we are forced to recognize that we are or could be like them in similar circumstances. We become angry, then, both at the women and at their oppression. Rhys never lets us identify with the oppressors, and she always clearly analyzes the forces that demean her heroes. We are constantly seeing her characters from the outside, as "them," then from the inside, as "us." The conventional distinction between good and bad women makes no sense. Bitter irony and self-hatred turn into compassion. The author who creates these characters never voices her own anger, yet we become enraged at the patriarchy and sympathetic to its victims of both sexes, reassured because we know that the author is herself a survivor, in control of her prose and of her heroes' destinies as none of them are. Thus as readers we oscillate between transient empathic identifications with these characters and defenses against them, defining ourselves through them in the process.

Many women writers feel that women remember what men choose to forget. If memory operates in the service of identity maintenance differently in the two sexes, it will appear differently in literature by women—both in the representation of characters' mental processes and in the representation of the narrative process itself.[21] In *The Golden*

21. I speculate that male memory operates differently from female memory, at least in terms of the memory of emotional states. If empathy is "vicarious introspection," then

Notebook, Doris Lessing uses memory to demonstrate gender difference in self-concept. Anna's effort to retain her memories despite the lack of validation by others is crucial to the construction of her self-concept and also to the construction of the golden notebook, her synthetic literary accomplishment. Her memory keeps her personality intact and saves her from madness. She controls her dreams so that instead of "making up stories about life," she goes "back and look[s] at scenes from my life, . . . touching for reassurance. . . . I had to 'name' the frightening things, . . . making past events harmless, by naming them, but making sure they were still there."[22] The repetitive, overlapping style of the novel imitates this process of remembering, as the narrator writes and reads herself, creating and discarding partial and alternative selves. The reassurance that the past and therefore her self are "still there" allows her to stop splitting herself up into four notebooks and to create one whole one, which is projected as a potential for the future rather than actualized in the text.

Finally, the study of female identity development can illuminate one other, and recently much-discussed, aspect of twentieth-century women's writing: androgyny. Women writers often draw characters in whom traditionally male and female attributes of personality form a real and infrangible union. Such deliberate literary androgyny does not reflect authorial confusion about gender identity. As we have seen, boys have more difficulty than girls in acquiring gender identity, and men exhibit more disturbances in gender identity than do women. The problems of female identity presented in women's poetry and prose are rarely difficulties in knowing one's gender; more frequently, they are difficulties in learning how to respond to social rules for what being female means in our culture.

In a male-dominated society, being a man means not being like a woman. As a result, the behavior considered appropriate to each gender becomes severely restricted and polarized. I have postulated that the primary identities of women remain relational throughout life, and girls form the gender identity that defines them as women easily, securely, and permanently. Since women do not, like men, experience gender itself as a problem, social attempts to make it a problem for them may cause confusion and anxiety. Many pioneering works of female modernism, like those of Woolf and Stein, create fictional universes which question patriarchal assumptions about the conformity between

---

memory may be seen as empathic introspection with one's past self. According to this thesis, men maintain a coherent sense of themselves by repression; that is, they change over time while suppressing self-knowledge of change. With less repression, women may be more conscious of change and hence more vulnerable to a feeling of identity loss or to the diminishing of self-concept without necessarily changing more. This hypothesis is congruent with Freud's view that Oedipal repression is more massive and total in boys than in girls.

22. Doris Lessing, *The Golden Notebook* (New York, 1973), p. 616.

gender ascription and other aspects of personality. Novels as different as Djuna Barnes' *Nightwood* and Carson McCuller's *The Heart Is a Lonely Hunter* use transvestite men to indicate how irrelevant conventions about gender are to human desire. In Jane Bowles' *Two Serious Women,* the affectionate, conventional wife Mrs. Copperfield finds peace of mind with a girl prostitute while the ascetic Miss Goering finds hers by picking up seedy men. Like Stein, Bowles shocks the reader by a deliberate flatness of tone, a refusal to ascribe motives or to psychologize her characters' alienation from the gender conventions of their culture.

The antiromantic treatment of heterosexuality in twentieth-century women's writing follows from this contrast between secure gender identity and a denial of cultural truisms for appropriate sexual emotions and behavior. The conventional old plots of heterosexual seduction and betrayal play a minimal role in contemporary women's fiction. Women in recent novels do not fear loss of their lovers, nor do they seriously resent male infidelity. The husband who goes off with another woman leaves his wife poorer but freer. The sexually active women heroes are not guilty, nor do they find sexual love redemptive. At best it offers women temporary warmth and sensual exhilaration; more often, it confuses women and alienates them from themselves.

A woman's sense of her gender, her sexuality, and her body may assume a different, perhaps a more prominent, shape in her conception of her self than these factors would for a man. Women are encouraged to judge their inner selves through their external physical appearance and to equate the two. At the same time, they are taught to create socially approved images of themselves by manipulating their dress, speech, and behavior. "Our identities can no more be kept separate from how our bodies look than they can be kept separate from the shadow selves of the female stereotype," according to philosopher Sandra Bartky, who defines "female narcissism" as a woman's alienated "infatuation with an inferiorized body."[23] Women writers interpret this alienation between outer and inner selves in various ways and thus give some distinctive turns to old verities about appearance and reality.

* * *

Incorporating feminist psychoanalytic insights, the concept of female identity shows us how female experience is transformed into female consciousness, often in reaction to male paradigms for female experience. The concept of female identity provides us with a sophisticated and multivariant theoretical apparatus with which to explain differences between writing by women and by men in matters of both form

---

23. Sandra Lee Bartky, "On Psychological Oppression," in *Philosophy and Women,* ed. Sharon Bishop and Marjorie Weinzweig (Belmont, Calif., 1979), pp. 41, 34, 38.

and content. "Female identity is a process," and writing by women engages us in this process as the female self seeks to define itself in the experience of creating art. "The hero is her author's daughter": bonds between women structure the deepest layers of female personality and establish the patterns to which literary identifications are analogous. Contemporary women's literature promises that a sense of full, valued, and congruent female identity may form in the continuing process of give and take that re-creates both self and other in a supportive community of women. This creation of a valid and communicable female experience through art is a collective enterprise. And we are its collaborative critics.

Costumes of the Mind: Transvestism as Metaphor in Modern Literature

Sandra M. Gilbert

> What is the current that makes machinery, that makes it crackle, what is the current that presents a long line and a necessary waist. What is this current.
>
> What is the wind, what is it.
>
> Where is the serene length, it is there and a dark place is not a dark place, only a white and red are black, only a yellow and green are blue, a pink is scarlet, a bow is every color. A line distinguishes it. A line just distinguishes it.
>
> —GERTRUDE STEIN, "A Long Dress"[1]

"There is much to support the view that it is clothes that wear us and not we them," declared Virginia Woolf in *Orlando* (1928), adding that "we may make them take the mould of arm or breast, but [clothes] mould our hearts, our brains, our tongues to their liking."[2] In the same year, however, W. B. Yeats published a collection of poems that included a very different, and far more famous, statement about costume: "An aged man is but a paltry thing, / A tattered coat upon a stick, unless / Soul clap its hands and sing, and louder sing, / For every tatter in its mortal dress." Where Woolf's view of clothing implied that costume is inseparable from identity—indeed, that costume creates identity—Yeats' metaphor, repeated often throughout his career, posits a heart's truth which stands apart from false costumes. For Woolf, we are what we wear, but for

---

1. "A Long Dress," *Tender Buttons: Selected Writings of Gertrude Stein* (New York, 1972), p. 467.

2. Virginia Woolf, *Orlando* (New York, 1928), p. 188.

Yeats, we may, like Lear, have to undo the last button of what we wear in order to dis-cover and more truly re-cover what we are.

It is not surprising that literary men and women like Yeats and Woolf should have speculated on the significance of costume, for both were living in an era when the Industrial Revolution had produced a corresponding revolution in what we have come to call "fashion." Though there has always been a tradition of theatricality associated with the expensive clothing of aristocrats and wealthy merchants as well as a long literary tradition exploring the implications of transvestism, until the middle or late nineteenth century most people wore what were essentially uniforms: garments denoting the one form or single shape to which each individual's life was confined by birth, by circumstance, by custom, by decree. Thus the widow's weeds, the peasant's Sunday embroidery, the governess' sombre gown, the servant's apron, and the child's smock were signs of class, age, and occupation as fated and inescapable as the judge's robes, the sergeant's stripes, and the nun's habit.[3]

With the advent of the spinning jenny and the sewing machine, common men and women, along with uncommon individuals from Byron to Baudelaire, began to experience a new vision of the kinds of costumes available to them and, as a corollary to that vision, a heightened awareness of the theatrical nature of clothing itself.[4] By 1833 Thomas Carlyle was writing obsessively about the mystical significance of tailoring, and by the 1890s *fin de siècle* literary circles were dominated by poets who defined themselves at least in part as dandies, poets whose art in-

3. Lawrence Langner, in *The Importance of Wearing Clothes* (New York, 1959), notes that in ancient Greece "women were not permitted . . . to wear more than three garments at a time. In Rome . . . the law restricted peasants to one color, officers to two, commanders to three. . . . In the reign of Charles IX of France, the ornamentation of clothing was regulated according to the rank of the wearer, and most of these laws remained in force until the French Revolution. In England Henry VIII insisted that a countess must wear a train both before and behind, while those below her in rank might not have this distinction" (p. 179).

4. The first of Yeats' visionary "Fragments," though probably intended as a comment on the Industrial Revolution, mythologizes the transformative power of the spinning jenny: "Locke sank into a swoon; / The Garden died; / God took the spinning-jenny / Out of his side" (*The Collected Poems of W. B. Yeats* [New York, 1955], p. 211).

Sandra M. Gilbert, professor of English at the University of California at Davis, is the author of *Acts of Attention: The Poems of D. H. Lawrence* and *In the Fourth World* and coauthor, with Susan Gubar, of *The Madwoman in the Attic: The Woman Writer and the Nineteenth-Century Literary Imagination*.

creasingly concerned itself with style in every sense of the word. In our own century that literary concern with costume has, of course, continued, accompanying and in a sense commenting on the rise and fall of hemlines and governments, houses of fashion and fashions of thought.

There is a striking difference, however, between the ways female and male modernists define and describe literal or figurative costumes. Balancing self against mask, true garment against false costume, Yeats articulates a perception of himself and his place in society that most other male modernists share, even those who experiment more radically with costume as metaphor. But female modernists like Woolf, together with their post-modernist heirs, imagine costumes of the mind with much greater irony and ambiguity, in part because women's clothing is more closely connected with the pressures and oppressions of gender and in part because women have far more to gain from the identification of costume with self or gender. Because clothing powerfully defines sex roles, both overt and covert fantasies of transvestism are often associated with the intensified clothes consciousness expressed by these writers. But although such imagery is crucially important in works by Joyce, Lawrence, and Eliot on the one hand, and in works by Barnes, Woolf, and H. D. on the other, it functions very differently for male modernists from the way it operates for feminist modernists.

Literary men, working variations upon the traditional dichotomy of appearance and reality, often oppose false costumes to true clothing. Sometimes, they oppose costume (seen as false or artificial) to nakedness (which is true, "natural," and the equivalent of a suitable garment or guise). Frequently, moreover, they see false costumes as unsexed or wrongly sexed, transvestite travesties, while true costumes are properly sexed. In defining such polarities, all are elaborating a deeply conservative vision of society both as it is and as it should be, working, that is, on the assumption that the sociopolitical world should be hierarchical, orderly, stylized. Often, indeed, in their anxiety about the vertiginous freedom offered by an age of changing clothes, these men seem nostalgic for the old days of uniforms, and so they use costumes in poems and novels in part to abuse them. Even more important, their obsessive use of sex-connected costumes suggests that for most male modernists the hierarchical order of society is and should be a pattern based upon gender distinctions, since the ultimate reality is in their view the truth of gender, a truth embodied or clothed in cultural paradigms which all these writers see as both absolute and Platonically ideal and which the most prominent among them—Joyce, Lawrence, Yeats, Eliot— continually seek to revive.

The feminist counterparts of these men, however, not only regard all clothing as costume, they also define all costume as false. Yet they don't oppose false costume to "true" nakedness, for to most of these writers that fundamental sexual self for which, say, Yeats uses nakedness as a metaphor is itself merely another costume. Thus where even the most theatrical male modernists differentiate between masks and selves, false costumes and true garments, most female modernists and their successors do not. On the contrary, many literary women from Woolf to Plath see what literary men call "selves" as costumes and costumes as "selves," in a witty revision of male costume metaphors that can be traced back to such nineteenth-century foremothers as Charlotte Brontë and Emily Dickinson. Moreover, just as male modernist costume imagery is profoundly conservative, feminist modernist costume imagery is radically revisionary in a political as well as a literary sense, for it implies that no one, male or female, can or should be confined to a uni-form, a single form or self. On the contrary; where so many twentieth-century men have sought to outline the enduring, gender-connected myths behind history, many twentieth-century women have struggled—sometimes exuberantly, sometimes anxiously—to define a gender-free reality behind or beneath myth, an ontological essence so pure, so free that "it" can "inhabit" any self, any costume. For the male modernist, in other words, gender is most often an ultimate reality, while for the female modernist an ultimate reality exists only if one journeys beyond gender.

I want to illustrate these points by considering both well-known male modernist transvestite fantasies and famous feminist fantasies which employ similar themes and plot devices but toward very different ends. One of the most dramatic transvestite episodes in modern literature, for example, appears in the Nighttown episode at the heart of Joyce's *Ulysses.* Here Leopold Bloom encounters a Circe named Bella Cohen, the whorehouse madam, who turns herself into a male named Bello and transforms Bloom first into a female, then into a pig, and finally into an elaborately costumed "charming soubrette." Significantly, it is the last of these transformations, the one depending upon costume, which is the seal of Bloom's humiliation, just as Bello's dreadful ascendancy is indicated by her/his clothing. "With bobbed hair, . . . fat moustache rings, . . . alpine hat . . . and breeches," Bello becomes a grotesque parody of masculinized female mastery, what she/he calls "petticoat government," hunting and beating the tremblingly masochistic Bloom.[5] Even more ludicrous clothing defines Bloom's disgrace. Pointing to the whores, Bello growls that "as they are now, so will you be, wigged, singed, perfumesprayed, ricepowdered, with smoothshaven armpits. Tape measurements will be taken next your skin. You will be laced with cruel force into vicelike corsets . . . to the diamond trimmed pelvis . . . while your figure, plumper than when at large, will be restrained in nettight frocks, pretty two ounce petticoats, and fringes . . ." (p. 523).

---

5. James Joyce, *Ulysses* (New York, 1934), p. 519; all further citations to this work will be included in the text.

These sadomasochistic passages are important for several reasons. Besides parodying fashion magazine descriptions of clothing and reminding us thereby that for the modernist both literary style *and* costume are often tools of ironic impersonation, Joyce is here specifically parodying Leopold von Sacher-Masoch's famous *Venus in Furs;* but in doing so, he is also parodying a distinctively nineteenth-century pornographic genre:

> Closely allied to [erotic histories of] spanking and whipping, were the underground Victorian epics about bondage that usually recount how recalcitrant and unmanageable boys were put into tight corsets and educated to be docile and feminine and lived more or less happily as women. Two such works are *Miss High Heels* and *Gynocracy*. . . . In the first, Dennis Evelyn Beryl is transformed under the supervision of his stepsister Helen into a properly trained young woman. As part of his corset discipline, he [is] sent to a girls' school, where he [is] punished with canes, riding whips, birch rods, and ever more restrictive corsets. . . . In the second novel, Julian Robinson, Viscount Ladywood . . . had showed too much energy as a boy, and so his parents shipped him to a [similar] school. The novel concluded: "The petticoat . . . I consider extremely beneficial. . . . I confess that I love my bondage. . . . There is a wonderful luxuriousness and sensuality in being made to bow down before a woman. . . . My lady's stockings and drawers upon me give me . . . an electrifying thrill. . . . This world is woman's earth, and it is petticoated all over. Theirs is the dominion, turn and twist the matter as you will!"[6]

In the dialogue between Bloom and Bella/Bello, Joyce almost literally echoes some of this language. ("Married, I see," says Bella to Bloom. "And the Missus is Master. Petticoat government"; "That is so," Bloom replies, adding encomia to Bella as "Powerful being" and "Exuberant female" [pp. 515–16].) Does Joyce's parody suggest a serious if covert acceptance of the original pornography, a reinterpretation of the work in a spirit in which it was not intended? Might we decide, for instance, as several recent critics have suggested, that the grotesque androgyny Joyce imagines for Bloom in Nighttown and elsewhere in *Ulysses* hints through veils of parody at the possibility of a nobler and more vital androgyny?[7] I would like to agree with such an optimistic, and implicitly feminist, interpretation of the Nighttown episode, but it strikes me as largely mistaken.

6. Vern Bullough, *Sexual Variance in Society and History* (New York, 1976), pp. 554–55.
7. See, e.g., Carolyn G. Heilbrun, *Toward a Recognition of Androgyny* (New York, 1974), p. 95, and Suzette Henke, *Joyce's Moraculous Sindbook: A Study of Ulysses* (Columbus, Ohio, 1978), pp. 7, 93, and 194–97.

For one thing, Bloom's female costume is clearly a sign that he has *wrongly* succumbed to "petticoat government" and thus that he has become weak and womanish himself; his clothing tells us, accordingly, not of his large androgynous soul but of his complete degradation. For Joyce's parodic narrative implies that to become a female or femalelike is not only figuratively but literally to be de-graded, to lose one's place in the preordained hierarchy that patriarchal culture associates with gender. If this is so, however, Joyce is also hinting that to *be* a woman is inevitably to be degraded, to be "a thing under the yoke." And certainly the language of the Nighttown episode supports this depressing notion, for as Joyce (and all his readers) knew perfectly well, it was not just Bella/Bello's whores who were "wigged, singed, perfumesprayed, ricepowdered," shaven, corseted, and "restrained in nettight frocks"; this degrading reality of female costume is in fact the reality at the heart of the pornography Joyce is parodying in *Ulysses*. (The sadism associated with the male/female role reversal in transvestite Victorian pornography suggests, moreover, that the pornography itself is perversely reversing, exaggerating, and thereby parodying the male dominance/female submission that the authors of these works believe to be quite properly associated with male/female relationships.)

In other words, just as Kate Millett extrapolated a true societal evaluation of femaleness from the parodic posturings of Jean Genet's male homosexual transvestites,[8] we can extrapolate Joyce's vision of society's vision of femaleness from Bloom's degraded androgyny. It is significant, therefore, that after this episode the traveling salesman returns home and, instead of increasing his commitment to nurturing wholeness, femaleness, and androgyny, he figuratively, if only temporarily, expels the suitors, gives the "viscous cream" ordinarily reserved for "his wife Marion's breakfast" to his mysteriously mystical son Stephen, and asserts his proper male mastery by ordering Molly to bring him eggs for his own breakfast the next morning. Casting off his false female costume, he has begun to dis-cover and re-cover his true male potency, his masterful male self. "From infancy to maturity he had resembled his maternal procreatrix," but from now on he will "increasingly

8. See Kate Millett, *Sexual Politics* (New York, 1970), pp. 336–61. Discussing Genet, Millett suggests that "as she minces along a street in the Village, the storm of outrage an insouciant queen in drag may call down is due to the fact that she is both masculine and feminine at once—or male, but feminine. [And thus] she has . . . challenged more than the taboo on homosexuality, she has uncovered what the source of this contempt implies—the fact that sex role is sex rank" (p. 343). See also Maria Ramas, "Freud's Dora, Dora's Hysteria: The Negation of a Woman's Rebellion," *Feminist Studies* (forthcoming), for a useful analysis of the connections between sex role, sex rank, and sadomasochistic fantasies. "Ultimately," Ramas suggests, "heterosexual desire cannot be separated from what psychoanalysis terms 'primal scene' phantasies [which] are sado-masochistic in content and have rigidly defined masculine and feminine positions. They are cultural and are perhaps the most profound ideology, precisely because they are erotised."

resemble his paternal creator" for he has at last taken his place in a patrilineal order of success and succession (p. 692).

Bloom's dramatic recovering of power is, however, curiously associated not only with his repudiation of the female and the female costume but also with his wearing of that costume. But this is not because his new power is in any way androgynous. On the contrary, Bloom's regained authority seems to have been energized by the sort of ritual sexual inversion that, as Natalie Davis notes, traditionally accompanied festive misrule. In sixteenth-century France, Davis tells us, the ceremonial functions of such sexual inversion were mostly performed by males disguised as grotesque cavorting females, and the primary purpose of their masquerades was usually to reinforce the sexual/social hierarchy.[9] Through enacting gender disorder, men and women learned the necessity for male dominant/female submissive sexual order. At the same time, through a paradoxical yielding to sexual disorder, the male, in particular, was thought to gain the sexual energy (that is, the potency) he needed for domination. For since women were traditionally defined as "the lustier sex"—the sex made for sex—it was only natural, if paradoxical, that a man could achieve sexual strength by temporarily impersonating a woman. Through grotesque submission, he would learn dominance; through misrule, he might learn rule; through a brief ironic concession to "petticoat government," he would learn not androgynous wholeness but male mastery.

Moreover, Bloom's revitalized male mastery might not derive just from the essentially conservative psychodramas of misrule that Davis describes but also from a transvestite enigma recently analyzed by the psychoanalyst Robert Stoller. Discussing the phenomenon of "the phallic woman," Stoller argues that the male transvestite uses the degrading apparatus of female costume to convert "humiliation" to "mastery" by showing himself (and the world) that he is not "just" like a woman, he is better than a woman because he is a woman with a penis. Unlike the transsexual, Stoller notes, the transvestite is constantly and excitedly "aware of the penis under his women's clothes and, when it is not dangerous to do so, gets great pleasure in revealing that he is a male-woman and [proving as it were] that there is such a thing as a woman with a penis. He therefore can tell himself that he is, or with practice will become, a better woman than a biological female if he chooses to do so."[10] Such a "phallic woman" does not merely, as Davis suggested, gain female sexual power by impersonating femaleness, he assimilates

9. Natalie Davis, "Women on Top," *Society and Culture in Early Modern France* (Stanford, Calif., 1975), p. 129.

10. Robert Stoller, *Sex and Gender*, 2 vols. (New York, 1975), 1:177. Significantly (in view of the connections I have been examining between sex role, sex rank, and transvestism), Stoller asserts that "fetishistic cross-dressing is almost non-existent in women" (1:143).

femaleness into his maleness—not his androgyny—so that he mysteriously owns the power of both sexes in a covertly but thrillingly male
body.

In an analysis of transvestite masochism which is also obviously important for understanding Leopold-von-Sacher-Masoch-Bloom's behavior, Stoller reviews the pornography "that repeatedly shows cruelly
beautiful [women] . . . bullying the poor, pretty, defenseless transvestite." This image is associated, he notes, with the terrifying ascendancy of
women (usually mothers or older sisters) in the lives of transvestites, Gea
Tellus-women—like Molly Bloom—who have made their man-children
impotent as little girls: "they hang those bosom-bombs heavily over his
head," says Stoller; "they are cruel and haughty; they are sure of themselves; their gigantically voluptuous bodies are strong, hard, slim, long,
and smooth, i.e., phallic. . . . [And] it takes little imagination," he remarks, "to recognize in the transvestite man's erotic daydream the little
boy's impression of the woman or older girl, who, in her greater power,
so damaged his masculinity." Yet, he adds, "by a remarkable tour de
force [the transvestite] takes the original humiliation and converts it into
an active process of sexual mastery and pleasure. . . . [For while the
archetypal pornographic] illustration makes him appear like a poor cow-
ering wretch, the fact is that the [transvestite] man who is excitedly
masturbating while looking at such a picture is . . . filled with a sense of
triumph as he is successful in producing an erection, excitement, and
orgasm."[11]

11. Because it is so important to an understanding of the phenomenon Joyce describes in Nighttown, here is Stoller's key passage on transvestism in toto:

> The transvestite, his sense of wholeness and worth in himself damaged, often *before*
> the Oedipal phase, by the powerful feminizing effect of the woman who dressed
> him or who otherwise scorned his maleness, has a disturbance in his sense of iden-
> tity, in his taken-for-granted feeling of wholeness as a male. Because of this, he
> senses that the prime *insignia* of maleness, his penis, is in danger. Then, knowing of
> the biological and social "inferiority" of women, and also knowing that within him-
> self there is a propensity toward being reduced to this "inferior" state, he denies that
> such creatures exist and invents the "phallic" woman. In a way, he does not have to
> invent such a person, for the living prototype actually has existed in his life—that is,
> the fiercely dangerous and powerful woman who already so humiliated him as a
> child. But he will have his triumph over her and all women, in the process of which
> he will reestablish his masculinity, the scar of the perversion remaining as a perma-
> nent sign of the original traumatic relationship. While it seems paradoxical, this
> triumph comes when he dresses up as a woman, for then, appearing like a woman,
> he can nonetheless say that he is a whole person, since he is the living proof that
> there is such a thing as a woman who has a penis. [P. 215]

For a slightly different but related analysis of compensatory transvestism, see Freud's
analysis of Senatspräsident Schreber, who believed that he had been magically transformed into a semidivine woman and even after his "cure" continued at times to cross-
dress ("Psycho-analytic Notes on an Autobiographical Account of a Case of Paranoia," *The
Standard Edition of the Complete Psychological Works of Sigmund Freud*, ed. James Strachey, 24
vols. (London, 1958), 12:3–82.

The transvestism in Joyce's Nighttown, like much of the costume play imagined by Victorian pornographers, almost exactly recapitulates the spirit of such sexually compensatory transvestism even while it depends upon the energy of the traditional ritual transvestism Davis analyzes. Because this transvestism is the parodic product of an age of costumes rather than an era of uniforms, both its private/neurotic and its public/ritual functions are of course disguised, ironic, and oblique compared to those implicit in Stoller's case histories and Davis' social histories. Nevertheless, Leopold Bloom's imaginary escapade in the Dublin whorehouse is a kind of parodic Feast of Misrule from which this exiled husband regains the strength for true rule. Recovering himself in his proper male costume, he finds a spiritual son (Stephen), remembers a lost real son (Rudy), and returns from his wanderings to a moderately welcoming Penelope. Just as the ritual magic plant *Moly* saved Homer's Ulysses from the degradation threatened by Circe, Joyce's Bloom saves himself from the depravations of Bella/Bello Cohen by not only having but ironically pretending to *be* his own *Molly,* a covertly but triumphantly phallic version of the recumbent *Ewig-Weibliche,* a "new womanly man" (p. 483) whose secret manliness must ultimately co-opt *and* conquer all insubordinate "new women."[12]

* * *

D. H. Lawrence's "The Fox," another transvestite work, tells the tale of Banford and March, two "new women" from the city who try to run a farm together but who fail when a literal fox attacks their chickens and a figurative fox, in the form of a young soldier, attacks them, first by making love to March and thus disrupting the women's relationship, and later by accidentally-on-purpose felling a tree in such a way that it kills Banford. Thus the foxy soldier, Henry, and his two vulnerable female opponents, Banford and March, form a love/hate triangle whose tension is resolved only when Henry manages to divest the transvestite March of her male clothing, her female companion, and her autonomous power.

In the beginning of the story, Lawrence tells us, March is dressed in "putties and breeches . . . belted coat and . . . loose cap," a costume in which "she looked almost like some graceful, loose-balanced young man." But he adds that "her face was not a man's face, ever," and it is not surprising that shrewd, foxily masculine Henry soon decides that he should marry her and take over the farm. "What if she was older than

---

12. It is quite clear that Joyce is referring consciously and sardonically to the turn-of-the-century idea of the "new woman." He even introduces a bit of comic dialogue for "a feminist" who comments on Bloom's fantasied achievements as a political leader (p. 472):

A Millionairess: (*Richly.*) Isn't he simply wonderful?
A Noblewoman: (*Nobly.*) All that man has seen!
A Feminist: (*Masculinely.*) And done!

he? It didn't matter. When he thought of her dark, startled, vulnerable eyes, he smiled subtly to himself. He was older than she, really. He was master of her."[13]

March's change of dress is the most dramatic sign that Henry's appraisal of her is correct. Coming in to tea one day, he finds her "in a dress of dull, green, silk crepe," and, as if to emphasize the sexual revelation this costume change represents, Lawrence comments that "if she had suddenly grown a mustache he could not have been more surprised" (p. 156). Despite the surprise, however, March's dress confirms Henry's mastery and definitively transforms the two of them into the true male and true female each had been all along.

> Seeing her always in the hard-cloth breeches . . . strong as armour
> . . . it had never occurred to [Henry] that she had a woman's legs
> and feet. Now it came upon him. She had a woman's soft, skirted
> legs, and she was accessible. . . . He felt a man, quiet, with a little of
> the heaviness of male destiny upon him. (P. 157)

But if March's dress emphasizes her true womanliness, it also reveals, by comparison, the unwomanliness of Banford, who, with her little "iron breasts" and her chiffon costumes, is a sort of grotesque female impersonator of a male impersonating a female (p. 155). Thus Henry's murder of Banford is his most powerful assertion of his "destiny" as well as the final sign that he has achieved the virility he needs in order to dominate March. Seeming "to flash up enormously tall and fearful" (p. 173), he fells Banford by felling "a weak, leaning tree" which had appeared, in its attempt at upright assertiveness, to impersonate the phallic strength that must by rights belong to him. Once again, though rather more painfully than in *Ulysses*, a male modernist has shown the way to rule by elaborating a costume drama of misrule. And once again, the hierarchical principle of an order based upon male dominance/female submission has been recovered from transvestite disorder.

That order undergoes a similar process of testing and regeneration in *The Waste Land*, a poem that is obviously about sexuality but not quite so clearly about the horrors of transsexuality. It is certain, of course, that, as Carolyn Heilbrun notes, Tiresias' androgyny "made him of spe-

13. D. H. Lawrence, "The Fox," *Four Short Novels* (1923; New York, 1965), p. 130; all further citations to this work will be included in the text. "Tickets, Please," which Lawrence wrote during World War I, is an interesting mirror image of "The Fox." In this tale, a group of uniformed young women tram conductors attack an inspector who is given the significant Lawrentian name of "John Thomas"; like vengeful Bacchae, they strip him of the official tunic that is a sign of his power over them, and the mock rape-murder they enact suggests, as dramatically as the scene in Bella Cohen's whorehouse, the horror and disorder associated with female ascendancy (see *The Complete Short Stories of D. H. Lawrence*, 3 vols. [New York, 1961], 2:334–46).

cial interest to Eliot."[14] But this is not necessarily because the author of *The Waste Land* wanted to elide traditional gender definitions. On the contrary, it seems likely that Eliot was using sexual costumes to promote a vision of rule and misrule comparable to the visions that underlie "The Fox" and *Ulysses*. For though androgyny—or, more accurately, hermaphroditism—of the sort Tiresias possesses is not quite the same as transvestism, metaphorically speaking the two are close indeed. Certainly when Tiresias describes himself as an "Old man with wrinkled female breasts," he is defining his sexuality in much the same way that Joyce defines Bloom's in Nighttown. But if, as Eliot himself noted, "what Tiresias *sees*, in fact, is the substance of the poem," we must assume that the vision offered by *The Waste Land* is in some sense a comment on the consciousness through which it is filtered. Just as a dream of Tiresias' would speak to us primarily of Tiresias, so "what Tiresias *sees*" must reveal more about Tiresias than about anyone else.

What Tiresias sees, however, is a Dantesque Inferno of sexual misrule, an unreal (and unroyal) City enthralled by the false prophetess Madame Sosostris and laid waste both by its emasculated king's infertility and by the disorderly ascendancy of Belladonna, the Lady of Situations (whose name, whether intentionally or not, echoes Bella Cohen's). Moreover, just as the perverse ceremonies of Joyce's female-dominated Nighttown inevitably organized themselves into a Black Mass in celebration of the unholy "Dooooog!" who is God spelled backward, Eliot's infertile London is haunted by a sinister Dog, who threatens to dig up corpses. For like Nighttown, this unreal City is a topsy-turvy kingdom where towers that should be upright hang "upside down in air" and babyfaced bats crawl "head downward down a blackened wall." And like Nighttown, it is ruled (and may indeed have been magically created) by a magical woman, a kind of sorceress, who draws "her long black hair out tight" and fiddles terrifyingly sacrilegious "whisper music on those strings."[15] Even the central scene Tiresias "sees" in the upside-down

14. Heilbrun, *Toward a Recognition of Androgyny*, p. 11.

15. It is interesting to speculate that some of the imagery of *The Waste Land* unconsciously (or consciously?) echoes the mythic imagery of Rider Haggard's extraordinarily influential *She* (1887; New York, 1976), the best-selling tale of a sinister, "upside-down" African matriarchy ruled by a semiimmortal, raven-haired *femme fatale* known as "She-who-must-be-obeyed." In addition, it is also interesting to consider the connection between Bram Stoker's *Dracula* and the upside-down bats described in "What the Thunder Said." In early drafts of *The Waste Land* these were "a man/form" which "crawled head downward down a blackened wall," and Valerie Eliot has noted the link between this figure and the scene in *Dracula* where the count crawls in a similar way (see Leonard Wolf, *The Annotated Dracula* [New York, 1975], p. 37 n. 29). Count Dracula is, of course, a dead man who must depend for sustenance on the blood of living women; after he has converted his female victims to vampires, moreover, they prey on infants, unnaturally reversing woman's maternal role. Finally, *The Waste Land*'s "voices singing out of empty cisterns and exhausted wells" are reminiscent of the voice of John the Baptist, who was the victim of yet another "woman on top"—Herodias' unruly daughter Salome.

world he describes—the seduction of the typist by the young man carbuncular—is merely a grotesquely disorderly parody of the male dominance/female submission that should be associated with fertility and order, for the young man is "One of the *low* on whom assurance sits / As a silk hat on a Bradford millionaire," and the typist is not really submissive but simply indifferent. Both, therefore, represent a society where everything and everyone are out of place, not just women on top but shopclerks unruly and carbuncular young men strutting in the false costume of the nouveau riche.

Some of the passages Pound and Eliot excised from the original manuscript of *The Waste Land* make it, finally, quite clear that both Tiresias' terrible vision and Eliot's vision of Tiresias' anomalous sexuality arise from sexual anxiety and specifically from anxiety about a blurring of those gender distinctions in which human beings ought properly to be clothed. The first draft of "The Burial of the Dead," for instance, begins with a description of a visit to a whorehouse called "Myrtle's Place," a house not unlike Bella Cohen's establishment—for Madame Myrtle proves frighteningly independent, even masterful. Announcing that "I'm not in business here for guys like you," she explains, as if anticipating Banford and March, that she's going to "retire and live on a farm."[16] And though she is ultimately kinder than Bella—refusing to give the speaker a woman, she does give him "a bed, and a bath, and ham and eggs"—her kindness is disturbingly matriarchal. "Now you go get a shave," she tells her would-be customer, as she turns him out into the barren nighttime streets of the wasteland. Her emasculating sexual autonomy foreshadows the frightening sexual dominance of sibylline Madame Sosostris, of enthroned Belladonna—that chess queen who moves in all directions, unlike her paralyzed king—and of the freewheeling, unladylike ladies in the pub. It also adumbrates the obscenely perverse power of another character who was summarily cut from the final draft: "white-armed Fresca."

Appearing voluptuously "between the sheets," like insubordinate Molly Bloom, Fresca "dreams of love and pleasant rapes" in a series of antiheroic "heroic couplets" that parody Pope's often equally disturbing eighteenth-century parodies of the lives and aspirations of "Blue Stockings." Fresca's perverse dreams comment interestingly on those literal and figurative rapes (of Philomel, the Thames daughters, and the typist) which actually occur in Eliot's Waste Land. When she enters her "steaming bath," moreover, she does not strip or purify herself; rather, costuming herself in deceptive "odours, confected by the artful French,"

16. Eliot, *The Waste Land: A Facsimile and Transcript of the Original Drafts Including the Annotations of Ezra Pound*, ed. Valerie Eliot (New York, 1971), p. 5; all further citations to this work will be included in the text. The Augustine allusions in "The Fire Sermon"—"To Carthage then I came" and "Burning burning"—also of course recall "unholy loves" in a sort of ancient Nighttown.

she willfully disguises what Eliot describes as her "good old hearty female stench."

Worse still, although Eliot/Tiresias tells us that "in other time or other place" Fresca would have been her proper self, a creature devised by male poets, "A meek and lowly weeping Magdalene; / More sinned against than sinning, bruised and marred, / The lazy laughing Jenny of the bard" (and at the same time "a doorstep dunged by every dog in town"), in the upside-down realm Fresca now rules she is, of all improper things, a woman poet, the inevitable product of an unnatural age of transvestite costumes, masks, disguises:

> Fresca was baptized in a soapy sea
> Of Symonds—Walter Pater—Vernon Lee. . . .
> From such chaotic misch-masch potpourri
> What are we to expect but poetry?
> When restless nights distract her brain from sleep
> She may as well write poetry, as count sheep.
>
> [P. 27]

Thus, "by fate misbred, by flattering friends beguiled, / Fresca's arrived (the Muses Nine declare) / To be a sort of can-can salonniere," and, significantly, the immediate consequence of her literary triumph for the speaker is that "at my back from time to time I hear / The rattle of the bones, and chuckle spread from ear to ear." For as this speaker—Tiresias, Eliot, the lost disinherited son of the Fisher King—had earlier reminded us, "Women grown intellectual grow dull, / And lose the mother wit of natural trull." Losing nurturing *mother* wit, however, and artificially separating themselves from the natural trull in themselves, such women separate their men from the fertile and properly mythologized order of nature, precipitating everyone, instead, into a chaotic No Man's Land of unnatural, transvestite women.

It is no coincidence, then, that the third in the series of nineteenth-century aesthetes who "baptized" Fresca into her unholy religion of art really was, in an important sense, a female transvestite: Vernon Lee was the male pseudonym under which a woman named Violet Paget achieved considerable literary success in the late nineteenth and early twentieth centuries. Her fleeting appearance here is yet one more detail which suggests that, rather than implying an optimistic vision of androgyny, *The Waste Land* is precisely the *Walpurgisnacht* of misplaced sexuality that a conservative male modernist like Eliot would define as the fever dream of the hermaphrodite, the nightmare of gender disorder. Ultimately, after all, Eliot yearns with Joyce and Lawrence for "the violet hour, the evening hour that strives homeward," to bring a thoroughly male Ulysses home from the sea to his soft-skirted, definitively female Penelope. Because both time and Tiresias are out of joint, such a consummation does not happen in *The Waste Land*. But it is devoutly wished, and thus it represents a patriarchal sexual rule which is as implicit in the sorrowful misrule that haunts Eliot's poem as it is in the Jovian voice of thunder that virtually concludes the work and in the triumphantly orderly endings of *Ulysses* and "The Fox."

* * *

Virginia Woolf knew, of course, these three works—*Ulysses*, "The Fox," and *The Waste Land*—and it is to her use of metaphorical transvestism that I will now turn, for her radical revisions of male costume dramas provide an extraordinarily useful paradigm of the gleeful skepticism with which feminist modernists questioned, subverted, and even repudiated the conservative, hierarchical views of their male counterparts.

When "Great Tom" Eliot came to Hogarth House and "sang" and "chanted" and "rhythmed" *The Waste Land*, Woolf was so impressed by its "great beauty" that Hogarth Press published the poem in book form the following year.[17] When Eliot defended *Ulysses* to her, however, her feelings about Joyce's novel were considerably less charitable. Though Eliot was eventually to praise not only Joyce's literary abilities but also his "ethical orthodoxy,"[18] Woolf insisted in her diary that *Ulysses* was "brackish" and "underbred," adding that "one hopes he'll grow out of it; but as Joyce is 40 this scarcely seems likely."[19] But she herself was forty when she made this remark, and, for herself, she considered the age advantageous: "At forty I am beginning to learn the mechanism of my own brain" (*WD*, p. 46). Clearly, then, Joyce's "orthodox" but "underbred" novel inspired her with sufficient irritation so that her thinking became uncharacteristically inconsistent. Could the sexual psychodrama embedded in *Ulysses* and manifested in its transvestite fantasies have anything to do with these feelings? Considering both Woolf's feminism and her developing "Sapphism," such a possibility seems reasonable. Certainly within a few weeks of her assertion that *Ulysses* was "underbred," she noted in her diary that when "Tom said '[Joyce] is a purely literary writer,'" she had scornfully responded that he was "virile—a he-goat . . ." (*WD*, p. 49). Five years later, when Woolf herself wrote a transvestite novel—*Orlando*—she seems to have deliberately set out to shatter the "he-goat" vision of male mastery upon which Joyce based *Ulysses*.

Orlando, a work that is nominally about a transsexual, depicts transsexualism through sardonic costume changes rather than through actual physical transformations. In fact, as if to emphasize that costume, not

17. See Quentin Bell, *Virginia Woolf: A Biography*, 2 vols. (New York, 1972), 2:86.

18. T. S. Eliot, *After Strange Gods* (London, 1934), p. 38.

19. Virginia Woolf, *A Writer's Diary*, ed. Leonard Woolf (New York, 1954), p. 48; all further citations to this work, abbreviated as *WD*, will be included in the text.

anatomy, is destiny, Woolf comically eschews specific descriptions of the bodily changes that mark Orlando's gender metamorphosis. As "man become woman," Orlando stands naked before a mirror, but Woolf merely remarks that he/she looks "ravishing," then brings on three parodic "virtues" personified as ladies—Chastity, Purity, and Modesty —who throw a towel at the unclothed being.[20] That the towel bearers are *ladies* suggests at once the connection between self-definition, sexual definition, and costume, a connection that Woolf makes more clearly as her narrative unfolds. Her transsexual, she argues, is no more than a transvestite, for though Orlando has outwardly become a woman, "in every other respect [she] remains precisely as he had been" (p. 138), and this not because sexually defining costumes are false and selves are true but because costumes *are* selves and thus easily, fluidly, interchangeable.

Unlike Leopold Bloom's humiliation, then, or the "corset discipline" imposed upon Dennis Evelyn Beryl and Viscount Ladywood, Orlando's metamorphosis is not a fall; it is simply a shift in fashion (so that Woolf associates it with shifts in literary style, shifts in historical styles, changing modalities of all kinds which remind us that, like Orlando, all is in flux, all is appearances, no fixed hierarchy endures or should endure). As a shift that is not a fall, moreover, Orlando's metamorphosis, and indeed the whole of her history, seems to comment on Bella/Bello Cohen's threat to Bloom that "As they are now, so shall you be"—wigged, powdered, corseted, de-graded. Although Orlando's female costume discomfits her at times, it never degrades her, for, declares Woolf, "it was a change in Orlando herself that dictated her choice of a woman's dress and of a woman's sex [because] different though the sexes are, they intermix" (p. 188). Orlando, in other words, really is androgynous (as Tiresias, for instance, is not) in the sense that she has available to her a sort of wardrobe of male and female selves, "far more" says Woolf, "than we have been able to account for . . . since a person may well have [thousands]" (p. 309). Making herself up daily out of such costumes, Orlando rejoices in the flux and freedom of a society where there need be no uni-forms, for indeed (as if confusing nakedness and costume) Woolf remarks that Orlando's own "form combined in one the strength of a man and a woman's grace" (p. 138).

Thus, unlike Tiresias, upon whom the worst of both sexes has been inflicted as if to suggest that any departure from the fixity of gender implies disorder and disease, Orlando has the best of both sexes in a happy multiform which she herself has chosen. And in accordance with this visionary multiplicity, she inhabits a world where almost anyone can change his or her sexual habits at any time. Yet this is not, like Tiresias' Waste Land, a kingdom of gender disorder but a realm of insouciant shiftings. After Orlando has become a woman, for instance, the Arch-

---

20. *Orlando*, p. 138; all further citations to this work will be included in the text.

duchess Harriet becomes Archduke Harry; he/she and Orlando act "the parts of man and woman for ten minutes with great vigour, and then [fall] into natural discourse" (p. 179). Similarly, marriage for Orlando need not be the affair of pure masterful maleness embracing pure submissive femaleness that it was for Lawrence's foxy Henry. Wed to the magical sea captain Marmaduke Bonthrop Shelmerdine, Orlando comically accuses her simpatico husband of being a woman, and he happily accuses her of being a man, "for . . . it was to each . . . a revelation that a woman could be as tolerant and free-spoken as a man, and a man as strange and subtle as a woman" (p. 258). Thus a question with which Bella Cohen's Fan surrealistically initiated the phantasmagoria of sick horror that overtook Bloom in Nighttown aptly summarizes not the disease but the delight of *Orlando:* "Is me her was you dreamed before? Was then she him you us since knew? Am all them and the same now we?" (*Ulysses,* p. 516).

Orlando is, of course, in one sense a utopia, a revisionary biography of society not as Woolf thinks it is but as she believes it ought to be; and in another sense *Orlando* is a kind of merry fairy tale, its protagonist an eternally living doll whose wardrobe of costume selves enables her to transcend the constraints of flesh and history. But though Woolf defined the book as a happy escapade, satiric and wild, *Orlando's* carefully plotted transvestism contrasts so strikingly with the transvestism we have seen in major works by male modernists that I believe we must consider this fantastic historical romance more than merely a lighthearted *jeu.* How, in fact, can we account for the extraordinary divergence between the transvestism depicted in *Ulysses,* "The Fox," and *The Waste Land,* on the one hand, and in *Orlando* on the other?

There is a major sense, of course, in which *Orlando* is first and foremost a costume drama of wish fulfillment, a literary pageant (comparable to the one in *Between the Acts)* designed to prove to Everywoman that she can be exactly who or what she wants to be, including Everyman. In this regard, it is significant that the tale forced its way out like a mirage of health just when Woolf was preparing to defend Radclyffe Hall's *The Well of Loneliness* and settling down to confront the painful problems of female subordination in the treatise on *Women and Fiction* that was to become *A Room of One's Own.* "How extraordinarily unwilled by me but potent in its own right . . . *Orlando* was!" she exclaimed in her diary. "As if it shoved everything aside to come into existence" (*WD,* p. 118). Yet if *Orlando* is primarily a fantasy of wish fulfillment which can be explained as a feminist pipe dream, a self-deceptive response to the anxieties instilled in women by a society structured around male dominance/female submission, what *male* anxieties energize the nightmare fantasies of *Ulysses,* "The Fox," and *The Waste Land?* And what engendered such anxieties in artists like Joyce, Lawrence, and Eliot, all of whom lived in a world that was still, as Woolf knew to her sorrow, comfortably patriarchal?

Obviously this last question is not one that can be answered hastily. Unique biographical irritants contributed, for instance, to the sexual worries of each of these men: Lawrence's mother-dominated childhood, and perhaps ambiguous sexuality, and maybe even his large, strong-willed motherly wife; Joyce's ambivalent relationship to his mother, his church, and his old gummy granny of a country; Eliot's clouded and cloudy first marriage, perhaps his somewhat beclouded relationship to the Frenchman Jean Verdenal, and maybe even his poet mother, who so strongly disapproved of the vers libre her son had been writing.[21] History, too, must have intensified these male anxieties, history which—as Eliot wrote in "Gerontion"—"gives with such supple confusions / That the giving famishes the craving." Certainly the nineteenth century's incessant contrivance of costumes may have bewildered these writers, along with what must often have seemed the threatening effeminacy of the decadent *fin de siècle* and the threatening rise of serious feminism in England and America. Yet another important irritant may have been the hidden but powerful attraction that the modernists' ancestors, the Romantic poets, felt for matriarchal modes and images.[22] In addition, many men of letters were obviously disturbed by the fact that "scribbling women" on both sides of the Atlantic had begun to appropriate the literary marketplace.[23] These speculations are necessarily vague, however, and in place of further generalities I would like briefly to consider one significant event which is in any case always associated with the characteristics displayed by modernism: World War I.

21. For a discussion of Eliot's relationship with Jean Verdenal, see James E. Miller, Jr., *T. S. Eliot's Personal Waste Land* (University Park, Pa., 1977).

22. See Leslie A. Fiedler, "The Politics of Realism: A Mythological Approach," *Salmagundi* 42 (Summer/Fall 1978): 31–43, and Northrop Frye, "The Revelation to Eve," in *Paradise Lost: A Tercentenary Tribute,* ed. Balachandra Rajan (Toronto, 1969), pp. 18–47. There is, of course, a significant nineteenth-century tradition of writing about androgyny, hermaphroditism, transvestism, and even transsexualism, with some key texts being Swinburne's lyric poem "Hermaphroditus" (1863) and Balzac's two short novels *Sarrasine* (1831) and *Seraphita* (1835). (For a brilliant, though in some respects evasive, reading of *Sarrasine,* see Roland Barthes, *S/Z,* trans. Richard Miller [New York, 1975].) In addition, Theodore Roszak has noted the powerful but neglected impact of nineteenth-century feminism in his "The Hard and the Soft: The Force of Feminism in Modern Times," in *Masculine/Feminine: Readings in Sexual Mythology and the Liberation of Women,* ed. Betty Roszak and Theodore Roszak (New York, 1969), pp. 87–104. An important twentieth-century transvestite fantasist who seems to have actually enacted many of Balzac's (and Joyce's) fictions was Marcel Duchamp. Photographed by Man Ray as Rose Sselavy, his female alter ego, Duchamp asked essential gender questions for many contemporary dadaists and surrealists (see Calvin Tompkins, *The World of Marcel Duchamp* [New York, 1966]).

23. For a discussion of Hawthorne's "scribbling women" and their appropriation of the literary marketplace in America, see Nina Baym, *Woman's Fiction: A Guide to Novels by and about Women in America, 1820–1870* (Ithaca, N.Y., 1978), esp. chaps. 1 and 2.

Surely that Great War which so haunts modern memory had something to do with the different costume metaphors I have been reviewing
here and with their very different implications: male gloom and female
glee; male sexual anxiety and female sexual exuberance; male yearnings
to get *back* to myth and female desires to get *behind* myth. For World War
I, after all, is a classic case of dissonance between official, male-centered
history and unofficial female history.[24] Not only did the apocalyptic
events of the war have very different meanings for men and women,
such events *were* in fact very different for men and women.

As Paul Fussell has shown, World War I fostered characteristically
"modernist" irony in young men by revealing to them exactly how spurious were their visions of heroism and, by extension, history's images of
heroism.[25] For these doomed young soldiers, history's "cunning passages" (Freudianly female!) had deceived "with whispering ambitions"
(like Belladonna's hair) and had guided "by vanities." But of course
young women had never had such illusions, either about themselves or
about history. Whether or not they consciously articulated the point,
almost all had always shared the belief of Jane Austen's Catherine Mor-
land that "history, real solemn history . . . tells me nothing that does not
either vex or weary me. The quarrels of popes and kings, with wars or
pestilences, in every page; the men all so good for nothing, and hardly
any women at all—it is very tiresome."[26] With nothing to lose, therefore,
women in the terrible war years of 1914 to 1918 had everything to gain.
And indeed, when their menfolk went off to the trenches to be literally
and figuratively shattered, the women on the home front literally and
figuratively rose to the occasion and replaced them in farms and fac-
tories. While their brothers groped through the rubble of *No Man's Land*
for fragments to shore against the ruins of a dying culture, moreover,
these women *manned* the machines of state, urging more men to go off to
battle. At times, in fact, these vigorous, able-bodied young women, who
had so often been judged wanting by even the weakest of young men,
became frighteningly censorious judges of their male contemporaries.
Speaking with some bewilderment and disgust of "the gratification that
war gives to the instinct of pugnacity and admiration of courage that are
so strong in women," Bernard Shaw complained that "civilized young
women rush about handing white feathers to all young men who are not
in uniform."[27] But though such behavior may have offended Shaw's (or

24. For a useful discussion of such "dissonance," see Joan Kelly-Gadol, "Did Women
Have a Renaissance?" in *Becoming Visible: Women in European History*, ed. Renate Bridenthal
and Claudia Koonz (Boston, 1977), pp. 137–64.

25. See Paul Fussell, *The Great War and Modern Memory* (New York, 1975), esp. chap. 1.
For equally telling analyses of the war, see also Eric J. Leed, *No Man's Land: Combat and
Identity in World War I* (Cambridge, 1979).

26. Jane Austen, *Northanger Abbey* (New York, 1965), chap. 14.

27. Shaw, quoted by Virginia Woolf in *Three Guineas* (New York, 1938), p. 182.

anyone's) pacifism, it is easy to understand once we recognize the different meanings World War I had for men and women. Every feather given
to a young man, after all, might mean another job, another *position*, for a
young woman.

This is hyperbolic, of course, but it is worth considering that even
the most conventionally angelic women's ministrations—jobs like rolling
bandages, nursing the wounded, and entertaining the troops—must
have reminded both sexes that while men were now wounded, partial,
invalid, maybe even in-valid, women were triumphant survivors, gold
star mothers who might inherit the very state which had for so long
disinherited them. Consciously or not, then, even the "best" of women
must have seen themselves as living out a tradition first imagined in
Victorian fiction by the male novelist Charles Dickens who was obsessed,
as Alexander Welsh has argued, by female angels of death, and by the
female novelist George Eliot who was obsessed, as several critics have
demonstrated, by female angels of destruction.[28] Indeed, in a triumph
of ambiguity, Eliot declared that the happiest hour of her life was the
hour she spent at her father's deathbed—and such a statement might
well have been made by even the most devoted of World War I sisters.
For to many of these women the war was, yes, a horror and a nightmare,
but it was also, alas, a nightmare from which they might awake (as Florence Nightingale did from the Crimean War) to find themselves on the
sofa, permanently invalid and in-valid. Thus, like Edith Wharton (whom
Henry James actually did shiveringly describe as an "Angel of Desolation"),[29] the noblest of women rushed about in the service of the Red
Cross, tending the wounded with the sinister tenderness displayed by
Isolde of the white hands in *Tristan and Isolde*—a work with which writers
like T. S. Eliot and D. H. Lawrence were obsessed.

In this connection it is surely significant that the women's movement
in England recognized quite early a connection—though, as Emily
Dickinson would say, a "slant" one—between feminist goals and the effects of the war. In 1915 *The Suffragette*, the newspaper of the Women's
Social and Political Union, was renamed *Britannia*, with a new dedica-
tion: "For King, For Country, For Freedom." At last, it must have
seemed, women could begin to see themselves as coextensive with the

28. See Alexander Welsh, *The City of Dickens* (London, 1971), pp. 182–90 passim. For a
discussion of Eliot's stance as an "angel of destruction," see Carol Christ, "Aggression and
Providential Death in George Eliot's Fiction," *Novel* (Winter 1976): 130–40, and Gilbert
and Susan Gubar, "George Eliot as the Angel of Destruction," *The Madwoman in the Attic:
The Woman Writer and the Nineteenth-Century Literary Imagination* (New Haven, Conn., 1979),
pp. 478–535.

29. See Cynthia Griffin Wolff, *A Feast of Words: The Triumph of Edith Wharton* (New
York, 1977), pp. 144–45. Henry James' epithets for Wharton included "The Princess
Lointaine, the whirling princess, the great and glorious pendulum, the gyrator, the devil-
dancer, the golden eagle, the Fire Bird, the Shining One, the angel of desolation or of
devastation, the historic ravager."

state, and with a female state at that, a Britannia not a Union Jack. And, as we know, the female intuition expressed in that renaming was quite accurate: in 1918, when World War I was over, there were 8.5 million European men dead, and there had been 37.5 million male casualties, including killed, wounded, and missing, while all the women in England over the age of thirty were finally, after a sixty-two year struggle, given the vote. For four years, moreover, a sizable percentage of the young men in England had been imprisoned in trenches and uniforms, while the young women of England had been at liberty in farm and factory, changing their clothes.

In an analysis of Austen's novels, Susan Gubar and I have used Rudyard Kipling's "The Janeites" to show that Austen's heroines inhabit "a tight place" not unlike the constricted trenches of World War I.[30] But of course the converse of the proposition is also true. If eighteenth- and nineteenth-century women occupied a place as narrow as a trench, the soldiers of World War I kept house in trenches as constricting as what had heretofore been woman's place.[31] Paradoxically, then, the war to which so many men had gone in the hope of becoming heroes ended up emasculating them, depriving them of autonomy, confining them as closely as any of Austen's heroines, or any Victorian women, had been confined. It is not surprising, therefore, that the heart of darkness Yeats confronts in "Nineteen Hundred and Nineteen" is the nightmare of the return of Herodias' castrating daughters together with the horror of the ascendance of that fiend Robert Artisson, a low and no doubt carbuncular creature "To whom the love-lorn Lady Kyteler brought / Bronzed peacock feathers, red combs of her cocks." For while the Jake Barneses of the early twentieth century were locked up like Victorian girls in the trenches of No Man's Land, their female counterparts were coming out of the closet as flappers, like Lady Brett, barelegged, short-haired, cor-

---

30. See *The Madwoman in the Attic*, pp. 110–12.

31. For a brilliant analysis of spatial symbolism in World War I, see Leed, *No Man's Land*, pp. 17–24. It is, of course, true that feminists like Woolf and Crystal Eastman were also passionate pacifists whose anger at patriarchal culture was often specifically channeled into contempt for masculine war-making, while such other literary women as Katherine Mansfield and H. D. hated the Great War because they had suffered severe personal losses. Nevertheless, the paradox of the war's asymmetrical effect on men and women must have unconsciously (if not consciously) struck all these women. To many of them, moreover, the devastation wrought by war may have seemed a punishment (for men) exactly fitted not only to the crime of (masculine) war-making but to other (masculine) crimes. In a draft of *Three Guineas* that is now part of the New York Public Library's Berg Collection, Woolf wrote: "you [men] must help us. because that is the only way we can help you. if you allow us to earn enough to live on to be independent you have a great instrument to prevent w. [war?] *We should say let there be war. We should go on earning our libings. We should say its is a ridiculous and barbarous but perhaps nec aary little popgun.* The atwould be a help. Then we should live oursleves the sight of happiness is very make you envious" (my italics; Woolf's spelling and punctuation).

setless, in simple shifts, knickers, and slacks.[32] For many, indeed, "wearing the pants" in the family or even stepping into "his" shoes had finally become a real possibility.

It is no wonder, then, that Lawrence's Henry, like Homer's Ulysses (if not Joyce's), is a soldier from the wars returning—and returning specifically to a home and farm that have been taken over by undutiful Penelopes. It is no wonder, too, that Joyce's Stephen feels himself haunted by the powerfully reproachful ghost of a mother who refuses to lie down in the grave where she belongs and no wonder that in one version of *The Waste Land* Eliot wrote that he had "spelt" these fragments from his ruin, as one would painfully spell truths out of the sibyl's leaves.[33] Finally, it is no wonder that toward the end of the last draft of *The Waste Land* a wounded voice babbles that "London Bridge is falling down falling down falling down," hinting at and simultaneously repressing the next line of the nursery rhyme: "Take a key and lock *her* up, My Fair *Lady*" (my italics). Coerced by women, at the mercy of women, bedded *down* in the terrible house of women, all these male modernists must have felt that they had painfully to extract the truth of their gender's ancient dominance from an overwhelming chaos of female leaves and lives and leavings. For the feminist redefinitions fostered by World War I had reminded them that even the brothel, ostensibly an institution designed to serve men, had served—as it does in *Ulysses*—both to test men and to reinforce female power, autonomy, sisterliness.[34] Finally, therefore, it is no wonder that when Woolf came to write those twin meditations on gender, *Orlando* and *A Room of One's Own,* she had to set herself against what Rebecca West astutely called "an invisible" but unfriendly "literary wind." Woolf's argument, wrote West in an early review of *A Room,* "is all the more courageous because anti-feminism is so strikingly the correct fashion of the day among the intellectuals." And West's explanation accurately summarizes what has been my speculation here: "Before the war conditions were different. The man in the street was anti-feminist but the writers of quality were pro-suffrage. Now the case is reversed. The man in the street accepts the emancipation of women. . . . But a very large number of the younger male writers adopt a [misogynistic] attitude."[35]

32. In the unpublished essay "Original Sin in 'The Last Good Country'; or, The Return of Catherine Barkley," Mark Spilka speculates, however, that Hemingway saw "Lady Brett's defiance" as an "implicit tribute to male superiority: the girls were more like men, they were copying male styles," and he adds that "androgyny . . . was for Hemingway a reassurance of manly superiority which allowed him to be womanly" (p. 25).

33. See *The Waste Land: A Facsimile,* p. 81.

34. For a discussion of the covertly feminist function of late nineteenth-century brothels, see Ruth Rosen, *The Lost Sisterhood: Prostitution in the American Past* (Ph.D. diss., University of Calif., Berkeley, 1976).

35. Rebecca West, "Autumn and Virginia Woolf," *Ending in Earnest: A Literary Log* (New York, 1971), pp. 212–13.

In fact, the misogyny (or, more accurately, the sexual anxiety) of these young male writers led them in the postwar years to just the obsession with false and true costumes, deceptive history and true myth, and transvestism and true "vestism" that we have observed in *Ulysses, The Waste Land,* and "The Fox." For inevitably, in the aftermath of the emasculating terrors of the war, the male modernist insists that the ultimate reality underlying history—the myth or ontology or, as Robert Scholes would put it, "cybernetic" pattern—is and must be the Truth of Gender.[36] In Joyce's system, Bloom and Molly can and must be boiled down, as it were, to Ulysses and Penelope, the "childman weary" and the "fulfilled, recumbent" woman, Sinbad the Sailor and Gea Tellus (*Ulysses,* pp. 720, 721). For Lawrence, all men, together with (or, more accurately, over against) all women, can and should be reduced to the paradigmatic polarities of "man-life and woman-life, man-knowledge and woman-knowledge, man-being and woman-being."[37] And Eliot, seeking beneath the sexual chaos of the Waste Land the ultimate beginning which is his true end, quite logically yearns toward the "significant soil" of gender, imagining that on a summer midnight he can hear the Ur-music "of the weak pipe and the little drum / And see them dancing around the bonfire / The association of man and woman / In daunsinge, signifying matrimonie— / A dignified and commodious sacrament."

Eliot's "East Coker," from which these last lines were drawn, is one of the major works to which Woolf was responding in *Between the Acts.* But this novel's Miss La Trobe, an ironic version of the lost Shakespearean sister Woolf imagined in *A Room,* holds many mirrors up to the nature of Western culture in order to show that all our roles, even those which appear most fated, are merely costumes. Indeed, rather than shoring up fragments of history against her ruin, Miss La Trobe, like a revisionary feminist Shakespeare, seems to want to fragment history in order to ruin it. Together, she and her author imply that to find real truth one must "tunnel" back, back to the night of the dinosaurs and the mud, the "night before roads were made,"[38] the night before costumes and gender, the sacred shamanistic night of what Djuna Barnes' Dr. O'Connor calls "the third sex."[39] Woolf insisted that her own novelistic art was based upon a "tunneling" process (*WD*, p. 60), but such tunneling has long been a technique common to female writers, many of whom wish either to identify "selves" with costumes or to strip away all cos-

36. Robert Scholes, *Structuralism In Literature: An Introduction* (New Haven, Conn., 1974), pp. 180–90.

37. Lawrence, *The Letters of D. H. Lawrence,* ed. Harry Moore, 2 vols. (New York, 1962), 1:280.

38. Woolf, *Between the Acts* (New York, 1941), p. 219.

39. Djuna Barnes, *Nightwood* (1937; New York, 1961), p. 146; all further citations to this work will be included in the text.

tumes (and selves) to reveal the pure, sexless (or third-sexed) being behind gender and myth.

As early as 1847, for instance, Charlotte Brontë's Rochester dresses himself as a female gypsy not to degrade himself but to try to "get at" the truth about Jane; in *Villette*, moreover, Brontë's Lucy Snowe discovers ultimate truths about herself, first, when she impersonates a man for the school play and, later, when she perceives that the nun who has haunted her is really no more than a costume worn by a transvestite male. Just as Rochester is trying to communicate with the "savage free thing" trapped in Jane, Lucy is trying to uncover that purely powerful element in herself and her life. Similarly, throughout the middle years of the century, Emily Dickinson defines herself variously as Emily, Emilie, Uncle Emily, Brother Emily, and Dickinson,[40] as if attempting to name not what is fixed but what is fluid in herself; in the same years Florence Nightingale continually calls herself a "man of action" or a "man of business."[41] Like latter-day gnostics, moreover, many of these women see the transformation or annihilation of gender as theologically necessary. "The next Christ will perhaps be a female Christ," writes Nightingale in *Cassandra* in 1852, and in 1917 the feminist theorist Olive Schreiner fantasizes a mystical encounter with "a lonely figure" standing "on a solitary peak," about whom she notes that "whether it were man or woman I could not tell; for partly it seemed the figure of a woman but its limbs were the mighty limbs of a man. I asked God whether it was man or woman. God said, 'In the least Heaven sex reigns supreme, in the higher it is not noticed; but in the highest it does not exist.'"[42]

More recent writers have elaborated the transvestite metaphors Brontë, Dickinson, Nightingale, and Schreiner only provisionally imagined. For example, Barnes' *Nightwood* (1937) hurls us back through tunnels of history and literature to the third-sexed figures of Robin Vote and Dr. O'Connor. Both star in a novel that was, ironically enough, introduced by Eliot himself, but despite the Jacobean eloquence that must have appealed to the admirer of Webster and Beaumont and Fletcher, Dr. O'Connor is an anti-Eliotian witch doctor or medicine man, half Circe half Ulysses, who wears women's skirts and wigs. Robin Vote,

40. See Dickinson, *The Letters of Emily Dickinson*, ed. Thomas Johnson, 3 vols. (Cambridge, Mass., 1965). In a few poems, Dickinson speaks of an "it" with which she seems to identify her ontological being, as if to emphasize a secret belief that ultimately her true self is gender-free. See, for instance, "Why make it doubt—it hurts it so—" and "I want—it pleaded—All its life—."

41. See Myra Stark's introduction to Florence Nightingale's *Cassandra* (Old Westbury, N.Y., 1979), p. 17.

42. Nightingale, *Cassandra*, p. 53; Olive Schreiner, *Stories, Dreams, and Allegories* (London, 1924), pp. 156–59. For further discussion of Schreiner's work, see Joyce Berkman, "The Nurturant Fantasies of Olive Schreiner," *Frontiers: A Journal of Women's Studies* 3, no. 3 (Fall 1977): 8–17.

moreover, is described as "outside the 'human type'—a wild thing caught in a woman's skin" (p. 146), whose first name connects her with nature and whose last name associates her with the triumphs of the women's movement and the voting powers of the sacred. She is "my heart," says Robin's lesbian lover Nora Flood, implying that Robin represents the wild reality beyond gender, the pure potency to be found in what Yeats, less optimistically, called "the rag and bone shop of the heart." "I, who want power," says Nora, "chose a girl who resembles a boy," and Dr. O'Connor glosses this line as follows: "The last doll, given to age, is the girl who should have been a boy, and the boy who should have been a girl! The love of that last doll was foreshadowed in that love of the first. The doll and the immature have something *right* about them, the doll because it resembles but does not contain life, and, the *third sex* because it contains life but resembles the doll" (p. 148). If we read *Nightwood* in the aftermath of this speech—the way it seems we must—as a revisionary response to male modernist touchstones like Nighttown and *The Waste Land,* it is not surprising that by the end of the novel Robin actually does become a kind of sacred Dog, a reversed God (or Goddess) of the third sex, parodically barking before a conventional statuette of the Madonna.

Even more recently, H. D.'s *Helen in Egypt* (1961) suggests that Helen and Achilles, the archetypal seductive female and the paradigmatic warrior male, must be redeemed as "New Mortals," a phrase that seems to be a revision of the earlier "New Woman." Their salvation begins in the sacred precincts of the Amen Temple and ends with a rediscovery of the lost androgyny they had as children.[43] Helen, for instance, recalls that as Helen of Sparta she spoke in a "heroic voice," praising war, while the narrator reminds us that Achilles' mother—the sea nymph Thetis—dressed her heroic boy as a girl to hide him from the men who would make him into a warrior, and she argues that such transvestism, far from being degrading, was appropriate and necessary. Indeed, at the end of this enigmatic epic, H. D. suggests that the vulnerable New Mortal Achilles, freed from the iron ring of his Myrmidons through his mother's lucky failure to dip his heel into the river Styx, will be reborn in Helen's arms as the potentially transvestite or third-sexed boy he once was, "the child in Chiron's cave" who cherished a wooden doll carved in his mother's image, a "Thetis-eidolon" (p. 284).

When we consider this last, fetishistic doll in the context of the dolls, witch doctors, and magical third-sexed beings of *Nightwood* as well as in connection with the visionary multiplicity of the costumes depicted in *Orlando* and *Between the Acts,* it becomes quite clear that many feminist/ modernist are concerned not only with "savage free things" or "wild things caught in women's skins" or "third sexes" but obsessed with a kind

43. H. D., *Helen in Egypt* (New York, 1961).

of utopian ceremonial androgyny whose purpose is very different from the ritual transvestism more "ethically orthodox" artists like Joyce, Eliot, and Lawrence have used to maintain or reassert a fixed social order. For in the view of such women as Woolf and Barnes, that social order is itself fallen or at least misguided. Thus the only redemption that they can imagine from the dis-order and dis-ease of gender is in the symbolic chaos of transvestism, a symbolic chaos that is related not to the narrow power of male mastery but, as in Miss La Trobe's play, to the androgynous wholeness and holiness of prehistory. For, as Mircea Eliade has noted, the ceremonial transvestism practiced in many non-Western societies is "a coming out of one's self, a transcending of one's own historically controlled situation . . . in order to restore, if only for a brief moment, the initial completeness, the intact source of holiness and power . . . the undifferentiated unity that preceded the Creation."[44]

Although Woolf would not have had access to most of the anthropological materials with which Eliade worked, she would have been introduced to such ideas by at least one contemporary thinker—and a thinker who links her not only with Schreiner but also with, of all unlikely peers, Lawrence. I am referring, of course, to Edward Carpenter, the well-known Fabian writer who was also in his own time a famous Whitmanite and a major homosexual theorist of gender. The friend of Havelock Ellis, Bernard Shaw, Lowes Dickinson, and E. M. Forster as well as of Schreiner, Carpenter wrote two widely read books on the so-called third-sexed beings he called "Uranians" or "Urnings," meaning "children of heaven": *The Intermediate Sex: A Study of Some Transitional Types of Men and Women* (1908) and *Intermediate Types among Primitive Folk* (1914). In both works, but especially in the latter, he postulated a connection between the third sex and what Eliade calls the ahistorical "Great Time" of the sacred, a link between the bisexual or "homosexual temperament and divinatory or unusual psychic powers."[45] Carpenter's notions of the "man-womanliness" of such artists as Shelley, Shakespeare, and Michelangelo clearly influenced Woolf (probably through Forster but perhaps more directly), for they are exactly analogous to the ideas she defines in *A Room of One's Own*.[46] Even more to the point here, the ameliorative and mystical vision of sacred transvestism that he offers in *Intermediate Types* seems closely connected to the magical transvestism depicted in *Orlando* and, by implication, in *Between the Acts*.

As Emile Delavenay has pointed out, Lawrence was also deeply influenced by Carpenter's sermons on sexuality, even by the Victorian theorist's beliefs in the undifferentiated sexual energy that manifests

---

44. Mircea Eliade, *Mephistopheles and the Androgyne* (New York, 1965), p. 113.

45. See Edward Carpenter, *Intermediate Types among Primitive Folk: A Study in Social Evolution* (New York, 1914), p. 48.

46. See Carpenter, *The Intermediate Sex* (London, 1908), pp. 170–71.

itself as "femaleness" in males and "maleness" in females.[47] At the same time, however, Delavenay has definitively demonstrated Lawrence's ambivalence about Carpenter's theories of androgyny, theories that were essentially elaborations of images of ceremonial transvestism and sacred bisexuality. Ultimately, Delavenay suggests, Lawrence withdrew as anxiously as Eliot or Joyce did from a final commitment to Carpenter's "intermediate sex"—leaving the concept free and powerful for feminist Carpenter disciples like Woolf.[48] For Lawrence, as for Eliot and Joyce, the "cybernetic" patterns of dominance/submission associated with paradigms of gender were not only inevitable but necessary, not just irrefutable but consoling.

That a male modernist should have wanted the consolation of orthodoxy is not surprising, for it is, after all, only those who are oppressed or repressed by history and society who want to shatter the established paradigms of dominance and submission associated with the hierarchies of gender and restore the primordial chaos of transvestism or genderlessness. Such political devotees of "the third sex" wish to say "I am not that fixed self you have restrained in those nettight garments; I am all selves—and no selves." Given even a modicum of power, as they were, for example, by the Great War, these women—for of course I am talking mainly about women—will enact their ceremonies of ritual transvestism with what we might call "a vengeance." Those to whom the social order has traditionally given power, however, will inevitably use ceremonies of transvestite misrule to recapture rule; they seek not a third sex but a way of subordinating the second sex, and in their anxiety they play with costumes to show that costumes are merely plays, seeking reassurance in what they hope is the reality behind appearances.

Though I do not have space here to bring this argumentative history up to the present, I want in conclusion to suggest that even for post-modernist women both the identification of self with costume and the search for an ontological "savage free thing," a third sex beyond gender, may be healthy rituals, enabling the sex that is still subordinated to stand ironically outside subordination, like customers in a dress shop refusing to buy uncomfortable clothes. In her marvelously witty *The Left Hand of Darkness*, Ursula K. Le Guin has created a ceremonial and gender-free planet whose inhabitants may be alternately described with the English pronouns "he" and "she"—as their author actually has described them in different versions of the same romance.[49] And although

47. Emile Delavenay, *D. H. Lawrence and Edward Carpenter* (New York, 1971), pp. 190–235.

48. Ibid., pp. 243–44.

49. See Ursula K. Le Guin, *The Left Hand of Darkness* (New York, 1969), esp. p. 17: "For it was impossible to think of him [Estraven] as a woman . . . and yet whenever I thought of him as a man I felt a sense of falseness. . . ." For a revision of an early story about Winter, in which Le Guin uses "she" instead of "he" to describe her androgynes, see

Sylvia Plath in one of the *Ariel* poems sees her world as a series of civilized suitcases "Out of which the same self unfolds like a suit / Bald and shiny, with pockets of wishes,"[50] in another poem this paradigmatic post-modernist transcends the pain of her own life by imagining her "selves dissolving [like] old whore petticoats"—the old whore petticoats, for instance, of the "tuppenny uprights" whose degradation Barnes describes with such nightmarish precision in *Nightwood*.[51] And in the fierce monologue of reborn "Lady Lazarus," Plath boasts that she is a "big striptease," a savagely naked shamanistic spirit who "eats men like air."

In the end, Plath may have been killed by the fixity of her situation, her imprisonment in an identity the world refused to see as a costume. But she fought by trying to throw away costumes, trying to redefine herself as a "savage free thing," sexless and "pure as a baby," rather than as "a thing under the yoke," like the masochistic female Bloom had impersonated (*Ulysses*, p. 523). In *The Bell Jar*, for instance, Plath has Esther Greenwood enact a Woolfian utopian fantasy on the roof of the Amazon Hotel in New York City. Biblically queenly in her first name, green with the untried chaotic power of forests and wishes in her last, this cynical but feminist heroine renounces both true and false costumes as casually as Orlando adopts them. "Piece by piece, I fed my wardrobe to the night wind, and flutteringly, like a loved one's ashes, the gray scraps were ferried off. . . ."[52] To Bella Cohen's "As they are so shall you be," she replies, like Orlando, *no I shall not.*

---

her "Winter's King," *The Wind's Twelve Quarters* (New York, 1976), pp. 85–108. See also Dorothy Gilbert, "Interview with Ursula Le Guin," *California Quarterly* 13/14: 48–51.

50. Sylvia Plath, "Totem," *Ariel* (New York, 1963), p. 76.

51. Plath, "Fever 103," *Ariel*, p. 55; Barnes, *Nightwood*, pp. 130–31.

52. Plath, *The Bell Jar* (New York, 1972), p. 91. From *Jane Eyre* and *The Mill on the Floss* to Kate Chopin's *The Awakening* and Margaret Atwood's *Surfacing*, ruining, tearing, or throwing away clothes is of course a general female metaphor for defiance of sex roles, but Plath, especially in her poems, presses it farther than most of her precursors and contemporaries.

Gertrude Stein, the Cone Sisters, and the Puzzle of Female Friendship

Carolyn Burke

For ten years, between 1903 and 1913, Gertrude Stein saw human relationships as painful mathematical puzzles in need of solutions. Again and again, she converted the predicaments of her personal life into literary material, the better to solve and to exorcise them. The revelation that relationships had a structural quality came to her during the composition of *Q.E.D.* (1903), when she grasped the almost mathematical nature of her characters' emotional impasse. Stein's persona in the novel comments on their triangular affair, "Why it's like a piece of mathematics. Suddenly it does itself and you begin to see."[1] The theory encouraged her to examine such situations as if they were case histories: she continued to study the same piece of mathematics from different angles in *Fernhurst* (1904), *Three Lives* (1905–6), and *The Making of Americans* (1906–11). But whatever the sexual arrangements in these triangles, the powerful generally managed to impose their wills upon the less powerful, and the triangles resolved themselves into oppositional structures, pitting two against one. Gradually, when the couple began to replace the triangle as her structural model, Stein composed numerous verbal portraits of couples and their relationships. In two of these, "Ada" and "Two Women," Stein applied her general theory of relationships to the particular puzzle of female friendships because, I think, she felt that women's characters were most intensely molded in same-sex involvements. Although she attempted to "prove" these theories in distanced, de-

1. Stein, *"Fernhurst," "Q.E.D.," and Other Early Writings*, ed. Leon Katz (New York, 1971), p. 67.

liberately depersonalized prose, we as readers must examine "the complex interplay of self-discovery and writing" from which her portraits emerged.[2]

Stein's portraits of women entangled in familial and erotic bonds seem to invite us into "the process whereby the self creates itself in the experience of creating art"; to read them, we must "join the narrator in reconstructing the other woman by whom we know ourselves."[3] This task of reconstruction implies that we must also rethink the place of biography—generally dismissed by New Criticism and its subsequent post-structuralist permutations as "mere" biography—in feminist critical projects. If it is true that "in reading as in writing, it is ourselves that we remake," then feminist critics have a special stake in understanding the biographical, and autobiographical, impulses at work in these activities.[4] Stein's portraits, which hover between fiction and biography, raise important questions about the ways in which biographical information can justify our suspicion that female writers may be "closer to their fictional creations than male writers are."[5] Recently, feminist critics have adapted psychoanalytic theory to examine the particular closeness of female characters in women's writing or to suggest a related closeness between the female author and her characters. We find it useful to speak of the pre-Oedipal structures and permeable ego boundaries that seem to shape women's relationships. Although Stein used very different psychological paradigms, she approached these same issues in her own studies of female friendships. Realizing that she preferred to write about women, she observed, "It is clearer . . . I know it better, a little, not very much better."[6] In spite of her qualifications, she knew that she could see

2. Elizabeth Abel, "Reply to Gardiner," *Signs* 6 (Spring 1981): 444. For a very useful critical discussion of this complex issue, see Abel, "(E)Merging Identities: The Dynamics of Female Friendship in Contemporary Fiction by Women," and Judith Kegan Gardiner, "The (US)es of (I)dentity: A Response to Abel on '(E)Merging Identities,' " in the same issue of *Signs* (pp. 413–35, 436–42).

3. Gardiner, "The (US)es of (I)dentity," p. 442.

4. Jonathan Morse, "Memory, Desire, and the Need for Biography: The Case of Emily Dickinson," *The Georgia Review* 35 (Summer 1981): 271. See also J. Gerald Kennedy's suggestive remarks on the "tension between personal confession and implacable theory" in Barthes' later work ("Roland Barthes, Autobiography, and the End of Writing," in the same issue of *The Georgia Review*, p. 381).

5. Abel, "Reply to Gardiner," p. 444.

6. Stein, *The Making of Americans*, cited in Richard Bridgman, *Gertrude Stein in Pieces* (New York, 1970), p. 78.

Carolyn Burke, an Affiliated Scholar at the Center for Research on Women, Stanford University, has published articles on French feminist writing and on Mina Loy.

the structuring principles of relationships with greater clarity when writing from her own perspective.

Furthermore, Stein knew that certain pivotal texts "were generated out of, and generate," important relationships.[7] For this reason, she insisted that "Ada" occupied a special place in her development: it was the first in her series of portraits, indeed, it was the discovery of the genre.[8] "Ada" celebrates Alice Toklas' arrival, in Stein's imagination, as the other woman by whom she knew herself. The portrait memorializes their relationship as an enabling union: by giving it such prominence in her own development, Stein hinted that her text had the power to generate more of its kind. She had little to say, however, about its companion text, "Two Women." Only her manuscript notes identify its subjects as her old friends, the Cone sisters of Baltimore. Furthermore, once she reached an understanding with Alice, who could not tolerate a rival, she carefully omitted from her writing any mention of her close relationship with Etta, the younger sister. After backing away from her long-standing friendship with both Cones, Stein could analyze the bond between them. Their portrait describes "existences of daughters spending a lifetime in freeing themselves from family fixations; old maid sisters housing drearily together and circling slowly about each other."[9] While "Ada" celebrates the female couple's mutual fulfillment, "Two Women" analyzes a case of arrested development. I intend to reconstruct Stein's friendship with the Cones in order to understand better how her portraits participate in the reflexive interplay of self-discovery and writing.

1

Like Leo and Gertrude Stein, Claribel and Etta Cone formed a couple apart within their own large, prosperous family.[10] Even more than Leo, Claribel was the dominant personality in her respective pair. As an

7. Abel, "Reply to Gardiner," p. 444.

8. Bridgman's "Key to the *Yale Catalogue*" of Stein's work lists "Two Women" as the third and "Ada" as the eleventh of the twenty-five portraits written between 1908 and 1912 (*Stein in Pieces*, p. 349). Although critics differ over the exact date of "Ada"'s composition, I think it likely that it was written in 1909 or 1910, following the composition of "Two Women" (see *Stein in Pieces*, p. 93 n).

9. Paul Rosenfeld, *By Way of Art* (New York, 1928), p. 117.

10. The following provide information on the Cones: Barbara Pollack, *The Collectors: Dr. Claribel and Miss Etta Cone* (Indianapolis, 1962), which includes the text of "Two Women"; Ellen B. Hirschland, "The Cone Sisters and the Stein Family," *Four Americans in Paris: The Collections of Gertrude Stein and Her Family* (New York, 1970), pp. 75–86; Edward T. Cone, "The Miss Etta Cones, the Steins, and M'Sieu Matisse: A Memoir," *The American Scholar* 42 (Summer 1973): 441–60; James R. Mellow, *Charmed Circle: Gertrude Stein & Company* (New York, 1974). Mellow's account of "Two Women" (pp. 165–66) stimulated my own interpretation.

older Cone child, she was always addressed as "Sister" by the younger ones, who recognized her importance in the use of this honorific. Edward Cone, their nephew, remembers Etta as the subordinate of the pair: "Where her sister was independent, brilliant and aggressive, she was painstaking and earnest."[11] Although they were both expected to marry within well-to-do Jewish circles, neither Claribel nor Etta did so. Instead, they formed a couple of their own, which appeared to work to the dominant member's advantage.

Claribel had already completed medical school when Gertrude and Leo first met the Cones in 1892. She impressed Gertrude, ten years her junior, as an independent spirit whose life was free of the usual domestic concerns of women. Because Etta took care of these matters for her, Gertrude concluded that the younger sister was "essentially a home-maker."[12] The Steins renewed their acquaintance with the Cones in 1897. When Gertrude began her own medical studies at Johns Hopkins, Claribel was doing research there as well as teaching at the Women's Medical College. Gertrude admired her and discussed medicine during their daily trolly car rides together. Although Etta was far more conventional, Gertrude also enjoyed her company, especially on shopping excursions. For years, Gertrude sought her advice on matters of taste. At social gatherings, however, everyone turned to Leo or Claribel. Gertrude and Etta had an intuitive understanding of each other's situation as the younger, less brilliant member of a pair.

Leo's descriptions of their summers in Florence inspired Etta to tour Italy under his guidance. When Leo held forth at churches or museums, Etta found his lectures "far more interesting and fully as expansive as Baedeker" (*TC*, p. 41). But when she joined Gertrude in Paris, Etta arranged to include numerous shopping expeditions, as well as visits to the Louvre. Leo was Etta's aesthetic tutor, but Gertrude's high spirits made her stay in Paris more delightful. She noted, "there is great talk *from* Leo, but friends talk *with* Gertrude."[13] Gertrude also initiated Etta into her latest psychological theories on the way to the shops:

> Immediately after lunch I was delighted when Gertrude suggested going to the dressmaker's with me. She was quite amused and interested in the funny conglomeration of French people there. We then wandered along the Rue de la Paix to look in the jewelry shops . . . talked with Gertrude on her pet subject of human intercourse of the sexes. [*TC*, p. 50]

11. Cone, "The Miss Etta Cones," p. 447; all further citations to this work, abbreviated as "EC," will be included in the text.

12. Stein, cited in Pollack, *The Collectors*, p. 149; all further citations to this work, abbreviated as *TC*, will be included in the text.

13. Etta Cone, cited in Hirschland, *Four Americans in Paris*, p. 16.

Although Leo delivered speeches "on the value of life in a European city and how to regard art," Gertrude was "truly interesting" (*TC,* p. 50).

When the two women returned to the United States on the same ship, they seemed to have reached a new stage of intimacy: Etta noted enigmatically, "Clear beautiful day which I spent mostly below in a beautiful state of mind, but one which brought out the most exquisite qualities of Gertrude. My vanity . . ." (*TC,* p. 51). In the months that followed, Gertrude was a frequent visitor. During the winter of 1901-2, however, she became involved with Mabel Haynes and May Bookstaver; this triangular relationship later formed the basis for the emotional mathematics of *Q.E.D.* Probably because of this situation, Gertrude grew so dissatisfied with medical school that she abandoned her plans to complete the degree. Although the facts are far from clear, it is likely that Gertrude's involvement with May, who was Mabel's protégée, was fairly obvious to their mutual friends.[14] Etta remained unaware of the intensity of the emotions generated by the affair only because she did not frequent their circles.

Furthermore, Etta's prudishness about sexual matters would have kept her from entertaining such notions. Unlike Claribel, she "never quite shed the timorousness of the Victorian maiden lady," which does not mean that sex, in some fashion, was not on her mind ("EC," p. 447). Family members told stories of Etta looking under her bed every night, and when a friend "remarked that she could never remember whether it's the 'w' or the 'h' in 'whore' that should be silent," Etta replied, "The whole word should be silent!" ("EC," p. 447). Her sexuality was, it seems, thoroughly and efficiently repressed. Unlike Gertrude, she did not yet appear to suffer from the contradictions between her emotions and her distrust of passion. Years later, however, Etta spoke to her niece of a matter that had troubled her for some time: "You know, . . . people say that there was something *between* Gertrude and Alice, but I never believed it. After all, what can two women *do?*" ("EC," p. 458). If Etta lacked the capacity to imagine what women might do, Gertrude was finding out, at considerable cost to her peace of mind.

Gertrude could not discuss with Etta her realization that she loved women, nor, for that matter, could she discuss it with anyone. But she could seek to understand the complex emotional drama whose structure seemed to be independent of the players. Gertrude spent the winter of 1902-3 in New York working on the first version of *Q.E.D.* When Etta met her next in Florence, she was still struggling with the manuscript. Gertrude had come from Rome especially to see Etta, and she wanted

14. For further information, see Katz's reconstruction of the affair in his introduction to *Fernhurst* (n. 1 above); Mellow's *Charmed Circle,* pp. 78–83; and Catharine R. Stimpson's "The Mind, the Body, and Gertrude Stein," *Critical Inquiry* 3 (Spring 1977): 489–506. Although my emphases are different from hers, I am indebted to Stimpson's persuasive analysis of this phase in Stein's development.

her friend to accompany her when she returned there for a reunion with May and Mabel. Although Gertrude and Etta resumed their habit of long talks in Etta's room, it is impossible to know how much she told Etta of the affair. It is quite likely that Gertrude hoped to produce Etta in Rome to demonstrate her emotional independence and show off her new involvement. In any case, Etta could have served as a kind of buffer or, perhaps, in spite of her timorousness, been brought out into the open about her feelings for Gertrude. However, whether or not she was capable of suspecting a lesbian love affair, Etta probably distrusted the intensity of Gertrude's feelings. Claribel's departure for Germany presented a reason to decline Gertrude's invitation, for she had to accompany her sister. "In those days it did not occur to Etta to accommodate herself even if it meant discommoding her sister" (*TC*, p. 54). And probably, an emotional retreat to the familiar patterns of sisterhood was preferable to being involved in a complex set of new relationships, even at Gertrude's side.

While Gertrude was in Florence, nevertheless, daily life had greater zest. In Etta's diary, Gertrude's name is associated with sensual pleasures. When she joined them on excursions, Etta's spirits lifted: "Gertrude and Sister Claribel came. . . . Had a table d'hôte dinner at Fiesole and all got drunk." "Gertrude and I lay there and smoked." "Gertrude is great fun." Of a trip to Vallombrosa, in the mountains above Florence, Etta noted: "Gertrude was at her best and we were all happy." While Claribel toured the forestry institute, Etta and Gertrude had lunch in the woods, like children playing hooky from the serious pursuits of their elders. Etta observed with reticence, "Were sad when we had to wend our way to the depot, for it meant leaving Gertrude" (*TC*, pp. 54–56). Whatever happened in Rome, Gertrude was able to finish *Q.E.D.* that autumn. She put the manuscript into a closet, however, where it remained for nearly thirty years.

By the following spring, Etta and Gertrude were making plans to sail together to Italy in June. Claribel was aware of her sister's devotion to Gertrude: "I sincerely trust your ocean trip may be a comfortable one . . . that you may enjoy it to the utmost—Also Gertrude (this may be taken in both ways)" (*TC*, p. 62). After four weeks with the Steins in Florence, the Cones resumed their travels with the idea of a reunion in Paris. They became friendly with Sarah and Michael Stein as well, but once again Claribel's decision to spend the winter in Frankfurt meant that Etta must accompany her. Gertrude teased Etta in the baby talk that she affected with close friends: "you are an ungrateful brute so you are and I won't never have anything more to do with you." The letter continued with information about her new corset covers, a friend's near miscarriage, and a new woman friend who writes plays and smokes. It concluded by scolding Etta for being "neglectful" and "an ungrateful cuss." Gertrude sent her love to Claribel, but "not to you cause you bad."

Later that year Gertrude tried to persuade Etta to meet her in London, although she must have felt that Etta could not be relied upon. The letter concludes: "be a good girl and do everything the way you are told." Gertrude's playfulness hints that Etta's obedience to Claribel implies her disobedience to Gertrude's own desire for her company. Another letter that year asks for advice about shirtwaist patterns: "Shall I have them made or shall I wait for your over-seeing eye what I axed about in my postal?" (*TC*, pp. 66–68). At this point, Gertrude was quite ready to be looked after.

Although Etta was flattered by her friend's request for her presence, her over-seeing eye was not available again until the autumn of 1905, when she took the unprecedented step of letting Claribel go to Frankfurt alone. Etta found a small flat in Sarah and Michael Stein's building at 58 rue Madame, around the corner from the rue de Fleurus. That autumn and winter she explored the Steins' Paris and made their interests her own. With Gertrude she strolled in the Luxembourg Gardens and made lengthy shopping trips to the Bon Marché. Together they attended the opening of the Salon d'Automne and saw the infamous fauve paintings with Claribel, who made a special trip for the occasion. The Cones' first impressions were that such art was "grotesque. We asked ourselves, are these things to be taken seriously" (*TC*, p. 70). But soon they took Matisse as seriously as did the Steins and became his patrons. Etta was also taken to meet Picasso, who called the sisters "les Miss Etta Cone," as if they were a married couple. Uncertain of his talent, Etta nevertheless bought several drawings when Gertrude, with this purchase in mind, took her to his studio.

From that point on, Gertrude seems to have regarded Etta as "something of a soft touch," whose responsiveness to her own taste could be turned to the support of the needy.[15] Etta's long experience of altruism in the service of Claribel and her desire to follow Gertrude's lead combined nicely on such occasions. Years later, in *The Autobiography of Alice B. Toklas,* Gertrude's version of the incident suggested her deliberate manipulation of the self-sacrificing Etta: "Etta Cone found the Picassos appalling but romantic. She was taken there by Gertrude Stein whenever the Picasso finances got beyond everybody and made to buy a hundred francs' worth of drawings. . . . She was quite willing to indulge in this romantic charity."[16] Soon, Etta was encouraging Gertrude to ask for more than advice about clothes and support for needy artists: "Don't you need some cash, don't hesitate and you needn't luxuriate in the feeling of poverty" (*TC*, p. 85). It was a delicate situation, for Gertrude was always aware that Etta's income was far more generous than her own and that Etta was only too willing to help.

15. Mellow, *Charmed Circle*, p. 83.
16. Stein, *The Autobiography of Alice B. Toklas,* in *Selected Writings of Gertrude Stein,* ed. Carl van Vechten (New York, 1962), p. 49.

Etta became more intimately involved in Gertrude's projects when she began to type her new manuscript, *Three Lives.* Gertrude wanted to send her stories to friends for advice, but typing made her nervous and the result was little better than her nearly illegible scrawl. Etta's support at this point was both practical and emotional. Although she offered crucial assistance at a time when Gertrude most needed it, she also, however, managed to maintain a certain distance. When Gertrude went to visit her, she found Etta copying the manuscript letter by letter because she had not received the author's explicit permission to read her stories. Gertrude recalled dryly: "Baltimore is famous for the delicate sensibilities and conscientiousness of its inhabitants. . . . Permission to read the text having been given the typewriting went on."[17] One wonders what the fastidious Etta made of "Melanctha," whose heroine prowls "in the streets and in dark corners to discover men" as she searches for sexual "wisdom."[18] Whatever she thought, Etta was pleased with her new occupation. She would have continued in this close relation to her friend but for Cone family projects.

That winter, her brother Moses, the head of the family, wrote to propose that Etta and Claribel accompany him on his first European tour. Soon thereafter, their biographer observes without comment, "around the time she finished typing Gertrude's stories, . . . Etta began to suffer from an old complaint—severe stomach pains." No remedy could be found for this nervous ailment. "In a state of considerable pain and unhappiness, Etta packed her bags, said good-bye to Gertrude, and went off to Munich in April, 1906, to consult a specialist Claribel had recommended" (*TC*, pp. 79–80). One may speculate that the impending return to the bosom of her family and the break in relations with Gertrude contributed to her distress. Etta kept up the correspondence, hoping to persuade Gertrude to meet her in Italy during the summer. They gossiped about the romance of their Baltimore relations, whose marriage would make them cousins. By then, Etta had assimilated the Stein epistolary style: she urged Gertrude to accompany her to Naples "because Mike didn't know my eldest brother and Gertrude didn't know my eldest brother and Sally didn't know my eldest brother, but little Etta did know Brother Mosie." The letter concludes with a revealing comment on what proximity to the family meant for her condition, diagnosed as stomach ulcers: "Well, sad be my lot, and sorry my tummy and weakly my nerves, but they is all got to go to Naples and that very soon" (*TC*, pp. 84–85). Her final appeal to Gertrude, in her own style, serves as an astute diagnosis of Etta's emotional condition.

Gertrude, however, did not mention what was on her mind during the spring and summer of 1906—that is, the resolution of her affair with

17. Ibid.
18. Stein, "Melanctha," in *Selected Writings of Gertrude Stein,* p. 347.

May Bookstaver, whose conduct with Mabel was still scandalizing their friends in Baltimore. A friend who kept Gertrude informed about "those two other misguided females" sent a card in August to announce May's wedding, which, presumably, put an end to the affair.[19] Soon thereafter Gertrude told Etta that she needed her in Paris to type a new manuscript. However, Etta could offer little encouragement. Although she hoped to return to Paris by October, "Goodness knows how long we will be there as when I leave Frankfurt I shall no longer be my own boss. Goodbye to little Etta's freedom, but somehow I never did mind being bossed by my biggest brother. . . . I see you have some misgivings." Another letter concludes ambivalently: "Well, adios, with much love and sort of glad at the prospect of seeing you soon even if I can do no typewriting as wants to" (*TC,* p. 86). Etta's typical omission of the first person singular voiced her unconscious realization that she would always sacrifice her own desires to the wishes of others, especially members of her own family.

The reunion did not take place until late autumn: the formality of the occasion was dictated by Etta's new occupation as her brother's tour guide. Her notes to Gertrude suggest her self-consciousness about the geographical and emotional distance between them, since she was staying with her brother at an expensive hotel on the Right Bank. Furthermore, she was kept busy by her family's numerous social calls and tourist activities. It was not easy to resume her habit of leisurely strolls around the Luxembourg Gardens or intimate talks with Gertrude. Etta felt the loss deeply. A letter written to Gertrude on the next leg of their trip suggests how much their former intimacy was on her mind. Wondering whether Gertrude had found someone else to type for her, Etta asked: "Has my successor done her duty by my place what she usurped and does she your typewriting & takes she care of that nice Mikey man. I am sometimes envious, but guess I am greedy, cause so far, this trip has not been at all a bad stunt. It's not Ameriky I am hankering arter" (*TC,* pp. 91–92). Her "greediness" for contact with Gertrude implies more than Etta realized, for in a postscript she added the news that Mabel Haynes would soon be married. The juxtaposition of her regret over losing her "place" with Gertrude and her reference to the emotional intrigue in which Gertrude had sought to involve her suggests an unconscious realization of the connections between these problematic friendships.

A few months later, Etta told Gertrude to "get the typewriter in good condition in case—but I don't know" (*TC,* p. 94). By then, both of them knew that she could not commit herself to being something other than "little Etta," whose identity was defined by her family position. It was not until the following autumn that Gertrude met Etta's real successor, who would do her typewriting and oversee her household until her

19. Emma Lootz Erving, cited in Mellow, *Charmed Circle,* p. 83.

death. When Alice Toklas took her place in Gertrude's life, she provided something far more important than Etta's personal and financial assistance, for she, rather than the vacillating Etta, could wholeheartedly say yes to Gertrude and her writing.[20] Etta drew back again into the mold of family life and her absorbing, though unsatisfying, relations with her older sister. A permanent relationship with anyone else was out of the question. Etta's affections for Gertrude were not sufficiently powerful for her to defy family obligation, habit, and convention all at once. And she did not like to think of herself as a sexual being, let alone a lesbian, if she even knew the word.

One is surprised, however, to learn that Gertrude's first impressions of Alice's character were far from flattering. She described her as "conscienceless," "sordid," and "without ideals of any kind."[21] Furthermore, she compared Alice with Claribel, both women having pride as their dominating characteristic. Gertrude noted that "Claribel sacrifices everything to preserve her pride," but Etta came out little better. Ruled by her vanity, she had barely any pride at all. Obviously, Gertrude's estimate of Alice's character went through some adjustment, but it is interesting to see that initially she compared her with the Cone sisters. Alice arrived in Paris at the right moment as far as Gertrude was concerned: May's and Mabel's marriages left her free to form a union of her own, and it was clear that Etta could not, or would not, overcome her reticence. Furthermore, Alice had daring and knew that she preferred women as sexual companions. In the complicated process of taking leave of old relationships while establishing a new one, Gertrude composed "Ada" and "Two Women." Their solutions to the puzzle of women's relationships could not have been more dissimilar.

Before she sat down to write, however, a curious event took place. In the summer of 1908, the Cones returned to Florence, where Gertrude and Alice were spending an idyllic summer. They reached the understanding that they would live together as if married, Gertrude as the husband, Alice as the wife. When all four women met for lunch, Alice found Claribel "handsome and distinguished, Miss Etta not at all so."[22] There ensued a tiff about who should pay the bill. Probably alluding to more than their immediate differences, Etta remarked that she "could forgive but never forget." Alice retorted that as for herself, she "could forget but never forgive."[23] Soon, Alice's strong dislike of Etta,

20. Stein speaks of the psychic relief when "at last 'some one says yes to it, to something you are liking or doing or making'" (cited in Bridgman, *Stein in Pieces*, p. 63).

21. Stein, cited in Katz, "The First Making of *The Making of Americans:* A Study Based on Gertrude Stein's Notebooks and Early Versions of Her Novel, 1902–8" (Ph.D. diss., Columbia University, 1963), p. 235; and in Bridgman, ibid., p. 109. Cf. Notebooks, Collection of American Letters, Yale University (YCAL), folio 2, DB56.

22. Alice B. Toklas, *What Is Remembered* (New York, 1963), p. 48.

23. Toklas, cited in Stein, *The Autobiography*, in *Selected Writings of Gertrude Stein*, p. 68.

colored by her resentment of her former intimacy with Gertrude, had influenced Gertrude's attitude as well. The emotional distance between Etta and Gertrude increased. Etta was relegated to her sterile relationship with her sister, but Gertrude and Alice would gradually invent their own version of the couple, "complete and complemented."[24] Gertrude would be the genius, and Alice, her audience and inspiration.

2

The Cone sisters could now be seen with detachment, and their relationship transformed into a subject for analysis. Picasso's ironic reference to "les Miss Etta Cone" presented them as a couple, but theirs was not the kind of union which Gertrude and Alice planned to imitate. Both sisters were trapped in the frustrating routines of a static relationship. However, during the time that she had known them, Gertrude's own perspective had undergone a crucial shift. If initially she saw herself as an Etta, in the shadow of an older, more brilliant sibling, she now was moving toward the substitution of lover for brother and toward the creation of a new kind of couple. The Cone sisters' duo and her "marriage" to Alice were like hinged mirrors set at different angles: they permitted related perspectives on the puzzle of female friendships. Gertrude's last word on the Cones was, "A revolving life is a sad sad life";[25] what she anticipated with Alice was an evolving life, one that allowed for personal fulfillment within its own conventions. Although to the outside world Alice would play Etta to Gertrude's Claribel, the private balance of power did not always correspond to the public image of their relationship.

Even before they reached this understanding, however, Gertrude initiated Alice into her obsession with the systematic classification of character types, her "characterology."[26] During the winter of 1907–8, they discussed her attempts to diagram psychological types and relationships. Gertrude's desire to understand the structural knots produced by the ties of family and friendship led logically to her portraits, a series of character analyses which began to detach themselves from the long family history, *The Making of Americans.* By then, Alice was playing an active role in the development of Gertrude's system: "Gertrude would

24. Gênet (Janet Flanner), "Letter from Paris," *New Yorker,* 25 March 1967, p. 174; cited in Stimpson's fine account of their symbiotic relationship, "Gertrice/Altrude," in *Mothering the Mind,* ed. Ruth Perry (forthcoming).

25. Stein, "Possessive Case," *As Fine as Melanctha* (New Haven, Conn., 1954), p. 129; all further citations to this work, abbreviated as *AF,* will be included in the text.

26. Katz uses this term in "Weininger and *The Making of Americans,*" *Twentieth Century Literature* 24 (Spring 1978): 11. This is a useful account of Stein's adaptations of Otto Weininger's rigid sexual psychology.

query Alice on her impressions of friends, relatives and casual visitors to the studio who were to become frozen in the glacierlike progress of the novel" or fixed on the page in the related portraits.[27] Both kinds of writing demonstrate Gertrude's obsession with her subjects' "relative success or failure at achieving identity or 'being.' "[28] Once Etta was consigned to the geometry of her "family living," it seemed that she, rather than Alice, was more suitably described as an "old maid mermaid."[29] But if Etta's feelings were doomed to frustration, Alice's were not.

Because "Ada" is as much a celebration of their union as it is a portrait of Alice, it suggests that her character is fulfilled only in this relationship. The portrait begins with her biography and ends with an ecstatic mimesis of her fusion with "some one," a storyteller who loves Ada and listens to her "charming stories." Indeed, "telling" and "listening" are intimately connected with "loving," which is also associated with Ada's escape from the demands of family life. Although "she and her mother had always told very pretty stories to each other," this dimension of her life is missing after her mother's death until she meets the unnamed "some one." The blissful consequence of their meeting concludes the portrait:

> Trembling was all living, living was all loving, some one was then the other one. Certainly this one was loving this Ada then. And certainly Ada all her living then was happier in living than any one else who ever could, who was, who is, who ever will be living.[30]

Her identity is fulfilled in becoming one with another like herself. As Nora discovers in Djuna Barnes' *Nightwood,* "A man is another person—a woman is yourself, caught as you turn in panic; on her mouth you kiss your own."[31] Paradoxically, to merge with the other is to discover the self.

It is not by chance that the Etta figure in "Two Women" is also called "Ada." The two portraits were probably written within a year of each other. However, while "Ada" 's prose rhythms enact emotional union, "Two Women" studies its subjects' inability to enter into rewarding relationships. The portrait begins by insisting that "there were two of them": the primary element of their identity is "twoness," belonging to a pair. That they are also sisters matters a great deal: "They always knew this thing, they always knew that one was the elder and one was the

27. Mellow, *Charmed Circle,* p. 161.

28. Bridgman, *Stein in Pieces,* p. 93.

29. Toklas recalls that Stein once called her this (*What Is Remembered,* p. 44). Aware of the sexual connotations, she adds, "But by the time the buttercups were in bloom, the old maid mermaid had gone into oblivion and I had been gathering wild violets."

30. Stein, *Geography & Plays* (New York, 1968), pp. 15–16.

31. Djuna Barnes, *Nightwood* (New York, 1961), p. 143.

younger." There is a related imbalance in their relationship: "The older one was more something than the younger one." The "something" remains opaque, and we learn only that the older one "did some things" while the younger one "was receiving everything" (*TC*, pp. 275–77). Slowly we come to see that the older of the pair is more active, that she *is* and *does* more than her younger sister. The example of the two women illustrates one of Stein's favorite psychological paradigms, the relationship of dominant and subordinate, active and passive, or "dependent independent" and "independent dependent." Such relationships could be reconstructed in prose through the slow, deliberate unfolding of relational patterns, and the absence of biographical specificity gave heightened significance to the few personal details that she chose to include.

The choice of names demonstrates how closely "Two Women" is related to "Ada" and *The Making of Americans*. At first, she planned to call the older one Bertha (the name of her older sister), possibly because of a buried sympathy for the younger member of the pair. In this case, Bertha-Claribel would also stand for Leo, the older sibling who seemed to have "more something" than Gertrude. During the composition of "Two Women," however, she changed her mind and called the older sister Martha, the name that she had given herself in *The Making of Americans*. As for the other member of the pair, "the older called the younger Ada" (*TC*, p. 276). There was an obvious parallel in Gertrude's mind between her first and second typists. Etta sensed that she would be replaced by Alice, and Gertrude realized that she, like Claribel, would profit from a relationship with a subservient "receiver." The dominant member of the pair names the other and creates her role, in the same way that Gertrude "created" a role for Alice. However, unlike the "some one" whose love of Ada makes them both happy, Martha-Claribel is apparently unconcerned about her sister's dissatisfaction. Relations between them are unbalanced because of Martha's egotism and Ada's self-sacrificing acceptance of it.

After the first four pages of "Two Women," we learn that "there were others connected with them" (*TC*, p. 278). Gertrude's marginal notations on the manuscript indicate that she planned to "go on with . . . their family and their relatives the number of brothers and sisters they had . . . and how their mother and father died" (*TC*, pp. 314–15). She intended to put their relationship in the context of family history, as she was doing with her own in *The Making of Americans*. However, the finished portrait offers few details, even though it does insist that "certainly sister Martha and Ada had been ones having family living and certainly they were ones having family living and certainly they were ones going to be having family living" (*TC*, p. 288). Past, present, and future are all shaped by the quality of their family living, which carries with it a feeling of connection and a recognition of "duties toward these connected with them" (*TC*, p. 279). The two women claim that in their family one develops "a finer feeling." Indeed, the narrator asserts, "such a family living made any one have a finer feeling" (*TC*, p. 289). But in what this finer feeling consists it is hard to say. Their inability to express any other feelings becomes the measure of their failure at "being living." The bond between the sisters cannot satisfy their deeper needs, yet its strength prevents them from seeking strong attachments to anyone else.

Stein plays on the element of "want" in their lives. Ostensibly they can both have whatever they want because they can purchase it. Nevertheless, "they both had not what they were wanting." Although what they lack is never made explicit, the reader comes to realize that they lack emotional connection with others, or, to put it in Stein's terms, they lack the possibility to express and receive "tender feeling" outside the family circle. The older sister does not feel this lack "because she was not wanting it," but the younger suffers from ambivalence "because she could not come to want it." In other words, Martha-Claribel appears not to want anything outside herself (as long as she can count on her sister's devoted service), and Etta-Ada cannot make up her mind about her own wants or needs. Their alternative to the recognition of this "wanting" is "buying things and living in a way" (*TC*, p. 280). With her usual circumspection, Stein speaks of their ability to "please" some. Although the older sister manages to be pleasing because she is a person "with some distinction," she is not particularly concerned with making herself agreeable (*TC*, p. 281). The younger one, however, is more aware of the dynamics of pleasing: "She was pleasing some and she was feeling something about this thing and feeling something about some pleasing her some." The portrait continues enigmatically, "She did not have what she wanted as she could not come to want it," presumably because she feels trapped in her primary relationship (*TC*, p. 281). Her role is to be her sister's mirror, to reflect her conviction that she is a person of distinction. However, for both of them, this situation offers limited satisfaction. As in "Ada," "telling" and "listening" are closely linked with emotional satisfaction, and "pleasing" acquires erotic overtones. Only Ada and Martha listen to each other, and that, Stein implies, out of obligation or family duty.

Because Ada must listen to Martha, the older sister is immune to "need." However, unlike Martha, Ada "needed to be one being living," but she has difficulty in expressing this desire (*TC*, p. 287). Her need for emotional sustenance cannot be met within the circumscribed limits of "family living." When an unnamed "some one" actually listens to the sisters, they realize "some connection between loving and listening between liking and listening." Martha is reassured about her own importance, but Ada worries: "She certainly was suffering in this thing in there being existing a connection between listening and liking and listening and tender feeling" (*TC*, pp. 290–91). Because she is ambivalent about "coming to want" this connection more actively, she "was going on suffering from this thing" (*TC*, p. 290). The older sister's independence is given even greater emphasis: she "was very often not with any one." Although the younger sister "was certainly needing being with some one," she was accustomed to filling that need with the company of her older sister (*TC*, p. 292). Toward the conclusion, this portrait of crippling emotional dependency becomes quite wicked. Possibly remembering Etta's characterization of herself as "little Etta," Stein emphasizes Ada's preoccupation with being the younger of the pair: "She had been a young one a quite young one and this had been completely enough interesting to her" (*TC*, p. 296). When Ada discovers that she would like to live differently, to enjoy life more fully, "she always could remember that she would enjoy some, that she would enjoy some things" (*TC*, pp. 297–98). However, she seems to live life largely in order to remember it. (One wonders whether this is a dig at Etta for having incurred Alice's anger when she said that she could forgive but never forget.)

The memory of past pleasures does not help Ada to seek a way out of the situation. Circling back to its opening, the portrait insists that the two women are sisters, that their living is bound up in being together, whether in each other's presence or apart. Each needs to know that the other acknowledges the primacy of this relationship so that she can go on with her "being living." The cumulative effect of Stein's semantic and rhythmic repetitions suggests, in contrast to the developing relationship celebrated in "Ada," another emotional impasse. And her typical pattern of making a statement about her subject's character and then restating the same idea in the negative is particularly well suited to the expression of ambivalent states of mind. There is more than one way in which the sisters cannot be lovers: because they do not really love each other, they are unable to love anyone else.

That Stein intended to say more about the connection between individual character and family living is clear from her marginal notes: "Tell about the others connected with them, their duties and how they did them, what effort they had when they were traveling, how they quarreled, how they spent money. . . . Stinginess, buying scarves . . . Etta and no father no mother. Sex in both" (*TC*, p. 314). The connection between the loss of parental affection and the absence of emotional capacity was clearly on her mind, even though the association was not pursued in the finished portrait. Reading between the lines, one can translate the crabbed vocabulary to interpret Stein's feelings about the lack of sex, or "pleasing," in the Cone sisters' lives.

Two works written about the same time as "Two Women" are also preoccupied with the structural dynamics of the pair. *A Long Gay Book* was to include "everybody I can think of ever, narrative after narrative of pairs of people." And *Many Many Women*, though far more impenetrable than "Two Women," intended to analyze "how women are lived and what they are," once again by studying her own friends.[32] Both works are like extended portraits, although in *A Long Gay Book*, Stein moves from her early, analytic style to the more lyrical tone of *Tender Buttons*. Richard Bridgman speculates that during this period, which culminated in her trip to Spain with Alice in 1912, Gertrude "had become reconciled to the nature of her affections."[33] She even announced this acceptance near the end of *The Making of Americans*:

> Some say alright all but one way of loving, another says alright all but another way of loving. . . . I like loving. I like mostly all the ways any one can have of having loving feeling in them. Slowly it has come to be in me that any way of being a loving one is interesting and not unpleasant to me.[34]

What mattered was that people express the "loving feeling" in whatever way possible. They should not fear "coming to want what they want," as Ada does in "Two Women," but be tolerant of the many ways of loving. Women's lives could be lived in any number of ways, she concluded, as long as one did not allow oneself to stay trapped in the frustrating emotional structures of family life.

If sisters could not be lovers, lovers might still resemble sisters. Although Stein often writes of herself and Alice as husband and wife, other possibilities present themselves in her erotic texts. Gertrude and Alice make a covert appearance as loving sisters in "Lifting Belly," which Virgil Thompson calls Stein's "hymn to the domestic affections."[35] The language of gender should be rethought to name their relationship, for "What is a man? What is a woman?"[36] Although conventional language does not adequately express their union, the lovers may be described as one who is "fierce and tender," the other "sister" and not "mistress." The loved one is at once "his wife and sister inside" (*AF*, p. 129). Although their unconventional marriage sustains and protects them, they "live in a house which is certainly not mentioned anywhere" (*AF*, p. 119). This reinvention of female relationships goes beyond the limits of family structures: the "man" of the house explains, "I measured a sister, I shall please" (*AF*, p. 112). As if evoked by the word "sister," one who cannot admit needing to be pleased in Stein's special sense makes her appearance some pages later. One speaker urges the other to "come at

32. Stein, cited in Bridgman, *Stein in Pieces*, pp. 99, 105.
33. Bridgman, ibid., p. 105.
34. Stein, cited in Bridgman, ibid., pp. 105–6.
35. Virgil Thompson, in Stein, *"Bee Time Vine" and Other Pieces (1913–1927)* (New Haven, Conn., 1953), p. 64. On Stein's erotic writing of this period, see Elizabeth Fifer, "Is Flesh Advisable? The Interior Theater of Gertrude Stein," *Signs* 4 (Spring 1979): 472–83.
36. Stein, "Lifting Belly," *Bee Time Vine*, pp. 93, 66, 77, 82.

once. Chamber music. Dr. Claribel invited us." The coyly enigmatic declaration which follows picks up the vocabulary of "Two Women": "I don't want to put in any reference to the best way to relieve actual and premeditated and perhaps debatable want I wish only to refer to the fact that in every way there can be reliance there is naturally meaning and clearly there was change" (*AF*, p. 143). In the way that their lives are lived, there has been meaningful change. However, of Dr. Claribel it can only be said that her "wants" go unrecognized and change is unlikely to occur.

Gertrude's study of stasis in the lives of the two women soon served her in another way. During the next two years (1910–12), she composed *Two*, the long, opaque piece subtitled *Gertrude Stein and Her Brother*. As Bridgman has observed, "the title itself has a dual meaning, for it refers first to brother and sister, then to sister and friend."[37] From 1909, when Alice joined their household, until 1913 or 1914, Alice was part of a triangular relationship with Gertrude and Leo. But its dynamics did not resemble the triangle that had caused Gertrude such pain and had stimulated her discovery that relationships resembled mathematical problems. Although Gertrude and Alice were a pair and Leo the odd man out, Gertrude still had to discover the means by which she would free herself of his authority. Analyzing her relations with her brother in much the same terms that she used in "Two Women," she worked out both an analysis and a solution to their impasse. Like Martha-Claribel, the brother in *Two* is the member of the pair with distinction. He is also the one who is "not yielding." Intensely involved in his intellectual pursuits, "he is not the one receiving any change."[38] The sister, on the other hand, "said it was the time to grow" (*T*, p. 135). That growth is made possible by the arrival in their lives of another "one," with whom the sister can learn a different way to be two. Having untied the knot of sibling dependency in "Two Women," she could then apply a similar analysis to her own situation. If "the number two represents brother and sister, unified but separate,"[39] it can also come to stand for a different pair: "There were two, she and she were there" (*T*, p. 135). The couple celebrated a few years earlier in "Ada" is given formal status in *Two*. Having played their role as counters in Stein's elaborate conceptual geometry, the Cone sisters could be removed from the center of her preoccupations.[40]

37. Bridgman, *Stein in Pieces*, p. 107.

38. Stein, *"Two: Gertrude Stein and Her Brother" and Other Early Portraits (1908–1912)* (New Haven, Conn., 1951), p. 139; all further citations to this work, abbreviated as *T*, will be included in the text.

39. Bridgman, *Stein in Pieces*, p. 113.

40. It is likely that three more early portraits in *Two*, "Rue de Rennes," "Bon Marché Weather," and "Flirting at the Bon Marché," draw on Stein's analysis of the Cone sisters, particularly Etta. "Rue de Rennes" is concerned with a "some one" whose chief charac-

3

Although Hugh Kenner gleefully asserts that "she's not even deconstructible," recent critics of Stein have begun to read her experimental texts of the 1908–14 period with greater ease.[41] It *is* possible to deconstruct her various codes—cubistic, erotic, and structural—and furthermore, she even offered careful readers an invitation to approach her writing in this way.[42] In a discussion of cubism, Stein once told Mina Loy, an early and sympathetic critic of her work, that its aim was "deconstruction preparatory to complete reconstruction of the objective."[43] What she meant by the term "deconstruction," which she appears to have coined, may be much simpler than what it is now understood to mean—yet, it is not so very different. Stein maintained that she, like Picasso, had in mind a thorough dismantling of both the structural principles of the subject and traditional, unexamined habits of perception. Her own writing in these years deconstructs her favorite subjects—pairs, triangles, and other geometric formulations of human relationships—in preparation for their "complete reconstruction." However, as I have tried to suggest, Stein's deconstruction and reconstruction are closely related, even simultaneous movements of her mind. If "Two Women" may be said to deconstruct one mode of relations between women, then "Ada" reconstructs the possibility of another in the fusion of its final paragraph.[44]

---

teristic is timidity and whose shopping expeditions to the antique shops of the rue de Rennes inspire the portrait (see Janet Flanner's intro. to *Two,* p. xiii). That the two Bon Marché portraits are related to "Two Women" is suggested by Stein's marginal notes, which mention "bon marché" as one of the details to include in their portrait (see *TC,* p. 314). "Bon Marché Weather" asserts that "some are ones needing to go very often to buy something" (*T,* p. 352), and "Flirting at the Bon Marché" begins, "some know very well that their way of life is a sad one" (*T,* p. 353): both statements use the vocabulary of "Two Women" and would seem to describe Etta, who, furthermore, was in the habit of buying lace for her extensive collection at the Bon Marché.

41. Hugh Kenner, *New York Times Book Review,* 21 December 1980, p. 5.

42. Among the most interesting essays are Marjorie Perloff, "Poetry as Word-System: The Art of Gertrude Stein," *American Poetry Review* 8 (1979): 33–43, on literary cubism; Stimpson, "The Mind, the Body, and Gertrude Stein" and "Gertrice/Altrude," and Fifer, "Is Flesh Available?," on sexuality and erotic language; and Marianne DeKoven, "Gertrude Stein and Modern Painting: Beyond Literary Cubism," *Contemporary Literature* 22 (1981): 81–95, which argues that Stein's writing of the 1910s is best understood in the terms proposed by deconstructive criticism.

43. Stein, cited in Mina Loy, "Phenomenon in American Art," unpublished essay, Loy papers, YCAL, p. 1.

44. Julia Kristeva's distinction between the semiotic and the symbolic modes of signification could also be applied in a discussion of Stein's early writing on women's relationships. The semiotic mode, in close relation to the unconscious, expresses the instinctual drives through the resources of rhythm, intonation, gesture, and melody. It is also, according to Kristeva, closely allied with the infant's pre-Oedipal (and presymbolic)

In 1915, Stein was again turning over in her mind the connections between biography and writing. Her lover's participation in her work combined the functions of subject and typist/reader: the ideal collaboration for her purposes. Appropriately, the dialogue of "Possessive Case" blends domestic banter and inventive verbal play in a kind of erotic grammar of relationships. The imminent arrival of "Doctor Claribel" in the speakers' private world provokes the observation that "A revolving life is a sad sad life a revolving life to mention," made presumably by the wife of the pair. The other speaker replies, "I think she has a history and you too Miss Polly." The process of association linking their stories continues in the questions, "How do they spell their name [Cohn or Cone]?" and "What's it say about us?" The answer comes in the husband's assertions that their own relations create the opposite of a sad life, for they envision "no not [a] knot again" but "amiable stepping." Furthermore, this reflection upon their domestic dance is "inspired by Claribel's portrait." By 1915, the passionate fusion of "Ada" had become an amiable two-step through the therapeutic operations of writing and related changes in domestic arrangements. Stein comments upon this phase of her writing in her next question, which provides its own reply: "What's the use of portraiture, to tranquilise your mind" (*AF,* pp. 129–30). Her experiments with portraiture had served to tranquilize her mind (and Alice's as well) by finding solutions to the painful puzzle of female relationships. In public they might play the roles of Gertrude Stein, writer and genius, and Alice Toklas, typist and overseeing eye, but in private, and in the privacy of such works as "Lifting Belly" and "Possessive Case," they could experiment with the endless possibilities of being "Gertrice and Altrude."[45]

They continued on good terms with Claribel, who was a frequent visitor at the rue de Fleurus. However, the more cautious tone of Etta's correspondence with Gertrude reflects the alteration in their relationship. Although Etta had once written to Gertrude as "the friend who has been one of the real inspirations in my life with the deepest love

---

attachment to the mother's body. Stein's enjoyment of the rhythmic sensations obtained through the minutely varied repetitions and variations of her early writing could be described as semiotic, in this sense. Furthermore, such mimetic and kinesthetic effects in language are especially appropriate in the description of emotional/sexual experiences of great intensity, such as Stein offers in the final paragraph of "Ada" (a portrait which emphasizes its subject's loss of affect following the death of her mother, as well as the importance of the "pretty stories" told by the women to each other).

45. Wendy Steiner discovered this "doodle," which expresses the couple's symbiotic relationship, in the manuscript of Stein's "Lend a Hand" (YCAL, no. 269); see Steiner, *Exact Resemblance to Exact Resemblance: The Literary Portraiture of Gertrude Stein* (New Haven, Conn., 1978), p. 187. (Steiner does not discuss "Two Women" and has little to say about "Ada," probably because her study is concerned with portraiture as a genre with affinities to cubism.)

and devoted friendship of Etta Cone," after 1908 they communicated "with an informality devoid of intimacy" (*TC*, p. 102). When Etta saw Gertrude again in 1912, she noted another change in the household. Leo no longer dominated the scene. "He was either moodily silent or absent from the gatherings. It was now Alice Toklas' job to talk to wives, initiates, and those wanting a guided tour of the studio" (*TC*, p. 105). The process enacted in *Two* was being translated into social reality, and soon Leo would leave the household. On one of these visits, Gertrude pulled out the manuscript of "Two Women" and had the pleasure of hearing the unsuspecting Claribel read aloud portions of her portrait. She carried it off majestically, never realizing that the portrait was less than flattering. However, seeing both Claribel and Gertrude at the center of attention, Etta could not help comparing them. She told Gertrude, "it is a tossup as to which, you or Sister Claribel, likes being lionized the most" (*TC*, p. 110). As for the implicit comparison between the quieter members of these two pairs, herself and Alice, she could say nothing. Her frequent references to her successor as "Miss Taklos" (tactless?) suggest that her method of revenge was to refuse to learn her name.

Claribel returned to Baltimore after many years of residence in Germany, but the sisters decided to live in separate apartments. The following year, Etta set sail for Europe. Nora Kaufman, a young woman who nursed Etta through a severe case of influenza, went along as her paid traveling companion: "Etta had become more decided in her ways in recent years and was tired of catering to Claribel's demands" (*TC*, p. 109). At last she had someone to cater to her needs. When Gertrude and Alice met Etta and Nora for tea, they found the new arrangement to their liking. Two sets of pairs provided a neat solution to the awkwardness of their meetings as a threesome.

The Cones and the Stein-Toklas ménage did not meet again for nearly ten years. During the 1920s, the Cones devoted their Paris visits to the acquisition of paintings for their growing collection of modern art. Once they had completed their purchases, Claribel remained at the Hotel Lutetia, while Etta traveled with Nora. A warm relationship developed between the two women, which included private endearments and nicknames in the style of Alice and Gertrude. Claribel continued to make purchases from Gertrude's own collection, which suited both parties: Gertrude could not afford to buy a new painting unless she sold an old one, and the Cones admired what they saw in the studio. In 1926, they acquired a portrait of Gertrude herself—not the famous Picasso, but an unflatteringly lifelike portrait by Félix Vallotton, painted in 1907. Claribel enjoyed writing to Etta about the awkward negotiations for such purchases and reported Gertrude's hesitations about the "indelicacy" of inviting Claribel to inspect her antiques. She still enjoyed being asked to read aloud Gertrude's latest work. Claribel wrote that Gertrude's attitude at such readings was one of "satisfied amplitude": "Amplitude is the word . . . a good Gertrudism for something she has written and sits in her chair listening to with great satisfaction beaming from her face and her whole ample form" (*TC*, p. 151). Claribel was amused that she too could express herself in Steinese.

Relations between Etta and Gertrude did not, however, continue so amiably. Shortly after her arrival in 1924, Etta received a note in which Gertrude announced that she wished to sell the manuscript of *Three Lives*. Moreover, she mentioned the sum of $1000 dollars. Her guilty feelings color the note:

> I don't suppose that you want to pay any such price for a manu-script but since you had a connection with that manuscript I want to tell you about it before I consider doing anything. I think it's kind of foolish but I wouldn't want you to think that I would sell it to anyone else without telling you about it first. [*TC*, p. 159]

Etta managed to refuse the offer politely but at the same time broke off a proposed visit to the rue de Fleurus. For many years she told the story of Gertrude's attempt to sell her the same manuscript that she had typed with such devotion. If Gertrude could think of exploiting their friendship for even more obvious gain, it must have counted for very little.

In the same year that Etta declined her offer, Gertrude settled some scores of her own in "A History of Having a Great Many Times Not Continued to Be Friends." This list of former friends had "been nicely planned by those who feel best and most" (*AF*, p. 292). Although it is announced that there will be "no names mentioned," the Cone sisters are recognizable in "Clara and Bell" and "Etta is a name" (*AF*, pp. 308, 292, 325). The following year Gertrude wrote to Etta, "You will be pleased will you be pleased that two sisters are being printed in a book along with a lot of other authors" (*TC*, p. 181). The book was Robert McAlmon's *Contact Collection of Contemporary Writers,* which also included work by Joyce, Hemingway, Barnes, and Loy, but Gertrude had good reason to wonder whether Etta would be pleased to see the portrait in print. Her ambivalent remark suggests that she still had a guilty conscience about the decline of their friendship.

Something of their old intimacy returned to the correspondence in 1929, however, when Gertrude sent her sympathy on learning of Claribel's death. She tried to make amends by giving Etta the typescript of "Two Women." Etta was touched but chose her words with care: "I was moved by your remembering my sister as you did, and I shall catalogue your manuscript among her other art books which eventually will go to a museum." She added, "Life continues very empty without her but I am trying to carry on as she would have wished done." Then, in a revealing association of ideas, she noted of a recent purchase, "The

Picasso picture of Leo will be an important addition to those we had and I am very glad to have it" (*TC*, p. 224). If Gertrude had "had" Etta and Claribel as literary material, then Etta, in turn, might "have" brother and sister together in her art collection. However, Etta never saw Gertrude again. After Gertrude called her "a distant connection" in *The Autobiography* and declined an offer of hospitality on her American tour, Etta went out of her way to avoid further snubs.[46] If Gertrude bothered to read between the lines, she must have understood Etta's reasons when she wrote in 1934: "I was very much flattered to see from your autobiography of Alice Toklas that you remembered my one-time remark as to my 'ability to forgive but not forget.'" Etta concluded, "I haven't changed" (*TC*, p. 226). As Natalie Barney, herself a cool observer of women's relationships, said of Gertrude's history of failed friendships, "It is obvious that . . . her friendships ceased from the causes already detected in their beginning" (*AF*, p. xviii). Another piece of emotional mathematics had solved itself but not, this time, at Gertrude's expense.

46. See *Selected Writings of Gertrude Stein*, p. 68.

Zero Degree Deviancy: The Lesbian Novel in English

Catharine R. Stimpson

In her poem "Diving into the Wreck" (1972), Adrienne Rich imagined a descent into the sea of history that might see the damage that was done and the treasures that prevail. The poem has been a mandate for feminist critics as they measure the damage patriarchal cultures have inflicted and the treasures that a female tradition has nevertheless accumulated. We have yet to survey fully, however, the lesbian writers who worked under the double burden of a patriarchal culture and a strain in the female tradition that accepted and valued heterosexuality.[1] It is these writers whom I want to ground more securely in the domain of feminist criticism.[2]

Early versions of this paper were read at Brown University, Hampshire College, the Columbia University Seminar on Women in Society, and the Modern Language Association. I am grateful to Adrienne Rich, Elizabeth Wood, and Elizabeth Abel for their comments.

1. The number of texts about lesbians, by lesbians and nonlesbians, is unclear. There are about twenty-three hundred entries in Gene Damon and Lee Stuart's *The Lesbian in Literature: A Bibliography* (San Francisco, 1967) and about nineteen hundred entries in the revised edition by Damon, Jan Watson, and Robin Jordan (Reno, Nev., 1975). While this second edition has more nonfiction entries and has been updated, the compilers have also cut over a thousand entries from the first edition because they referred to "trash" men had written for male readers (p. 26). The pioneering survey of the figure of the lesbian in Western literature remains Jeannette H. Foster's *Sex Variant Women in Literature: A Historical and Quantitative Survey* (London, 1958), but adding to it now is Lillian Faderman's valuable *Surpassing the Love of Men* (New York, 1981).

2. For a study of the French literary tradition, see Elaine Marks, "Lesbian Intertextuality," in *Homosexualities and French Literature*, ed. George Stambolian and Marks (Ithaca, N.Y., 1979), pp. 353–77. Several of the articles on female sexuality which were collected in *Women—Sex and Sexuality*, ed. Stimpson and Ethel Spector Person (Chicago, 1980), have insights into modern lesbianism.

My definition of the lesbian—as writer, as character, and as reader—will be conservative and severely literal. She is a woman who finds other women erotically attractive and gratifying. Of course a lesbian is more than her body, more than her flesh, but lesbianism partakes of the body, partakes of the flesh. That carnality distinguishes it from gestures of political sympathy with homosexuals and from affectionate friendships in which women enjoy each other, support each other, and commingle a sense of identity and well-being. Lesbianism represents a commitment of skin, blood, breast, and bone. If female and male gay writings have their differences, it is not only because one takes Sappho and the other Walt Whitman as its great precursor. They simply do not spring from the same physical presence in the world.

To my lexicographical rigidity I will add an argument that is often grim. Because the violent yoking of homosexuality and deviancy has been so pervasive in the modern period, little or no writing about it can ignore that conjunction. A text may support it, leeringly or ruefully. It may reject it, fiercely or ebulliently. Moral or emotional indifference is improbable. Few, if any, homosexual texts can exemplify writing at the zero degree, that degree at which writing, according to Roland Barthes, is ". . . basically in the indicative mood, or . . . amodal . . . [a] new neutral writing . . . [that] takes its place in the midst of . . . ejaculation and judgements; without becoming involved in any of them; [that] . . . consists precisely in their absence."[3] Lesbian novels in English have responded judgmentally to the perversion that has made homosexuality perverse by developing two repetitive patterns: the dying fall, a narrative of damnation, of the lesbian's suffering as a lonely outcast attracted to a psychological lower caste; and the enabling escape, a narrative of the reversal of such descending trajectories, of the lesbian's rebellion against social stigma and self-contempt. Because the first has been dominant during the twentieth century, the second has had to flee from the imaginative grip of that tradition as well.

3. Roland Barthes, *Writing Degree Zero,* trans. Annette Lavers and Colin Smith (Boston, 1970), pp. 76–77. Barthes has claimed that a recent novel, Renaud Camus' *Tricks* (trans. Richard Howard [New York, 1981]), which I read in manuscript, exemplifies homosexual writing at the degree zero. In his preface, Barthes says that homosexuality is ". . . still at that stage of excitation where it provokes what might be called feats of discourse," but "Camus' narratives are neutral, they do not participate in the game of interpretation." I suggest that *Tricks* does interpret a pattern of male homosexual activity as a fascinating, intense, limited, and only apparently permissible form of experience.

Catharine R. Stimpson, professor of English at Rutgers University, is the former editor of *Signs: Journal of Women in Culture and Society.* The author of both critical essays and fiction, she recently coedited, with Ethel Spector Person, *Women—Sex and Sexuality.*

If the narratives of damnation reflect larger social attitudes about homosexuality, they can also extend an error of discourse about it: false universalizing, tyrannical univocalizing. Often ahistorical, as if pain erased the processes of time, they can fail to reveal the inseparability of the twentieth-century lesbian novel and the twentieth century: ". . . in the nineteenth century . . . homosexuality assumed its modern form," which the next century was to exhibit.[4] One sympton of modernization, of the refusal to exempt the lesbian from the lurching logic of change, was a new sexual vocabulary. Before the end of the nineteenth century, homosexuality might have been subsumed under such a term as "masturbation."[5] Then lesbians became "lesbians." The first citation for lesbianism as a female passion in *The Shorter Oxford English Dictionary* is 1908, for "sapphism" 1890.

The public used its new language with pity, hostility, and disdain.[6] The growing tolerance of an optionally nonprocreative heterosexuality failed to dilute the abhorrence of a necessarily nonprocreative homosexuality, especially if practicing it threatened to mean social as well as sexual self-sufficiency. In her study of birth control, Linda Gordon states: "We must notice that the sexual revolution was not a general loosening of sexual taboos but only of those on nonmarital heterosexual activity. Indeed, so specifically heterosexual was this change that it tended to intensify taboos on homosexual activity and did much to break patterns of emotional dependency and intensity among women."[7] Both female and male writers absorbed such strong cultural signals. If "guilt and anxiety rarely appear in homosexual literature until the late nineteenth century, . . . [they] become the major theme of *Angst* . . . after 1914."[8] Evidently, freedom in one place may serve as an innoculation against its permissible appearance elsewhere. The more autonomy women claim in one sphere, the more they may enter into an obscure balancing act that may lead to tighter restrictions upon them in another.

4. Gayle Rubin, introduction to Renee Vivien's *A Woman Appeared to Me*, trans. Jeannette H. Foster (Reno, Nev., 1976), p. v.

5. See Vern L. Bullough and Martha Voght, "Homosexuality and Its Confusion with the 'Secret Sin' in Pre-Freudian America," *Journal of the History of Medicine and Allied Sciences* (Spring 1973): 143–55; rpt. in Bullough, *Sex, Society, and History* (New York, 1976), pp. 112–24. My thanks to Mari Jo Buhle for bringing this article to my attention.

6. See Bullough, *Sexual Variance in Society and History* (New York, 1976), p. 605.

7. Linda Gordon, *Woman's Body, Woman's Right: A Social History of Birth Control in America* (New York, 1976), p. 164.

8. Rictor Norton, "The Homosexual Literary Tradition," *College English* 35, no. 6 (March 1974): 677; see also *College English* 36, no. 3 (November 1974), "The Homosexual Imagination," ed. Norton and Louis Crew. For an enthusiastic survey of lesbian writing, see *Margins* 23 (August 1975), "Focus: Lesbian Feminist Writing and Publishing," ed. Beth Hodges, esp. Julia P. Stanley, "Uninhabited Angels: Metaphors for Love" (pp. 7–10), which makes several points similar to mine here. For critical studies of the literature about male homosexuals, see Roger Austen, *Playing the Game: The Homosexual Novel in America* (Indianapolis, 1977), and Robert K. Martin, *The Homosexual Tradition in American Poetry* (Austin, Tex., 1979).

Such an environment nurtured external and internal censorship. During a century in which the woman writer as such became less of a freak, the lesbian writer had to inhibit her use of material she knew intimately but which her culture might hold to be, at best, freakish. She learned that being quiet, in literature and life, would enable her to "pass." Silence could be a passport into the territory of the dominant world. In a quick-witted recent novel, June Arnold's *Sister Gin,* an aging mother responds to her middle-aged daughter's attempt to talk to her about her lesbianism: "But she shouldn't say that word. It isn't a nice word. 'People don't care what you do as long as you don't tell them about it. I know that.' "[9] Such silence signifies a subterranean belief in the magical power of language. If the lesbian were to name herself, her utterance might carry a taint from speaker to listener, from mouth to ear. Silence is also a shrewd refusal to provoke punitive powers—be they of the family, workplace, law, or church. Obviously this survival tactic makes literature impossible. Culture, then, becomes the legatee of linguistic zeros, of blank pages encrypted in tombs critics will never excavate.

If the lesbian writer wished to name her experience but still feared plain speech, she could encrypt her text in another sense and use codes.[10] In the fallout of history, the words "code" and "zero" lie together. The Arabs translated the Hindu for "zero" as *sifr* ("empty space"), in English "cipher." As the Arabic grew in meanings, *sifr* came to represent a number system forbidden in several places but still secretly deployed, and cipher became "code." In some lesbian fiction, the encoding is allegorical, a straightforward shift from one set of terms to another, from a clitoris to a cow. Other acts are more resistant to any reading that might wholly reveal, or wholly deny, lesbian eroticism.

Take for example "the kiss," a staple of lesbian fiction. Because it has shared with women's writing in general a reticence about explicitly representing sexual activity, the kiss has had vast metonymic responsibilities. Simultaneously, its exact significance has been deliberately opaque. Look at three famous kiss scenes:

> It was a very real oblivion. Adele was roused from it by a kiss that seemed to scale the very walls of chastity. She flung away on the instant filled with battle and revulsion. [Gertrude Stein, *Q. E. D.*]

9. June Arnold, *Sister Gin* (Plainfield, Vt., 1975), p. 82. For an account of a facade that a lesbian community kept up, see Vern and Bonnie Bullough, "Lesbianism in the 1920s and 1930s: A Newfound Study," *Signs* 2, no. 4 (Summer 1977): 895–904.

10. I have written about coding by those who consider themselves sexual anomalies in "The Mind, the Body, and Gertrude Stein," *Critical Inquiry* 3, no. 3 (Spring 1977): 489–506. Detailed work on Stein's codes includes: Richard Bridgman, *Gertrude Stein in Pieces* (New York, 1970); Linda Simon, *Biography of Alice B. Toklas* (Garden City, N.Y., 1977); William Gass, *World within the Word* (New York, 1978), pp. 63–123; and Elizabeth Fifer, "Is Flesh Advisable: The Interior Theater of Gertrude Stein," *Signs* 4, no. 3 (Spring 1979): 472–83.

Julia blazed. Julia kindled. Out of the night she burnt like a dead white star. Julia opened her arms. Julia kissed her on the lips. Julia possessed it. [Virginia Woolf, "Slater's Pins Have No Points"]

Then came the most exquisite moment of her whole life passing a stone urn with flowers in it. Sally stopped; picked a flower; kissed her on the lips. The whole world might have turned upside down! . . . she felt that she had been given a present, wrapped up, and told just to keep it, not to look at it—a diamond, something infinitely precious, wrapped up . . . she uncovered, or the radiance burnt through the revelation, the religious feeling! [Woolf, *Mrs. Dalloway*]

Does the kiss encode transgression or permissibility? Singularity or repeatability? Impossibility or possibility? The same character, "O," can stand for both the zero of impossibility and for the possibilities of female sexuality.[11] Does the kiss predict the beginning of the end, or the end of the beginning, or a lesbian erotic enterprise? Or is it the event that literally embraces contradictions?

Still, the overt will out. As if making an implicit, perhaps unconscious pact with her culture, the lesbian writer who rejects both silence and excessive coding can claim the right to write for the public in exchange for adopting the narrative of damnation. The paradigm of this narrative is Radclyffe Hall's *The Well of Loneliness*—published, banned in England, and quickly issued elsewhere in 1928, by which time scorn for lesbianism had hardened into orthodoxy.[12] Novelist as well as novel have entered minor mythology. Hall represents the lesbian as scandal and the lesbian as woman-who-is-man, who proves "her" masculinity through taking a feminine woman-who-is-woman as "her" lover. In a baroque and savage satire published after *The Well of Loneliness*, Wyndham Lewis excoriates a den of dykes in which a woman artist in "a stiff Radcliffe-Hall collar, of antique masculine cut" torments a heterosexual fellow and dabbles with a voluptuous mate.[13] He is too jealous and enraged to recognize either the sadness of costume and role reversal (the stigmatized seeking to erase the mark through aping the stigmatizers) or the courage of the masquerade (the emblazoning of defiance and jaunty play).[14] Be it mimicry or bravery, the woman who would be man reaches for status and for freedom. The man who would be woman, because of

11. See Nina Auerbach, *Communities of Women: An Idea in Fiction* (Cambridge, Mass., 1978), pp. 186–87, for more comment on the "O."

12. See Blanche Wiesen Cook, " 'Women Alone Stir My Imagination': Lesbianism and the Cultural Tradition," *Signs* 4, no. 4 (Summer 1979): 718, and Lillian Faderman, "Love between Women in 1928" (paper delivered at the Berkshire Conference, Vassar College, Poughkeepsie, N.Y., 18 June 1981).

13. Wyndham Lewis, *The Apes of God* (New York, 1932), p. 222.

14. My comments footnote Sandra M. Gilbert's "Costumes of the Mind: Transvestism as Metaphor in Modern Literature."

the devaluation of the female and feminine, participates, in part, in a ritual of degradation.

Comparing *The Well of Loneliness* to Hall's life reveals a discrepancy between the pleasures she seems to have found with her lover, Una Taylor, Lady Troubridge, and the sorrows of her hero, Stephen Gordon. Hall offers a parallel to the phenomenon of the woman novelist who creates women characters less accomplished and successful than she. In addition, the novel is more pessimistic about the threat of homosexuality *as such* to happiness than Hall's earlier novel, *The Unlit Lamp* (1924). Set in roughly the same time period as *The Well of Loneliness, The Unlit Lamp* dramatizes a triangle of mother, daughter, and governess. The daughter and governess have a long, unconsummated, ultimately ruptured lesbian relationship. Their grief is less the result of a vile passion and the reactions to it than of the daughter's failure of nerve, her father's patriarchal crassness, her mother's possessive manipulations, and the constrictions provincial England places on the New Woman.

In brief, *The Well of Loneliness* tends to ignore the more benign possibilities of lesbianism. Hall projects homosexuality as a sickness. To deepen the horror, the abnormal illness is inescapable, preordained; an ascribed, not an achieved, status. For Stephen is a "congenital invert," the term John Addington Symonds probably coined around 1883 and Havelock Ellis later refined: "Sexual inversion, as here understood, means sexual instinct turned by inborn constitutional abnormality towards persons of the same sex. It is thus a narrower term than homosexuality, which includes all sexual attractions between persons of the same sex." The congenital female invert has male physical traits—narrow hips, wide shoulders—as "part of an organic instinct."[15] Stephen also has a livid scar on her cheek. Literally, it is a war wound; socially, a mark of the stigmatized individual who may blame the self for a lack of acceptability;[16] mythically, the mark of Cain. *The Well of Loneliness* stresses the morbidity of a stigma that the politics of heaven, not of earth, must first relieve.

Yet Hall planned an explicit protest against that morbidity. Indeed, having Stephen Gordon be a congenital invert who has no choice about her condition strengthens Hall's argument about the unfairness of equating homosexuality with punishable deviancy. The novel claims that God created homosexuals. If they are good enough for Him, they ought to be good enough for us. Hall cries out for sacred and social toleration, for an end to the cruelties of alienation. In the novel's famous last paragraph, Stephen gasps, "God . . . we believe; we have told You we believe.

15. Havelock Ellis, "Sexual Inversion," *Studies in the Psychology of Sex*, 2 vols. (1901; New York, 1936), 1:1, 122.
16. Erving Goffman's *Stigma: Notes on the Management of Spoiled Identity* (Englewood Cliffs, N.J., 1963), pp. 8–9, has influenced my analysis here.

. . . We have not denied You, then rise up and defend us. Acknowledge us, oh God, before the whole world. Give us the right to our existence."[17] Ironically, the very explicitness of that cry in a climate increasingly harsh for lesbians, combined with the vividness of Hall's description of homosexual subworlds, propelled *The Well of Loneliness* into scandal while the far more subversive, if subtle, *Unlit Lamp* was a success. To double the irony, Hall's strategies of protest against damnation so entangle her in damnation that they intensify the sense of its inevitability and power. The novel's attack on homophobia becomes particularly self-defeating. The text is, then, like a Janus with one face looming larger than the other. It gives the heterosexual a voyeuristic tour and the vicarious comfort of reading about an enforced stigma—in greater measure than it provokes guilt. It gives the homosexual, particularly the lesbian, riddling images of pity, self-pity, and of terror—in greater measure than it consoles.

The Well of Loneliness lacks the intricacies of Djuna Barnes' *Nightwood,* another parable of damnation, published eight years later. Its lack of intricacy, plus its notoriety and the way in which it inscribes damnation, helped to transform its status from that of subject of an obscenity trial to that of an immensely influential, token lesbian text. As one historian writes, "most of us lesbians in the 1950s grew up knowing nothing about lesbianism except Stephen Gordon."[18] Despite, or perhaps because of, its reputation, critics have ignored its structural logic, an error I want to remedy now.

Each of the novel's five sections (or acts) ends unhappily, the parts replicating and reinforcing the movement of the whole. Book 1 begins with Stephen's birth to a loving, rich couple.[19] The happiness of their legitimate, heterosexual union is the positive term that opposes the woe lurking in wait for illegitimate, homosexual ones. Although Sir Philip Gordon had wanted a son, he loves his daughter. Wise, courageous, kind, honorable, attentive, athletic, he embodies a fantasy of the perfect father Hall never had, the perfect man she could never become. Lady Anna, however, who had simply wanted a baby, instinctively repudiates her "unnatural" daughter. Though mother and child are of the same sex, they share neither gender nor love. Hall's idealization of Sir Philip and her regrets about Lady Anna are early markers of a refusal to link a protest against homophobia with one against patriarchal values.

During her late adolescence, Stephen meets a visiting Canadian,

17. Radclyffe Hall, *The Well of Loneliness* (1928; New York, 1950), p. 437; all further references to this work will be included in the text.

18. Cook, " 'Women Alone,' " p. 719.

19. Though Hall's father deserted her mother around the time of Hall's birth, he left the child a generous inheritance. She was one of several aesthetic lesbians whose incomes permitted them to do more or less as they pleased. Class cannot abolish the stigma of homosexuality, but it can mitigate some of the more painful impressions.

Martin Hallam. They become the best of brotherly friends—until Martin falls in love with Stephen. His emotions shock her; her shock stuns him; he leaves the neighborhood. Stephen's introduction to heterosexual passion, to her a form of homosexual incest, confirms her inability to pass even the most benign of initiation rites for girls. The loss of her "brother," however, is far less painful than the accidental death of her father, which ends book 1: it deprives her of "companionship of mind, . . . a stalwart barrier between her and the world, . . . and above all of love" (p. 121).

So bereft, Stephen behaves blindly. She falls in love with Angela Crosby, fickle, shallow, and married. As Angela strings Stephen along with a few of those conventional kisses, she sets her up as a rival of two men: husband Ralph and lover Roger. The masculinized lesbian has few advantages in competition with natural males. To keep Ralph from finding out about Roger, Angela shows him a love letter from Stephen and claims to be the innocent victim of odd affections. Ralph takes the letter to Lady Anna, who gives Stephen the choice of leaving her beloved ancestral estate or watching Lady Anna leave it. Finding her "manhood," Stephen accepts exile. With a loyal governess, a favorite horse, and a private income, she abandons Eden for London. Hall concludes book 2 with the punishment of expulsion, proving that even the aristocratic homosexual must suffer.

In the city, Stephen completes the rites of maturity for inverts. She finds a home: Paris, the center of literary lesbianism in the first part of the twentieth century. She finds work: literature itself. She writes a wonderful and famous novel. As Cain's mark was from God, so both Ellis and Hall give their inverts some compensations: intelligence and talent. If the body is negatively deviant, the mind is positively so. Hall demands that the invert use that intelligence and talent. Hard work will be a weapon against the hostile world; cultural production an answer to the society that repudiates a Stephen because she has been forced to repudiate reproduction. Finally, serving a larger cause, Stephen becomes a valiant member of a World War I women's ambulance corps. (Hall here explores, if peripherally, that standard setting of the lesbian text: a community of women.) But despite the personal bravery of both female and male warriors, the war is a wasteland. Stephen's personal anguish and confusion over her sexuality, then, find a larger, historical correlative in the trenches, as Hall ends book 3 with a lament for the dead.

During the war, however, Stephen has met a poorer, younger, Welsh woman, Mary Llewellyn, whom she takes to a Mediterranean villa. For a while they suppress their physical longing. In Stephen's fears that sex will destroy love, ecstasy intimacy, Hall is suggesting that the stigma of homosexuality is tolerable as long as the erotic desire that distinguishes the lesbian remains repressed. The conclusion—that a released eros will provoke the destructive potential of the stigma—places Hall in that Western cultural tradition that links sex and death. In addition, she is attributing to lesbianism a conventional belief about female sexuality in general: that women prefer love and romance to physical consummation. Ultimately Mary's needs overwhelm Stephen's chivalrous hope to protect her from them. Though their bodies, like those of any homosexual couple, are anatomically similar, their relationship embodies a number of dyadic roles. Into their closed and exclusive world they structure multiple polarized differences, primarily that between female and male. Hall exults:

> Stephen as she held the girl in her arms, would feel that indeed she was all things to Mary; father, mother, friend and lover, all things; and Mary all things to her—the child, the friend, the beloved, all things. But Mary, because she was perfect woman, would rest without thought, without exultation, without question; finding no need to question since for her there was now only one thing—Stephen. [P. 134]

Seeking metaphors for their passion, Hall, like many lesbian novelists, turns to nature, both tamed and untamed: to vineyards, fruit trees, flowers, the four elements, the moon. Such standard tropes carry the implicit burden of dissolving the taint of "unnatural" actions through the cleansing power of natural language.[20]

Most idylls, even those of refound Edens, must end. Hall concludes book 4 with the ominous "And thus in a cloud of illusion and glory, sped the last enchanted days at Orotava" (p. 317). Stephen and Mary return to Paris. There, with their loving dog, they are happy—for a while; but Mary, restless, begins to seek diversion with other lesbians and in the homosexual underworld, particularly in the bars that modern cities nurture. Bars can serve as a source of warm, egalitarian *communitas* for the marginal homosexual who must also aspire to the far more prestigious heterosexual world that is a structural reference group.[21] But the fearful, puritanical Stephen despises them; like many fictive lesbians, she finds security in a sanctified domesticity. Though a friend reasonably tells Stephen that Mary has too little to do, especially when Stephen is obsessively writing, Hall just as reasonably locates the primary source of strain between the lovers in the tension between their little world and the larger world of society and family that fears them.

20. As late as 1974, when the American Psychoanalytic Association voted to declassify homosexuality as a mental illness, lesbian writers were still dipping into the reservoir of such romantic tropes, as in Kate Millett's *Flying* (New York, 1974): "Taste of salt. Catching it in my mouth. A thirst to suckle it. . . . Very small thing. Pain of tenderness. . . . Fire. The vulva a sun setting behind trees" (p. 536).

21. I am gratefully adapting these terms from Victor Turner's "Passages, Margins, and Poverty," *Dramas, Fields, and Metaphors: Symbolic Action in Human Society* (Ithaca, N.Y., 1974), p. 233.

Whatever the cause, Mary mopes and hardens. Then, a secular *deus ex machina*, Martin Hallam returns. Stephen's alter ego, he, too, has been wounded in the war. He, too, falls in love with Mary. The two fight it out for her. Though Stephen wins, the price is too high: where she once had Mary's soul but feared possession of the body, she may now possess the body but not the soul. For God's scheme includes congenital heterosexuals as well as congenital inverts. Mary has, somewhat belatedly, realized that she is one of them. Martyring herself in the religion of love, Stephen pretends to be having an affair with a woman friend, Valerie Seymour. She stays out for two nights. When she returns, her mock confession of infidelity drives the distraught Mary into the night and the arms of the waiting Martin, whom Stephen has posted in the street below.

Throughout book 5, Hall's religiosity has become more and more omnipresent: her attraction to Catholic theology, architecture, and liturgy; her anxious queries about God's real allegiance in the war between Stephen's little world and that which would damn it. As Stephen renounces Mary, she has a compensatory vision, at once hallucination, inspiration, and conversion experience. She will become the voice of the voiceless stigmatized; she will help them break through to a new, sympathetic recognition. So willing, Stephen finds that "her barren womb became fruitful—it ached with its fearful and sterile burden" (p. 437).

That juxtaposition of fruitfulness and aching burdens is a final bit of information about the unevenly balanced duality of Hall's text. Yet she does create the figure of Valerie Seymour, a charismatic teetotaler who keeps a famous Parisian salon. Amidst the volatile gloom of Stephen's histrionics, she is serenely sunny. She, too, finds homosexuality congenital, but she lyrically interprets fate as a friendly boon: "Nature was trying to do her bit; inverts were being born in increasing numbers, and after a while their numbers would tell, even with the fools who still ignored Nature" (p. 406). Though Hall does little with Valerie, she signifies the presence of a second consciousness about lesbianism that *The Well of Loneliness* and the forces surrounding it helped to submerge, screen, and render secondary during the mid twentieth century. This consciousness, aware of the labelling of lesbianism as a pollutant, nevertheless chose to defy it.

The "Kinsey Report" suggests the existence of such a mentality. Of 142 women with much homosexual experience, 70 percent reported no regrets.[22] This consciousness has manifested itself in literature in two ways. First, in lesbian romanticism: fusions of life and death, happiness and woe, natural imagery and supernatural strivings, neoclassical paganism with a ritualistic cult of Sappho, and modern beliefs in evolu-

---

22. Alfred C. Kinsey et al., *Sexual Behavior in the Human Female* (1953; New York, 1965), p. 477. I am sure that this secondary consciousness will appear in autobiographical texts that scholars have previously ignored or been ignorant of. See, e.g., Elsa Gidlow, "Memoirs," *Feminist Studies* 6, no. 1 (Spring 1980): 103–27.

tionary progress with a cult of the rebel. At its worst an inadvertent parody of *fin de siècle* decadence, at its best lesbian romanticism ruthlessly rejects a stifling dominant culture and asserts the value of psychological autonomy, women, art, and a European cultivation of the sensuous, sensual, and voluptuous. Woolf's *Orlando* is its most elegant and inventive text, but its symbol is probably the career of Natalie Barney, the cosmopolitan American who was the prototype of Valerie Seymour.[23]

The second mode is lesbian realism: the adaption of the conventions of the social and psychological novel to appraise bonds between women and demonstrate that such relationships are potentially of psychic and moral value. The slyest realistic text is Stein's *Autobiography of Alice B. Toklas,* but less tricky examples include *The Unlit Lamp* and another ignored novel, Helen R. Hull's *Labyrinth* (1923). There one sister marries an ambitious, egocentric man. A second sister lives with an ambitious, generous woman. The first sister is unhappy and confined; the second happy and productive.[24] What *Labyrinth* implies, other realistic texts state explicitly: even though the lesbian may have children whom she loves, she must reject the patriarchal family, which the stigma against her helps to maintain, if she is to reject repression as well. The tension between the role of mother, which the lesbian may desire, and the traditional family structure, in which women are subordinate, is obviously far more characteristic of lesbian than gay-male writing. A man may have both paternity and power, but a woman must too often choose between maternity and comparative powerlessness.

In 1963 Mary McCarthy's *The Group* brought that submerged, screened, secondary consciousness to public prominence. Second on the fiction best-seller list for its year, selling well over 3,000,000 copies by 1977, *The Group* showed that lesbianism could be an acceptable, even admirable, subject—particularly if a writer of unquestioned heterosexuality served as the gatekeeper. Moreover, McCarthy was tactfully judicious about the erotic details of lesbian sexuality. Cleverly, if perhaps inadvertently, McCarthy fused lesbian romanticism and lesbian realism. In characterization, setting, style, and some of its assumptions, *The Group* was realistic, but its heroine was wonderfully romantic. For Lakey is self-assured, intelligent, beautiful, charitable, and anti-Fascist; she wears violet suits; she has lived in Europe; she has an affair with a baroness. In brief, she personifies the most glamorous of enabling escapes from stigma and self-contempt. The members of The Group, all Vassar graduates, also prefigure the possible response of liberal readers of this

23. See Rubin, introduction to Vivien's *A Woman Appeared to Me,* and George Wickes, *The Amazon of Letters: The Life and Loves of Natalie Barney* (New York, 1976).

24. A more ironic and subtle English equivalent is Elizabeth Bowen's *The Hotel* (New York, 1928). Patricia Highsmith's ("Claire Morgan") *The Price of Salt* (New York, 1952), like *Labyrinth,* is about the family and the lesbian's need to leave it even if she is a mother.

novel to the claims of this secondary consciousness to primary status. Lakey, after she returns from Europe, cannot be damned; indeed, she must be respected. Yet The Group finds encounters with her awkwardly enigmatic and strange; strangely and enigmatically awkward.

Since *The Group,* a far less tormented lesbian has surfaced—to supplement, if not wholly supplant, the Stephens and the Marys. In some texts by nonlesbians, she is little more than a romp, a sexual interlude and caper. Like masturbation and the orgy, homosexuality has become a counter in the game of erotic writing. Trade fiction has claimed the provinces of pornography and sexology. Other texts, however, primarily by lesbians and sympathetic feminists, damn the lesbian's damnation. Their appearance in strength is the result of a confluence of forces. Certainly a material cause was the founding of several journals, magazines, and presses that could publish the products of a more audacious sexual ideology and practice. Among the most substantial, for the lesbian novel, was the small trade house, Daughters, Inc. Its subtitle, "Publishers of Books by Women," reflects its founders' theory that feminism would create new genres. Existing in that climate, which might have a certain early crudity, would be a "freer lesbian novel, and Daughters would be a medium that lesbian novelists could count on."[25] Among the social causes of the reappearance of a submerged consciousness and its narrative of the enabling escape have been the women's movement, more flexible attitudes toward marriage (so often contrasted favorably to the putative anarchy of homosexual relations), the "modernization of sex," which encourages a rational, tolerant approach to the complexities of eros,[26] and the growing entrance of more women into the public labor force, which gives a financial autonomy inseparable from genuine sexual independence.

The new texts are hopeful about homosexuality and confident about the lesbian's power to name her experience and experiment with literary form.[27] These novels invert the application of the label of deviant: the lesbian calls those who would call her sinful or sick themselves

25. Bertha Harris (personal interview, New York, 3 August 1977); unless otherwise indicated, all further quotations from Harris are from this interview. See also Lois Gould, "Creating a Women's World," *New York Times Magazine,* 2 January 1977, pp. 34, 36–38.

26. I am indebted for this concept to Paul Robinson's *The Modernization of Sex* (New York, 1976). I have written in more detail about the relationship of the women's movement to American culture in "Women and American Culture," *Dissent* 27, no. 3 (Summer 1980): 299–307.

27. Ann Allen Shockley has suggested that the taboo on such a lesbian voice has been stronger in the black community than in the white, but even there the gags have loosened; see Shockley, "The Black Lesbian in American Literature: An Overview," in *Conditions Five, The Black Women's Issue,* ed. Lorraine Bethel and Barbara Smith (1979): 133–42. The entire issue is courageous and important. See also J. R. Roberts, *Black Lesbians: An Annotated Bibliography* (Tallahassee, 1981), with a foreword by Smith.

sinful or sick; she claims for herself the language of respectability. In a sweet novel of the 1960s, Elana Nachman's *Riverfinger Woman,* the protagonist fantasizes about enlightening some benighted heterosexuals. She and her lover will make a movie "so that people would see that lesbians are beautiful, there is nothing, nothing at all unnatural about them, they too can have weddings and be in the movies."[28] Mingling fiction, journalism, autobiography, and polemic, Jill Johnston declares in her book *Lesbian Nation* that "that awful life of having to choose between being a criminal or going straight was over. We were going to legitimatize ourselves as criminals."[29] Obviously these dreams and manifestos are still enmeshed in older vocabularies of value. A few books approach indifference. Less attracted to acts of reversal, they hint at a Barthian writing degree zero.[30]

Among the first of the more hopeful lesbian novels was *A Place for Us,* which its author (using the name Isabel Miller) published privately in 1969 and which a commercial press reissued as *Patience and Sarah* in 1972. That was the year of the Stonewall Resistance, the defense of a New York gay bar against a police raid that symbolizes the beginning of the Gay Liberation movement. The history of *A Place for Us*—the pseudonym, the dual publication—shows both the presence and the dissolution of a fear of lesbian material. Its author's comments about *The Well of Loneliness* reveal both the influence of and a resistance to Hall's earlier gesticulations: "I think Radclyffe Hall was antihomosexual. . . . I first read *The Well of Loneliness* when I was about seventeen. . . . I was very excited. But I didn't like the characters, I didn't like the arrogance of the heroine."[31] Gentle, kindly, *A Place for Us* tells of two nineteenth-century women who run away together from patriarchal brutalities to build their farm in New York State. Almost immediately after *A Place for Us,* the most successful of the new texts appeared, Rita Mae Brown's *Rubyfruit Jungle* (1973), which during the 1970s replaced *The Well of Loneliness* as the one lesbian novel someone might have read. In *Rubyfruit Jungle* (the title alludes to the female genitals), Molly Bolt (a name that alludes to

---

28. Elana Nachman, *Riverfinger Woman* (Plainfield, Vt., 1974), p. 13.

29. Jill Johnston, *Lesbian Nation: The Feminist Solution* (New York, 1973), p. 97.

30. For example, in Linda Crawford's *A Class by Herself* (New York, 1976), pills and booze compel a far greater renunciatory attention than does the stigma of lesbianism.

31. Alma Routsong ("Isabel Miller"), interview in Jonathan Katz, *Gay American History: Lesbians and Gay Men in the U.S.A.* (New York, 1976), p. 442. The career of one professional novelist replicates the historical shift from a stress on the stigmatized text to its rejection. As "Ann Aldrich," Marijane Meaker wrote widely read novels about the romances and difficulties of the lesbian subculture. Then under her own name she published *Shockproof Sydney Skate* (New York, 1972). Profitable, well received, it is about a triangle consisting of a woman, the younger woman with whom she has an affair, and her son, who is in love with the younger woman as well. The lesbian circles are little more absurd than any other subject of a comedy of manners.

freedom and flight) escapes from a seedy provincial background to triumph over mean men, shallow women, bad schools, menial jobs, and lesbian-baiting.

If *A Place for Us* adapts the narrative of the enabling escape to the pastoral domestic idyll, *Rubyfruit Jungle* integrates it with the picaresque and the *Bildungsroman*. Together these novels dramatize two contradictory attitudes about sex and gender that pervade the contemporary lesbian novel. The first of these attitudes is a bristling contempt for sexual role playing (*A Place for Us* is an exception here). The protagonist in *Riverfinger Woman* asserts: "we were too modern already to believe that one of us was the man and the other . . . the woman. We felt like neither men nor women. We were females, we were queers. . . . We knew we had the right to love whomever we loved."[32] Under the influence of an existential ethic that praises the freely forged self and of a feminist ideology that negates patriarchal practices, such novels abandon the customs of a Radclyffe Hall. Yet they are simultaneously conscious of sex. Males, particularly traditional ones, are in disrepute. Some novels, such as Arnold's *Sister Gin*, articulate punitive fantasies—some violent, some playful—which they justify as catharsis or self-defense. The female and the female world are honorable, as structural reference and source of *communitas*. Women ask not only for equality but for self-celebration; less for the rehabilitation of men than for independence from them.

Lesbian novels thus map out the boundaries of female worlds.[33] Some of the bonds within these boundaries are erotic, a proud isosexuality that separates the lesbian novel from other, more guarded explorations, such as Charlotte Perkins Gilman's *Herland*. Characters also search, however, for alter egos, moral and psychological equivalents, which the term "sister" signifies. Poignantly, painfully, they seek the mother as well.[34] A mother waits at the heart of the labyrinth of some lesbian texts. There she unites past, present, and future. Finding her, in herself and through a surrogate, the lesbian reenacts a daughter's desire for the woman to whom she was once so linked, from whom she was then so severed. Because the mother was once a daughter, a woman approaching her can serve as the mother's mother even as she plays out the drama of a daughter. In such complex mother/daughter exchanges and

32. Nachman, *Riverfinger Woman*, p. 13.

33. For a scrupulous exploration of lesbianism and women's worlds in the poetry of the 1960s and 1970s, see Mary Carruthers, "Imaging Women: Notes Towards a Feminist Poetic," *Massachusetts Review* 20, no. 2 (Summer 1979): 281–407.

34. See, e.g., Joan Winthrop, *Underwater* (New York, 1974), p. 256. Winthrop has her central character indulge in a good deal of masculine role playing, which occurs with a certain *esprit* but is only one aspect of personality, not a controlling force as it is in *The Well of Loneliness*. That the role playing takes place after a radical mastectomy is a point Winthrop does not explore. She does, however, say that her heroine's fantasies of being male were the product of years of her own "repression" (personal interview, Sag Harbor, N.Y., 28 July 1976).

interchanges, the women explore both narcissistic and anaclitic love. Of course lesbianism is far more than a matter of mother/daughter affairs, but the new texts suggest that one of its satisfactions is a return to primal origins, to primal loves, when female/female, not male/female, relationships structured the world. A lesbian's jealousy, then, spurts like blood from the cut of terror at the possibility of losing again the intimacy that has at last been regained.

To focus on mothers and daughters—or on any personal bonds—is too narrow; psychology hardly defines the totality of our lives. In several texts the world of women is also a political center of solidarity and resistance. As such it can perform social experiments that the larger culture might regard attentively. To name such communities, the lesbian writer calls on myth: prehistorical matriarchies; the Amazons; Sappho and her school. The myths, also current in contemporary feminist ideology, were popular in stylish lesbian circles in the earlier part of the twentieth century. Part of their value is their ability to evoke atemporal resonances within narratives that are separate from such patriarchal religious structures as the Catholic church before which Hall knelt. When novelists grant myths the status of history (easier to do with Sappho than with Amazons and primeval matriarchs), their error, because it occurs in the freewheeling context of fiction, is more palatable than in the stricter context of programmatic ideology, political theory, and "herstory."

The most ambitious and the cleverest of the new novels in English is perhaps Bertha Harris' *Lover* (1976). The lesbian novel has tended to be, and remains, formally staid, a conventionality that has served both a homosexual and heterosexual audience. The lesbian, as she struggles against the hostilities of the larger world, can find comfort in the ease of reading. Between text and self she may also establish a sense of community. The heterosexual, as she or he nears unfamiliar and despised material, can find safety in the same ease of reading. The continued strength of literary form can stand for the continued strength of the larger community's norms. However, Harris, an American equivalent of Monique Wittig, experiments with narrative pattern as a possible coefficient of her vision of sexuality. A modernist, she fragments and collapses characters, settings, chronology, and states of mind. Her central presence appears as Veronica (also the name of the second wife of Veronica's bigamist grandfather); as Flynn; as Bertha; and as "I." In each guise the voice is both fiction and the author in the act of writing fiction. In brief, *Lover* is another book about becoming a book.

Harris is ingenious, sardonic, parodic—an economical comic intelligence. Another cultural consequence of the stigma against the lesbian is that it deforms comedy. Those who support the stigma, such as Wyndham Lewis, may freely assault the homosexual with hostile satire and burlesque. Those who internalize the stigma use the same weapons as a form of self-assault. Only when the stigma is simultaneously comprehended and despised can the comedy of a Harris, or of a Barnes before her, emerge.[35] It is a satire, often elaborate, even grotesque and baroque, that ultimately adorns rather than mutilates its subject. Barnes' enigmatic and rich prose has deeply influenced Harris, but more immediately, so has Nabokov's, his "tricking and fooling and punning and literary joking."

Some people in the feminist and lesbian press have criticized Harris and others for these adventures. Harris has been called inaccessible, as if modernism were itself an indecipherable code. She is, therefore, supposedly ideologically unsound, stopping that illusory creature, the average lesbian, from using literature to articulate her experience and urge rebellion against its nastier aspects. Harris has explanations for such prescriptive reviews. She believes that the feminist and lesbian press still lacks an informed criticism to mediate between texts and a large audience, and she finds too few "well-read reviewers, conscious of literary traditions." The press must learn to do what modern art has done: to create a self-explanatory body of criticism. Furthermore, "the lesbian readership" wants a "positive image" in its novels. Part of the huge popularity of *Rubyfruit Jungle* is due to its ebullient self-admiration. Such easy hedonism and heroism is, of course, didactically helpful and politically worthwhile, but it also "prevents a deeper look into the nature of things and the nature of lesbianism."

The baffled response to *Lover* is ironic, for few writers have given the lesbian a more lyrical identity. Harris explores the various roles women have played: grandmother, mother, daughter, sister, wife and second wife, businesswoman in man's clothing, prostitute, factory worker, movie star, muse and tutelary spirit, warrior, artist, fake saint, martyr. She codifies difference of role in order to assess similarities of the players and to find a common basis for a community of women. There the primary difference will be between lover and beloved— though lovers can be loved and the beloved lovers. The phallus may not be unwelcome, especially if necessary for breeding, but the nonphallic lesbian has a privileged status. In loving women she exalts both self and other. Harris also anoints this paradigm and paramour as an omnipotent cosmic spirit. Capable of anything and everything, she is polymorphic, amorphic, transmorphic, and orphic. She both pictures margins and escapes them. She is the principle of creativity, of a fertility of both mind and body. As such she incarnates the genesis of the world itself, once

35. A notable example is Barnes' *Ladies Almanack: Written and Illustrated by a Lady of Fashion* (1928; New York, 1972) A dazzling analysis of this work is Susan Sniader Lanser's "Speaking in Tongues: *Ladies Almanack* and the Language of Celebration," *Frontiers* 4, no. 3 (Fall 1979): 39–46. The issue devotes itself to lesbian history and culture.

suppressed, which might be reappearing now. In an essay about Barnes and lesbian literature, Harris might be talking about *Lover* itself:

> There is not a literature that is not based on the pervasive sexuality of its time; and as that which is male disappears (sinks slowly in the west) and as the originally all-female world reasserts itself by making love to itself, the primary gesture toward the making at last of a decent literature out of the experience of a decent world might simply be a woman like myself following a woman like Djuna Barnes, and all she might represent down a single street on a particular afternoon.[36]

Not everyone will accept Harris' only partially ironic apocalyptic fantasy. Her picture of the damned does, however, reverse that of *The Well of Loneliness*. The lesbian novel has offered up Hall's vision, but it has also sheltered and released the rejection of that vision, offering an alternative process of affirmation of the lesbian body and transcendence of a culturally traced, scarring stigma. It has been a deviant voice that has both submitted to deviancy and yearned to nullify that judgment. Feminist critics, zeroing in on that voice, can serve as its acoustical engineers. We can listen for its variations, fluctuations, blurrings, coded signals, and lapses into mimicry or a void. As we do, we must also try to hear, in wonder and in rage, words and phrases that might explain what is now a mystery: why people wish to stigmatize, to dominate, to outlaw, and to erase a particular longing for passion and for love.

36. Harris, "The More Profound Nationality of Their Lesbianism: Lesbian Society in Paris in the 1920s," in *Amazon Expedition: A Lesbian Feminist Anthology*, ed. Harris et al. (Washington, N.J., 1973), p. 88; see also "What We Mean to Say: Notes Toward Defining the Nature of Lesbian Literature," *Heresies* 3 (Fall 1977): 5–8, an issue of exceptional interest.

"Draupadi" by Mahasveta Devi

Translated with a Foreword by Gayatri Chakravorty Spivak

Translator's Foreword

I translated this Bengali short story into English as much for the sake of its villain, Senanayak, as for its title character, Draupadi (or Dopdi). Because in Senanayak I find the closest approximation to the First World scholar in search of the Third World, I shall speak of him first.

On the level of the plot, Senanayak is the army officer who captures and degrades Draupadi. I will not go so far as to suggest that, in practice, the instruments of First World life and investigation are complicit with such captures and such a degradation.[1] The approximation I notice relates to the author's careful presentation of Senanayak as a pluralist aesthete. In *theory*, Senanayak can identify with the enemy. But pluralist aesthetes of the First World are, willy-nilly, participants in the production of an exploitative society. Hence in *practice*, Senanayak must destroy the enemy, the menacing other. He follows the necessities and contingencies of what he sees as his historical moment. There is a convenient colloquial name for that as well: pragmatism. Thus his emotions at Dopdi's capture are mixed: sorrow (theory) and joy (practice). Correspondingly, we grieve for our Third World sisters; we grieve and rejoice that they must lose themselves and become as much like us as possible in order to be "free"; we congratulate ourselves on our specialists' knowledge of them. Indeed, like ours, Senanayak's project is interpretive: he

---

1. For elaborations upon such a suggestion, see Jean-François Lyotard, *La Condition post-moderne: Rapport sur le savoir* (Paris, 1979).

looks to decipher Draupadi's song. For both sides of the rift within himself, he finds analogies in Western literature: Hochhuth's *The Deputy*, David Morrell's *First Blood.* He will shed his guilt when the time comes. His self-image for that uncertain future is Prospero.

I have suggested elsewhere that, when we wander out of our own academic and First World enclosure, we share something like a relationship with Senanayak's doublethink.[2] When we speak for ourselves, we urge with conviction: the personal is also political. For the rest of the world's women, the sense of whose personal micrology is difficult (though not impossible) for us to acquire, we fall back on a colonialist theory of most efficient information retrieval. We will not be able to speak to the women out there if we depend completely on conferences and anthologies by Western-trained informants. As I see their photographs in women's-studies journals or on book jackets—indeed, as I look in the glass—it is Senanayak with his anti-Fascist paperback that I behold. In inextricably mingling historico-political specificity with the sexual differential in a literary discourse, Mahasveta Devi invites us to begin effacing that image.

My approach to the story has been influenced by "deconstructive practice." I clearly share an unease that would declare avant-garde theories of interpretation too elitist to cope with revolutionary feminist material. How, then, has the practice of deconstruction been helpful in this context?

The aspect of deconstructive practice that is best known in the United States is its tendency toward infinite regression.[3] The aspect that interests me most is, however, the recognition, within deconstructive practice, of provisional and intractable starting points in any investigative effort; its disclosure of complicities where a will to knowledge would

2. See my "Three Feminist Readings: McCullers, Drabble, Habermas," *Union Seminary Quarterly Review* 1–2 (Fall-Winter 1979–80), and "French Feminism in an International Frame" (forthcoming in *Yale French Studies*).

3. I develop this argument in my review of Paul de Man's *Allegories of Reading: Figural Language in Rousseau, Nietzsche, Rilke, and Proust* (forthcoming in *Studies in the Novel*).

Mahasveta Devi teaches English at Bijaygarh College in Jadavpur, India, an institution for working-class women. She has published over a dozen novels, most recently *Chotti Munda ebang Tar Tir* ("Chotti Munda and His Arrow"), and is a prolific journalist, writing on the struggle of the tribal peasant in West Bengal and Bihar. **Gayatri Chakravorty Spivak** is professor of English at the University of Texas at Austin. The translator of Derrida's *De la grammatologie,* she has published essays on Marxist feminism, deconstructive practice, and contemporary literature.

create oppositions; its insistence that in disclosing complicities the critic-as-subject is herself complicit with the object of her critique; its emphasis upon "history" and upon the ethico-political as the "trace" of that complicity—the proof that we do not inhabit a clearly defined critical space free of such traces; and, finally, the acknowledgment that its own discourse can never be adequate to its example.[4] This is clearly not the place to elaborate each item upon this list. I should, however, point out that in my introductory paragraphs I have already situated the figure of Senanayak in terms of our own patterns of complicity. In what follows, the relationship between the tribal and classical characters of Draupadi, the status of Draupadi at the end of the story, and the reading of Senanayak's proper name might be seen as produced by the reading practice I have described. The complicity of law and transgression and the class deconstruction of the "gentlemen revolutionaries," although seemingly minor points in the interpretation of the story as such, take on greater importance in a political context.

I cannot take this discussion of deconstruction far enough to show how Dopdi's song, incomprehensible yet trivial (it is in fact about beans of different colors), and ex-orbitant to the story, marks the place of that other that can be neither excluded nor recuperated.[5]

"Draupadi" first appeared in *Agnigarbha* ("Womb of Fire"), a collection of loosely connected, short political narratives. As Mahasveta points out in her introduction to the collection, "Life is not mathematics and the human being is not made for the sake of politics. I want a change in the present social system and do not believe in mere party politics."[6]

Mahasveta is a middle-class Bengali leftist intellectual in her fifties. She has a master's degree in English from Shantiniketan, the famous experimental university established by the bourgeois poet Rabindranath Tagore. Her reputation as a novelist was already well established when, in the late '70s, she published *Hajar Churashir Ma* ("No. 1084's Mother"). This novel, the only one to be imminently published in English translation, remains within the excessively sentimental idiom of the Bengali

4. This list represents a distillation of suggestions to be found in the work of Jacques Derrida: see, e.g., "The Exorbitant. Question of Method," *Of Grammatology*, trans. Spivak (Baltimore, 1976); "Limited Inc abc," trans. Samuel Weber, *Glyph* 2 (1977); "Ou commence et comment finit un corps enseignant," in *Politiques de la philosophie*, ed. Dominique Grisoni (Paris, 1976); and my "Revolutions That as Yet Have No Model: Derrida's 'Limited Inc,' " *Diacritics* 10 (Dec. 1980), and "Sex and History in Wordsworth's *The Prelude* (1805) IX-XIII" (forthcoming in *Texas Studies in Literature and Language*).

5. It is a sign of E. M. Forster's acute perception of India that *A Passage to India* contains a glimpse of such an ex-orbitant tribal in the figure of the punkha puller in the courtroom.

6. Mahasveta, *Agnigarbha* (Calcutta, 1978), p. 8.

novel of the last twenty-odd years.[7] Yet in *Aranyer Adhikar* ("The Rights
[or, Occupation] of the Forest"), a serially published novel she was writing almost at the same time, a significant change is noticeable. It is a
meticulously researched historical novel about the Munda Insurrection
of 1899–1900. Here Mahasveta begins putting together a prose that is a
collage of literary Bengali, street Bengali, bureaucratic Bengali, tribal
Bengali, and the languages of the tribals.

Since the Bengali script is illegible except to the approximately 25
literate percent of the about 90 million speakers of Bengali, a large
number of whom live in Bangladesh rather than in West Bengal, one
cannot speak of the "Indian" reception of Mahasveta's work but only of
its Bengali reception.[8] Briefly, that reception can be described as a general recognition of excellence; skepticism regarding the content on the
part of the bourgeois readership; some accusations of extremism from
the electoral Left; and admiration and a sense of solidarity on the part of
the nonelectoral Left. Any extended reception study would consider that
West Bengal has had a Left-Front government of the united electoral
Communist parties since 1967. Here suffice it to say that Mahasveta is
certainly one of the most important writers writing in India today.

Any sense of Bengal as a "nation" is governed by the putative identity of the Bengali language.[9] (Meanwhile, Bengalis dispute if the purest
Bengali is that of Nabadwip or South Calcutta, and many of the
twenty-odd developed dialects are incomprehensible to the "general
speaker.") In 1947, on the eve of its departure from India, the British
government divided Bengal into West Bengal, which remained a part of
India, and East Pakistan. Punjab was similarly divided into East Punjab
(India) and West Pakistan. The two parts of Pakistan did not share
ethnic or linguistic ties and were separated by nearly eleven hundred
miles. The division was made on the grounds of the concentration of
Muslims in these two parts of the subcontinent. Yet the Punjabi Muslims
felt themselves to be more "Arab" because they lived in the area where
the first Muslim emperors of India had settled nearly seven hundred
years ago and also because of their proximity to West Asia (the Middle

---

7. For a discussion of the relationship between academic degrees in English and the
production of revolutionary literature, see my "A Vulgar Inquiry into the Relationship
between Academic Criticism and Literary Production in West Bengal" (paper delivered at
the Annual Convention of the Modern Language Association, Houston, 1980).

8. These figures are an average of the 1971 census in West Bengal and the projected
figure for the 1974 census in Bangladesh.

9. See Dinesh Chandra Sen, *History of Bengali Language and Literature* (Calcutta, 1911).
A sense of Bengali literary nationalism can be gained from the (doubtless apocryphal)
report that, upon returning from his first investigative tour of India, Macaulay remarked:
"The British Crown presides over two great literatures: the English and the Bengali."

East). The Bengali Muslims—no doubt in a class-differentiated way—felt themselves constituted by the culture of Bengal.

Bengal has had a strong presence of leftist intellectualism and struggle since the middle of the last century, before, in fact, the word "Left" entered our political shorthand.[10] West Bengal is one of three Communist states in the Indian Union. As such, it is a source of considerable political irritation to the central government of India. (The individual state governments have a good deal more autonomy under the Indian Constitution than is the case in the U.S.) Although officially India is a Socialist state with a mixed economy, historically it has reflected a spectrum of the Right, from military dictatorship to nationalist class benevolence. The word "democracy" becomes highly interpretable in the context of a largely illiterate, multilingual, heterogeneous, and unpoliticized electorate.

In the spring of 1967, there was a successful peasant rebellion in the Naxalbari area of the northern part of West Bengal. According to Marcus Franda, "unlike most other areas of West Bengal, where peasant movements are led almost solely by middle-class leadership from Calcutta, Naxalbari has spawned an indigenous agrarian reform leadership led by the lower classes" including tribal cultivators.[11] This peculiar coalition of peasant and intellectual sparked off a number of Naxalbaris all over India.[12] The target of these movements was the long-established oppression of the landless peasantry and itinerant farm worker, sustained through an unofficial government-landlord collusion that too easily circumvented the law. Indeed, one might say that legislation seemed to have an eye to its own future circumvention.

It is worth remarking that this coalition of peasant and intellectual—with long histories of apprenticeship precisely on the side of the intellectual—has been recuperated in the West by both ends of the polarity that constitutes a "political spectrum." Bernard-Henri Lévy, the ex-Maoist French "New Philosopher," has implicitly compared it to the May 1968 "revolution" in France, where the students joined the workers.[13] In France, however, the student identity of the movement had remained clear, and the student leadership had not brought with it sustained efforts to undo the privilege of the intellectual. On the other hand, "in much the same manner as many American college presidents

10. See Gautam Chattopadhyay, *Communism and the Freedom Movement in Bengal* (New Delhi, 1970).

11. Marcus F. Franda, *Radical Politics in West Bengal* (Cambridge, Mass., 1971), p. 153. I am grateful to Michael Ryan for having located this accessible account of the Naxalbari movement.

12. See Samar Sen et al., eds., *Naxalbari and After: A Frontier Anthology*, 2 vols. (Calcutta, 1978).

13. See Bernard-Henri Lévy, *Bangla Desh: Nationalisme dans la révolution* (Paris, 1973).

have described the protest of American students, Indian political and social leaders have explained the Naxalites (supporters of Naxalbari) by referring to their sense of alienation and to the influence of writers like Marcuse and Sartre which has seemingly dominated the minds of young people throughout the world in the 1960s."[14]

It is against such recuperations that I would submit what I have called the theme of class deconstruction with reference to the young gentlemen revolutionaries in "Draupadi." Senanayak remains fixed within his class origins, which are similar to those of the gentlemen revolutionaries. Correspondingly, he is contained and judged fully within Mahasveta's story; by contrast, the gentlemen revolutionaries remain latent, underground. Even their leader's voice is only heard formulaically within Draupadi's solitude. I should like to think that it is because they are so persistently engaged in undoing class containment and the opposition between reading (book learning) and doing—rather than keeping the two aesthetically forever separate—that they inhabit a world whose authority and outline no text—including Mahasveta's—can encompass.

In 1970, the implicit hostility between East and West Pakistan flamed into armed struggle. In 1971, at a crucial moment in the struggle, the armed forces of the government of India were deployed, seemingly because there were alliances between the Naxalites of West Bengal and the freedom fighters of East Bengal (now Bangladesh). "If a guerrilla-style insurgency had persisted, these forces would undoubtedly have come to dominate the politics of the movement. It was this trend that the Indian authorities were determined to pre-empt by intervention." Taking advantage of the general atmosphere of jubilation at the defeat of West Pakistan, India's "principal national rival in South Asia"[15] (this was also the first time India had "won a war" in its millennial history), the Indian prime minister was able to crack down with exceptional severity on the Naxalites, destroying the rebellious sections of the rural population, most significantly the tribals, as well. The year 1971 is thus a point of reference in Senanayak's career.

This is the setting of "Draupadi." The story is a moment caught between two deconstructive formulas: on the one hand, a law that is fabricated with a view to its own transgression, on the other, the undoing of the binary opposition between the intellectual and the rural struggles. In order to grasp the minutiae of their relationship and involvement, one must enter a historical micrology that no foreword can provide.

14. Franda, *Radical Politics*, pp. 163–64. See also p. 164 n.22.
15. Lawrence Lifschultz, *Bangladesh: The Unfinished Revolution* (London, 1979), pp. 25, 26.

Draupadi is the name of the central character. She is introduced to the reader between two uniforms and between two versions of her name: Dopdi and Draupadi. It is either that as a tribal she cannot pronounce her own Sanskrit name (Draupadi), or the tribalized form, Dopdi, is the proper name of the ancient Draupadi. She is on a list of wanted persons, yet her name is not on the list of appropriate names for the tribal women.

The ancient Draupadi is perhaps the most celebrated heroine of the Indian epic *Mahabharata*. The *Mahabharata* and the *Ramayana* are the cultural credentials of the so-called Aryan civilization of India. The tribes predate the Aryan invasion. They have no right to heroic Sanskrit names. Neither the interdiction nor the significance of the name, however, must be taken too seriously. For this pious, domesticated Hindu name was given Dopdi at birth by her mistress, in the usual mood of benevolence felt by the oppressor's wife toward the tribal bond servant. It is the killing of this mistress' husband that sets going the events of the story.

And yet on the level of the text, this elusive and fortuitous name does play a role. To speculate upon this role, we might consider the *Mahabharata* itself in its colonialist function in the interest of the so-called Aryan invaders of India. It is an accretive epic, where the "sacred" geography of an ancient battle is slowly expanded by succeeding generations of poets so that the secular geography of the expanding Aryan colony can present itself as identical with it and thus justify itself.[16] The complexity of this vast and anonymous project makes it an incomparably more heterogeneous text than the *Ramayana*. Unlike the *Ramayana,* for example, the *Mahabharata* contains cases of various kinds of kinship structure and various styles of marriage. And in fact it is Draupadi who provides the only example of polyandry, not a common system of marriage in India. She is married to the five sons of the impotent Pandu. Within a patriarchal and patronymic context, she is exceptional, indeed "singular" in the sense of odd, unpaired, uncoupled.[17] Her husbands, since they are husbands rather than lovers, are *legitimately* pluralized. No acknowledgment of paternity can secure the Name of the Father for the child of such a mother. Mahasveta's story questions this "singularity" by placing Dopdi first in a comradely, activist, monogamous marriage and then in a situation of multiple rape.

In the epic, Draupadi's legitimized pluralization (as a wife among husbands) in singularity (as a possible mother or harlot) is used to demonstrate male glory. She provides the occasion for a violent transaction between men, the efficient cause of the crucial battle. Her eldest hus-

16. For my understanding of this aspect of the *Mahabharata*, I am indebted to Romila Thapar of Jawaharlal Nehru University, New Delhi.

17. I borrow this sense of singularity from Jacques Lacan, "Seminar on 'The Purloined Letter,' " trans. Jeffrey Mehlman, *Yale French Studies* 48 (1972): 53, 59.

band is about to lose her by default in a game of dice. He had staked all he owned, and "Draupadi belongs within that all" (*Mahabharata* 65:32). Her strange civil status seems to offer grounds for her predicament as well: "The Scriptures prescribed one husband for a woman; Draupadi is dependent on many husbands; therefore she can be designated a prostitute. There is nothing improper in bringing her, clothed or unclothed, into the assembly" (65:35–36). The enemy chief begins to pull at Draupadi's *sari*. Draupadi silently prays to the incarnate Krishna. The Idea of Sustaining Law (Dharma) materializes itself as clothing, and as the king pulls and pulls at her *sari*, there seems to be more and more of it. Draupadi is infinitely clothed and cannot be publicly stripped. It is one of Krishna's miracles.

Mahasveta's story rewrites this episode. The men easily succeed in stripping Dopdi—in the narrative it is the culmination of her political punishment by the representatives of the law. She remains publicly naked at her own insistence. Rather than save her modesty through the implicit intervention of a benign and divine (in this case it would have been godlike) comrade, the story insists that this is the place where male leadership stops.

It would be a mistake, I think, to read the modern story as a refutation of the ancient. Dopdi is (as heroic as) Draupadi. She is also what Draupadi—written into the patriarchal and authoritative sacred text as proof of male power—could not be. Dopdi is at once a palimpsest and a contradiction.

There is nothing "historically implausible" about Dopdi's attitudes. When we first see her, she is thinking about washing her hair. She loves her husband and keeps political faith as an act of faith toward him. She adores her fore*fathers* because they protected their women's honor. (It should be recalled that this is thought in the context of American soldiers breeding bastards.) It is when she crosses the sexual differential into the field of what could *only happen to a woman* that she emerges as the most powerful "subject," who, still using the language of sexual "honor," can derisively call herself "the object of your search," whom the author can describe as a terrifying superobject—"an unarmed target."

As a tribal, Dopdi is not romanticized by Mahasveta. The decision makers among the revolutionaries are, again, "realistically," bourgeois young men and women who have oriented their book learning to the land and thus begun the long process of undoing the opposition between book (theory or "outside") and spontaneity (practice or "inside"). Such fighters are the hardest to beat, for they are neither tribal nor gentlemen. A Bengali reader would pick them out by name among the characters: the one with the aliases who bit off his tongue; the ones who helped the couple escape the army cordon; the ones who neither smoke nor drink tea; and, above all, Arijit. His is a fashionable first name, tinsel Sanskrit, with no allusive paleonymy and a meaning that fits the story a bit too well: victorious over enemies. Yet it *is* his voice that gives Dopdi the courage to save not herself but her comrades.

Of course, this voice of male authority also fades. Once Dopdi enters, in the final section of the story, the postscript area of lunar flux and sexual difference, she is in a place where she will finally act *for* herself in *not* "acting," in challenging the man to (en)counter her as unrecorded or misrecorded objective historical monument. The army officer is shown as unable to ask the authoritative ontological question, What is this? In fact, in the sentence describing Dopdi's final summons to the *sahib*'s tent, the agent is missing. I can be forgiven if I find in this an allegory of the woman's struggle within the revolution in a shifting historical moment.

As Mahasveta points out in an aside, the tribe in question is the Santal, not to be confused with the at least nine other Munda tribes that inhabit India. They are also not to be confused with the so-called untouchables, who, unlike the tribals, are Hindu, though probably of remote "non-Aryan" origin. In giving the name *Harijan* ("God's people") to the untouchables, Mahatma Gandhi had tried to concoct the sort of pride and sense of unity that the tribes seem to possess. Mahasveta has followed the Bengali practice of calling each so-called untouchable caste by the name of its menial and unclean task within the rigid structural functionalism of institutionalized Hinduism.[18] I have been unable to reproduce this in my translation.

Mahasveta uses another differentiation, almost on the level of caricature: the Sikh and the Bengali. (Sikhism was founded as a reformed religion by Guru Nanak in the late fifteenth century. Today the roughly 9 million Sikhs of India live chiefly in East Punjab, at the other end of the vast Indo-Gangetic Plain from Bengal. The tall, muscular, turbanned, and bearded Sikh, so unlike the slight and supposedly intellectual Bengali, is the stereotyped butt of jokes in the same way as the Polish community in North America or the Belgian in France.) Arjan Singh, the diabetic Sikh captain who falls back on the *Granth-sahib* (the Sikh sacred book—I have translated it "Scripture") and the "five Ks" of the Sikh religion, is presented as all brawn and no brains; and the wily, imaginative, corrupt Bengali Senanayak is of course the army officer full of a Keatsian negative capability.[19]

The entire energy of the story seems, in one reading, directed toward breaking the apparently clean gap between theory and practice in

18. As a result of the imposition of the capitalist mode of production and the Imperial Civil Service, and massive conversions of the lowest castes to Christianity, the invariable identity of caste and trade no longer holds. Here, too, there is the possibility of a taxonomy micrologically deconstructive of the caste-class opposition, functioning heterogeneously in terms of the social hierarchy.

19. If indeed the model for this character is Ranjit Gupta, the notorious inspector general of police of West Bengal, the delicate textuality, in the interest of a political position, of Senanayak's delineation in the story takes us far beyond the limits of a reference *à clef*. I am grateful to Michael Ryan for suggesting the possibility of such a reference.

Senanayak. Such a clean break is not possible, of course. The theoretical production of negative capability is a practice; the practice of mowing down Naxalites brings with it a theory of the historical moment. The assumption of such a clean break in fact depends upon the assumption that the individual subject who theorizes and practices is in full control. At least in the history of the Indo-European tradition in general, such a sovereign subject is also the legal or legitimate subject, who is identical with his stable patronymic.[20] It might therefore be interesting that Senanayak is not given the differentiation of a first name and surname. His patronymic is identical with his function (not of course by the law of caste): the common noun means "army chief." In fact, there is the least hint of a doubt if it is a proper name or a common appellation. This may be a critique of the man's apparently self-adequate identity, which sustains his theory-practice juggling act. If so, it goes with what I see as the project of the story: to break this bonded identity with the wedge of an *unreasonable* fear. If our certitude of the efficient-information-retrieval and talk-to-the-accessible approach toward Third World women can be broken by the wedge of an unreasonable uncertainty, a feeling that what we deem gain might spell loss and that our practice should be forged accordingly, then we would share the textual effect of "Draupadi" with Senanayak.

* * *

The italicized words in the translation are in English in the original. It is to be noticed that the fighting words on both sides are in English. Nation-state politics combined with multinational economies produce war. The language of war—offense *and* defense—is international. English is standing in here for that nameless and heterogeneous world language. The peculiarities of usage belong to being obliged to cope with English under political and social pressure for a few centuries. Where, indeed, is there a "pure" language? Given the nature of the struggle, there is nothing bizarre in "Comrade Dopdi."[21] It is part of the undoing of opposites—intellectual-rural, tribalist-internationalist—that is the wavering constitution of "the underground," "the wrong side" of the law. On the right side of the law, such deconstructions, breaking down national distinctions, are operated through the encroachment of king-emperor or capital.

20. The relationship between phallocentrism, the patriarchy, and clean binary oppositions is a pervasive theme in Derrida's critique of the metaphysics of presence. See my "Unmaking and Making in *To the Lighthouse*," in *Women and Language in Literature and Society*, ed. Sally McConnell-Ginet, Ruth Borker, and Nelly Furman (New York, 1980).

21. "My dearest Sati, Through the walls and the miles that separate us I can hear you saying, 'In Sawan it will be two years since Comrade left us.' The other women will nod. It is you who have taught them the meaning of Comrade" (Mary Tyler, "Letter to a Former Cell-Mate," in *Naxalbari and After*, 1:307; see also Tyler, *My Years in an Indian Prison* [Harmondsworth, 1977]).

The only exception is the word "*sahib.*" An Urdu word meaning "friend," it came to mean, almost exclusively in Bengali, "white man." It is a colonial word and is used today to mean "boss." I thought of Kipling as I wrote "Burra Sahib" for Senanayak.

In the matter of "translation" between Bengali and English, it is again Dopdi who occupies a curious middle space. She is the only one who uses the word "counter" (the "n" is no more than a nasalization of the diphthong "ou"). As Mahasveta explains, it is an abbreviation for "killed by police in an encounter," the code description for death by police torture. Dopdi does not understand English, but she understands this formula and the word. In her use of it at the end, it comes mysteriously close to the "proper" English usage. It is the menacing appeal of the objectified subject to its politico-sexual enemy—the provisionally silenced master of the subject-object dialectic—to encounter—"counter"—her. What is it to "use" a language "correctly" without "knowing" it?

We cannot answer because we, with Senanayak, are in the opposite situation. Although we are told of specialists, the meaning of Dopdi's song remains undisclosed in the text. The educated Bengali does not know the languages of the tribes, and no political coercion obliges him to "know" it. What one might falsely think of as a political "privilege"—knowing English properly—stands in the way of a deconstructive practice of language—using it "correctly" through a political displacement, or operating the language of the other side.

It follows that I have had the usual "translator's problems" only with the peculiar Bengali spoken by the tribals. In general we educated Bengalis have the same racist attitude toward it as the late Peter Sellers had toward our English. It would have been embarrassing to have used some version of the language of D. H. Lawrence's "common people" or Faulkner's blacks. Again, the specificity is micrological. I have used "straight English," whatever that may be.

Rather than encumber the story with footnotes, in conclusion I shall list a few items of information:

Page 393: The "five Ks" are *Kes* ("unshorn hair"); *kachh* ("drawers down to the knee"); *karha* ("iron bangle"); *kirpan* ("dagger"); *kanga* ("comb"; to be worn by every Sikh, hence a mark of identity).

Page 396: "Bibidha Bharati" is a popular radio program, on which listeners can hear music of their choice. The Hindi film industry is prolific in producing pulp movies for consumption in India and in all parts of the world where there is an Indian, Pakistani, and West Indian labor force. Many of the films are adaptations from the epics. Sanjeev Kumar is an idolized actor. Since it was Krishna who rescued Draupadi from her predicament in the epic, and, in the film the soldiers watch, Sanjeev Kumar encounters Krishna, there might be a touch of textual irony here.

Page 397: "Panchayat" is a supposedly elected body of village self-government.

Page 399: "Champabhumi" and "Radhabhumi" are archaic names for certain areas of Bengal. "Bhumi" is simply "land." All of Bengal is thus "Bangabhumi."

Page 399: The jackal following the tiger is a common image.

Page 400: Modern Bengali does not distinguish between "her" and "his." The "her" in the sentence beginning "No comrade will . . ." can therefore be considered an interpretation.[22]

Page 401: A *sari* conjures up the long, many-pleated piece of cloth, complete with blouse and underclothes, that "proper" Indian women wear. Dopdi wears a much-abbreviated version, without blouse or underclothes. It is referred to simply as "the cloth."

Draupadi

Name Dopdi Mejhen, age twenty-seven, husband Dulna Majhi (deceased), domicile Cherakhan, Bankrajharh, information whether dead or alive and/or assistance in arrest, one hundred rupees . . .

An exchange between two liveried *uniforms.*

FIRST LIVERY: What's this, a tribal called Dopdi? The list of names I brought has nothing like it! How can anyone have an unlisted name?

SECOND: Draupadi Mejhen. Born the year her mother threshed rice at Surja Sahu (killed)'s at Bakuli. Surja Sahu's wife gave her the name.

FIRST: These officers like nothing better than to write as much as they can in English. What's all this stuff about her?

SECOND: *Most notorious* female. *Long wanted in many . . .*

Dossier: Dulna and Dopdi worked at harvests, *rotating* between Birbhum, Burdwan, Murshidabad, and Bankura. In 1971, in the famous *Operation* Bakuli, when three villages were *cordonned* off and *machine gunned,* they too lay on the ground, faking dead. In fact, they were the main culprits. Murdering Surja Sahu and his son, occupying upper-caste wells and tubewells during the drought, not surrendering those three young men to the police. In all this they were the chief instigators. In the morning, at the time of the body count, the couple could not be found. The blood-sugar level of Captain Arjan Singh, the *architect* of Bakuli, rose at once and proved yet again that diabetes can be a result of anxiety and depression. Diabetes has twelve husbands—among them anxiety.

Dulna and Dopdi went underground for a long time in a *Neanderthal* darkness. The Special Forces, attempting to pierce that dark by an armed search, compelled quite a few Santals in the various districts of West Bengal to meet their Maker against their will. By the Indian Con-

22. I am grateful to Soumya Chakravarti for his help in solving occasional problems of English synonyms and archival research.

stitution, all human beings, regardless of caste or creed, are sacred. Still, accidents like this do happen. Two sorts of reasons: (1), the underground couple's skill in self-concealment; (2), not merely the Santals but all tribals of the Austro-Asiatic Munda tribes appear the same to the Special Forces.

In fact, all around the ill-famed forest of Jharkhani, which is under the jurisdiction of the police station at Bankrajharh (in this India of ours, even a worm is under a certain police station), even in the southeast and southwest corners, one comes across hair-raising details in the eyewitness records put together on the people who are suspected of attacking police stations, stealing guns (since the snatchers are not invariably well educated, they sometimes say "give up your *chambers*" rather than give up your gun), killing grain brokers, landlords, moneylenders, law officers, and bureaucrats. A black-skinned couple ululated like police *sirens* before the episode. They sang jubilantly in a savage tongue, incomprehensible even to the Santals. Such as:

> Samaray hijulenako mar goekope

and,

> Hende rambra keche keche
> Pundi rambra keche keche

This proves conclusively that they are the cause of Captain Arjan Singh's diabetes.

Government procedure being as incomprehensible as the Male Principle in Sankhya philosophy or Antonioni's early films, it was Arjan Singh who was sent once again on *Operation Forest* Jharkhani. Learning from Intelligence that the above-mentioned ululating and dancing couple was the escaped corpses, Arjan Singh fell for a bit into a *zombie*like state and finally acquired so irrational a dread of black-skinned people that whenever he saw a black person in a ballbag, he swooned, saying "they're killing me," and drank and passed a lot of water. Neither uniform nor Scriptures could relieve that depression. At long last, under the shadow of a *premature and forced retirement,* it was possible to present him at the desk of Mr. Senanayak, the elderly Bengali specialist in combat and extreme-Left politics.

Senanayak knows the activities and capacities of the opposition better than they themselves do. First, therefore, he presents an encomium on the military genius of the Sikhs. Then he explains further: Is it only the opposition that should find power at the end of the barrel of a gun? Arjan Singh's power also explodes out of the *male organ* of a gun. Without a gun even the "five Ks" come to nothing in this day and age. These speeches he delivers to all and sundry. As a result, the fighting forces regain their confidence in the *Army Handbook.* It is not a book for everyone. It says that the most despicable and repulsive style of fighting is guerrilla warfare with primitive weapons. Annihilation at sight of any and all practitioners of such warfare is the sacred duty of every soldier. Dopdi and Dulna belong to the *category* of such fighters, for they too kill by means of hatchet and scythe, bow and arrow, etc. In fact, their fighting power is greater than the gentlemen's. Not all gentlemen become experts in the explosion of "chambers"; they think the power will come out on its own if the gun is held. But since Dulna and Dopdi are illiterate, their kind have practiced the use of weapons generation after generation.

I should mention here that, although the other side make little of him, Senanayak is not to be trifled with. Whatever his *practice,* in *theory* he respects the opposition. Respects them because they could be neither understood nor demolished if they were treated with the attitude, "It's nothing but a bit of impertinent game-playing with guns." *In order to destroy the enemy, become one.* Thus he understood them by *(theoretically)* becoming one of them. He hopes to write on all this in the future. He has also decided that in his written work he will demolish the gentlemen and *highlight* the message of the harvest workers. These mental processes might seem complicated, but actually he is a simple man and is as pleased as his third great-uncle after a meal of turtle meat. In fact, he knows that, as in the old popular song, turn by turn the world will change. And in every world he must have the credentials to survive with honor. If necessary he will show the future to what extent he alone understands the matter in its proper perspective. He knows very well that what he is doing today the future will forget, but he also knows that if he can change color from world to world, he can represent the particular world in question. Today he is getting rid of the young by means of *"apprehension and elimination,"* but he knows people will soon forget the memory and lesson of blood. And at the same time, he, like Shakespeare, believes in delivering the world's *legacy* into youth's hands. He is Prospero as well.

At any rate, information is received that many young men and women, *batch by batch* and on jeeps, have attacked police station after police station, terrified and elated the region, and disappeared into the forest of Jharkhani. Since after escaping from Bakuli, Dopdi and Dulna have worked at the house of virtually every landowner, they can efficiently inform the killers about their targets and announce proudly that they too are soldiers, *rank and file.* Finally the impenetrable forest of Jharkhani is surrounded by real soldiers, the *army* enters and splits the battlefield. Soldiers in hiding guard the falls and springs that are the only source of drinking water; they are still guarding, still looking. On one such search, army informant Dukhiram Gharari saw a young Santal man lying on his stomach on a flat stone, dipping his face to drink water. The soldiers shot him as he lay. As the .303 threw him off spread-eagled and brought a bloody foam to his mouth, he roared "Ma—ho" and then went limp. They realized later that it was the redoubtable Dulna Majhi.

What does "Ma—ho" mean? Is this a violent slogan in the tribal language? Even after much thought, the Department of Defense could not be sure. Two tribal-specialist types are flown in from Calcutta, and they sweat over the dictionaries put together by worthies such as Hoffmann-Jeffer and Golden-Palmer. Finally the omniscent Senanayak summons Chamru, the water carrier of the *camp*. He giggles when he sees the two specialists, scratches his ear with his "bidi," and says, The Santals of Maldah did say that when they began fighting at the time of King Gandhi! It's a battle cry. Who said "Ma—ho" here? Did someone come from Maldah?

The problem is thus solved. Then, leaving Dulna's body on the stone, the soldiers climb the trees in green camouflage. They embrace the leafy boughs like so many great god Pans and wait as the large red ants bite their private parts. To see if anyone comes to take away the body. This is the hunter's way, not the soldier's. But Senanayak knows that these brutes cannot be dispatched by the approved method. So he asks his men to draw the prey with a corpse as bait. All will come clear, he says. I have almost deciphered Dopdi's song.

The soldiers get going at his command. But no one comes to claim Dulna's corpse. At night the soldiers shoot at a scuffle and, descending, discover that they have killed two hedgehogs copulating on dry leaves. Improvidently enough, the soldiers' jungle scout Dukhiram gets a knife in the neck before he can claim the reward for Dulna's capture. Bearing Dulna's corpse, the soldiers suffer shooting pains as the ants, interrupted in their feast, begin to bite them. When Senanayak hears that no one has come to take the corpse, he slaps his *anti-Fascist paperback* copy of *The Deputy* and shouts, "*What?*" Immediately one of the tribal specialists runs in with a joy as naked and transparent as Archimedes' and says, "Get up, *sir!* I have discovered the meaning of that 'hende rambra' stuff. It's Mundari *language.*"

Thus the search for Dopdi continues. In the forest *belt* of Jharkhani, the *Operation* continues—will continue. It is a carbuncle on the government's backside. Not to be cured by the tested ointment, not to burst with the appropriate herb. In the first phase, the fugitives, ignorant of the forest's topography, are caught easily, and by the law of confrontation they are shot at the taxpayer's expense. By the law of confrontation, their eyeballs, intestines, stomachs, hearts, genitals, and so on become the food of fox, vulture, hyena, wildcat, ant, and worm, and the untouchables go off happily to sell their bare skeletons.

They do not allow themselves to be captured in open combat in the next phase. Now it seems that they have found a trustworthy courier. Ten to one it's Dopdi. Dopdi loved Dulna more than her blood. No doubt it is she who is saving the fugitives now.

"They" is also a *hypothesis.*
Why?

How many went *originally?*

The answer is silence. About that there are many tales, many books in press. Best not to believe everything.

How many killed in six years' confrontation?

The answer is silence.

Why after confrontations are the skeletons discovered with arms broken or severed? Could armless men have fought? Why do the collarbones shake, why are legs and ribs crushed?

Two kinds of answer. Silence. Hurt rebuke in the eyes. Shame on you! Why bring this up? What will be will be. . . .

How many left in the forest? The answer is silence.

A *legion?* Is it *justifiable* to maintain a large battalion in that wild area at the taxpayer's expense?

Answer: *Objection.* "Wild area" is incorrect. The battalion is provided with supervised nutrition, arrangements to worship according to religion, opportunity to listen to "Bibidha Bharati" and to see Sanjeev Kumar and the Lord Krishna face-to-face in the movie *This Is Life.* No. The area is not wild.

How many are left?

The answer is silence.

How many are left? Is there anyone *at all?*

The answer is long.

Item: *Well, action* still goes on. Moneylenders, landlords, grain brokers, anonymous brothel keepers, ex-informants are still terrified. The hungry and naked are still defiant and irrepressible. In some *pockets* the harvest workers are getting a *better wage.* Villages sympathetic to the fugitives are still silent and hostile. These events cause one to think. . . .

Where in this picture does Dopdi Mejhen fit?

She must have connections with the fugitives. The cause for fear is elsewhere. The ones who remain have lived a long time in the primitive world of the forest. They keep company with the poor harvest workers and the tribals. They must have forgotten book learning. Perhaps they are *orienting* their book learning to the soil they live on and learning new combat and survival techniques. One can shoot and get rid of the ones whose only recourse is extrinsic book learning and sincere intrinsic enthusiasm. Those who are working practically will not be exterminated so easily.

Therefore *Operation* Jharkhani *Forest* cannot stop. Reason: the words of warning in the *Army Handbook.*

2

Catch Dopdi Mejhen. She will lead us to the others.

Dopdi was proceeding slowly, with some rice knotted into her belt.

Mushai Tudu's wife had cooked her some. She does so occasionally. When the rice is cold, Dopdi knots it into her waistcloth and walks slowly. As she walked, she picked out and killed the lice in her hair. If she had some *kerosene,* she'd rub it into her scalp and get rid of the lice. Then she could wash her hair with baking *soda.* But the bastards put traps at every bend of the falls. If they smell *kerosene* in the water, they will follow the scent.

Dopdi!

She doesn't respond. She never responds when she hears her own name. She has seen in the Panchayat office just today the notice for the reward in her name. Mushai Tudu's wife had said, "What are you looking at? Who is Dopdi Mejhen! Money if you give her up!"

"How much?"

"Two—hundred!"

Oh God!

Mushai's wife said outside the office: "A lot of preparation this time. A—11 new policemen."

Hm.

Don't come again.

Why?

Mushai's wife looked down. Tudu says that Sahib has come again. If they catch you, the village, our huts . . .

They'll burn again.

Yes. And about Dukhiram . . .

The Sahib knows?

Shomai and Budhna betrayed us.

Where are they?

Ran away by train.

Dopdi thought of something. Then said, Go home. I don't know what will happen, if they catch me don't know me.

Can't you run away?

No. Tell me, how many times can I run away? What will they do if they catch me? They will *counter* me. Let them.

Mushai's wife said, We have nowhere else to go.

Dopdi said softly, I won't tell anyone's name.

Dopdi knows, has learned by hearing so often and so long, how one can come to terms with torture. If mind and body give way under torture, Dopdi will bite off her tongue. That boy did it. They countered him. When they counter you, your hands are tied behind you. All your bones are crushed, your sex is a terrible wound. *Killed by police in an encounter . . . unknown male . . . age twenty-two . . .*

As she walked thinking these thoughts, Dopdi heard someone calling, Dopdi!

She didn't respond. She doesn't respond if called by her own name. Here her name is Upi Mejhen. But who calls?

Spines of suspicion are always furled in her mind. Hearing "Dopdi" they stiffen like a hedgehog's. Walking, she *unrolls the film* of known faces in her mind. Who? Not Shomra, Shomra is on the run. Shomai and Budhna are also on the run, for other reasons. Not Golok, he is in Bakuli. Is it someone from Bakuli? After Bakuli, her and Dulna's names were Upi Mejhen, Matang Majhi. Here no one but Mushai and his wife knows their real names. Among the young gentlemen, not all of the previous *batches* knew.

That was a troubled time. Dopdi is confused when she thinks about it. *Operation* Bakuli in Bakuli. Surja Sahu arranged with Biddibabu to dig two tubewells and three wells within the compound of his two houses. No water anywhere, drought in Birbhum. Unlimited water at Surja Sahu's house, as clear as a crow's eye.

Get your water with canal tax, everything is burning.

What's my profit in increasing cultivation with tax money?

Everything's on fire.

Get out of here. I don't accept your Panchayat nonsense. Increase cultivation with water. You want half the paddy for sharecropping. Everyone is happy with free paddy. Then give me paddy at home, give me money, I've learned my lesson trying to do you good.

What good did you do?

Have I not given water to the village?

You've given it to your kin Bhagunal.

Don't you get water?

No. The untouchables don't get water.

The quarrel began there. In the drought, human patience catches easily. Satish and Jugal from the village and that young gentleman, was Rana his name?, said a landowning moneylender won't give a thing, put him down.

Surja Sahu's house was surrounded at night. Surja Sahu had brought out his gun. Surja was tied up with cow rope. His whitish eyeballs turned and turned, he was incontinent again and again. Dulna had said, I'll have the first blow, brothers. My greatgrandfather took a bit of paddy from him, and I still give him free labor to repay that debt.

Dopdi had said, His mouth watered when he looked at me. I'll pull out his eyes.

Surja Sahu. Then a *telegraphic message* from Shiuri. *Special train. Army.* The *jeep* didn't come up to Bakuli. *March-march-march.* The *crunch-crunch-crunch* of gravel under hobnailed boots. *Cordon up. Commands* on the *mike.* Jugal Mandal; Satish Mandal, Rana *alias* Prabir *alias* Dipak, Dulna Majhi-Dopdi Mejhen *surrender surrender surrender. No surrender surrender. Mow-mow-mow down the village.* Putt-putt putt-putt—*cordite* in the air—putt-putt—*round the clock*—putt-putt. *Flame thrower.* Bakuli is burning. *More men and women, children . . . fire—fire. Close canal approach. Over-over-over by nightfall.* Dopdi and Dulna had crawled on their stomachs to safety.

They could not have reached Paltakuri after Bakuli. Bhupati and Tapa took them. Then it was decided that Dopdi and Dulna would work around the Jharkhani *belt.* Dulna had explained to Dopdi, Dear, this is best! We won't get family and children this way. But who knows? Landowner and moneylender and policemen might one day be wiped out!

Who called her from the back today?

Dopdi kept walking. Villages and fields, bush and rock—*Public Works Department* markers—sound of running steps in back. Only one person running. Jharkhani *Forest* still about two miles away. Now she thinks of nothing but entering the forest. She must let them know that the *police* have set up *notices* for her again. Must tell them that that bastard Sahib has appeared again. Must change *hideouts.* Also, the *plan* to do to Lakkhi Bera and Naran Bera what they did to Surja Sahu on account of the trouble over paying the field hands in Sandara must be cancelled. Shomai and Budhna knew everything. There was the *urgency* of great danger under Dopdi's ribs. Now she thought there was no shame as a Santal in Shomai and Budhna's treachery. Dopdi's blood was the pure unadulterated black blood of Champabhumi. From Champa to Bakuli the rise and set of a million moons. Their blood could have been contaminated; Dopdi felt proud of her forefathers. They stood guard over their women's blood in black armor. Shomai and Budhna are half-breeds. The fruits of the war. Contributions to Radhabhumi by the American soldiers stationed at Shiandanga. Otherwise, crow would eat crow's flesh before Santal would betray Santal.

Footsteps at her back. The steps keep a distance. Rice in her belt, tobacco leaves tucked at her waist. Arijit, Malini, Shamu, Mantu—none of them smokes or even drinks tea. Tobacco leaves and limestone powder. Best medicine for scorpion bite. Nothing must be given away.

Dopdi turned left. This way is the *camp.* Two miles. This is not the way to the forest. But Dopdi will not enter the forest with a cop at her back.

I swear by my life. By my life Dulna, by my life. Nothing must be told.

The footsteps turn left. Dopdi touches her waist. In her palm the comfort of a half-moon. A baby scythe. The smiths at Jharkhani are fine artisans. Such an edge we'll put on it Upi, a hundred Dukhirams—Thank God Dopdi is not a gentleman. Actually, perhaps they have understood scythe, hatchet, and knife best. They do their work in silence. The lights of the *camp* at a distance. Why is Dopdi going this way? Stop a bit, it turns again. Huh! I can tell where I am if I wander all night with my eyes shut. I won't go in the forest, I won't lose him that way. I won't outrun him. You fucking jackal of a cop, deadly afraid of death, you can't run around in the forest. I'd run you out of breath, throw you in a ditch, and finish you off.

Not a word must be said. Dopdi has seen the new *camp*, she has sat in the *bus station*, passed the time of day, smoked a "bidi" and found out how many *police convoys* had arrived, how many *radio vans*. Squash four, onions seven, peppers fifty, a straightforward account. This information cannot now be passed on. They will understand Dopdi Mejhen has been countered. Then they'll run. Arijit's voice. If anyone is caught, the others must catch the *timing* and *change* their *hideout*. If *Comrade* Dopdi arrives late, we will not remain. There will be a sign of where we've gone. No *comrade* will let the others be destroyed for her own sake.

Arijit's voice. The gurgle of water. The direction of the next *hideout* will be indicated by the tip of the wooden arrowhead under the stone.

Dopdi likes and understands this. Dulna died, but, let me tell you, he didn't lose anyone else's life. Because this was not in our heads to begin with, one was countered for the other's trouble. Now a much harsher rule, easy and clear. Dopdi returns—good; doesn't return—*bad. Change hideout*. The clue will be such that the opposition won't see it, won't understand even if they do.

Footsteps at her back. Dopdi turns again. These 3½ miles of land and rocky ground are the best way to enter the forest. Dopdi has left that way behind. A little level ground ahead. Then rocks again. The *army* could not have struck *camp* on such rocky terrain. This area is quiet enough. It's like a maze, every hump looks like every other. That's fine. Dopdi will lead the cop to the burning "ghat." Patitpaban of Saranda had been sacrificed in the name of Kali of the Burning Ghats.

Apprehend!

A lump of rock stands up. Another. Yet another. The elderly Senanayak was at once triumphant and despondent. *If you want to destroy the enemy, become one.* He had done so. As long as six years ago he could anticipate their every move. He still can. Therefore he is elated. Since he has kept up with the literature, he has read *First Blood* and seen approval of his thought and work.

Dopdi couldn't trick him, he is unhappy about that. Two sorts of reasons. Six years ago he published an article about information storage in brain cells. He demonstrated in that piece that he supported this struggle from the point of view of the field hands. Dopdi is a field hand. *Veteran fighter. Search and destroy.* Dopdi Mejhen is about to be *apprehended.* Will be *destroyed.* Regret.

Halt!

Dopdi stops short. The steps behind come around to the front. Under Dopdi's ribs the *canal* dam breaks. No hope. Surja Sahu's brother Rotoni Sahu. The two lumps of rock come forward. Shomai and Budhna. They had not escaped by train.

Arijit's voice. Just as you must know when you've won, you must also acknowledge defeat and start the activities of the next *stage*.

Now Dopdi spreads her arms, raises her face to the sky, turns toward the forest, and ululates with the force of her entire being. Once, twice, three times. At the third burst the birds in the trees at the outskirts of the forest awake and flap their wings. The echo of the call travels far.

3

Draupadi Mejhen was apprehended at 6:53 P.M. It took an hour to get her to *camp*. Questioning took another hour exactly. No one touched her, and she was allowed to sit on a canvas camp stool. At 8:57 Senanayak's dinner hour approached, and saying, "Make her. *Do the needful*," he disappeared.

Then a billion moons pass. A billion lunar years. Opening her eyes after a million light years, Draupadi, strangely enough, sees sky and moon. Slowly the bloodied nailheads shift from her brain. Trying to move, she feels her arms and legs still tied to four posts. Something sticky under her ass and waist. Her own blood. Only the gag has been removed. Incredible thirst. In case she says "water" she catches her lower lip in her teeth. She senses that her vagina is bleeding. How many came to make her?

Shaming her, a tear trickles out of the corner of her eye. In the muddy moonlight she lowers her lightless eye, sees her breasts, and understands that, indeed, she's been made up right. Her breasts are bitten raw, the nipples torn. How many? Four-five-six-seven—then Draupadi had passed out.

She turns her eyes and sees something white. Her own cloth. Nothing else. Suddenly she hopes against hope. Perhaps they have abandoned her. For the foxes to devour. But she hears the scrape of feet. She turns her head, the guard leans on his bayonet and leers at her. Draupadi closes her eyes. She doesn't have to wait long. Again the process of making her begins. Goes on. The moon vomits a bit of light and goes to sleep. Only the dark remains. A compelled spread-eagled still body. Active *pistons* of flesh rise and fall, rise and fall over it.

Then morning comes.

Then Draupadi Mejhen is brought to the tent and thrown on the straw. Her piece of cloth is thrown over her body.

Then, after *breakfast*, after reading the newspaper and sending the radio message "Draupadi Mejhen apprehended," etc., Draupadi Mejhen is ordered brought in.

Suddenly there is trouble.

Draupadi sits up as soon as she hears "Move!" and asks, Where do you want me to go?

To the Burra Sahib's tent.

Where is the tent?

Over there.

Draupadi fixes her red eyes on the tent. Says, Come, I'll go.

The guard pushes the water pot forward.

Draupadi stands up. She pours the water down on the ground. Tears her piece of cloth with her teeth. Seeing such strange behavior, the guard says, She's gone crazy, and runs for orders. He can lead the prisoner out but doesn't know what to do if the prisoner behaves incomprehensibly. So he goes to ask his superior.

The commotion is as if the alarm had sounded in a prison. Senanayak walks out surprised and sees Draupadi, naked, walking toward him in the bright sunlight with her head high. The nervous guards trail behind.

What is this? He is about to cry, but stops.

Draupadi stands before him, naked. Thigh and pubic hair matted with dry blood. Two breasts, two wounds.

What is this? He is about to bark.

Draupadi comes closer. Stands with her hand on her hip, laughs and says, The object of your search, Dopdi Mejhen. You asked them to make me up, don't you want to see how they made me?

Where are her clothes?

Won't put them on, *sir.* Tearing them.

Draupadi's black body comes even closer. Draupadi shakes with an indomitable laughter that Senanayak simply cannot understand. Her ravaged lips bleed as she begins laughing. Draupadi wipes the blood on her palm and says in a voice that is as terrifying, sky splitting, and sharp as her ululation, What's the use of clothes? You can strip me, but how can you clothe me again? Are you a man?

She looks around and chooses the front of Senanayak's white bush shirt to spit a bloody gob at and says, There isn't a man here that I should be ashamed. I will not let you put my cloth on me. What more can you do? Come on, *counter* me—come on, *counter* me—?

Draupadi pushes Senanayak with her two mangled breasts, and for the first time Senanayak is afraid to stand before an unarmed *target,* terribly afraid.

Critical Response

I

Writing and Sexual Difference:
The Difference Within

Jane Gallop

This volume entitled *Writing and Sexual Difference* began as the Winter 1981 issue of *Critical Inquiry* (vol. 8, no. 2), edited by Elizabeth Abel. Her introduction concludes that: "In addition to refining our mythologies of difference, this moment of feminist inquiry allows new figures to provide a different and enabling mythology" (p. 6). In "this moment," winter 1981, *Critical Inquiry* has become "feminist inquiry," and the momentary substitution of terms—"feminist" for "critical"—allows new figures (the guest editor, for example) to provide a different and en-Abel-ing mythology.

The word "mythology" might remind us that, in the same issue, Nina Auerbach celebrates how the poet H. D. aimed "to metamorphose the woman's selfhood into an infinitely shifting myth" (p. 128). Late in the issue, Judith Kegan Gardiner—whose work is very close to Abel's—writes that "the woman writer uses her text . . . as part of a continuing process involving her own self-definition" (p. 187). According to Gardiner, the autobiographical critical essay is one manifestation of the tendency in women's writing to "blur the public and private," a tendency which stems from the "continual crossing of self and other" that is peculiar to female psychology (p. 185).

My reading of the "autobiographical" component in Abel's editor-

1. This can be deduced from evidence internal to the issue. Elaine Showalter says that Abel applies Nancy Chodorow's theory to contemporary women's novels (see "Feminist Criticism in the Wilderness," pp. 26–27. This is essentially what Gardiner does in her contribution to the issue. Not only is the work of these two women close, but they work on the closeness between women.

ship might lay it open to accusations of self-indulgence if it were not that, with a "continual crossing of self and other," it becomes quite difficult to pin down the self that is being indulged.[2] In other words, there is an alien presence within Abel's text which makes it impossible for her to "use" it as Gardiner suggests a woman does. Just as Abel and Gardiner, following Nancy Chodorow, see the woman's self as inextricably mixed up with the identity of another woman (the mother), so too the alien presence within Abel's moment is the text of another woman. The other woman's name is Barbara Johnson. A quotation from Johnson's book *The Critical Difference* appears as the epigraph to the editor's introduction. If the substitution of "feminist" for "critical" allows an en-Abel-ing, the epigraph already occasions a return of the dethroned term "critical."

There is one other mention of Johnson and *Critical Difference* in the issue. Mary Jacobus describes a "love language between two women" as "a language of desire whose object . . . is that internal (in)difference which, in another context, Barbara Johnson calls 'not a difference between . . . but a difference within. Far from constituting the text's unique identity, it is that which subverts the very idea of identity' " (pp. 50–51). Writing about this internal difference, Jacobus enacts it. Johnson's words, although within Jacobus' text, remain marked as different, marked as belonging to "another context." In its position as epigraph, *The Critical Difference* functions precisely as such a dis-Abel-ing "difference within" the entire issue.

The beginning of the epigraph promises to repeat a commonplace about literature and sex: "If human beings were not divided into two biological sexes, there would probably be no need for literature. And if literature could truly say what the relations between the sexes are, we would doubtless not need much of it then, either." At this point, Abel elides part of Johnson's text, and on the other side of the elision we encounter a quite startling formulation which reverses the terms of the expected truism: "It is not the life of sexuality that literature cannot capture; it is literature that inhabits the very heart of what makes sexuality problematic for us speaking animals." Sexual difference is a mystery; literature is concerned with that mystery. The reader expects another

2. It is, of course, not literally autobiographical but rather auto-graphical, a writing of the self. Nor do I mean to suggest that Abel consciously intends to write her name into the new mythology. What I wish to get at through this play on words is what we might call the text's unconscious. My hope is that attention to such marginal yet symptomatic moments might uncover some powerful, but not explicitly thematized, forces in the text.

Jane Gallop, associate professor of French at Miami University, is the author of *Intersections: A Reading of Sade with Bataille, Blanchot, and Klossowski* and *The Daughter's Seduction: Feminism and Psychoanalysis.*

rendition of the refrain that literature is unable to "capture" the mystery of sex, but instead Johnson claims that literature is already at the heart of what constitutes sex as enigma. Literature could be called the difference within sexuality.

This is very puzzling, very hard to understand. Abel says nothing in the introduction to explain it, and nothing in the issue explicitly serves to assimilate this internal difference. But because of it, from the very first page, *Writing and Sexual Difference* (the title) becomes troubling. Does "sexual difference" mean the *difference between* the sexes or the *difference within* sex? Are "sexual difference" and "writing" two distinct domains which intersect, or is writing interior to sexual difference?

Johnson's puzzling remark could best be explained by recourse to Lacanian psychoanalysis. According to Jacques Lacan, desire springs from the fact that the articulated demand always necessarily exceeds the instinctual needs one might wish to communicate.[3] The common view of language—that which underwrites the expected refrain about literature's inadequacy to capture sex—is that language is inadequate to express human needs. But according to Lacan, language is not only adequate but overabundant: it presents a surplus. In a formulation closer to Johnson's, Jean Laplanche, another French psychoanalyst, writes that sexual excitation is an "alien internal entity" and that this entity is precisely "parental fantasies and above all maternal fantasies."[4] If we understand fantasies as a form of literature, then sexual excitation, for Laplanche, is the alien internal presence of literature.

My attempt to explain Johnson's provocative remark is far from satisfactory, but even this cursory gesture demonstrates that any assimilation of these words necessitates a foray into "another context." My concern here, however, is not with what the epigraph might mean in the context of Johnson's book but rather with its effect within the bounds of the Winter 1981 issue of *Critical Inquiry*. Earlier, via Chodorow, I compared *The Critical Difference* within the "feminist inquiry" to the mother internal to the daughter's self; now I would construe it as a maternal fantasy, an unassimilated internal difference which, like sex itself, creates a tension, an instability, a subversion of identity, threatening, for example, the identity "feminist."

In the introduction Abel writes, "The analysis of female talent grappling with a male tradition translates sexual difference into literary differences" (p. 2). Literary difference is a "translation" of sexual difference which is, by implication, an original. This suggests the standard model in which sexuality is prior to literature, whereas the epigraph enigmatically implies that literature is already operative within

3. See Jacques Lacan, "The Signification of the Phallus," *Ecrits: A Selection*, trans. Alan A. Sheridan (New York, 1977), pp. 286–87.

4. Jean Laplanche, *Life and Death in Psychoanalysis*, trans. Jeffrey Mehlman (Baltimore, 1976), p. 24.

sexuality. But "translation" is also a potentially resonant term in the network of disabling internal alterity which I am here attempting to trace.

Although Johnson is mentioned only twice in the issue, her name does make one other appearance between its covers. In the pages of advertising at the end of the journal, in the ad for *Critical Inquiry*'s own publisher, the University of Chicago Press, we read that Johnson has translated Jacques Derrida's *Dissemination*. From the biographical notes on the contributors, we learn that the issue includes another translator of Derrida, Gayatri Chakravorty Spivak. Moreover, Spivak's contribution is itself a translation.

Spivak translates the Bengali story "Draupadi," written by Mahasveta Devi. Within the issue, the story occasions some uncertainty about the authority of original over translation: both in the table of contents and in the running heads, Spivak's name appears in the position of author. The editor's introduction, as we have seen, links the priority of original over translation with the anteriority of sexuality to literature. Not only does "Draupadi" call into question the authority of the original, it also raises the question of what is sexuality, or what is the body, outside of or anterior to literature.

Abel writes that "the fragmented female body shifts from metaphor to fact. 'Draupadi' lays bare the physical violence sublimated in metaphors of textual production" (p. 6). "From metaphor to fact": it looks like the Bengali story is going to take the journal from literature to life, to the real body, the real world, outside of rhetoric. This shift from metaphor to fact is in fact, however, a shift from nonfiction to fiction. "Draupadi" is the only piece of fiction in the issue; so when Abel says we switch from metaphor to fact, we must take "fact" as a metaphor.

Abel writes "the fragmented female body," but Draupadi (the heroine of the story) is not literally fragmented but rather mutilated. The metaphorical use of "fragmented" serves to link the story with Nancy J. Vickers' article on the Petrarchan tradition of fragmentary descriptions of the female body. According to Vickers, Petrarch's rhetorical fragmentation of Laura's body reverses the classical myth of the literal fragmentation of Actaeon as punishment for his view of Diana's naked body. One could say that "Draupadi" reverses the reversal: the naked female body, albeit mutilated, has once again the power to threaten the male.

Although Abel presents the story as a break with the rest of the volume, a shift "from West to East, . . . from implicit to explicit political perspective" (p. 6), she also sutures this break. Moreover, she links the Bengali story to probably the most traditional criticism in the volume, a study of variations on a classical myth in Renaissance poetry. Petrarch and Ovid might be said to represent the mainstream of our Western tradition, and yet they are linked to this gesture outside. Rather than simply dismissing this link as an imperialistic appropriation, might we not also see this resemblance between the exotic other and the very heart of the same as another manifestation of the difference within?

Continuing my analysis of Abel's statement about "Draupadi," I read the phrase " 'Draupadi' lays bare the physical violence" as a piece of black humor when I recall that in the story the heroine, after being multiply raped and mutilated, tears up her clothes and refuses to cover her mangled, bleeding body. She literally "lays bare the physical violence," which then reminds us that Abel is not using the phrase literally but figuratively. Abel's sentence implies that metaphor is a "cloth" veiling physical violence and that to expose violence demands that we tear the metaphor, render it inoperative, as Draupadi does her "cloth." Yet in order to speak this violent literalization, she necessarily has recourse to metaphor. In fact, the play on "Draupadi" as title and Draupadi as character allows us to see Draupadi's defiant exhibition after her rape as an allegory or a metaphor for reading, for a certain kind of ideological criticism.

At the very moment when she would proclaim the shift from metaphor to fact, the feminist critic cannot help but produce metaphors. I say "the feminist critic," rather than "Abel" because this is a moment that recurs in various texts of this issue, the moment when, in reaching for some nonrhetorical body, some referential body to ground sexual difference outside of writing, the critic produces a rhetorical use of the body as metaphor for the nonrhetorical.

At the beginning of her article on the lesbian novel, Catharine R. Stimpson states that her "definition of the lesbian . . . will be conservative and severely literal." We are prepared for the nonrhetorical, a shift from literary metaphor to sexual fact. It turns out that the "severely literal" is the domain of the body: "She is a woman who finds other women erotically attractive and gratifying. Of course a lesbian is more than her body, more than her flesh, but lesbianism partakes of the body, partakes of the flesh" (p. 244). Although the phrase "finds other women erotically attractive and gratifying" is vague and does not necessarily denote any specific activity, Stimpson is somewhat apologetic about her restriction of the lesbian to the body: "of course she is more" but. . . . Yet we have been warned that she will be "conservative" and severe, that we might not find her definition gratifying.

"Partakes of the body, partakes of the flesh" is still quite vague. She needs to go on and make it clear what she does and does not mean: "That carnality distinguishes it from gestures of political sympathy with homosexuals and from affectionate friendships in which women enjoy each other, support each other, and commingle a sense of identity and well-being. Lesbianism represents a commitment of skin, blood, breast, and bone" (p. 244). She is quite specific about what she does *not* mean. Political sympathy and affectionate friendships are excluded from the literal definition, however severe we might find that exclusion. They are only figuratively or symbolically lesbian. Literal lesbianism is "a commitment of skin, blood, breast, and bone." Actually Stimpson writes that "lesbianism represents" this commitment, that is, lesbianism symbolizes it. The literal definition turns out to give a figurative sense of lesbianism. Moreover, what it symbolizes is "a commitment of skin, blood, breast, and bone"; that is, it symbolizes something that is already rhetorical. Are any of these items literally committed? How, and to what or to whom? Not only is the list highly alliterative but each of the terms has a long history of metaphoric use. She does not include more shocking, more severely unliterary terms such as kidney or even clitoris. Despite her proclamation of severe literality, her definition ultimately remains within the rhetorical tradition for designating the body. This implicit contradiction has potentially far-reaching implications for an article that, on the one hand, decries a tradition of oppression that has kept the lesbian from directly and explicitly "naming her experience" and yet finally regrets that the lesbian and feminist press is ignorant of literary traditions and rejects novels that are too literary.

Elaine Showalter has other sorts of problems with the metaphor of the body. She writes: "While feminist criticism rejects the attribution of literal biological inferiority, some theorists seem to have accepted the *metaphorical* implications of female biological difference in writing." Again the literal and the metaphoric body are at stake. A question from Sandra Gilbert and Susan Gubar's *Madwoman in the Attic* seems a point of focus for Showalter's discomfort: " 'If the pen is a metaphorical penis, from what organ can females generate texts?' " (p. 17).

Showalter gives a derisive, dismissive answer to the question: "critics . . . like myself . . . might reply that women generate texts from the brain or that the word-processor of the near future, with its compactly coded microchips, its inputs and outputs, is a metaphorical womb" (p. 17). But the dismissal does not work; the question returns to haunt her text, appearing in two nervously jocular parentheses: "(If to write is metaphorically to give birth, from what organ can males generate texts?)"; "(could this [the bladder] be the organ from which females generate texts?)" (pp. 18, 24). I submit that the persistence of this question bespeaks a difficulty in accepting the body as metaphor, a demand that metaphors of the body be read literally. This difficulty with bodily metaphors has various important implications. For example, although she recognizes that Lacanian psychoanalysis uses castration as a "total metaphor" for the subject's relation to language, she misconstrues it as only referring to the female subject, thereby assuming that "castration" even as metaphor must still refer to the literal lack of male organs (p. 24).

An example of some sort of trouble around literal and metaphoric bodies might be found in almost any of the articles in *Writing and Sexual*

Difference. I would say that the metaphoricity of the body, what appears in this context as the inescapable metaphoricity of the body, comes close to Johnson's statement that literature inhabits the very heart of sexuality. At the moment when Stimpson, for example, would separate the sexual life from literature and turn to the purely flesh, she willy-nilly produces more literature.

Yet must we then conclude that the literal body, the real world, is no concern of the critic, that everything is metaphor or rhetoric or literature? This bodes ill for feminist criticism or indeed any nonformalist criticism. It seems to argue for apolitical criticism which has historically been politically conservative.

Abel suggests that we read formalistic differences as translations of sexual difference. Translation, like metaphor, is imbued with the difference within, for it is never simply itself but must represent another text and thus includes another within its identity. Not only is literature at the heart of sexual difference, but sexual difference is at the heart of literature as the absent original to which the translation must refer. I would accept the statement that literature is a translation of sexuality if I could add that we have no direct access to the original, that the best we ever have available is a good translation. Perhaps that is the purport of Spivak's name in the place for the author.

Abel endorses Spivak's contribution to the issue as not only an explicit difference within but an unsettling one: "With this story the volume shifts from West to East, from criticism to fiction, from implicit to explicit political perspective. . . . Our interpretative strategies should be shaken by Draupadi" (p. 6). Yet what is perhaps most unsettling about this text is not the shift from metaphor to fact but rather that the switch to an explicit political perspective corresponds to a switch from nonfiction to fiction.

I have identified two alien internal presences in *Writing and Sexual Difference:* one explicitly recognized and celebrated as foreign and unsettling, the other pursuing her subversive effect in silence. They would seem to be not only at opposite ends of the volume but also at opposite ends of a spectrum. "Draupadi" is literature; the epigraph, not even criticism but rarefied theory. The Bengali story is explicitly political, not just feminist but Third World revolutionary; Johnson's statements find their context in the most esoteric achievements of First World thought and would seem to deny feminism and other real-world concerns in favor of a formalistic concern with literature. Yet there might be, despite their blatant opposition, some similarity between these poles, like red and violet on the color spectrum.

The epigraph and the final entry ("Draupadi") could be said to represent the two allegiances between which "this moment of feminist inquiry" is torn: the literary and the political. Abel writes in her introduction that "concern with textual conventions dispels one litany of familiar accusations: reductiveness, dogmatism, insensitivity to literary values. . . . Such sophisticated reading . . . may also generate a litany of new accusations: that the concern with textuality augurs a return to formalism; that feminist critics have betrayed [their] political commitments" (p. 2). The repeated phrase "litany of accusations" is the tip-off that the feminist critic's relations to these two stern authorities are structurally the same. Like the child whose two parents have differing values, she is caught in a balancing act, trying to stave off disapproval on two fronts.

Although Showalter suggests that we choose political commitment and stop trying to please the "white fathers" of literary criticism, she also presents a model of the girl's necessary balancing act: "If a man's text . . . is fathered, then a woman's text is not only mothered but parented; it confronts both maternal and paternal precursors and must deal with the problems and advantages of both lines of inheritance" (p. 33). In our culture, we have a singular identity, one name, the name of the father. For the purpose of consolidating an identity, one-half of our parentage is denied.

That one is the child of two parents is another way of formulating the difference within. The feminist critic in her inheritance from both feminism and criticism lives the at once enabling and disabling tension of a difference within. We write in sexual difference. That is the critical difference in feminist inquiry.

Critical Response

II

A Response to *Writing and Sexual Difference*

Carolyn G. Heilbrun

In this response to *Writing and Sexual Difference,* I shall concentrate on the idea of "difference," wondering where, once the neglected worlds of female culture and female texts have been illuminated, feminist critics might expect their studies to take them. Some of these essays speak of strategies for literary criticism, and, while recognizing that these strategies are useful at the moment, I ask whether they may not fail, in the longer run, to energize feminism or extend the possibilities of life for women. I worry about the effects of a feminist criticism or history that necessarily focuses on the constraints of female life, constraints that, however overcome or subverted or subtly recognized in novels and in life, remain nonetheless crippling and are, of course, neither necessary nor desirable.

I shall respond to only a few of the essays, though all of them seem to me impressive, indeed, thick with meaning to a degree hardly imaginable when Kate Stimpson and I, as Elaine Showalter mentions, set out for Kentucky in 1973 to debate the possibilities of feminist criticism. Feminist critical essays such as these are not only of a high standard: they challenge, in their skill, daring, and vitality, any criticism offered today.

Mentioned with Stimpson, then, at the beginning of these essays, and impelled to debate her over her own moving and persuasive essay, I find what is to me one of the most appealing characteristics of feminist criticism: in deconstructing literature and life, we ourselves become novelists, making fictions out of the texts, and lives, other women have left us.[1] I, like others, find myself a character in a novel entitled *Writing and Sexual Difference.*

Showalter's essay "Feminist Criticism in the Wilderness" will inevitably be required reading for every student of feminist theory. Certainly I concur in her admonition that there is not much future for us in the androcentric critical tradition. I honor feminist criticism not least because it avoids the most dehumanizing quality of androcentricism: the individualistic ambition which fears those similarly engaged. The editors of the recent *Yale French Studies* issue on feminist texts report that they found themselves "participating in what may be seen as a countertradition in academia, or a new tradition emerging in feminist studies—that of reading collectively, of speaking in a plural voice, of contributing individual work to a group product." This process, they report, has "been observed with a degree of amazement by our male colleagues."[2] The introduction to *The Woman's Part,* a collection of feminist essays on Shakespeare, also suggests how important to feminist critics is the sense they have of working for a common purpose. I do not mean to imply that feminists are achieving that will-o'-the-wisp, the ideal academic community. The failure of the ideal community of feminism to come into existence is, to judge from her prolix admonitions in *The Second Stage,* what has driven Betty Friedan to embrace the language and phallocentricism of feminism's opponents. As academics and critics, we are less easily discouraged, more willing to experiment with new feminist modes.

Showalter makes brilliantly clear, however, that while trying to expand the resources of language available to us, we are torn between using the language of male discourse, in which we have all been trained, and our own gestures toward what Elizabeth Abel, in her introduction, calls "unthinkable alternatives." Have we not, in fact, the perfect mode of female discourse that questions male discourse in *Alice,* both in wonderland and through the looking glass? Alice is not by accident female, nor so only because of Charles Dodgson's sexual quirks. She embodies

1. Peggy Brawer first suggested to me the idea that women critics create novels from other women's texts.

2. Introduction to *Feminist Readings: French Texts: American Contexts, Yale French Studies* 62 (1981): 2, 3.

Carolyn G. Heilbrun, professor of English at Columbia University, is the author of *Toward a Recognition of Androgyny* and *Reinventing Womanhood* and the editor, with Margaret Higonnet, of the volume of English Institute Essays entitled *Representation of Women in Fiction.*

the female use of male logic against itself. Jane O'Reilly has well described how we all began our discovery of feminism: "After all, why was it necessary to go on and on about it. The principle, once noticed, seemed so obvious. Women were not equal. Women should be equal. There had been some strange oversight which, once explained—Hey Guys, something seems to be unfair here—would be remedied."[3] Even by the time Stimpson and I made our way to Kentucky, it was clear that the "guys" were not going to see the logic of feminist words, though Alice's have continued to echo. Today, feminist criticism is recognized by Terry Eagleton as the paradigm for a revolutionary literary criticism: "Feminist criticism is spontaneously aware of the ideological nature of received literary hierarchies, and struggles for their reconstruction."[4] Feminist critics have grown weary, meanwhile, of pointing out "logical" constrictions on female destiny. Mary Jacobus, in "The Question of Language," wonderfully illuminates Maggie's struggle with male maxims in *The Mill on the Floss.* But we must not overlook the female cry for vocation modeled upon male possibilities: Maggie wants a "steady purpose" in life and says to her brother: "You are a man, Tom, and have power, and can do something in the world," and Tom replies, "Then if you can do nothing, submit to those who can."

In a surprisingly short time, feminist criticism moved on from Maggie's cry, went beyond the task of revealing the ways in which the patriarchy oppressed and misused women. That work was too easily done, too repetitive, and, of course, too ineffective. Many of the essayists in this volume have moved on to the great untouched subject (untouched, that is, by critics in the androcentric tradition): the texts of women. Nonetheless, the only paragraph with which I quarrel in Showalter's essay is that in which she relegates to the past those who do not take women's writing as "the central project of feminist literary study" (p. 185). The earlier project of revising male readings of male literature may indeed be over. But I agree with Myra Jehlen's view of the central problem in analyzing female texts: one discovers inevitably that women must be depicted not in "actual independence but [in] action despite dependence."[5] I do not deny our need to explore the vast hidden culture of women, as Gerda Lerner and others have urged us to do. But I believe there is a danger in the approach suggested by Showalter of underestimating the force of the oppression women writers suffered, the terrible degree of restriction upon their lives. Abel attributes the "survival" of women to "resilience" and "ingenuity." True enough. But these are the only weapons of the oppressed. Those with power and autonomy

3. Jane O'Reilly, *The Girl I Left Behind Me* (New York, 1980), p. xi.
4. Terry Eagleton, *Walter Benjamin; or, Towards a Revolutionary Criticism* (London, 1981), pp. 98–99.
5. Myra Jehlen, "Archimedes and the Paradox of Feminist Criticism," *Signs* 6 (Summer 1981): 581.

may also use them but need not depend upon them for survival. Nina Auerbach's marvelous demonstration in "Magi and Maidens" of the force some women had upon men who dominated them does not alter the source of that force as woman's embodiment of deep psychic male fears and, perhaps, hidden hopes for a female autonomy that might release men from those fears. Froma Zeitlin's essay "Travesties of Gender and Genre in Aristophanes' *Thesmophoriazousae*" is similarly perceptive.

Androcentric criticism offers us no temptations to mimesis—and Showalter's characterization of "the tight-lipped Olympian intelligence" of Elizabeth Hardwick and the "arid and strained" texts of Susan Sontag seem to free us, in a phrase, from a terrible burden. What I wonder about, however, is an emphasis on female difference so acute that we must discover it in female texts. Jacobus' demonstration of how George Eliot "makes vividly legible what the critical institution has either ignored or acknowledged only under the sign of inferiority" is sharp and unarguable (p. 39). At the same time, are we not in danger of forgetting that for Maggie, as for D. H. Lawrence's Ursula, education itself seemed to hold the promise of that knowledge which was the necessary if not sufficient condition of autonomy? We now know that even a measure of autonomy brings choices, and choices bring pain, particularly for women who do not, like men, have wives licensed for comfort on the premises. Does this, however, deny for heroines like Maggie and Ursula the importance of those adventures long restricted to males? Men, taking unto themselves all adventure, leaving women each other, the children, and the laundry, will further enslave women if women identify all adventure as "male" and not for them. Women must discover their difference and their own culture. No doubt that, as Showalter knows, is the next important phase for feminist criticism. But if women forfeit the culture men have dubbed "male" when it is, in fact, human, they will have deprived themselves of too much. In Ruth Prawer Jhabvala's novel *Heat and Dust*, Olivia's husband explains women's restrictions in the use of language: "It's a man's game, strictly." "What isn't?" Olivia asks.

For this reason I feel troubled by the emphasis on genitalia. The analogy between pens and penises, between wombs and creativity, must be recognized, as Sandra Gilbert and Susan Gubar have, in various publications, pointed out. But surely we must develop other metaphors for creativity. Let me risk the personal statement that, insofar as I have been creative, the act has resembled neither childbirth nor the guilty assumption of a "penis." Rather, creation is allied with, if not identical to, sexuality: they are both energy at its most concentrated. Libido in both sexes is aroused by identical hormones. Aside from that of pregnant females, the urine of stallions is reputed to contain the largest amounts of estrogen. I mention this to suggest that while women celebrate their particular sexuality, they must also recognize that, as female sexuality has been muted by culture, male sexuality has been deformed into hideous aggression. Both deformations are of an energy which sexuality properly expresses. I do not contradict Gubar's analysis of how women have been used as the "blank page" of male artists, nor of women's long and desperate need to be artists in their own flesh and blood. Is not the eventual aim, however, to free sexuality as a source of energy from gender restrictions?

In Annette Kolodny's suggestion that "women, too, required imaginative constructs through which to accommodate themselves to the often harsh realities," she hints at the usefulness of women's accepting certain "male" models of survival (p. 161). She goes on to discuss, in "Turning the Lens on 'The Panther Captivity,' " the problem women faced in mastering "the skills requisite for survival at the edge of the frontier without becoming . . . masculinized" (p. 167). But what exactly is the problem? Either "femininity" is inherent and cannot be lost, or it is a matter of choice. Kolodny recognizes the "catch 22" dilemma: skills are masculine by definition; to be helpless is to be feminine. Surely in emphasizing "difference" and uniquely female culture, we should avoid the trap of depriving ourselves of male discourse altogether while we attempt to subvert it. The fact is that the discourse of males is not all "male" discourse: much of it is human discourse that society has denied to women. Feminist theory must be able to comprehend that which men and women share as well as that which is, or is accounted, intrinsically feminine.

It is by now clear, I trust, that I offer these remarks as addenda, not rebuttals, to the essays I have mentioned. The only essay which seems to me to oversimplify the question of difference is Judith Kegan Gardiner's, "On Female Identity and Writing by Women." This is not only, I hope, because she argues directly with me more than once. The problem, I think, is that she renders too distinct the question of female identity as opposed to male identity, thus exaggerating the difference in the potentialities of women and men. Gardiner speaks, for example, of the "autobiographical critical essay" mode adopted by some feminists as "personal and intense." Yet are those essays she mentions more personal and intense than the essays of Lionel Trilling? What *is* different, and indicates the intent behind the autobiographical mode (certainly true in my case), is the desire to free oneself from the androcentric critical attitude which delights to divide the world into "them" and "we." Trilling's "we"—males of his class and political beliefs—dictates the same Olympian tone Showalter finds distressing in Sontag and Hardwick. The autobiographical mode, on the other hand, denies, in revealing the author's experience, that she divides herself from "them." To judge another while reserving one's own moral experience and transgressions seems to me elitism in its most objectionable form.

Gardiner goes on to identify my model for the "full range of human experience" as the "linear male quest" (p. 185). I have certainly written of the male quest; "linear," however, is Gardiner's term, not mine, and misses my intent. To my mind, the quest is a marvelously stimulating trope. Far from being linear, it is an enterprise that takes the quester into the world on a path that may be highly circuitous. Along the way all manner of women, men, and beasts are encountered. The quest is to be valued not only because one arrives ultimately at the goal but also because one lives fully in the world along the way. In writing about fairy tales in *Reinventing Womanhood,* I recall pointing to the youngest of the three brothers in the tales as a model: the one who has time for animals, and nature, and helping others, who does not follow his quest like an arrow shot from a bow, but who yet seeks a distant objective that orders his passage through life; unlike a woman's, his life is not ordered *for* him by an erotic plot.

Gardiner is insightful when she declares that in antiromantic novels today "sexually active women heroes are not guilty, nor do they find sexual love redemptive. At best it offers women temporary warmth and sensual exhilaration" (p. 190). When she adds that such women may also be confused or alienated from themselves, she understands that these heroes are in danger of falling into what I have dubbed the "Friedan trap" of wanting choices and then condemning the inevitable pains and perplexities that follow.

Lesbian writing, like the lesbian experience, is of particular significance to feminist criticism as a whole. For only here have women writers not appeared to internalize the patriarchal view of their subservience nor accepted, even superficially, their "feminine role" and their ancillary position. If gynocriticism as a whole analyzes the way women writers covertly express their anger, the lesbian writer alone insists that women must dramatically explode from the constricted fate that they will not accept, even superficially, to render their lives less painful. Stimpson's article on the lesbian novel, "Zero Degree Deviancy," concludes these essays (I count the powerful story Gayatri Spivak translates as fiction) and does so with a moving plea that we ponder the mystery "why people wish to stigmatize, to dominate, to outlaw, and to erase a particular longing for passion and for love" (p. 259). I would like to extend that final sentence, and indeed her whole argument, to women as a sex and as a whole, to allow them passion, love, purpose, beyond any restrictions imposed by others' sense of rectitude. As Stimpson herself says: "To focus on mothers and daughters—or on any personal bonds—is too narrow; psychology hardly defines the totality of our lives" (p. 257).

Yet Stimpson too insists upon the importance of difference. For her, the relevant difference is between a "woman who finds other women erotically attractive and gratifying" and women who rejoice in friendships where they enjoy and support each other, commingling "a sense of identity and well-being" (p. 244). I understand the necessity of defining lesbian love as different from female friendship; but need that necessity be reified? Homophobics fear that gay people will develop a wild passion for everyone of the same sex, a fear modeled upon the miserable male heterosexual habit of viewing women as sexual prey. Yet we who are not lesbians are isolated between the fearful homophobic to our right and those lesbians to our left who insist on distinguishing themselves from "safer" feminists. Let me hasten to admit that I recognize the naiveté of this statement, the futility as of an Englishman urging the Irish to love one another. There are deep reasons for these divisions, and certain loyalties demand precedence. Yet when Stimpson writes of Wyndham Lewis, "He is too jealous and enraged to recognize either the sadness of costume and role reversal (the stigmatized seeking to erase the mark through aping the stigmatizers) or the courage of the masquerade (the emblazoning of defiance and jaunty play)," she writes for more women than lesbians: she writes for me (p. 247). Nor, if the detective novel is any indication, are all women who adopt male dress lesbians. The sense of being oppressed and stigmatized by the male world (even if one sleeps with it) is something that unites women beyond sexual preference. I fear lesbians who insist upon what separates them from other feminists, even from more conciliatory lesbians. I, who am in a position of security, academically and sexually, and have little to risk, feel compelled to say this even at the risk of angering lesbians who would divide us. What Abel calls "the shifting boundaries of sexual difference" must not, at any arbitrary point, be prevented from shifting (p. 2).

When Stimpson and I went to Kentucky in 1973, the conference that Josephine Donovan had organized beckoned like a lighted house in a dark wood. I was told that women students were, at that very moment, "entertaining" football players who might thus be tempted to attend the University of Kentucky. I'm not sure how much the university, or the world, has changed since then, but I am certain that feminist criticism has gained a strength and developed a power of illumination far beyond anything we could have anticipated. Yet while our theorists brilliantly extend the possibilities of gynocentric criticism—and, inevitably, the possibilities of all criticism—I suggest that we resolve not to limit ourselves to modes hitherto only female, whether these be semiotic, pre-Oedipal, cultural, maternal, or lesbian. There are alternatives to the choice between seeking more space for women in the patriarchy and moving out of the patriarchy altogether. This collection of essays forces us to recognize the speed with which feminist criticism develops and changes. We ought not to confine ourselves even within temporarily necessary definitions.

Critical Response

III

Feminist(s) Reading: A Response to Elaine Showalter

Carolyn J. Allen

In an earlier formulation of the issues Elaine Showalter raises in her article "Feminist Criticism in the Wilderness," she recounts the dichotomy many feminists feel between our academic and political selves: "We are both the daughters of the male tradition . . . and sisters in a new women's movement."[1] I certainly experience that division in responding to her article. From my place in the academy, I am troubled by her summary of current feminist criticism, with its misleading taxonomy and resulting omission of theoretical possibilities. As my second self looks up at the isolation of the Tower, I wonder whether we have forgotten the political beginnings of our enterprise and withdrawn from the task of addressing the world outside the academy.

Because she is writing an overview, Showalter must present considerable information in the space of a few pages. In doing so, though she successfully describes much recent work, she invites challenges to her categories from other feminist critics and risks confusing those unfamiliar with the work she cites. She begins by separating feminist reading (critique) from studies of women writing (gynocritics) and suggests that feminist reading examines male-centered texts, both literary and critical, that it has an ideological emphasis, and that it "is in essence a mode of interpretation" (p. 12). But, clearly, feminist reading is not limited to androcentric texts; further, it seems to me that all feminist criticism is ideological and that gynocritics is as readily a mode of interpretation or, conversely, that feminist reading is as open to a theoretical, culturally conscious theory of process as gynocritics. What she schematically jux-

1. Elaine Showalter, "Towards a Feminist Poetics," in *Women Writing and Writing about Women*," ed. Mary Jacobus (London, 1979), p. 39.

taposes as the problem of pluralistic readings of androcentric texts versus a need for consensual theoretical study of gynocentric texts is really less an opposition than a somewhat too arbitrary assigning of features to her two modes. Though I agree with Showalter that the interest of feminist criticism has shifted, I would revise her terms and say it has shifted to feminists reading women writers. I will return both to the ideology of feminist criticism and to the possibilities inherent in a theoretical investigation of the feminist reading process, but first let me quibble with one further, though less significant, taxonomic problem.

Having divided feminist critical practice into feminist critique and gynocritics, she summarizes the kinds of interests we have evidenced. While she acknowledges that like other contemporary critics we care about theory as well as praxis, she misleads the uninitiated by putting forth as "schools" and "models of sexual difference" widely varying studies whose terms and methodologies (or lack thereof) hardly make recognizable schools. Though this problem recurs in all her summaries, it is especially clear in her description of "biological criticism." She refers to practitioners as disparate as Adrienne Rich, Hélène Cixous, and Sandra Gilbert and Susan Gubar. Surely the use of a biological metaphor or the surveying of biological images in literary texts and the attempt to create an *écriture féminine* that "articulates the female body" do not constitute anything like a school or model or even an "approach." Though it is helpful to have all bases covered, Showalter suggests that schools exist where none do.

Her categories are dismissive because, like every good critic, she wants to clear the way for her own theory. When she arrives at it, she notes that her own interest in a theory of culture incorporates the biological, linguistic, and psychological "models" of difference that she has critiqued earlier. This strategy seems a bit like eating one's cake and having it, but beyond questions of strategy is the larger issue of why we need or would want a single model for all feminist criticism just now when we have finally begun to move away from close reading to investigate a range of theoretical directions. Nonfeminist discourses are not monolithic, so it is difficult to see the value or purpose in limiting the theoretical basis of our work.

Even if we were to agree to such a limitation, Showalter's proposal is inadequate on two grounds: (1), by referring to women's culture as something that encompasses arguments about sexual differences based on biology, language, and psychology, she has made her model too general to have much force; (2), by defining women's culture as women's

Carolyn J. Allen is an associate professor of English and director of graduate studies at the University of Washington.

experience, she does not suggest the plurality of those cultures. She sidesteps the long-standing feminist debate about whether the origin of oppression is gender or class to assume a women's culture, but even then she does not sufficiently account for differences in race, class, and sexual preference, complicated matrices without which the term "women's culture" seems unexamined and too quickly posited. She acknowledges that race and class are equally as important as gender, but when she goes on to say that those issues can be set aside, she opens herself to the charges of ethnocentrism that have been leveled against feminist criticism in both its classic and recent phases.[2]

Showalter has long been interested in the idea of women's culture, so it is not clear why she introduces Shirley and Edwin Ardener's work in anthropology in her present essay, except to join the recent and often valuable trend toward using social science models to support work in literary criticism.[3] In a 1975 review of feminist criticism, Showalter notes the usefulness of the idea of a female subculture for a consideration of women's literature "because it provides a coherent framework for studying the development of writers in a separable tradition, without either denying their participation in a larger cultural system or involving questionable assumptions of innately feminine modes of perception and creativity."[4] Her book *A Literature of Their Own* is just such a study and an invaluable source of revisionist literary history, especially in its consideration of nineteenth-century writers. But the historical ideas of "woman's sphere" and "feminine ideal," important in that diachronic study and used in her present essay to help define woman's culture, cannot account for the contemporary plurality of cultures based on differences of race, class, sexual preference, age, religion, and geography, to name only some of the variables.

Her failure to address this issue adequately in her essay may again be a consequence of the polarity of her construct, and it brings us to the problem of ideology. She identifies feminist critique as ideological but does not describe gynocritics as equally so. Surely all feminist criticism is ideological by definition. Though we who practice it may not agree on the particulars of that ideology, we cannot forget its origins in a largely nonacademic women's movement. In fact, we might give equal time to

2. For an early critique of the problem, see Lillian Robinson, "Dwelling in Decencies: Radical Criticism and the Feminist Perspective," *Sex, Class, and Culture* (Bloomington, Ind., 1978), pp. 3–21. For a recent criticism, see Elly Bulkin, "A Response to Annette Kolodny's 'Dancing through the Minefield: Some Observations on the Theory, Practice, and Politics of a Feminist Literary Criticism,' " *Feminist Studies* 8 (Summer 1982).

3. For the bias of Edwin Ardener's theory toward European political and social history, see his essays in *Nature, Culture, and Gender,* ed. Carol P. MacCormack and Marilyn Strathern (London, 1980).

4. Showalter, "Literary Criticism," *Signs* 1 (Winter 1975): 445.

wondering whether we speak at all anymore to women outside the academy. In several of her essays, Showalter quotes Adrienne Rich's hope that feminist criticism "would take the work first of all as a clue to how we live, to how we have been . . . trapped as well as liberated . . . ; and how we can begin to see—and therefore live—afresh."[5] Rich's recent poetry and prose makes clear that by "we" she means all women, not simply those who have "mastered" or in some cases been "mastered" by the various coterie languages of critical theory.

Which returns me to the dilemma of the dual selves who read Showalter's essay. Even as my academic impulses lead me to raise questions about the structure of her argument while my feminist ones question the ethnocentrism of her model, so I am at once stimulated by plunges into the theoretical wilderness and troubled by how few people I meet there. It is not a split easily made whole, but feminist critics might use the resulting tension to pursue a direction that at least permits theoretical and political concerns to be addressed in the same context. In her division of feminist criticism into two modes, Showalter never asks about the process and cultural contexts of reading the way she does of writing. If we consider the reading process, we can bring a feminist perspective to the critical debate about the reader's role in the making of meaning.[6] Feminist critics, with the exception of Judith Fetterley, have not been interested in any sustained way in the woman as reader, but such an approach invites perspectives both theoretical and political.[7]

When the dust from the fray settles, when we are through describing implied, inscribed, real, and ideal readers, surely most critics will agree that readers have a part to play in determining textual meaning. The questions for feminist critics then become: Do women and men create different meanings? and Do they create meanings differently? Judith Kegan Gardiner insists that they do in "On Female Identity and Writing by Women." She suggests that the maternal metaphor of female authorship, "the hero is her author's daughter," applies as well to the relationship between women readers and characters. Gardiner does not

5. Adrienne Rich, "When We Dead Awaken: Writing as Re-Vision," quoted in Showalter, "Literary Criticism," p. 437.

6. Showalter might respond by pointing to my androcentric sources, especially Jonathan Culler and Stanley Fish, but I believe that these things are a matter of degree. She's right, for example, to point out the reverence given Jacques Lacan in some French feminist formulations. But, like Mary Jacobus, I think that "feminist colonizing" of current work on the reader and the text is a necessary "rewriting of a critical fiction in which issues of gender have been ignored" (Jacobus, "The Difference of View," in *Women Writing and Writing about Women*, p. 21).

7. See Judith Fetterley, *The Resisting Reader: A Feminist Approach to American Fiction* (Bloomington, Ind., 1978). See also Dorin Schumacher, "Subjectivities: A Theory of the Critical Process," in *Feminist Literary Criticism*, ed. Josephine Donovan (Lexington, Ky., 1975), pp. 29–37.

elaborate on her suggestion, but we might profit from exploration of it and of other such metaphors about the relations among women authors, characters, and readers.[8]

Formulations about gender-based differences in readers are, however, open to charges like those I make above about women's culture. The concept "woman as reader," like the terms "women's style" and "women's culture," is too general to be useful.[9] Further, women do not read in a cultural vacuum any more than they write in one. Obviously women raised and taught in cultures where male institutions and power structures prevail do not let go of that bias when they read simply because they're women. We might think more productively about feminist readers than about women readers. Clearly all feminists don't make meaning in the same way either; individual personal, political, and cultural differences are central. Yet by assuming, however broadly, an ideological base, then specifying its parameters, we can learn something about politics and reader response and perhaps also more about feminism and feminist criticism.

Of course there are readers and readers or, more accurately, readers and critics. Focusing on feminist readers outside the academy and feminist critics inside it might help us bridge the division between the applied and the theoretical. If we imagine a spectrum with the feminist reader as critic at one end and the feminist reader as political activist at the other, we can create a context within which to examine various intricacies of the reader-text interchange—reading as critical process, reading as personal fiction, reading as social construct. As we think about reading and politics, we can inquire how politics influence not only how we fill Iserian gaps in our reading but how we recognize them as gaps at all. In wondering how to communicate our theoretical discoveries to readers across the continuum, we must continue to develop new sensitivities in teaching and learn to use the nonacademic feminist press as well as scholarly mediums for our translations. Despite Showalter's assertion that it is "very difficult to propose theoretical coherence" in interpretation, feminist critics within the academy can focus on our critical processes and discover in our "interpretive community" common strategies in constructing interpretations and in conceiving ap-

8. See also the exchange between Gardiner and Elizabeth Abel in *Signs* 6 (Spring 1981): Abel, "(E)Merging Identities: The Dynamics of Female Friendship in Contemporary Fiction by Women" (pp. 413–35); Gardiner, "The (US)es of (I)dentity: A Response to Abel on '(E)Merging Identities'" (pp. 436–42); and Abel, "Reply to Gardiner" (pp. 442–44).

9. For a discussion of the problems with the term "women's style," see my "'Dressing the Unknowable in the Garments of the Known': The Style of Djuna Barnes' *Nightwood*," in *Women's Language and Style*, ed. Douglass Butturff and Edmund Epstein (Akron, Ohio, 1978), pp. 106–18.

proaches to the question of sexual difference (p. 12).[10] This kind of self-reflection, in which our criticism becomes our text, will in no way substitute for investigations both theoretical and pragmatic of literary works, but it will contribute to an understanding of our hermeneutic principles and a recognition that every critical performance—feminist and nonfeminist—is a political act.

10. Annette Kolodny makes some observations on her own critical practices in "Turning the Lens on 'The Panther Captivity': A Feminist Exercise in Practical Criticism." For "interpretive communities," see Stanley Fish, *Is There a Text in This Class?* (Cambridge, Mass., 1980). I am currently writing a study of the relation between this and other reader/text considerations and feminist criticism.

Critical Response

IV

Reply to Carolyn J. Allen

Elaine Showalter

Despite its youth, feminist criticism has been around long enough to have generated its own myth of origins and of a Golden Age. In this imaginary past, a "largely nonacademic women's movement" gave birth to an ideological feminist criticism, one in which "all women, not simply those who have 'mastered' . . . the various coterie languages of critical theory" could and did participate. But then feminist critics abjured their mothers, entered the "isolation of the Tower," forgot the "political beginnings of our enterprise," and withdrew "from the task of addressing the world outside the academy."

This melancholy fable, retold by Carolyn J. Allen in her response to my "Feminist Criticism in the Wilderness," will be familiar to many readers, male as well as female, who will recognize in its contours the archetypal form of academic self-recrimination, the standard myth of the Fall. I have extrapolated it from Allen's text because her disagreement with me is framed and shaped by her assumptions about the development and obligations of American feminist critical theory. Although she and I share an intense concern for the role of the feminist critic in academic and political life, we have a different understanding of the process by which feminist theory developed in this country and of the methods by which it is most likely to proceed.

First of all, Allen's misgivings seem to be occasioned by a view of the Tower of academia as lofty and remote from "real life." This argument strikes me as dated and even sentimental. Life in the university, especially in the humanities, was in the 1970s, and will continue to be in the 1980s, a struggle for survival whose accompanying stresses can be matched against the most authentically bracing—or destructive—careers the society has to offer. And I am puzzled by the implications throughout her commentary that feminist criticism is in some way limiting itself to elite publications (like *Critical Inquiry?*) and that "we must . . . learn to use the nonacademic feminist press as well as scholarly mediums." Those of us who have already spent more than a decade writing about feminist criticism for *MS,* the Feminist Press, and women's movement publications as far back as *Notes from the Second Year,* will have another perspective. We will recall, for example, that (although to say so may be to contradict mythic pieties about how movements *should* begin) feminist criticism along with the civil rights and antiwar movements and the New Left, was one of the *mothers* of the American women's liberation movement. Feminist criticism helped form the ideologies of the new feminism; we are people of the Book, and we had our origins as much in the library as in the streets. It's not an anomaly that the most widely read books of the early years of women's liberation, from Simone de Beauvoir to Betty Friedan to Mary Ellmann, were wholly or in part analyses of literary texts. It's not an aberration that Kate Millett's *Sexual Politics* was originally a Ph.D. dissertation for the Columbia University English department, nor that so many early leaders of the movement were scholars, writers, and editors.

The fact that feminist criticism has now expanded to include interdisciplinary and international problems of theory does not mean that it has abandoned its early and intense commitment to sexual politics or to the plurality of women's culture. Quite the contrary. My anthropologically based theory of sexual difference has evolved over the past five years in *response* to the plurality of women's culture. I am keenly aware of the significance of race, class, and nationality and would never suggest that these issues can be set aside. My essay is an effort, however incomplete, to respond to the valid criticism of black and lesbian women, for example, about the omissions of feminist theory. These are issues I intend to pursue and explore.

But we cannot answer all our questions and solve all our theoretical problems at once and alone. In order to sharpen our definitions of women's culture, to free ourselves from ethnocentrism, and still come up with a model specific enough to have some force, we need much more than a raised consciousness and good intentions. We need to expand and enlarge the boundaries of our own thought, seek out debate, test, discard, and rebuild ideas. Edwin Ardener's elegant model of the relation of dominant and muted cultures, which I first encountered in 1977, strikes me as an intellectually provocative formulation of a problem with which historians and critics had long been struggling. It is further developed in Shirley Ardener's introduction to *Defining Females* (1978), lectures on the nature of women in society which were presented at Oxford as part of a yearlong series.[1]

1. Shirley Ardener, "The Nature of Women in Society," in *Defining Females* (New York, 1978), pp. 9–48; see esp., her comments on mutedness, pp. 20–27.

It will be obvious, I am sure, that I have also been deeply influenced by the brilliant feminist historiography of Gerda Lerner. And in a new collection, *Victorian Women,* the historians Leslie Parker Hume and Karen M. Offen have mapped an elaborate and fascinating "geography of women's work" which shows women's sphere wholly contained within men's sphere but expanding into it in early industrial times.[2] Nonetheless, the views of women's sphere defined in social history lack the flexibility and the theoretical potential of current work in cultural anthropology, precisely because they are fixed to the economic and social conditions of the nineteenth century. Ardener's theory, while it may not be able to escape the ethnocentricity that comes from being born a white European male, is nonetheless based on fieldwork on women's rituals in Africa. I have no intention, as I have said, of canonizing Ardener or any other theoretician, so I am quite willing to grant him his flaws. The point is not the perfection of the work but its usefulness in moving us forward.

I would hope that the problem of defining sexual difference and cultural relation will be addressed by the widest possible group of scholars and critics and that it will be found to have relevance to our ongoing discussions of women's writing. Sylvia Plath wrote in her *Journals,* in 1952 as a sophomore at Smith agonizing over the conflict between writing and love, between her roles in literary and in women's culture:

> *Never* will there be a circle, signifying me and my operations, confined solely to home, other womenfolk, and community service, enclosed in the larger worldly circle of my mate, who brings home from his periphery of contact with the world the tales only of vicarious experience to me, like so: ⊙   No, rather, there will be two overlapping circles, with a certain strong riveted center of common ground, but *both* with separate arcs jutting out into the world. A balanced tension, adaptable to circumstances, in which there is an elasticity of pull, tension, yet firm unity. Two stars polarized: ∞   like so. In moments of communication that is complete almost, like so ⊚   almost fusing into one. But fusion is an undesirable impossibility—and quite nondurable. So there will be no illusion of that.[3]

I am encouraged by discovering in Plath a formulation so similar to Ardener's model. My real purpose is to construct a theory not just of feminist writing, or Victorian writing, or American or avant-garde writ-

2. See "Introduction to the Adult Woman: Work," in *Victorian Women: A Documentary Account of Women's Lives in Nineteenth-Century England, France, and the United States,* ed. Erna Olafson Hellerstein, Leslie Parker Hume, and Karen M. Offen (Stanford, Calif., 1981), pp. 272–91.

3. Sylvia Plath, *The Journals of Sylvia Plath, 1950–1962,* ed. Frances McCullough (New York, 1982), p. 43.

ing but of women's writing; and at the same time to avoid the prescriptive tone of criticism that insists that "not all writing by women, about women, can be called women's literature."[4] This may be an impossible task. When I read form letters like the following one I received from *Writer's Digest* magazine, I confess to despair:

> Dear Friend,
>
> I cordially invite you to join Pearl Buck, Shana Alexander, Edna St. Vincent Millay, Gloria Steinem, Erma Bombeck, Joyce Carol Oates, and thousands of other women who have commanded the attention and respect of the world as writers. . . . Today's great demand for writers is being met by people from all walks of life. If any single group has a competitive edge, it would be women. We are generally more perceptive of details, sensitive to undercurrents, and attentive to character than men.

This piece of grass-roots feminist criticism may not be quite what Allen has in mind. And we know that outside the academy most women are not even reading Erma Bombeck, let alone Joyce Carol Oates or Adrienne Rich. Apparently most women, when they are not buying books about preppies, diets, and cats, read the Harlequin and Silhouette romances that are marketed in exquisitely precise demographic calibrations. Yet a theory of feminist reading which would exclude these women, their literary tastes, their relation to culture, and the way they create meaning would teach us very little about the world outside the academy. I'm not in the least opposed to theories of reading, but I am skeptical about a theory of feminist reading that would not be narrow or prescriptive.[5] In the end, I suppose, we have to risk working out these unwieldly theories, rather than merely suggesting that someone should come up with them, and "[invite] challenges . . . from other feminist critics"—the best and only way, I think, for ideas to grow.

4. Elizabeth Janeway, "Women's Literature," in *The Harvard Guide to Contemporary American Writing*, ed. Daniel Hoffman (Cambridge, Mass., 1979), p. 345.

5. For a provocative analysis of the relationship between feminist interpretation and political and critical conventions of the 1960s and 1970s, see Jean E. Kennard, "Convention Coverage; or, How to Read Our Own Lives," *New Literary History* 13 (Autumn 1981).

Index